D0204717

TECHNOLOGY
& SOCIETY

Second Edition

TECHNOLOGY & SOCIETY

Social Networks, Power, and Inequality

Anabel Quan-Haase

OXFORD
UNIVERSITY PRESS

OXFORD

UNIVERSITY PRESS

Oxford University Press is a department of the University of Oxford.
It furthers the University's objective of excellence in research, scholarship,
and education by publishing worldwide. Oxford is a registered trade mark of
Oxford University Press in the UK and in certain other countries.

Published in Canada by
Oxford University Press
8 Sampson Mews, Suite 204,
Don Mills, Ontario M3C 0H5 Canada
www.oupcanada.com

Copyright © Oxford University Press Canada 2016

The moral rights of the author have been asserted

Database right Oxford University Press (maker)

First Edition published in 2013

All rights reserved. No part of this publication may be reproduced, stored in
a retrieval system, or transmitted, in any form or by any means, without the
prior permission in writing of Oxford University Press, or as expressly permitted
by law, by licence, or under terms agreed with the appropriate reprographics
rights organization. Enquiries concerning reproduction outside the scope of the
above should be sent to the Permissions Department at the address above
or through the following url: www.oupcanada.com/permission/permission_request.php

Every effort has been made to determine and contact copyright holders.
In the case of any omissions, the publisher will be pleased to make
suitable acknowledgement in future editions.

Library and Archives Canada Cataloguing in Publication
Quan-Haase, Anabel, author
Technology and society : social networks, power, and
inequality / Anabel Quan-Haase. — Second edition.

(Themes in Canadian sociology)
Includes bibliographical references and index.
ISBN 978-0-19-901471-2 (paperback)

1. Technology—Social aspects. I. Title. II. Series: Themes in
Canadian sociology

T14.5.Q36 2015   303.48'3   C2015-904239-9

Cover illustrations: © iStock/DrAfter123 and © iStock/KristinaVelickovic

Quote from *Star Trek* on page 4 used with the permission of
CBS Broadcasting Inc./CBS Television Studios.

Printed and bound in Canada

4 5 6 — 20 19 18

Contents

Preface

A key motivation for writing *Technology and Society* was a mixed sense of euphoria and concern. As I continued to adopt various technologies and to test new applications on the Web, I felt excited to be witnessing a time of technological transformation—the era of *digital tools and apps*. News stories on Reddit and the Huffington Post featured new apps, and my Twitter feed seemed to increase in volume daily. I often had the sense that things were happening faster and that if I was not tethered to my various devices, I could miss out on important events, news, or opportunities. This anxiety has been referred to as FOMO, the fear of missing out. How could I best organize my day and my technology habits to keep up with this ever-increasing flow of information? Harvey referred to this fundamental change in lifestyle as a time–space compression in his 1989 book *The Condition of Postmodernity*, which describes, among other things, an acceleration of social and capitalist dynamics resulting from digital communication. Key questions that emerged for me included: What does the time–space compression consist of? What are its social implications? And how can I keep up with transformative changes resulting in an increase of messages, the speedy circulation of news stories, and new social norms around communication?

There is no doubt that we have witnessed an unprecedented proliferation of social media tools, such as Twitter, Facebook, Tumblr, and Pinterest. The Pew Research Center found that Americans spend more time on social media than on any other Internet activity, with 73 per cent of adults online using at least one **social networking site** (SNS), and as many as 42 per cent using more than one. Social media adoption and use has become an important part of the presentation of the self, of connecting with friends and family, and of keeping up with the news and with world events, work, and everyday life. Even traditional institutions and organizations have made the move toward embracing digital technologies; for instance, the majority of mainstream media outlets have adopted at least one social media tool.

The purpose of this book, then, is to slow down and step back for a moment to make technology the object of sociological inquiry and to try to uncover the intricacies of our socio-technical existence. By taking a socio-technical perspective, the book makes readers aware of the pervasiveness of technology in our everyday lives and encourages an understanding of how technology interacts with and is embodied in society. Technology is both the driving force behind societal change as well as the output of our technological imagination. It is this dichotomy that we want to present. The focus of the book is on the high dependence on all things technological, combined with the problems, social issues, and socio-political realm in which these technologies are embedded. As Marshall McLuhan so eloquently pointed out, technology is not neutral. It affects our society and we need to be able to discuss and scrutinize these effects. This book provides the necessary background to start such an analysis by defining the parameters around technology.

The book as a whole has three goals. The first is to examine how technology and society intersect. The book investigates how technological change is interlinked with inequality, power, and social networks. It is about connecting issues of relevance at both local and global, micro and macro levels. In exploring these connections, this book raises and attempts to answer a number of central questions: How is technology leading toward social change? What is the nature of this social change? Who is being affected by the technologies? Are various social groups being affected differently? How are people using the technologies in different regions? Does the global digital divide continue to exist?

The book's second goal is to draw on readers' own experiences as a means to make sense of the link between technology and society. What is unique about this book is its focus on experiential learning, which emphasizes gaining meaning from direct experience. Aristotle was among the first to recognize the value of experience in gaining knowledge: "For the things we have to learn before we can do, we learn by doing" (Bynum & Porter, 2006). The book serves as a bridge, then, between abstract, theoretical thinking and real-life events and experiences. Throughout the book, on-the-ground examples are utilized to demonstrate the relevance of concepts and ideas. These real-life examples also demonstrate the relevance of studying technology in its specific social context, be it historical, geographic, regional, linguistic, age-based, or ethnic. Technology is about context. To understand better the contextual nature of technology, the book strongly encourages students to bring their personal experiences and voices to bear on the material. This helps to put the concepts and theories in perspective and give them meaning, immediacy, and relevance.

The final goal of the book is to encourage curiosity and to find out more about technologies. The book should give readers an urge to do something about the material: share it, post it, comment on it, and make a difference in the world. Technology has become such an intrinsic part of our everyday lives in the West that we need to care about these social problems and the questions that open from the critical analysis of text, theory, and experience.

What is difficult about any study of technology is to step back and look at technology as neutral, critical observers. But doing so allows us to examine technology in many different ways: technology as a technical device, as a social force, as an agent for warfare, as a tool for health care, as a device for fun, or as a force behind job losses and deskilling. Can we actually step back as neutral observers? It is hard to imagine a world without technology. Indeed, technology has been a part of human existence since the Stone Age, when humans used stones, bones, and sticks as tools for survival. But studying technology can help us become more aware of its role in our personal lives, in the lives of other social groups and their struggles, and in our society as a whole. Moreover, systematic analysis of design, implementation, and use allow us to develop theories of the intersection of technology and society. This type of analysis provides us with necessary background knowledge and tools to embark on social, socio-political, and cultural studies of our own socio-technical existence. As a result, this book provides a solid understanding of technology's role in society and gives students the tools they need to embark on a critical and in-depth inquiry of our technological society.

Overview of the Book

Technology and Society: Social Networks, Power, and Inequality is aimed at students in undergraduate courses on technology in a range of disciplines in the social sciences (in particular, sociology and anthropology), arts and humanities, communication studies, and information science. This book is also appropriate for management or business classes because of its focus on technology design, innovation, and labour in Web 2.0 contexts. The book does not require any previous knowledge of technology or statistics. Theories and concepts are explained in great depth, and the glossary provides definitions of new and specific terminology. *Technology and Society* relies on current interdisciplinary work from sociology, the history of technology, science and technology studies (STS), communications, and related fields.

The chapters are organized to help students understand and learn the material. Each chapter starts with a set of learning goals, continues with a general overview or introduction to guide the readers through the material, and ends with a conclusion, a set of study questions, and further readings. What distinguishes the book from other similar works is its focus on contemporary examples and case studies. The book brings concepts and theories to life by showing how they relate to current discussions in the media and in academia with regard to policy, changes in the law, and pressing critical issues of our digital age. Through its comprehensive list of further readings and additional/supplemental Web content, the book encourages readers to seek out further resources, to obtain additional current information, to deepen their knowledge of topics, and to explore new topics of their own interest. Next, we present a short overview of each chapter to give readers an idea of some of the topics covered.

Chapter 1: The Technological Society

Chapter 1 investigates the contentious question of how to best define *technology*. The chapter outlines and critically discusses several approaches. Considering the depth and pervasiveness of technology in our society, this introductory chapter stresses the relevance of studying the intersection of technology and society—what is often referred to as the **socio-technical perspective**. The chapter includes a discussion of how technologies lead to large-scale, widespread social change and issues, such as social and economic inequality. The key argument is that social change occurs not as a result of technology alone but as a blending of micro-, meso-, and macro-level processes. In addition to established approaches to understanding technology, the chapter also covers two of the main contemporary perspectives surrounding the use of technology in modern society. The first is simulation, which is geared toward the development of tools that can resemble or outperform human faculties. The second perspective is augmentation, which attempts to integrate machines and humans into new hybrid actors with added capabilities. Both of these perspectives highlight the many points of intersection of the human and the technological, raising important questions about the ethical, moral, and societal implications of endeavours such as augmentation and simulation.

Chapter 2: Technology in Society: A Historical Overview

To comprehend fully how technology and society intersect in our modern society, we need to first take a look at the history of technology. The aim of Chapter 2 is to provide a broad overview of this history by tracing the roots of technological development, discussing key periods of technological innovation, and outlining our present-day high-tech society. Technology is the strongest force of change in society and, as such, its development, transformation, and diffusion directly shape many aspects of society, such as work, community, and social relationships. We examine these technological transformations over time and demonstrate the impacts they have had on past societies. This chapter further attempts to link technologies, inventors, and historical moments to provide an in-depth examination of the socio-political context in which technologies emerge. Chapter 2 shows how technology is ingrained in society, affecting all aspects of our lives, and outlines the merits of taking a sociological perspective when studying the history of technology.

Chapter 3: Theoretical Perspectives on Technology

Chapter 3 covers a plurality of theoretical perspectives, which seek to shed light on the nature of the relationship between technology and society, as well as on those elements of society most affected by technology. First, the chapter contrasts the utopian and dystopian approaches, which each highlight a different side of how technology transforms society. Second, Chapter 3 also reviews the key premises underlying the theories of technological and social determinism and discusses their strengths and weaknesses. Third, the chapter introduces the field of STS as an alternative framework, which stresses that artifacts are socially constructed, mirroring the society that produces them. Then the chapter reviews the two most prominent approaches of STS: social construction of technology (SCOT) and actor network theory (ANT).

Chapter 4: Gendered Technology

The book would not be complete without a critical engagement with the topic of gender and technology. Often gender is ignored in the design, adoption, and use of tools and apps, despite the fact that an analysis of gender provides rich insights into fundamental differences between men and women and how they approach technology. The chapter looks at historical and contemporary theoretical and methodological approaches to the study and critique of gendered technologies. Of particular interest is the relation between household technologies and physical and mental labour. The chapter aims to discern the similarities and differences in how men and women adopt and use digital technologies. This analysis reveals that there is a gap between men and women in terms of their digital skills, perceptions of competency, and uptake of digital tools. Based on these differences, the chapter goes on to examine the role of women in the IT industry and provides an overview of current interventions, such as Ladies Learning Code, aimed at increasing gender equality in this field. Finally, the chapter investigates how the gendered body becomes reintegrated into the digital world in the form of images, discourse, media depictions, and user-generated content.

Chapter 5: Techno-Social Designing

The topic of Chapter 5 is the impact of social factors on the design of technology. Users of technology are often oblivious to the complexity underlying technological design because not much knowledge is available on how this process unfolds. The aim of this chapter, then, is to uncover these often hidden creative processes by examining developers' visions and the challenges experienced in research and development (R&D), including the pressures that exist in R&D teams and the ways that innovation occurs in these teams. As well, Chapter 5 introduces the term *technopole* to describe specialized cities dedicated solely to technological innovation. Silicon Valley is presented as an example of a technopole that combines a highly educated workforce with military and economic interests. The chapter also examines in more detail the inner workings and the outer pressures of software development, which is one type of R&D that has come to occupy a central role in the world economy.

Chapter 6: The Adoption and Diffusion of Technological Innovations

Chapter 6 investigates how technology diffuses in society. The chapter provides an overview of the key concepts, theories, and research findings in the diffusion of innovations literature and discusses them in relation to the diffusion of specific technologies, such as water boiling, the QWERTY keyboard, and the iPhone. The aim of the chapter is to examine key adopter groups, how they differ, and their salient characteristics. Everett Rogers's classic model of the diffusion of innovations, the stages of the innovation-decision process, and his categorization of adopter groups are elucidated in great detail to provide students with the necessary foundations in the field of diffusion of innovations. As part of this overview, change agents and early adopters are discussed as being among those who play active roles in promoting and diffusing new tools.

Chapter 7: The Labour of Technology

The complex interrelation between technology and labour is the topic of this chapter. The focus here is on the changes in the nature, context, and structure of work that result from new technologies and the associated power imbalances. Historically, these changes occurred as early as the Industrial Revolution when machines replaced skilled workers, creating social upheaval, dissatisfaction, and unrest. We use the historical context to help readers better grasp current trends in how Web 2.0 technologies facilitate new forms of production that are based on principles of collaboration, sharing, and open source. We discuss key concepts of the Web 2.0 mode of work, including *prosumer, produsage,* and *perpetual beta.* Wikipedia and Facebook are used as examples to illustrate current trends in how users become producers of content. Most users would not consider this work, rather, they view it as art, pleasure, fun, or leisure time. But these new forms of work do have consequences for the new economy and for labour relations. The main point of this chapter is that technology is not neutral but, rather, becomes an active force that changes the nature of work itself, working conditions, and the structure of society as a whole.

Chapter 8: Technology and Inequality

In Chapter 8 issues specifically linked to digital inequality are covered to provide an overview of the social, economic, and cultural consequences that result from a lack of access to the Internet. The chapter covers the historical developments of the digital divide concept, examines the complexity of its measurement, and considers its relevance to policy in Canada and the United States. A key argument is that inequalities in the use of digital technologies reflect not only problems associated with access to networked computers but also differences in skill level among users. Another central term covered in this chapter is the *global digital divide,* which describes the gap in access to the Internet that exists between developing and developed nations.

Many developing nations continue to falter in their efforts to become digital, having to overcome numerous barriers of access, skill, and infrastructure. China is discussed as a prime example of a newly industrializing nation that has struggled to join the information society and in the process has developed an ambivalent relationship with the Internet.

Chapter 9: Community in the Network Society

Chapter 9 examines how the notion of community has changed as a result of the introduction of new technologies in society. The chapter starts with a brief overview of *Gesellschaft* and *Gemeinschaft* as two of the most central concepts in the study of the structure of society. What follows is a critical examination of the debate about how industrialization, urbanization, and globalization have affected community. The community-lost, community-saved, and community-liberated perspectives are reviewed to contrast competing theories on the nature of these changes. The chapter also considers the recent concerns expressed about the impact of the Internet on the patterning of social relationships and presents various competing perspectives. Chapter 9 concludes with a discussion of how information and communication technologies have affected the public sphere. As part of this discussion, we take an in-depth look at the events that unfolded in Egypt in February of 2011 and analyze the role of social media in the protests.

Chapter 10: Technology-Mediated Social Relationships

In Chapter 10, we briefly outline the early beginnings of mediated communication and address how they impact society. Then, we review recent trends in how people form and maintain personal connections via the Internet. While most discourse focuses on the benefits of mediated communication, scholars have also warned about the potential negative effects on people's social life. Can personal relations maintained online provide as much social support as those maintained in person? The chapter then focuses on how social media have redefined our notion of friendship and the implications of these changes for community and social networking. What follows is an analysis of romance 2.0, investigating how people form and terminate romantic relations by using social media. The chapter ends with an exploration of the concept of virtual mourning and how people renegotiate online the meaning of death. To explore this new concept in depth, we examine the unprecedented online response to Michael Jackson's death and the supportive online community that formed around Canadian Eva Markvoort during her struggles with cystic fibrosis.

Chapter 11: The Surveillance Society

The topic of Chapter 11 is surveillance and how it has become a central concern of our digital age. The goal of this chapter is to define the multifaceted term by contrasting different perspectives available in the literature. The chapter then provides an overview of the concept and architecture of the Panopticon and its means of exerting control and imposing disciplinary action. The chapter discusses the new modes of surveillance made possible by recent technological developments, which show how technologies have changed not only the practices of surveillance but also the very nature of surveillance, reducing individuals' privacy rights to a large extent. We end the chapter with a review of innovative methods of counter-surveillance that aim at increasing awareness of the pervasiveness of surveillance in our society and provide means for personal resistance.

Chapter 12: Ethical Dimensions of Technology

The goal of the final chapter is to summarize the three key themes that run through the book. The first theme stresses the need to take a socio-technical perspective that allows for an in-depth examination of the social context of technology design, use, and implementation. The second theme demonstrates how innovation is associated with economics and as a result has consequences for our understanding of inequality and power relations. The last theme shows the many ways in which technological developments lead toward social change, impacting community, social networks, and social relations. The final chapter also embarks on a critical examination of the ethical and moral dimensions of humans' engagement with technology. The following themes are explored: the neutrality of technology, technology as human destiny, and technology as progress. Through this discussion, the chapter emphasizes the unexpected consequences of technology with which society must, ultimately, come to terms.

Acknowledgements

I am very grateful to Lorne Tepperman and Susan McDaniel for giving me the opportunity to contribute to the *Themes in Canadian Sociology* series; this has been a great honour and privilege. I would also like to thank Meg Patterson and Darcey Pepper at Oxford University Press for all of their advice and encouragement during the writing and editing of the book. The manuscript has benefited enormously from the constructive and helpful feedback received from Barry Wellman at the University of Toronto and Laurie Forbes at Lakehead University. I thank them for their time and their commitment to high standards in scholarship. This project would not have come to fruition without the love of my family—the Mortons and the Quans. They bring many of the examples in the book to life with their devotion to and skepticism of all things technological. I would also like to express my indebtedness to my research assistants—Becky Blue, Gary Nicholas Collins, Michael Haight, Kim Martin, and Jonathas Mello—who helped with literature reviews, drafts, editing, graphics, and humour. Chapter 1 greatly benefited from discussions with my colleague Victoria L. Rubin, whose sharp insights helped me better organize the chapter. Chapter 7 benefited from discussions with Brian Brown, while Chapter 11 received input from surveillance expert John Reed.

Anabel Quan-Haase
July 2015

Abbreviations

AI	artificial intelligence
ANT	actor network theory
CANARIE	The Canadian Advanced Network and Research for Industry and Education
CAP	Community Access Program
CBC	Canadian Broadcasting Corporation
CCTV	closed circuit television
CF	cystic fibrosis
CGE	Compagnie Générale d'Electricité
CNNIC	China Internet Network Information Centre
DD	digital divide
DIY	do-it-yourself
EDF	Électricité de France
FCC	Federal Communications Commission
GDP	gross domestic product
GERD	gross domestic product expenditure on research and development
GSS	General Social Survey
ICTs	information and communication technologies
ICT4D	information and communication technologies for development
IM	instant message
ISP	Internet service provider
IT	information technology
ITU	International Telecommunications Union
KME	Knowledge Management Enterprises
LAN	local area network
NPOV	neutral point of view
NRA	National Rifle Association of America
NTIA	National Telecommunications and Information Administration
OECD	Organisation for Economic Co-operation and Development
OLPC	One Laptop per Child
PC	personal computer
R&D	research and development
ROI	return on investment
SCOT	social construction of technology
SNSs	social network sites
STS	science and technology studies
UNDP	United Nations Development Programme
WELL	Whole Earth 'Lectronic Link
WSIS	World Summit on the Information Society

1   The Technological Society

Learning Objectives

◎   to understand the challenges in defining and studying technology;

◎   to obtain an overview of historical definitions of technology and their strengths and limitations;

◎   to learn about the complexity of defining technology as not merely material substance, but rather as a complex assemblage;

◎   to examine contemporary perspectives of technology that blur the boundaries of machine and human elements.

Introduction

This introductory chapter highlights the relevance of investigating the intersection of technology and society. It is easy to dismiss technology as a mere object, without giving much consideration to how it is woven into our everyday lives. Technology provides a means for us, its users, to get things done. Without giving it much thought, we leave our homes every morning with our cellphones (often more than one), laptops, MP3 players (such as iPods), headphones, watches, and other gadgets. Only when our technology fails us do we suddenly realize the depth of our dependence on that technology. There is frustration and sometimes even a sense of panic when we forget our cellphone at home (or worse, when we lose it!). Our cellphones' digital address books have become an extension of our memory, storing hundreds of names, phone numbers, and email addresses. Facebook pictures, posts, and updates are digital footprints of our e-identity, our digital selves. This ubiquity of and dependence on technology raises questions about its use as a means to enhance, complement, or even substitute human faculties and the ethical implications this close interlink has for our society. As long as technology works smoothly, it is simply part of our daily life, part of what keeps society as a whole functioning. But when it fails, or when its use crosses ethical boundaries, we come to realize that it is actually another "actor," even if non-human, in a complex web of relations. To demonstrate this balance between ethics and technological use, this chapter presents and discusses the Facebook experiment on social contagion as an example of an ethical dilemma not only for users but also for Facebook developers.

The aim of this initial chapter is to introduce readers to the topic of *technology* by critically discussing and comparing its various definitions. In addition, the chapter introduces and contrasts two perspectives of technology that define our current times. The first is **simulation**, which is geared toward the development of tools that can resemble or outperform human faculties. The second perspective is **augmentation**, which attempts to integrate machines and humans into new hybrid actors with added capabilities. Both of these perspectives highlight the many points of intersection of the human and the technological, raising important questions about the ethical, moral, and societal implications of endeavours such as augmentation and simulation.

The Social and Ethical Dimensions of Studying Technology

The study of technology has typically been approached from a material standpoint, consisting of the examination of tools and tool use. Early scholars of technology paid little attention to the social and ethical implications of technology, as illustrated in the definition of technology as material substance, discussed later in this chapter. The focus on how the social, ethical, and technological come together and influence one another started to become an object of study in the **Marxist tradition** around 1850 with its focus on **inequality**, which spurred interest in understanding how machines affect labour. For instance, the textile industry introduced machines to simplify and speed up work processes, resulting in the employment of non-skilled workers at lower wages (Berg, 1994); Marxist scholars examined how the growing use of machinery was a central factor in deskilling (i.e., the elimination, reduction, or downgrading of skilled labour because of the introduction of technologies within the workplace) and how it increased tensions in labour relationships. At this time, then, a transition occurred, away from the study of technology itself—as merely an object—toward an interest in how technology changes social structure and brings about social change. Now, examining the social side of technology is essential as our society moves toward greater integration, what Ellul (1964) has described as a **technological society**. The concept of a technological society does not describe technology merely as a tool that exists as an extension of our human faculties, however: it is far more complex than that. An example of how the social, ethical, and technological shape one another is the Facebook experiment discussed in Box 1.1.

Box 1.1 shows how technology that we trust, and that we do not think too much about when engaging with it, can potentially influence our lives, emotions, and self-worth in unexpected ways. In the case of the Facebook experiment, we learned that emotional contagion occurs on social media

**Box
1.1**

The Facebook Experiment

In the July 2014 issue of *Proceedings of the National Academy of Sciences of the United States of America*, an article was published providing evidence of **emotional contagion** through the exposure to content on social networking sites such as Facebook. The article described how in 2012 a team consisting of two scholars, Jeffrey T. Hancock and Jamie Guillory, and a Facebook computational social scientist, Adam D.I. Kramer, conducted a series of large-scale experiments to debunk an assumption widely held by users. The assumption was that watching Facebook friends post content with positive emotionality made people feel resentful, leading to feelings of inadequacy, envy, and perhaps even depression. In other words, seeing others having fun, being popular among peers, and enjoying themselves may stir negative emotions in onlookers.

To test this assumption, Kramer et al. (2014) manipulated the content that a select group of Facebook users viewed on their news feeds. The experiments ran for a one-week period from 11 January to 18 January 2012. To avoid bias, participants were randomly selected, yielding a sample of about 155,000 per condition. In one condition, negative content was removed from participants' news feeds; in the other, positive content was removed. Hence, the selected Facebook users saw content biased toward either positive or negative emotionality. The researchers then recorded the emotionality of the posts made under each condition.

The findings are illuminating in several ways. First, through the manipulation of content, users' posts can be influenced. Those Facebook users who saw less negative content posted more positive content themselves and vice versa. This clearly shows that through manipulating content on these sites, users' emotionality can also be controlled. Second, the more emotional the content, the more engagement was observed in general. The authors concluded that the lack of emotionality on these sites is probably the single most detrimental factor for engagement:

> We also observed a withdrawal effect: People who were exposed to fewer emotional posts (of either valence) in their news feeds were less expressive overall on the following days, addressing the question about how emotional expression affects social engagement online. (p. 8790)

Finally, there are ethical questions concerning how the experiments were conducted, which ultimately led Facebook to apologize to its users. Of course, conducting experiments is not necessarily a problem in and of itself, in principle, and is common practice in many disciplines. For example, much of what we know about drug efficacy for the treatment of mental health comes from knowledge gained through experimental design. However, the media, academics, and the general public all harshly criticized how this particular experiment was conducted because of its ethical implications and methodological shortcomings. The primary reason for the upheaval centred on the fact that those who were included in the experiment were not informed about their participation, something referred to as **informed consent**, nor were they properly debriefed. **Debriefing** is a central part of experimental design,

Continued

as it gives those who partake (voluntarily) in experiments the opportunity to learn exactly what the experiment intended to manipulate and how this may or may not affect them. It is also problematic for academics to engage in research that does not follow the protocols and guidelines put forth by universities, as this creates a general distrust in research and negatively affects the relationship between researchers and the individuals who participate in their studies.

sites in general, and that what we see can easily be manipulated and modified through computer algorithms.

Historical Definitions of Technology

Defining technology is no easy task. In the 2009 movie *Star Trek*, Scotty suggests that "transwarp beaming" is "like trying to hit a bullet with a smaller bullet, whilst wearing a blindfold, riding a horse" (Abrams, 2009).[1] Defining *technology* presents a similar challenge, and scholars have proposed many different definitions of the concept. In this section, we will review five different definitions, from the narrowest to the broadest, which view technology as (1) material substance, (2) knowledge, (3) practice, (4) technique, and (5) society.

1. Technology as Material Substance

Until the nineteenth century, the study of technology was primarily the focus of the technical fields or applied sciences; little work on technology was done in, for example, the social sciences or humanities. In technical fields technology was primarily defined as consisting of technical components; little attention was paid to the interplay of technology and society. Within this very materialistic approach, technology is viewed as "a radical other to humanity" (Feist, Beauvais, & Shukla, 2010, p. 8), an entity that exists outside of the social realm. This approach sees technology, then, as a passive object, a tool created by humans to be used under our control (Feist et al., 2010).

By examining technology as only **material substance**, the complex interplay of technology and society is disregarded. This tunnel vision limits our understanding of technology and does not allow for an examination of social change resulting from technology. This view has been largely discredited and a number of alternative definitions have been proposed.

2. Technology as Knowledge

In the same way that technology is closely interlinked with science, it is also closely connected to knowledge. At the most basic level, "[t]echnology is based upon, utilizes, and generates a complex body of knowledge, part of which may reasonably be called specifically technological knowledge" (McGinn, 1978, p. 186). In contrast to scientific knowledge, technological knowledge stems from human activity, often in relation to an **artifact** (Hershbach, 1995). *Artifacts*[2] are defined as all objects that have been modified, modelled, or produced according to a set of humanly imposed attributes. Examples of artifacts are tools, weapons, ornaments, utensils, and buildings. Technological knowledge is therefore focused on the ability to create, utilize, or transform objects with the aim of facilitating certain activities or achieving specific goals (McGinn, 1978). This distinguishes technological knowledge from scientific knowledge, which can be applied to the design and building of artifacts but is not directly linked with practical applications (see the discussion in Chapter 2). Scientific knowledge, in contrast, is abstract and consists of our understanding of the natural world. For instance, calculus, as a branch of mathematics, provides an understanding of limits, functions, derivatives, and integrals, and at the same time we can observe its value in real-world applications. Hence, calculus provided to a large extent the foundation for a practical **invention**, namely the introduction of the steam engine (Restivo, 2005).

The metaphor of technology as knowledge can, however, be limiting in two ways. First, it does not consider that the knowledge required to create, utilize, and transform objects is a different entity than the object itself, even if the object was invented based on this knowledge. Second, the metaphor disregards the impact that technology has on society by limiting technology to expertise, skill, and know-how. Layton's model of technology and knowledge is useful to examine next because it overcomes some of these limitations.

While also using the metaphor of technology as knowledge, in his model Layton distinguishes between the technology itself and the knowledge available about the technology. At the centre of **Layton's model of technology** is the process of technological development in which "technological ideas must be translated into designs" which then "must be implemented by techniques and tools to produce things" (Layton, 1974, p. 38). From this viewpoint, a model of technology emerges in which technology is not a single entity but, rather, embodies three different elements:

1. *Ideas*: Ideas are at one end of the spectrum, representing the thought processes that precede the tool, which is often referred to as the *technological imagination*. Ideas about what objects are useful motivate design and development.
2. *Design*: Design is in the middle of the spectrum, mediating between the abstract idea and the object. Design is the step that is required to go from idea to tool development and is where craftsmanship is needed.

3. *Techniques*: Technique describes the actual artifact, and lies at the other end of the spectrum. The artifact is made up of material substance and allows humans to complete tasks.

Layton's model of technology has two advantages. First, the definition of *technology* goes beyond a pure consideration of artifact. The model explicitly distinguishes between the artifact and the knowledge from which it arises. Second, the model also incorporates design as a middle stage that lies between the idea of a tool and the artifact itself (discussed in Chapter 5). This creates a link between how we envision tools and their actual realization, which are often two different things. One disadvantage of the model, however, is that there is no explanation of how technology and technological knowledge are linked to society. In this view, technology remains conceptualized as an artifact, drawing only on knowledge and design and in isolation from culture, economics, power, etc. That is, as in other theories of technology as knowledge, the socio-technical is largely disregarded.

3. Technology as Practice

A third set of definitions have broadened the meaning of technology. Canadian scholar Ursula Franklin (1992) has chosen to define *technology* in the context of the real world. For her, technology is not limited to the apparatus, to the material substance, or to the artifact. Nor is it just "the sum of the artifacts"; instead, it is "a system" involving organization, procedures, symbols, new words, and most importantly, a mindset (p. 2). Hence, technology needs to be understood as practice, as embedded in the everyday activities of humans.

Franklin's view is rather pessimistic in that the "real world of technology seems to involve an inherent trust in machines and devices ('production is under control') and a basic apprehension of people" (p. 25). Franklin criticizes society's simplistic view of technology, namely that people create problems and are unpredictable, while machines provide solutions to problems and are always controllable (1992). Hence, technologies are always idealized because any problems that arise from them can be easily blamed on people, on those who designed, produced, or consumed a given technology. Franklin (1992) believed that a technology that is perceived as being able to "liberate its users" often ends up enslaving them by creating a dependence on that technology. For instance, the iPod allows users to listen to music on the go and, consequently, creates a barrier between users and their external environment. Franklin argues that these tools have contributed to a world of "technologically induced human isolation" (p. 46).

Instead of conceptualizing technology as an external force that functions outside the everyday realm, viewing technology as practice places technology within people's everyday lives. This is the strength of this approach:

it emphasizes how technology becomes normalized within society over time and thereby points out how technology is a structuring force in how we live, play, and work. Simply put, we do not question our routines but, rather, take them for granted as part of our everyday lives. When we put on our running shoes and tie our laces, this is a *normalized* behaviour. We do not realize that shoes are an invention (as the Bata Shoe Museum in Toronto documents) and that shoelaces are a complex technology that developed over centuries (Tenner, 2003).

The limitation of Franklin's view is that technology is analyzed primarily as a negative force. This viewpoint asserts that it is technology that determines how social change occurs in society and neglects to examine human agency (see Chapter 3 for a discussion of technological determinism). Such an interpretation limits how we view technology because it does not allow for people's capacity to make decisions about which technologies they want to use, how they want to use them, and how these technologies affect their lives.

4. Technology as Technique

A different approach to defining *technology* comes from scholars who look at the problem from an action-oriented point of view. These thinkers aim to identify the essence of technology by distinguishing between *technology* and *technique*, which is a translation of the German word *Technik* (Hanks, 2010). **Technique**, then, describes an abstract concept and not an object. Martin Heidegger (2010) describes *technique* as a human activity and further divides it into **goal** (*Zweck* in German) and **mechanism** (*Mittel* in German). The goal is what humans want to achieve with the technique. It can be either something concrete, like an activity, or something more abstract, like a state of existence. The mechanism provides the means to realize the goal—this includes materials, procedures, know-how, and societal norms. Heidegger argues that the activity of technique and its products have an impact on every aspect of life.

Jürgen Habermas also describes technology in terms of the realization of goals. He sees technology as **strategic action** because it provides the means for the realization of human endeavours (Simpson, 1995). Habermas (1984) identifies a strategic action as a social action that is "oriented towards success" and that has considered "the aspect of following rules of rational choice and assess[ing] the efficacy of influencing the decisions of a rational opponent" (p. 285).

The emphasis on technology as goal was also present in Jacques Ellul's study of technology, where he defined *technique* as a standardized means for attaining a predetermined goal in society (Merton, 1964). Ellul also described technique as a mechanism characterized by efficiency: "the totality of methods rationally arrived at, and having absolute efficiency (for a given stage of development) in every field of human activity" (1964, p. xxv).

Ellul (1964) was interested in examining the lasting effect of efficient techniques, and in this context he viewed technique as the "defining force of a new social order in which efficiency is no longer an option but a necessity imposed on all human activity" (p. 17). His critique of technique focuses on the intricate link between technology and its social, psychological, moral, and economic consequences, which are not necessarily in agreement with human ethics. Hence, according to Ellul, technology imposes the principle of efficient ordering on society at the expense of other considerations.

In these conceptualizations of technology as technique, technology is examined in relation to human activity. Technology is no longer "just a tool"; it becomes a mechanism for achieving human needs and wants through efficient systems. While these thinkers take our understanding of technology a step further and acknowledge the lasting impact of technology on society, they do not elaborate on the mechanisms by which social change occurs. Again, technology continues to be an agent, a force external to society.

5. Technology as Society

When we define *technology* as material substance, knowledge, practice, or technique, we limit our ability to analyze the technological in society. Definitions of *technology* need to be broader to allow for a comprehensive examination of its close interplay with society. Narrow definitions limit our ability to see the realms in which technology has left a mark. Simpson (1995) provides a comprehensive definition, stating that technology encompasses knowledge, mechanisms, skills, and apparatus that are geared toward controlling and transforming society. In this perspective, technology goes beyond merely being machinery or practice—it becomes an agent of change that can control and alter humanity.

Jean Baudrillard goes even further by arguing that technology does more than effect change in society: "[i]t doesn't push things forward or transform the world, it becomes the world" (Baudrillard & Gane, 1993, p. 44). Baudrillard is not the only one to argue that technology and society become one and the same entity. For Herbert Marcuse, technology is "a social process, in which technics proper (that is, the technical apparatus of industry, transportation [and] communication) is but a partial factor" (1982, p. 138). As part of his critique of consumerism, Marcuse believes that the introduction of new technologies brought about new standards as well as cultural and social change, which were not purely the effect of technology but "rather themselves determining factors in the development of machinery and mass production" (1982, p. 138). This critique is perhaps one of the most relevant analyses of the technology–society link because it highlights the complex interdependence between cultural and social change and technological developments.

Like Baudrillard, Marcuse points to diminishing critical thought in society as the clamour for material goods increases. The radical view that technology is equal to society points out that our technological society cannot exist outside the framework of technology. Technologies are not only ubiquitous in our daily lives (e.g., transport, communication, food provision, and consumption), but even our way of seeing the world is mediated by technology. There is no escaping it. However, this view is also problematic because it does not allow us to study how technology intersects with society. In order for us to be able to study technology, we need to define it as something separate from society itself. If our definition of technology argues that it has become so intertwined with society that the two are in fact a single unit, this precludes any kind of serious investigation of how they influence each other.

Making Sense of These Definitions

It is important to understand the range of existing definitions of technology because this will provide the basis of our discussions of how technology intersects with society in the remainder of the book. Each of the five different definitions of technology reviewed has its merits, helping us understand one aspect of technology. Nevertheless, it is equally important to realize that no single definition can fully capture the meaning of such a complex concept. Hall has argued that we have to recognize the rich technological bases of modern cultural production, which enable us to endlessly simulate, reproduce, reiterate, and recapitulate. But there is all the difference in the world between the assertion that there is no one, final, absolute meaning of technology and the assertion that meaning does not exist (Grossberg, 1996, p. 137).

The definitions of technology as material substance, knowledge, practice, and technique are all rather limiting and do not show sufficiently how technology links to society. On the other hand, the definition of technology as society is broad in scope and directly attempts to understand how society and technology come together. The problem, though, with broad conceptualizations such as those of Baudrillard is that they fuse society and technology into one and the same thing: "[i]t doesn't push things forward or transform the world, it becomes the world" (Baudrillard & Gane, 1993, p. 44). This makes it impossible to study how the two are linked and also neglects to include the technology–society interdependence.

The definition of technology that we will adapt in this book is simple and draws on elements from the five definitions discussed above:

> Technology is an assemblage of material objects, embodying and reflecting societal elements, such as knowledge, norms, and attitudes, that have been shaped and structured to serve social, political, cultural, and existential purposes.

Despite its simplicity, the definition has three advantages: (1) it separates technology from society sufficiently enough to allow for an investigation of the technology–society interdependence; (2) it does not include technology as an element of society, rather it sees technology as serving social purposes; and (3) it views technology as embodying and reflecting knowledge, social norms, **social structures**, political interests, and so forth. This definition will guide our inquiry in the remainder of the book.

We conclude that technology has multiple definitions as it is a word that, applied in different social, historical, and cultural contexts, means different things. As a result, providing a simple definition is an effective way to distinguish the uniqueness of technology by trying to separate it from society while also taking into account how the social factors affect technological and scientific developments. Doing so, in turn, leads the way toward a more in-depth understanding of how technology intersects with other social realms. Additionally, in Box 1.3 we will examine in more detail the challenges inherent in studying technology. In the next section, we explore two contemporary definitions of technology that move the discussion of what technology is a step further.

Contemporary Discussions of Technology

In addition to the definitions of technology we have discussed so far, there also exist contemporary conceptualizations that are directly influenced by computational advancements and the digital age. These contemporary definitions show how the evolution of technology leads to changes in how we define technology, as well as to changes in the value and relevance we ascribe to technology in society. We discuss the two most prominent approaches here to show how radically different the notion of technology is in simulation and augmentation, where the material and the human start to blur and slowly become indistinguishable. Simulation is the attempt to develop technologies that can imitate the human mind and/or body. By contrast, augmentation is based on the integration of technology with the human body to enhance or strengthen certain capabilities or functions. These two perspectives question our view of technology as an external force because technology either becomes another actor in a social system or is seamlessly integrated with the human mind and body.

Simulation

Artificial intelligence (AI) started as a discipline in the late 1940s, when computing was still in its infancy, with the aim of developing tools that could resemble or outperform human intelligence. While debate continues today as to what it means to have an intelligent machine, the general goal in AI is to simulate in any way or form human faculties, often including emotionality.

Alan Turing (1950) was the first to discuss the idea of a "thinking machine" and to propose ways in which we could test whether machines can "think" or at least simulate thinking. His most central contribution to the field was the idea that AI could be achieved through computation instead of machinery. Early attempts to simulate human faculties had focused on building complex machines that physically resembled humans. However, according to Turing, what determines whether a machine qualifies as intelligent is the extent to which it can imitate the capabilities of the human brain.

Turing (1950) argued that machines have the ability to imitate human cognitive processes to such an extent that it is impossible to distinguish between human and machine. He devised the **Turing Test**, or imitation game, for two purposes: (1) to test a machine's potential to show intelligent behaviour and (2) to assess a human's ability to differentiate between human and machine intelligence. In the Turing Test, three players—an interrogator, a human, and a machine—are visually separated from one another and the goal of the game is for the interrogator to discriminate between machine and human through a series of queries using natural language. If the interrogator cannot distinguish machine from human, the machine has successfully passed the test. In June 2014, there were claims that the first computer AI had passed the Turing Test during a competition at the University of Reading in the United Kingdom. The program simulated a 13-year-old Ukrainian boy named Eugene Goostman and appeared convincingly human to 33 per cent of judges at the event. However, some question whether "Eugene" acted within the parameters of the test by openly limiting conversation topics beyond the expected knowledge of a teenage boy, as well as holding conversations lasting only about five minutes, which provided less time for judges to search for non-human elements. The Turing Test has had a profound impact on the field of artificial intelligence and computing in general, as it demonstrates the complexity of distinguishing what is profoundly human and what is in essence technological.

Even though computers can perform complex tasks mimicking humans or even outperforming them, John McCarthy (2007), one of the founders of the field of AI, argues that computers and humans are still fundamentally different in the way they solve problems: "Computer programs have plenty of speed and memory but their abilities correspond to the intellectual mechanisms that program designers understand well enough to put in programs" (para. 17). Hence computers can easily perform certain types of tasks—those based on algorithms—while other human abilities, even those that a two-year-old can easily master, cannot yet be programmed. Underlying this complexity is the lack of understanding in cognitive science about exactly what makes up human intelligence and how to program these components. In addition, McCarthy argues that a fundamental difference between humans and computers is that "[v]ery likely the organization of the intellectual mechanisms for AI can usefully be different from that in people" (para. 15).

Not surprisingly, the early dream of creating a machine that resembles humans has been largely abandoned even though it continues to persevere in science fiction. (Examples from science fiction movies of machines that simulate human faculties and even resemble human appearance abound and include *A.I. Artificial Intelligence*, *The Terminator*, and *Sleeper*). Instead, much effort is now devoted toward building machines that can perform complex tasks that humans have difficulty with or are unable to perform because of limited memory and computational resources. These intelligent machines do not need to resemble humans in their appearance or in their emotionality.

One of the most successful recent developments in AI is that of **intelligent agents** or **chatterbots**, which are computational systems based on **algorithms** that can process complex and large amounts of data (Russell & Norvig, 2003). While there is much debate around whether Web-based agents can qualify as intelligent, some chatterbots have reached a high level of sophistication and usefulness. Joseph Weizenbaum in 1966 developed a prototype of a chatterbot, which he named ELIZA, that could convincingly simulate a Rogerian psychotherapist (Rubin, Chen, & Thorimbert, 2010). ELIZA was designed on the premise that patients direct the conversation, and as a result the chatterbot primarily relied on external input to hold a conversation. (To interact with ELIZA, go to www.masswerk.at/elizabot/eliza.html.)

More sophisticated bots are autonomous, that is, able to act without external input. An example is the chatterbot that greets visitors at the U.S. Army website: **SGT STAR** is able to provide, in addition to basic information about the army, responses to more complex queries. To the question "Who are you?" SGT STAR responds: "My name is SGT STAR, which stands for Strong, Trained and Ready. I'm an artificial intelligence agent created for

"Chatterbot": SGT STAR, the U.S. Army's virtual guide.

the U.S. Army to provide you with information about Army life." SGT STAR reflects the army's voice and has been programmed to provide responses that fit with the army's norms and values. After testing SGT STAR with a wide array of questions, it becomes apparent that he is a machine, as some responses are quirky. Nonetheless, SGT STAR demonstrates advances in computing as he can act much more autonomously than ELIZA, who relies almost completely on external inputs to carry on a conversation.

Modern AI systems show the current technological limitations in building intelligent machines and more fundamentally demonstrate that the question as to when a machine can be considered intelligent is very difficult to answer. Intelligent systems are becoming more prevalent as they can act autonomously without the need for human input.

Augmentation

More recent discussions of technology have focused less on AI and more on ways to create augmented environments and bodies. Whereas AI is based on principles of simulation and replication between human and nonhuman entities, augmentation is based on principles of connectedness and responsiveness (Viseu, 2002). In augmentation, actors do not change their physical appearance and body shape, as is the case in simulation. In this approach, "[r]ather than building self-contained machines or leaving the body behind, machines and humans are coupled together into new hybrid actors with added capabilities" (Viseu, 2002). The physical body is augmented by connecting it to digital components with computational and communicational capabilities.

Augmentation can occur in many ways. An example of augmentation is **wearable computing, where** portable computers aid in the decision-making process by providing additional information, enhanced **surrounding awareness capabilities,** and real-time data streaming. A cellphone is a wearable computing device because it augments our capacities to communicate by bridging space and time constraints and allows us to access data on demand (Klemens, 2010).

While the aim of artificial intelligence is to *re-create* the human experience, augmentation attempts to *intensify* human qualities. One such example of augmentation is the **cyborg,** a merging of human and machine through seamless connectivity. Clynes and Kline introduced the term *cyborg* in the 1960s to describe the ways that long-distance space travel would require astronauts to transform their human qualities to robot-like qualities, which are fully automated. These transformations would allow astronauts to master the challenges presented in extraterrestrial environments. For Clynes and Kline (1960), the main objective of the cyborg was "to provide an organizational system in which such robot-like problems are taken care of automatically and unconsciously, leaving man free to explore, to create, to think, and to feel" (p. 27).

Science fiction writers then adapted the cyborg concept, which became a part of our popular culture as presented in books, movies, and television programs. A cyborg—a robot-like machine with human characteristics—is featured in the movie series *The Terminator*, in which Arnold Schwarzenegger plays Terminator, who has super-human strength and is indestructible by contemporary weapons. The latest Terminator model, the T1000, is superior to its predecessor model in many ways. It consists of a mimetic polyalloy, which is a kind of liquid metal that can emulate anything that surrounds it, giving the cyborg enormous flexibility and superiority. Interestingly, the cyborg also displays feelings that allow it to blend in well with humans, unlike the first Terminator, which was devoid of any human-like emotions.[3] Box 1.2 describes the cyborg experience as an example of an artifact built to augment reality through the merging of human and machine.

Significantly, the cyborg concept is moving from the annals of science fiction into the mainstream with the development of a number of man–machine systems that are geared toward practical goals, such as dealing with medical conditions. Such a prototype is the **C-Leg** system, which allows individuals with an amputated leg to walk again.

Futurists predict that augmentation and the coming together of human and machine are inevitable. One of the more controversial possibilities is **transhumanism**, which is characterized by the "surpassing of the biological limitations of our bodies, be they our lifespans or the capabilities of our brains" (Dewdney, 1998). Transhumanism is the product of a quasi-religious movement dedicated to the belief in the "futuristic technological change of human nature for the achievement of certain goals, such as freedom from suffering and from bodily and material constraints, immortality and 'super-intelligence'" (Schummer, 2006, p. 430). According to Schummer (2006), transhumanists have "an existential interest in nanotechnology, as a means for the ends of personal and/or societal Salvation" (p. 432). The transhumanist position toward nanotechnology raises pertinent ethical questions about the role of technology in transforming and prolonging the lifespan of the human body. Moreover, transhumanism aims to use scientific discoveries to enhance human faculties. The Kurzweil Accelerating Intelligence blog (www.kurzweilai.net/) showcases recent technological discoveries and inventions that have the potential to radically transform the human body. For instance, findings are reported from a study that shows how mice learn faster and remember better after PKR (an immune molecule that signals viral infections to the brain) is inhibited. From a transhumanist perspective, PKR is seen as a potential smart drug that boosts our cognitive capacities.

Developments such as the cyborg C-Leg and the inhibition of PKR illustrate the advancements in augmentation and the ways that science and technology can become a part of the human body, making it increasingly difficult to delineate the boundaries between what is human and what is technological.

Box 1.2

Augmentation through Wearable Computing: The Birth of the Cyborg

The cyborg dream is no longer just science fiction. The first attempts to link human and machine occurred in the 1980s when Steve Mann started using a wearable computing system that he called the WearComp. This system integrates wires, sensors, and computers with the aim of increasing users' memory, enhancing their vision, and allowing them to stay perpetually connected to data (Mann & Niedzviecki, 2001). The cyborg state raises an intriguing question: What is it like to live as part machine and part human? Does doing so fundamentally change human nature?

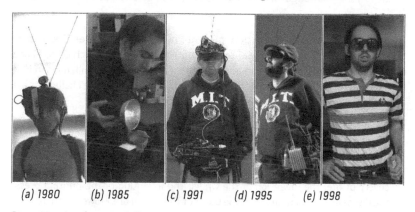

(a) 1980   (b) 1985   (c) 1991   (d) 1995   (e) 1998

Steve Mann's cyborg evolutions.

The five images show the development of Mann's equipment from the early 1980s to the late 1990s. These early prototypes are in stark contrast to the current incarnation of his WearComp system, which is so minute that it is barely noticeable and consists of three main features. First, it includes a digital camera that allows Mann to upload a video stream of his daily experiences in real time to the Internet, giving new meaning to the concepts of privacy and surveillance (this will be discussed in more detail in Chapter 11). In addition, a small camera is attached to his eyeglasses, providing him with a split real-to-Web experience, connecting him to the Internet and mobile devices 24/7. Finally, the camera also allows him to block out stimuli from his environment, such as advertisements, presenting an edited image of his surrounding world.

As a result of the device, Mann experiences the world as an amalgamation of the physical environment that surrounds him and the digital world that streams in front of his eyes at all times through his Web interface (Mann & Niedzviecki, 2001). This divided existence shows that "Mann inhabits a different world than you or I, a 'cyborgspace' that he claims is inevitable for all of us" (Dewdney, 2001, D7). To what extent human and machine will be integrated is still an open question; however, the concept has already garnered many followers and the community of cyborgs has reached about 80,000 worldwide (Dewdney, 2001).

Source: Photos are from Mann, Steve (2012) "Wearable Computing" in Soegaard, Mads and Dam, Rikke Friis (eds.). *Encyclopedia of Human-Computer Interaction.* Aarhus, Denmark: The Interaction-Design.org Foundation. Available online at http://www.interaction-design.org/encyclopedia/wearable_computing.html. Used with permission.

Box 1.3 discusses five challenges present in any inquiry of the relationship between technology and society. In addition, new technologies continue to emerge, creating new challenges for scholars. In the previous section, simulation and augmentation were discussed as two recent technological developments that illustrate how our perspective of what technology is continues to evolve and that also reveal the ethical, moral, and societal implications of these endeavours.

Box 1.3   Challenges in the Study of Technology and Society

The study of technology and society presents numerous challenges. The first of these stems from the complexity of the concepts themselves, as each is broad and difficult to define and measure. In addition, there are numerous challenges in how to approach research problems in the area. The five most prevalent challenges are as follows:[4]

1. *Rapid technological advances*: Technology evolves at a rapid pace. Not only do existing technologies transform, often becoming more complex, efficient, and fast, but there are also moments in history where technological revolutions have occurred. The key technological revolutions usually discussed include the discovery of fire; the invention of the wheel; the invention of the printing press; the discovery of electricity; and the dawn of the digital era. However, there is no definitive list of technological revolutions. We could include many other technological developments in our list, such as early tool use, navigation, metallurgy, functional magnetic resonance imaging (fMRI), etc. The point is that technologies evolve quickly and a single invention can lead to an infinite number of further developments.

2. *Unprecedented social change*: New technologies lead to unprecedented social change in many realms of society, affecting many aspects of social, cultural, and economic life, including how we work, live, communicate, and travel. Studying these changes is difficult because we cannot easily capture new forms of behaviour, thought, attitude, and belief with existing frameworks and methodologies. Thus, to assess the full impact of technology on society, researchers need to develop new theories and forms of measurement that complement existing ones.

3. *Direction and type of effect*: Determining the direction of effect is a major challenge because it is difficult to determine the extent to which technology affects society or society affects technology. Some analysts have argued that a mutual shaping of society and technology occurs (Bijker, Hughes, & Pinch, 1999) that is complex and non-linear (Chapter 3 covers this point in more detail). Moreover, researchers in the field aim to uncover an effect, regardless of whether the type of effect is positive or negative. However, in many cases no directional effect can be observed because technology becomes normalized and is then a part of everyday life.

4. *Target group*: When examining technology, we must keep in mind the target group. Many social changes associated with technology are specific to a particular social group, social class, ethnic group, or religious belief, which is the root of technological inequality. For example, industrialization affected workers in different ways than it affected managers and owners. For workers, industrialization meant deskilling, lower wages, and inferior working conditions. By contrast, employers saw advantages in streamlining work processes, reducing error, and increasing efficiency. Further, the use of machinery allowed employers to hire unskilled labour for lower wages. Hence, the particulars of a group have to be examined to understand how that group is appropriating the technology and how the technology has an impact on members' lives.

5. *Changing uses*: The uses of technology also change over time. The cellphone, for example, started out as a portable device to communicate one-to-one independently of location. It quickly transformed into a more complex tool, allowing users also to access the Web, take pictures, listen to music, store information, and play games. Hence a single technology often mutates into a technology serving multiple purposes.

Conclusions

With advancements in science and technology, the level of interaction between society and technology continues to grow rapidly. The prevailing theoretical perspectives on this subject have supplied a rich foundation of debate and criticism in this area. Yet, as the technology–society relationship deepens in complexity and intimacy, our definition of technology also becomes more and more opaque. In Western societies, the dominance of technology in everyday life has greatly altered conceptions of work and play. Yet such dominance has also profoundly affected and shaped notions of human existence in ways that earlier critics could not have imagined. Whereas early opponents of industrial technology were suspicious of hulking steel machines displacing the skilled craftsperson, contemporary critics are assailed with new ethical and moral challenges, as infinitesimal technologies enter the economic marketplace and the politico-cultural spheres of our secular, consumerist society.

The philosophical implications of classifying and clarifying present and forthcoming technologies will arguably be intertwined with how contemporary and future generations of citizens and scholars view technology as a whole. Indeed, it will be interesting to see how members of Generation Z (those born between 1990 and 2010) will rationalize, critique, and characterize technology, especially when considering the indelible role of, and their dependence upon, technology in their lives.

Questions for Critical Thought

1. Discuss the challenges associated with studying technology. Choose a specific technology that interests you to illustrate the discussed challenges.

2. How is technology described in the definition of technology as practice? What are the strengths and limitations of this conceptualization?

3. Compare and contrast the theoretical view of technology as power with that of technology as mechanization.

4. Critically examine the concept of the cyborg and discuss its ethical implications.

Suggested Readings

Bostrom, N. (2014). *Superintelligence: Paths, dangers, strategies.* Oxford: Oxford University Press. This book explores the new boundaries of transhumanism by looking at human and machine intelligence both as a possibility to new paths as well as a critique.

Franklin, U.M. (1992). *The real world of technology.* Concord, ON: House of Anansi. This book critically examines the relation of society to technology through the framework of practice.

Mann, S., & Niedzviecki, H. (2001). *Cyborg: Digital destiny and human possibility in the age of the wearable computer.* Toronto: Doubleday. An exploration of the wearable computer and how it affects humans and society.

Honeysett, A. (2014, 4 August). The Facebook experiment: What it means for you. *Forbes.* Retrieved October 25, 2014, from www.forbes.com/sites/dailymuse/2014/08/04/the-facebook-experiment-what-it-means-for-you/. The article provides an overview of the Facebook experiment and discusses some of its implications for businesses and users.

Online Resources

Steve Mann's laboratory at the University of Toronto
www.eecg.toronto.edu/~mann/
> The webpage compiles papers, presentations, and video footage of Mann's research about technology, privacy, and digital tools. It also includes information on his book and the movie made about his life as a cyborg.

Computer AI passes Turing Test in "world first"
www.bbc.com/news/technology-27762088
> This BBC story provides an overview of the most recent attempt to pass the Turing Test and includes a link to a video previewing the event.

What Is Artificial Intelligence?
www-formal.stanford.edu/jmc/whatisai/whatisai.html
> John McCarthy, the founder of artificial intelligence, provides a brief introduction to the topic.

Ask SGT STAR
www.goarmy.com/ask-sgt-star.html
> This is the intelligent agent of the U.S. Army, which answers questions about army life for those visiting the website.

2

Technology in Society: A Historical Overview

Learning Objectives

◎ to obtain a broad overview of the history of technology;

◎ to critically examine in a historical context how technology and society have mutually shaped each other;

◎ to provide an alternative view of the history of technology by taking a sociological perspective of technological transformations;

◎ to learn about how digital tools have led to the development of a high-tech society characterized by customization, individualism, and privatization.

Introduction

This chapter provides a broad overview of the history of technology by tracing the roots of technological development, discussing key periods of technological innovation, and outlining our present-day, high-tech society. The primary aim of the chapter is not to comprehensively cover technological developments over time, but to outline on-the-ground examples that illustrate how technology and society intersect. This chapter further attempts to link technologies, inventors, and historical moments to provide an in-depth examination of the socio-political context from which technologies emerge. This analysis will illustrate how we need to understand technology as a complex process instead of viewing it as a purely material entity disembodied from any societal influence. This chapter shows how technology is ingrained in society, becoming a part of all aspects of our lives. It outlines the merits of taking a sociological perspective of the history of technology.

Why Study the History of Technology?

Before we embark on historical details, we need to reflect on why it is important for us to understand the history of technology in our society. Technology is seen as a key mechanism of social change, moving society forward into new social, cultural, political, and economic milieus. For example, it is technology that makes it possible for humans to subsist in **megacities**, such as

Tokyo, with a population of 37.8 million, or Mexico City, with a population of 21 million. But megacities did not emerge overnight; in fact, there is no evidence of large human settlements in prehistoric times. The creation of megacities was possible only through the constant advancement of technology over centuries. This process occurred simultaneously with the evolution of advanced forms of construction, chains of mass distribution of goods, and new forms of social and political organization. While the evolutionary process of technology was not always straightforward, understanding that process and its link to social change is important.

Scholars of the history of technology describe the history of tool use as following an **evolutionary model of technological development** because tools build upon existing knowledge, making their development incremental. Throughout history, inventors did not work in complete isolation but instead drew upon earlier designs, often combining existing pieces into new forms. George Basalla (1988), in *The Evolution of Technology*, provides a good explanation of how this evolutionary model unfolds: he compares the process of innovation to the way biological evolution occurs in the natural world. The comparison is based on the diversity of tools that exists in the world of manufactured objects, which he argues is similar to the diversity of life forms that exists in nature. Central to Basalla's argument is the idea that novel tools arise only from earlier ones and "that new kinds of made things are never pure creations of theory, ingenuity or fancy" (Basalla, 1988, pp. vii–viii). Eugene Ferguson (1992) uses the example of the automobile to illustrate how technology is evolutionary instead of revolutionary, as the main components constituting the automobile were based on existing inventions. The pistons, cylinders, and nozzles used in cars formed part of a pump designed by Hero of Alexandria two millennia before. What made the automobile different from previous technologies was its unique blend of components, including modern electrical parts. This example shows that the integration of existing ideas in new ways is often what makes a tool innovative.

That technology develops in an evolutionary way, rather than in a revolutionary manner, may suggest that the study of technology is straightforward. Nonetheless, two key issues make understanding the history of technology difficult. First, there is a gap in time that exists between when an inventor first develops a new technology and when this technology is revealed and examined. Because social, cultural, and technological transformations are so extensive, people find it difficult to imagine what life was like in previous eras without their ideas being at least partly coloured by the technology and ideas we take for granted now. And the farther back in time one travels, the more true that is. The **Stone Age**, for example, began approximately 2.6 million years ago, while the medieval period ended only approximately 600 years ago. If we find it challenging today to relate to the medieval period, it is even more difficult to imagine events dating back millions of years.

The second issue that makes it difficult for us to understand the history of technology is our reliance on artifacts as evidence. Artifacts can be considered the basic components of **material culture** and are usually contrasted with elements encountered in nature, such as leaves, trees, caves, etc. *Material culture* refers to the interrelation that exists between an artifact and the social relations, cultural attitudes, and norms that are present in the society that uses the artifact.

Using artifacts as sole evidence of how societies evolved, however, is limiting because identifying all the existing tools of the time period under study is a daunting task. Moreover, studying the artifacts alone does not take into account how they shaped social norms, attitudes, and behaviours. The first tools were primitive and consisted of bones, flint, stones, and sticks, making it difficult for scholars to distinguish tools from naturally occurring objects. In order to make the past accessible, then, scholars study how previous societies used artifacts and what their social significance was.

We begin our examination of the history of technology with an overview of these different technological periods and the associated socio-political and cultural contexts. We define seven distinct periods of technological evolution: (1) the early beginnings of technological ingenuity, (2) ancient technology, (3) the Renaissance, (4) the Enlightenment and French Revolution, (5) the Industrial Revolution, (6) electronic times, and (7) the information society.

The Stone Age: The Early Beginnings of Technological Ingenuity

The earliest evidence of technology is traced back to the use of tools during the Stone Age, about 2.6 million years ago. There are two reasons why the study of early tool use in prehistoric times is significant. First, tool use suggests that humans reached an awareness of themselves as separate from the world around them, allowing for the development and use of external objects to accomplish tasks. This represents the earliest manifestation of human behaviour as intelligent and goal-oriented. Second, tool use is linked to human social and cultural evolution in terms of setting the foundation for a wide range of task-oriented behaviours, such as cutting, scratching, and manipulating (Plummer, 2004). These kinds of behaviours, even though simple, allow for complex interactions with the environment and other individuals and indicate the early beginnings of consciousness and thought. A set of socio-cultural behaviours directly results from tool use—users feel a sense of ownership over objects and, as a result, protect these from potential intruders. Therefore, even early tool use necessitates a sociological and cultural understanding of the relationship among tools, humans, and social systems.

In the Stone Age, communities would subsist on meat, obtained by hunting prey, and produce, obtained by gathering berries and other edible plants; this is how the term **hunter-gatherer societies** was coined. Hunter-gatherers lived in **nomadic tribes** that were highly dependent on climate and food availability. During this period, stone tools started to emerge as the first key technological development. Plummer (2004) describes how Oldowan archaeological sites in Eastern, Southern, and Northern Africa provided the first concrete evidence of material culture. Beginning around 2.6 million years ago, stone cores were struck to make sharp-edged chips of stone known as flakes. Tool use at the time was limited to animal butchery and possibly preparing plant foods and working with wood. These materials developed from single all-purpose tools to an assemblage of varied and highly specified ones, demonstrating the high level of complexity involved in early tool development. Though there is an assumption that the hunter-gatherer lifestyle was deprived, lonely, and brutish, Late Stone Age societies had a rich social and spiritual life—as evidenced in cave paintings, rock engravings, and other existing artifacts.[1] The domestication of plants and animals, considered a technological invention, marked a radical departure from the hunter-gatherer lifestyle. This shift took place over the course of several thousand years during what scholars have termed the **Neolithic period,** derived from the Greek words *neo,* meaning "new," and *lithic,* which refers to "stone"—that is, the New Stone Age. Having conducted a careful investigation of the archaeological record in the Middle East, influential archaeologist V. Gordon Childe concluded that the move from hunter-gatherer societies to the reliance on tools for agriculture was the most significant change in human cultural and social evolution (Ratnagar, 2001). To denote the impact of the introduction of agriculture on human societies, Childe introduced the term **Neolithic Revolution,** often also referred to as the **Agricultural Revolution**.

The Agricultural Revolution did not occur concurrently around the world. Rather, agricultural development originated in and spread from several regions at different times (Smith, 1995). The first area to witness the domestication of plants and animals was the Fertile Crescent in the Near East, approximately 10,000 years ago. Agriculture then arose in eastern China some 8,500 years ago, followed by sub-Saharan Africa and the Americas between 4,000 and 5,000 years ago.

In each of these settings, the Agricultural Revolution began with the transition from hunter-gatherer societies to **horticultural** and **pastoral societies**. In horticultural societies, simple hand tools are used to plant and tend crops. Relatively small plots of arable land are cleared of wild vegetation and used to grow food. When the topsoil becomes barren, new plots are cleared and planted, and the old plots lie fallow until the soil's nutrients have been replenished. This shows that horticultural societies require some degree of planning and organization and are a precursor to the **green revolution**, a term that denotes an exponential increase in innovation and transfer of technology in the realm of agricultural production. The "father of the green revolution," Norman Borlaug, is credited with saving millions from starvation in the mid-nineteenth century while also radically transforming the means of food production. The social and economic consequences of the green revolution still remain a controversial topic to date, with many ethical repercussions.

Conversely, in pastoral societies, animals are domesticated and bred for food. Pastoral societies tend to be more prominent in marginal regions where the soil is less fertile and populations must travel with animal herds to where grazing land is available. Generally, both horticulturalists and pastoralists find a more reliable means of acquiring food through the domestication of plants and animals.

In those areas where crops are readily grown, **agrarian societies** often come to replace horticultural societies. In agrarian societies, plows harnessed to animals are used in farming, which affords more efficient, larger-scale agriculture. Because the soil is being turned, fields remain fertile for longer periods of time, allowing people to remain in the same area for many years. In addition, food production increases substantially.

The Neolithic Revolution witnessed unprecedented social change. With the advent of horticultural, pastoral, and especially agrarian methods of food production, larger populations could be sustained. Where permanent settlements were established around food sources, towns and later cities developed. For sociological inquiry, this is a turning point, because settlements allow for the study of place as a social phenomenon, and lead to the introduction of sociological concepts, such as identity, sense of belonging, **community**, and social structure. In such **sedentary societies**, economic and social complexity increased (Barker, 2006). Food surpluses allowed for trade and the payment of tribute or tax. In addition, as it was no longer necessary that everyone be involved in food production, settlements were able to support merchants, craftspeople, warriors, and religious and political leaders. Surpluses also led to greater disparities in wealth and consequently social status. The Neolithic Revolution thus marked the emergence of social roles, class, and work relations. Gender inequality also became more pronounced with the rise of agrarian societies, as the production of food became a more exclusively male responsibility. Women, who had contributed significantly to their families' nourishment as gatherers or small-scale gardeners, were not as involved in larger-scale agriculture using plows and draft animals. As a result, they developed new social roles and these roles became more specialized.

Ancient Technology: The Development of the Scientific Method

As technologies such as the smelting of iron and the invention of the screw and the lever emerged in Greece around 500 to 336 BCE and in Rome around 509 BCE to 190 CE, social organization changed radically. Technology facilitated certain forms of life—concentration in cities and improved food production—and helped in the creation of complex government structures. While Greece and Rome basically continued threads of technological progress that had begun in earlier times, the most important contribution to science and technology from that time period comes from the premise that thought forms the basis for practical action.

Indeed, Fowler (1962) starts his book *The Development of Scientific Method* with a comprehensive overview of ancient Greek philosophy, where he illustrates that it was the ideas and thought processes of the time that represented the early beginnings of technological innovations—not the tools themselves. Then, once the appropriate knowledge was in place, technologies developed as practical solutions to everyday problems. While ancient civilization may be known for its great thinkers, not all inquiry was abstract; in fact, certain ideas also had practical significance. For example, the study of **perspective effects**, which refers to an array of techniques designed to provide the impression of depth and symmetry, had an impact on building construction, first in Greece and then in Rome. Moreover, the Romans were innovators in building technology by using materials such as fired brick, tile, and stone. To shore up their construction, they also invented a new type of cement that was strong and that also set under water. The Romans designed seminal architectural features, such as the arch, the vault, and the dome, each adding considerably to the possibilities in construction. These techniques allowed them to build large structures, such as amphitheatres, aqueducts, and tunnels, some of which still exist today. The amphitheatres allowed for social interaction and were some of the first venues geared specifically toward mass entertainment. These developments had enormous social significance as they allowed for new forms of social organization to emerge, such as the gathering of townspeople in social spaces for debate and entertainment, the development of more densely populated cities, and the emergence of increased traffic and trade.

Many of the ideas around science and technology that were formulated in ancient Greek philosophy remain influential in the twenty-first century. This is particularly true in the case of **basic research**, the idea of scientific inquiry not as specific practical applications but, rather, as the development of knowledge about the world. The Perimeter Institute for Theoretical Physics in Waterloo, Canada, exemplifies this emphasis on basic research, with about half a billion dollars of public and private funding invested into examining the fundamentals of physics.

© Dorin_S/iStockphoto

The University of Waterloo's Perimeter Institute for Theoretical Physics is dedicated to studying fundamentals about the world around us and sparking innovation. It attracts international scholars with its dynamic research atmosphere and conducts outreach programs for youth, teachers, and the general public. Its architecture—pictured here—is part of its atypical, articulated facade and reflects its forward-thinking principles.

Applying the scientific method of inquiry to the study of social processes is not new; it emerged in ancient Greece and was further developed during the Roman era. The tension between basic and applied research continues to exist in the twenty-first century and is visible both in society's approach to funding research and in the mandate of universities, which seek to balance the need for technological innovations with programs geared toward simply acquiring and diffusing new knowledge that has no direct economic impact.

The Renaissance: The Awakening of the Mind through Technology

Historians often characterize the invention of Johannes Gutenberg's printing press in the mid-fifteenth century as groundbreaking. As a tool, its use reshaped history and helped bring about early elements of modernity, including mass production, mass distribution, and the notion of a mass audience. The printing press has also been linked to the spread of literacy and to the diffusion of new ideas throughout Europe, which were crucial in promoting the development of novel religious, scientific, nationalist, and secular thought. Indeed, the printing press proved to be an instrument of great political, economic, social, and cultural power by (1) enabling the spread of ideas, which circumvented traditional institutional bodies, such as the Roman Catholic Church; (2) codifying language; and (3) bringing about the commoditization of information.

Before the development of Gutenberg's printing press and prior to the onset of print culture, manuscript or scribal culture was the primary source of written texts. In workshops, trained scribes would carefully and painstakingly copy texts to produce hand-copied books (Edmunds, 1991). These books, often of a religious nature, were expensive and time-consuming to produce because of the measured and methodical nature of scribes. As a result, books were accessible only to a select group of people who were literate and affluent, and could read Latin or Greek.

Gutenberg's printing press combined his own innovations with preexisting technologies into a new tool. Prior to Gutenberg, woodblock printing, which had originated in China, was the most popular form of printing in Europe. However, the methods originating in China lacked uniform standardization and required skilled craftspeople to develop individual wooden blocks. Inferior or worn blocks often distorted lettering and produced errors (Eisenstein, 1979). Gutenberg, who was a goldsmith from the German city of Mainz, developed Europe's first movable metal type by applying his knowledge of metallurgy—a process that had originated in Korea that same century (Füssel, 2005). Gutenberg split the text into individual components, such as letters and punctuation marks, which were cast in metal and assembled to form specific words. This yet again is evidence of how techniques develop in an evolutionary manner rather than following a revolutionary pattern, borrowing from existing techniques and adding new elements to yield new forms of production.

The printing press led to an era in which oral culture gave way to print culture. Marshall McLuhan proposed that the development of the printing press coincided with a change in how information was transmitted and received: from oral transmissions that relied upon "the magical world of the ear" to processing information from textual communications that emphasized visual cognition (1962, p. 18). Elizabeth Eisenstein (1979), one of the most influential scholars of the effects of print on society, agreed with McLuhan; she also saw print as revolutionary and as changing society. She argued that the shift from script to print "created conditions that favored new combinations of old ideas at first and then, later on, the creation of entirely new systems of thought" (p. 75).

The development of the printing press brought with it changes in how texts were used, distributed, and marketed, once again demonstrating the link between technology and society. Over time, the individualistic, producer-oriented approach of manuscript culture yielded to a consumer-oriented typographical print culture. This enabled the production of greater quantities of a single item within a much shorter time frame. Whereas manuscripts were primarily produced according to the literary interests of a single individual or institution, print texts could be manufactured according to the broad and diverse interests of a wider audience. The printing press altered the economics of the book industry by lowering the cost of purchasing books, which allowed individuals to assemble personal libraries, accrue new ideas, and educate themselves about subjects of interest. Although it was not an entirely error-free technology, the printing press brought about increased uniformity and encouraged the standardization of languages, as well as a surge in texts written in the vernacular (Febvre & Martin, 1997; McLuhan, 1962).

Without the printing press, it is arguable whether or not the dissemination of information via controversial texts and pamphlets during historical movements, such as the Reformation, the Scientific Revolution, and the Enlightenment, could have taken place. Some scholars, such as Haas (1996) and Johns (1998), have suggested that, as mentioned earlier, the printing press was more evolutionary than revolutionary, the product of a series of cultural, social, and technological changes occurring in European society during this period, whose influences were gradual rather than immediate. Others have noted that the printing press's effectiveness was largely restricted to areas of Western Europe (remember that China had been using movable type 500 years prior to Gutenberg's printing press) (Lorimer, Gasher, & Skinner, 2010). Regions consisting of largely oral-based cultures or those that used non-phonetic alphabets in fact eluded the socio-cultural and political upheavals typically associated with the printing press in Western Europe (Briggs & Burke, 2009).

In conclusion, it is likely that the spread of new ideas about science, politics, and religion in Western Europe was the product of technological diffusion. The cultural, political, and economic conditions of mid-fifteenth-century Western Europe were ripe to absorb and transform this technology into a powerful instrument of change. In addition, the printing press allowed new ideas about technological developments to spread more rapidly, leading to enormous advances in science and technology.

Enlightenment and Revolution: Systematic Knowledge in Action

As the decades and centuries progressed following the invention and subsequent proliferation of Gutenberg's printing press, technologies continued to evolve, often faster than ever before. As technologies changed, their impact on society changed as well, as did societal views on technology. The publication of Denis Diderot's *Encyclopédie* in mid-eighteenth-century France proved an important milestone during this period. A massive undertaking, the *Encyclopédie* was intended to be a universal dictionary of human knowledge. Upon completion, it comprised 28 volumes, which had been published over 21 years beginning in 1751. Though most often remembered for its contribution to the controversial **Enlightenment** movement, the *Encyclopédie* was also important for its presentation of technologies and technical processes, usually through detailed diagrams. An example is presented in Figure 2.1, which shows the underlying science of how to hatch a chicken through detailed representations of the chicken in the egg and the apparatus utilized for this purpose. Further examples are available online at http://quod.lib.umich.edu/d/did/title_plate/A.html.

By presenting these alongside articles on the sciences and liberal arts, the *Encyclopédie* encouraged the reader to see the mechanical arts as equal in importance to the more traditional, academic disciplines. Technologies

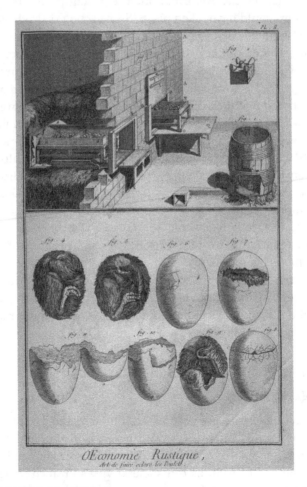

Figure 2.1 The Art of Hatching Chickens
Source: ARTFL Encyclopédie Project, University of Chicago

are shown to be complex, requiring skill and intelligence to design and use (Smentek, 2010). The *Encyclopédie* thus helped to shift European attitudes concerning technologies and artisans' work specifically. The work of artisans was no longer dismissed as insignificant, but was perceived as a valuable skill that was worth studying and improving. This also led to the notion of **technology transfer** both within and across trades, that is, the idea that one artisan can learn through careful observation and study the best practices of another.

The latter half of the eighteenth century in Europe also witnessed dramatic political and social upheaval during the **French Revolution**. There is no doubt that technological advances are often closely interlinked with military objectives and war, and the French Revolutionary and subsequent Napoleonic Wars serve as useful examples. During and after the French Revolution of 1789, the development of new and improved military technologies made it clear that technology was to play an even more central role in warfare than it already had. While the early eighteenth century had seen relative stability in terms of the tools utilized in war (Cohen, n.d.), this radically changed following the revolution.

The use of the guillotine by revolutionary governments as a method of punishment was perceived to be a technological change of societal significance. Public displays of punishment were not uncommon during the medieval period, but the guillotine allowed for a much faster means of ending a person's life, one that the public believed was more humane. The large-scale conflicts waged during and after the revolution led toward innovations in war--in terms of both strategy and tool use, which tend to go hand in hand. Cohen (n.d.) describes these drastic changes as follows:

> On land the advent of the rifle—modified and improved by the development of breech loading, metal cartridges, and later smokeless gunpowder—was accompanied as well by advances in artillery and even early types of machine guns. At sea changes were even more dramatic: steam replaced sail, and iron and steel replaced wood and canvas. Obsolescence now occurred within years, not decades, and technological experts assumed new prominence.

Interestingly, most analysis of these new military technologies assumed that existing frameworks could be utilized to examine their implications. Generally, however, they underestimated the unprecedented threats posed by such military technologies as mines, torpedoes, and submarines, and the human price of their use in warfare. Today, of course, there are still many ethical questions surrounding the use of technology in warfare, for example, the increasing international reliance on **armed drones**. (For a discussion of this, see www.thebureauinvestigates.com/category/projects/

drones/drones-war-drones/.) Thus technological advances in warfare bring with them increased hegemony for highly developed societies but also greater human detachment from the effects of war itself, as well as increased fatalities.

The Industrial Revolution: Revolting against Technology

Beginning in mid-eighteenth-century England, the **Industrial Revolution** advanced technology in three key industries: textile, steam, and steel. The era of industrialization was significant for changing the production and distribution of goods and had a major impact on workers as well as consumers. The era brought with it radical changes in people's work processes, man–machine interaction, and worker–employer relationships. The introduction of machines coincided with an increase in the number of individuals being employed in various sectors, such as weaving in the textile industry (Berg, 1994). The enlarged pool of workers, now with the addition of an "unregulated" workforce of women's and children's labour, coupled with simplified technological processes associated with new machinery, drove down wages and led to an increase in the number of unemployed yet highly skilled craftspeople (Berg, 1994).

A new phenomenon also emerged during this time. Machines were no longer seen as neutral but, were perceived as "actors" within a complex socio-technical system. In this system, technology was identified as the key force in producing social disparity and disrupting work conditions. To retaliate, workers directed their anger toward the machines that they perceived were taking away their jobs; the term **machine breaking** was introduced to describe workers' destruction of technology (Hobsbawn, 1952). These acts were organized by workers because they viewed the machines as threats to standards of living, employment, wages, and working conditions (Dinwiddy, 1979; Hobsbawn, 1952). Hobsbawn (1952) identifies two primary motivations for machine breaking: (1) to put pressure on employers to improve wages and working conditions, and (2) to direct hostility toward the machines themselves, especially those perceived as labour-saving. For worker groups without a tradition of trade or union organization, "machine breaking and violence proved effective methods of protest" (Randall, 1991, p. 149).

The Industrial Revolution was an era of unprecedented social change. Much of the upheaval taking place during this era was linked to the introduction of technological innovations in Europe. However, technologies alone do not lead to social change; we need to study their effect on society as parts of complex social systems (for more details see Chapter 3). That is, it was not technology that led to craftspeople losing their jobs, as machine breakers at the time concluded. It was, rather, the interplay between technology and the existing social system that radically transformed social structure. From a historical standpoint, industrialization was only the beginning of large-scale change linked to technological innovation. Next, we discuss how innovations in mass media, such as cinema and television, transformed the flow of information in society, created new forms of mass cultural production, and introduced new notions of entertainment and propaganda.

Electronic Times: Hot and Cool Media

The Industrial Revolution was a time of upheaval as new technologies infiltrated the workplace, creating major disruptions for workers. The pace of technological development did not halt with the industrial era, however. Major changes were observed in the late nineteenth and early twentieth centuries in particular in what we now refer to as the mass media or the electronic media. The widespread use of mass media and their impact on daily life have only recently become topics of much public debate and scholarly attention. Earlier, users of mass media did not generally reflect much upon its effects on family life, civic engagement, the diffusion of information, and community. Marshall McLuhan (1962, 1964) was among the first to draw attention to the effects mass media had on society, commenting on how these tools shaped our thinking processes as well as our understanding of the world. At the time, mass media encompassed radio, cinema, and television, and together they created a new era of electronic communication.

In order to help readers understand the close link between mass media and society, McLuhan used provocative, bold aphorisms that he termed **probes**. His probes are ideas that challenge us to think more deeply about the link between messages, media, and audiences, and are not to be taken literally but metaphorically. Perhaps McLuhan's most well-known probe is **"the medium is the message,"** which expresses the idea of media having a direct effect on how people make sense of information. McLuhan (1962, 1964) argued that media have different characteristics, thus engaging the audience in different ways. The essence of "the medium is the message" is that most analysis of the effect of media on society focuses on content. For example, while Albert Bandura's (1973) well-known experiments examined how children learn aggressive behaviour from exposure to images on a screen, McLuhan argued that attention to the effects of the medium itself was often neglected. For McLuhan, then, the medium was as important as the content, if not more so, because it framed how society interacted with information. This understanding of the effect of media led McLuhan toward a deep exploration of both the relationship between media and society, as well as the effect that different media have on society. To exemplify these links between media and society, Box 2.2 examines the way cinema was used in the early twentieth century as a means of propaganda.

Box 2.2   Cinema as a Propaganda Tool in Society

Originating in the late nineteenth century, the cinema became a mass medium that attracted people to the moving image. Film can be described as a technology-based art form that creatively expresses the world around us and that can be utilized to influence political or social change. Roebuck notes that "the importance of the cinema to social development lay in its national coverage and the enormous size of its audience" (1982, p. 119). Soon, cinema's ubiquitous presence became "a great standardizing agent which brought huge numbers of people together through vicariously shared experiences and promoted a general worship of the same heroes and the formation of similar dreams" (Roebuck, 1982, p. 119). Early in the medium's history, films were also used to express views supporting a specific ideology, such as the films of Sergei Eisenstein in Soviet Russia, or a revisionist take on history as exemplified by D.W. Griffith's 1915 film *The Birth of a Nation*.

The intricate connection between cinema and society can be demonstrated in the case of Nazi Germany. In an era before the widespread popularization of television, the cinema performed a crucial role in providing people with visual slices of information and entertainment through newsreels and feature films. Under Nazism, the German film industry was controlled through the *Reichsfilmkammer* (the Film Chamber of the Reich), which was governed by the Ministry of Propaganda, led by Joseph Goebbels. Films could only be created and used in accordance with the guidelines and objectives set by the Nazi party. A "popular medium and vehicle of mass culture, film preserved old forms of identity while offering a new (and powerful) instrument of consensus-building" (Rentschler, 1996, p. xi). Hitler argued that film and other similar media "could be instrumental in winning followers and propagating Nationalist Socialist ideas" (Hake, 2002, p. 77), and, at the same time, Goebbels "sought to transform the film apparatus into a tool of the state, a medium of myth, legend, and fantasy which would relieve reality of its dialectical complexity" (Rentschler, 1996, pp. 67–8).

As Minister of Propaganda, Goebbels wanted German films to "conceal the intentions" of the works by emphasizing presentation rather than content (Hake, 2002). As a result, the films produced under Goebbels aimed to "convey their messages as inconspicuously as possible" (Trimborn, 2007, p. 79). Even though some films were openly propagandistic, "most popular film genres carefully avoided references to the regime" yet continued to serve "it by promoting the sexist, nationalist and racist ideologies essential to its existence" (Hake, 2002, p. 77). This was accomplished by using the seductive language of cinema to create emotive films designed to collectively connect people to the shared experiences of the films' clichéd characters, as well as to the traditional values and illusory fantasies expressed in these motion-picture spectacles. The cinema thus became a mass medium adeptly utilized to placate or arouse the emotions of the masses.

Similar to cinema, television is an electrical device that provides information and entertainment to a large audience. By 1970, many North Americans had a television set in their homes and the average person was watching TV nearly four hours a day (Bogart, 1972). Nielsen data show that in 2009 Americans continued to spend large amounts of time watching TV in the home, including time-shifted TV, Internet TV, online videos, and TV via cellphones. In fact, in 2009 the average American watched about 153 hours every month, a 1.2 per cent increase from the previous year (Nielsen, 2009).

McLuhan (1962, 1964) saw television as a unifying force that provides viewers with a sense of connectivity. To describe the social connections created by television, he introduced the notion of the **global village**. The global village represents the possibility that electronic forms of communication and media, such as television, can compress the rigours of spatial distance by enabling people to remain connected to activities going on anywhere in the world. McLuhan explains in an interview that "[t]he global-village conditions being forged by the electric technology stimulate more discontinuity and diversity and division than the old mechanical, standardized society; in fact, the global village makes maximum disagreement and creative dialog inevitable" (E. McLuhan & Zingrone, 1995, p. 259).

To better understand the nature of electronic media, McLuhan distinguished between **hot** and **cool media** or "cold" media. For him, media could be differentiated in terms of the degree to which they engage a consumer. Books were categorized as being "hot" because they engage a single sense, in this case the visual system, providing readers with large amounts of information that is processed at lower sensory levels.[2] By contrast, television was considered to be "cool" because it requires greater effort to determine meaning. In addition to the cool–hot dimension, McLuhan also introduced the concepts **high-** and **low-definition media** to characterize how electronic media were processed by their audience. Crisply detailed and well-defined information, such as detailed images, that required little effort to be processed were referred to as "high definition" and were found in hot media. By contrast, "low-definition media," such as cartoons, provided users with less information and thus required a greater participation from the senses in order to be understood.

An implication of McLuhan's theories is that over time existing and emerging forms of media transform personalized experiences and societal structures. Previously popular media formats, for example, often give way to new technologies, which repackage older forms of content in a manner responsive and applicable to the changing information demands and experiences of their audience. For instance, contemporary communication technologies and media, such as cellphones or social networking sites, offer users a greater degree of mobility, reach, and instantaneity than their predecessors (Klemens, 2010). As a result, these new devices have changed social modes of interaction and societal expectations as to how communication can and should be conducted in the twenty-first century.

This section outlined the significance of electronic media or mass media in the history of technology. The developments in mass media that occurred at the end of the nineteenth century and the first half of the twentieth century transformed the flow of information in society, created new forms of mass cultural production, and introduced new notions of entertainment and propaganda. Clearly, the cinema became a new means of reaching mass audiences and served not only as a form of entertainment but also as a means of dispersing political propaganda. Some analysts stipulate that mass-produced cultural goods lead to standardization and uniformity in content, and additionally destroy individuality and multiplicity of choice (Gasher, Skinner, & Lorimer, 2012). In their view, exposure to standardized cultural goods—for example, movies produced in Hollywood—caused members of society to become a homogenous, uncritical, and passive mass with little willpower to resist the appeal and influence of the mass media. While some of these extreme views have been dismissed, there is no doubt that these technologies have had a large-scale impact on the production, dissemination, and interpretation of cultural goods. Perhaps the most fundamental social change is the link between mass media production and consumption and the emergence of a mass audience on a scale that did not exist prior to the media of mass communication.

The Information Society: The Bits and Bytes Revolution

What does living in a high-tech society entail? To what extent do technologies impact who we are as individuals, as nations, and as a society? Sociological work has extensively scrutinized the effect of industrialization and urbanization on cities, communities, family structures, and work. To illustrate the kinds of societal changes brought about by current technologies (Haigh, 2011), we discuss here the iPod and the cellphone. We examine the iPod as a form of entertainment that has become a force of individualization, privatization, and customization among youth. It allows young people to feel empowered and to make individualized decisions about music choices in a private space away from the adult world. By contrast, we examine the cellphone in reference to the have-nots, to those in society who only marginally interact with technology but yet are still struck by it.

iPod Culture

Released in October 2001, the iPod ushered in a new era of portable media devices and quickly transformed Apple from a niche computer manufacturer into an international media provider (Hartley, 2009). By 2008, Apple was the world's biggest music retailer and had captured 70 per cent of the market share in digital music-player devices (Hartley, 2009). Initially designed to allow users to carry their favourite songs on a small compact transportable unit, the iPod is an example of a product that evokes the principles generally associated with twenty-first-century technologies of the information society, including mobility, speed, multi-media interactivity, ease of use, customization, and multi-purpose usage.

With its signature aesthetic appearance, evidenced in its click wheel and white earbuds, the iconic iPod is a clearly identifiable product that along with its offshoots—the iPod Shuffle and the iPod Touch—has transformed the manner in which media is consumed, transmitted, transported, and received. Part of the iPod's initial popularity can be traced back to changes within the music and telecommunications industry. In 1993, the MP3 file format became popular for storing digital audio because of its relatively small size and versatility. Simultaneously, peer-to-peer networks and BitTorrent sites, such as Napster, Kazaa, and The Pirate Bay, provided Internet users with the ability to (often illegally) download music files. Subsequently, the iPod became a convenient device that allowed users to take their music collections with them.

iPods have brought about new forms of customization, which can reflect their users' unique personalities. The diverse selection of media content stored on the device is in itself reflective of individuals' interests, from the soundtrack collection to their choice of podcasts and applications (a.k.a. "apps"). Additionally, the exterior of the device can be altered according to the respective user's tastes by purchasing an iPod featuring a favourite colour, by adding a personalized engraving, or by adding stick-on artwork known as "skins."

The new forms of control and customization that iPods render go beyond the look and feel of the devices themselves and extend to users' ability to shape their experiences of the urban environment. Michael Bull (2008) writes about this extreme form of individualization:

> It is a hyper-post-Fordist culture in which subjects construct what they imagine to be their own individualized schedules of daily life—their own daily soundtrack of media messages, their own soundspace as they move through shopping centres, their own work-out soundtrack as they modulate the movement of their bodies in the gym. (p. 3)

In a **post-Fordist culture** (i.e., a system of production and consumption that features greater technical and individual specificity in production and labour roles), by contrast, consumers can design a consumer product with their personal touch through personalized specifications; in a **hyper-post-Fordist culture** customization goes much further, allowing users to customize their interactions with the urban space. Bull (2008) describes how through the creation of an imaginary sound bubble, the iPod culture allows individuals to regain some control over their urban space. And, as megacities continue to grow, the iPod has come to epitomize the possibility of withdrawing from the hectic life of urbanization and retreating into one's own personal and controlled space. The 2001 comedy *Bubble Boy*, directed by Blair Hayes, depicts what life would be like if we each lived enclosed in an artificial bubble that separates us from our urban surroundings.

Perhaps more so than other popular contemporary technological devices, such as cellphones, the iPod necessitates acquiring other related technologies in order to be properly used. People must have, at the very least, access to a computer and a broadband Internet connection. Thus, despite its diverse functional benefits, the iPod is a device whose diffusion, practicality, and adoption is severely limited to societies that are able to readily support a strong, computer-based, and Internet-intensive technological infrastructure, as well as a populace that is able to afford to purchase digital leisure products and to demonstrate an above-average degree of technical sophistication.

Cellphones as Empowerment

The second example of twenty-first-century technology is the cellphone or mobile phone, which lies in stark contrast to the iPod because it is a communication device that serves a clear utilitarian purpose rather than being an entertainment

© Razvan/iStockphoto

Do you think MP3 players like the iPod provide people with convenient, custom ways to connect with media and control their interaction with urban space, or do they encourage a withdrawal from urbanization and daily interactions?

tool. The Western mainstream assumption is that technologies have pervaded all aspects of society and are a part of our everyday lives. However, this is clearly not the case for most individuals in developing countries.

The **International Telecommunications Union (ITU)**, the **information technology (IT)** stream of the United Nations, is dedicated to recording and observing **technological inequality** around the globe. In its most recent study, it found that inequality along the lines of computers and the Internet continues to persist but has rapidly narrowed regarding cellphone use. Indeed, the penetration rate for cellphones increased in developing countries from about 10 per cent in 1995 to almost 80 per cent in 2005, when there were approximately 23 mobile cellular subscriptions per 100 inhabitants in the developing world (ITU, 2014). Since 2005, this number has again increased drastically, to an estimated 90 per cent in 2014 (ITU, 2014). This is particularly surprising considering that developing countries continue to lag behind Western countries when it comes to penetration rates of **fixed lines** or land lines (see Figure 2.2). However, the unique characteristics of the cellphone make it a technology that can easily disseminate, even in developing countries, providing a means of empowerment to those with limited economic resources.

Several factors allow cellphone use to spread more widely in comparison to other technologies:

1. *Infrastructure requirements*: Cellphones do not require the same kind of infrastructure that other technologies do, and, most importantly, they do not require wires. Even remote places can potentially get a signal if a **cellular network** exists.

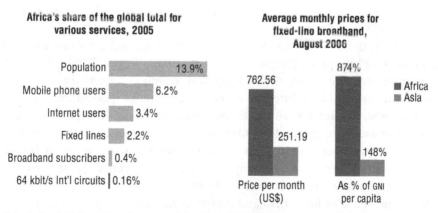

Note: In the right chart, the price sample is based on the 22 African economies that had fixed-line broadband service at the end of 2005. The average value is inflated, since in a high proportion of the economies in this sample, broadband is offered through leased lines and is priced as a business service, rather than for residential users.

Figure 2.2 Use of Communication Technologies in Africa
Source: International Telecommunication Union, *World Information Society Report 2007: Beyond WSIS* (Geneva: ITU, 2007), p. 27.

2. *Economic factors*: The cost to purchase a cellphone is lower than that to acquire a computer, laptop, or other electronic device, greatly reducing the initial investment in hardware. Moreover, cellphones do not require the payment of monthly fees, like a telephone or an Internet connection does— they can be used flexibly on a pay-per-use basis.

3. *Literacy prerequisites*: Cellphones fit well in oral societies, where literacy levels are low.

4. *Skill levels*: No computing skills are required to use a basic cellphone because a mouse, buttons, and navigation are unnecessary.

5. *Help and support*: In the context of developing countries, technical help for cellphones is easier to obtain than it is for other more complex and less widely available technologies, such as computers, the Internet, and other digital devices.

6. *Cultural norms*: These are the social norms and attitudes that influence how we use and make sense of various technologies. The cellphone fits well with many cultural norms because it allows individuals to maintain their social connections.

Most research examining the diffusion of cellphone use has focused on developed countries, in particular, the United States, Japan, and Norway. Recently, however, with increased penetration rates of cellphones in the developing world, interest in its impact on these countries has been growing. Unfortunately, the majority of studies produced so far have had a narrow focus, looking at either penetration rates or economic development. The book *Txt-ing Selves* by Pertierra et al. (2003) is unique in that it aims to further our understanding of how Filipinos use cellphones in everyday life, and how the unique cultural context shapes the social effects of this technology on Philippine society.

In 2004, there were 10.5 million cellphone users and 2 million Internet users in the Philippines (Regional Surveys of the World, 2004). In 2009, these numbers increased to 74.5 million cellphone users in comparison to almost 6 million Internet users (International Telecommunication Union, 2009). Pertierra et al. (2003) interviewed ordinary Filipinos to learn about their use of the technology. One case study focuses on Vilma, a retired woman who uses her cellphone as an alternative way to keep in touch with friends and relatives. She feels empowered by the technology because she can now continue to be socially active from the comfort of her home, which reduces her sense of loneliness and increases her feelings of self-worth. On the basis of various similar case studies, Pertierra and his team conclude that cellphones provide users with a sense of empowerment and are typically used for social and information purposes, helping to maintain existing relationships, and are not used much for creating new ones.[3]

Pertierra et al. (2003) also discuss the role of the cellphone in the context of recent political events. The authors focus primarily on EDSA 2, which refers to the large-scale protest organized on one of Manila's most central streets, Epifanio de los Santos Avenue. This protest was pivotal in the removal of former president Joseph Estrada from power, and the media depicted the cellphone as playing a key role in mobilizing large numbers of protesters through text messages. However, Pertierra et al. (2003) question that notion, arguing that in the media portrayals, the cellphone is presented as the principal agent of the revolt, ultimately leading to the mobilization of the masses and the demise of ex-president Estrada. In their opinion, a critical analysis needs to go beyond the technology and its capabilities, and ask questions about the origins of *texting during the protests*: "who their authors and initial disseminators were, and how such messages facilitated the coordination of the actions" (Pertierra et al., 2003, p. 107). This discussion parallels the debate about the role of social media in the Middle East protests, which we will discuss further in Chapter 9.

Technologies are often characterized in utopian terms as a means to overcome inequalities between rich and poor, educated and uneducated, and to support social movements in their quest for social change. While technologies do provide a means to improve individuals' quality of life, technologies can also increase divisions between the haves and the have-nots, thereby exacerbating the inequality gap, which we will discuss in more detail in Chapter 8. While many extant studies focus on technology's impact on development and economic growth, *Txt-ing Selves* takes a less deterministic view of technology, seeing it as blending in and becoming a natural part of modernity in the Philippines.

Conclusions

This chapter provided an overview of technological achievements from the early stages of humanity to the present. Understanding the close relationship between the introduction of a new technology and social change is not a straightforward task. McLuhan argued that society tends to approach technological developments with a rear-view mirror approach, where "[w]e march backwards into the future" and a new social order is not perceived until it is already in place (McLuhan & Quentin, 2003, p. 68). Hence, we tend to look backward to make sense of how we have changed as a society instead of looking ahead toward how transformations are occurring.

To counteract such an approach, this chapter presented on-the-ground examples showing how technological transformations intersect with cultural, political, economic, and social change. The examples demonstrate how technologies can be examined as social agents in a socio-technical system. From this viewpoint, technology has transformative power and can shape society. Nonetheless, it is important to keep in mind that technologies alone are not the single causal factor in enabling societal change. We demonstrated how technology shapes society in a social context, where many factors come together to create social change. For instance, the divergent effects of the printing press on Europe and Asia demonstrate this coming together of multiple factors to provide the necessary context for social change.

Questions for Critical Thought

1.   Can we understand technological developments in the past by looking at them through today's lens? What are the biases that can emerge? How do we take them into account?

2.   How does McLuhan's probe "the medium is the message" characterize the effect of media on society?

3.   Describe how the iPod feeds into the creation of a hyper-post-Fordist culture and how this is different from a post-Fordist culture.

4.   Think of how you use the cellphone to communicate with friends and relatives. Do you think the technology functions as a means of empowerment? How does it transform your ways of socializing? Do you think this change is best described as revolutionary or evolutionary?

Suggested Readings

Bull, M. (2008). *Sound moves: IPod culture and urban experience*. New York: Routledge. An in-depth investigation into the iPod culture and its ramifications for society.

Haigh, T. (2011). The history of information technology. *Annual Review of Information Science and Technology, 45*, 431–487. This article explores the literature and key ideas in the history of information technology.

McLuhan, M. (1962). *The Gutenberg galaxy: The making of typographic man*. Toronto: University of Toronto Press. A comprehensive analysis of the complex interplay of communication technology, cognition, and society.

Online Resources

Marshall McLuhan: The Man and His Message. CBC Digital Archives
www.cbc.ca/archives/
The Canadian Broadcasting Corporation (CBC) has put together a digital archive of McLuhan's interviews with the media, including radio and television programming.

Maclean's: Mind-Bending Mysteries at the Perimeter Institute
www2.macleans.ca/2010/09/17/solving-the-universe/
An overview of the Perimeter Institute for Theoretical Physics in Waterloo, Ontario.

McLuhan Interviews on YouTube
www.youtube.com/watch?v=ImaH51F4HBw&feature=related
A series of interesting interviews with Marshall McLuhan have been posted on YouTube dealing with a wide range of topics related to the effect of media on society.

MIT's six-minute video on Diderot's *Encyclopédie*
http://techtv.mit.edu/videos/5141-mind-and-hand-mens-et-manus-illustrated-in-diderots-encyclopdie

An interesting video put together by MIT of the development of Diderot's *Encyclopédie* and its implications for science and technology.

3 Theoretical Perspectives on Technology

Learning Objectives

◎ to address the fundamental difference between utopian and dystopian views of technology;

◎ to compare and critically examine a wide range of theories on the complex interrelationship between society and technology;

◎ to learn about the field of science and technology studies (STS) and its unique socio-technical perspective;

◎ to analyze how video games are developed for children and what understandings of play influence their design.

Introduction

A wide range of theoretical perspectives have been proposed that seek to show the ways in which technology and society are linked, as well as the elements of society most affected by technology. The plurality of perspectives shows that there is no single approach for examining this complex interrelationship; rather, a range of divergent perspectives have been proposed that each shed light on a different aspect of technological society. A long-standing debate exists between those who see technology as having only positive effects—the utopians—and those who see technology as having primarily negative effects—the dystopians. In addition, early discussions in the field centred on whether technology determines society or society determines technology. In the literature, these two views are referred to as **technological** and **social determinism**, respectively. The core assumption of the former is that technology has a unidirectional, strong effect that is not, or only minimally, mediated by other factors, while the latter ascribes these effects to society. We will review the key premises underlying these theories and discuss their strengths and weaknesses.

These early theoretical perspectives represent a rather simplified view of the technology–society interrelationship; recent perspectives are more complex and attempt to provide a more detailed view of how technology and society intersect. We discuss the field of **science and technology studies (STS)**, which emphasizes that artifacts are socially constructed, mirroring the society that produces them. At the same time, tools shape society itself, as well as its values, norms, and practices (Bijker et al., 1999; Callon & Law, 1997; Latour, 1993). As a result, according to the theories postulated by STS, social change needs to be understood in relation to technological developments. In this chapter, we review the most prominent theories within the field of STS: **actor network theory (ANT)** and **social construction of technology (SCOT)**. We will look at concrete examples—for instance, how video games like BarbieGirls and GalaXseeds are developed specifically for children and what understandings of play underlie their design.

Utopian versus Dystopian Views of Technology

The utopian and dystopian perspectives are two opposing views of how technology affects our everyday lives. Utopians embrace technology as a new means of achieving progress and improving efficiency. The idea of progress emerged in the seventeenth and eighteenth centuries, particularly in Europe and North America, and became something desirable, a sign of civilization. The *utopian view* reflects the assumption of technology as "the realization of science, revealing itself in ever increasing control over nature" (Street, 1992, p. 20). In this view, technology allows us to dominate and manage nature, making our lives easier, and leads to advancements in the production of material goods, thereby reducing costs and increasing efficiency. Progress is not limited to the production of material goods alone but extends to the accomplishment of societal goals, including higher levels of security, better means of communication over time and space, improved health care, and increased autonomy (Hill, 1989). Overall, "technical change serves to improve the quality of life" (Street, 1992, p. 20) and makes many aspects of life easier.

The other main viewpoint is the **dystopian perspective**. For Street, technology "threatens established ways of life" and is thus seen as a **regressive force** (1992, p. 20). This means that technology is not seen as helping society move forward; rather, it hinders the combat of key problems of our times like environmental sustainability, health care, and education. In the realm of education, for example, it is argued that cellphones, laptops, and other mobile devices easily distract students during school lectures and study time, reducing their ability to concentrate, which then has implications for their learning outcomes (Campbell, 2007; Quan-Haase & Collins, 2008). In a study by Campbell (2007), students indicated that the ringing of cellphones during class time was distracting and they strongly supported the implementation of guidelines to help reduce this. This response seems to indicate an understanding that classroom time is governed by social norms that facilitate learning and focused attention, unlike other social situations where inattention is not such a crucial issue.

While not all scholars advocate for simply embracing dystopian views of technology, many scholars do argue that the study of technology needs to go beyond a focus on the immediate and intended benefits of technological inventions, and should also analyze the often **unintended effects** that result in the long run—for example, the effects of industrialization and globalization on the environment. To return to the example of cellphones, an unintended effect of their use is taking students' attention away from material presented in lectures. Cellphones are social technologies, but the sociability they foster may be less desirable in some environments than others.

Tenner (1996) sees many technological solutions to societal problems as creating new problems, often larger in scale. He has termed the unintended consequences resulting from technology as **revenge effect** and analyzes these problems in depth through a series of case studies. An example of a revenge effect is when a drug used to induce hair growth actually accelerates hair loss under certain conditions. If the likelihood of cancer increases, this is considered a **side effect** rather than a revenge effect because it manifests itself in a different area. Side effects occur in an area unrelated to the one within which the technology was supposed to function and thus is surprising, whereas revenge effects occur directly in the area of intervention but are unintended. To use our example of cellphones again, a revenge effect would be an increase in our level of social alienation instead of an increase in our connections with other people. For instance, a family goes out for dinner and the mother is constantly checking her cellphone. The side effect (a positive one) in this case might be that she is using the cellphone to check the time and to determine when she should leave the restaurant to get her children home and in bed on schedule. The revenge effect is that that action disconnects her from her surroundings and her family.

The utopian and dystopian viewpoints provide a rudimentary understanding of how technology affects society. In the next section, we present the various theories that examine in more detail how technology and society intersect.

Theories of Technology and Society

Numerous theories of technology and society have been proposed. To examine these varied theories in more detail, Feenberg (1999) has developed a theoretical model (see Figure 3.1), in which he distinguishes between two central dimensions: (1) neutral (as in the **neutrality of technology argument**) versus **value-laden**; and (2) **autonomous** versus **human controlled**. In this section, we first describe the two dimensions and then discuss each of the four theoretical frameworks that result from the two-by-two matrix depicted in Figure 3.1.

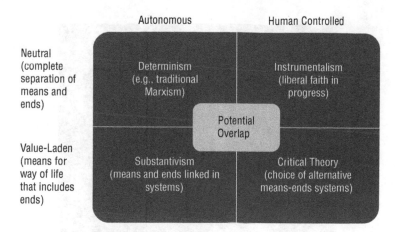

Figure 3.1 Theories of Technology and Society
Source: Adapted from Feenberg, A. (1999). *Questioning technology* (p. 9). New York: Routledge, p. 9.

Neutral versus Value-Laden

The first dimension encompasses theories that view technology as falling in the category of either neutral or value-laden. Theories of neutrality describe technology as separate from human activity and with no effect on natural ends—that is, on the fundamental elements of human nature (e.g., ethics, morality, forgiveness, and happiness). Feenberg argues that this neutralization of technology hinders any in-depth analysis of social change because "if technology merely fulfills nature's mandate, then the value it realizes must be generic in scope" (1999, p. 2).

Box 3.1 gives an example that demonstrates that technology is far from neutral. In this example, social media platforms are utilized to discuss moral and ethical dilemmas in our society and to inform and mobilize others for a social cause.

Box 3.1

Are Technologies Neutral? #50dollarsnot50shades

Just before the movie *Fifty Shades of Grey* was set to be released, a social media campaign was started on Facebook (www.facebook.com/50dollarsnotfiftyshades) and Twitter (#50dollarsnotfiftyshades) that encouraged followers to donate fifty dollars to shelters and Institutions that help abused women instead of spending the money on a ticket for the movie *Fifty Shades of Grey*, popcorn, and drinks (Couch, 2015). There were three primary sponsors of the campaign: the National Center on Sexual Exploitation, London [Ontario] Abused Women's Centre, and the agency Stop Porn Culture.

Continued

Figure 3.2 Twitter Activity related to #50dollarsnot50shades

On the one hand, Twitter is a neutral platform for the relay of information and the exchange of messages: anyone with a Twitter account can tweet, retweet and "favourite" content. On the other hand, Twitter can also act as a catalyst for social change by facilitating awareness of social issues, mobilizing individuals to partici-pate in campaigns, and facilitating discussion around controversial topics. To better understand how Twitter can become a part of a social campaign, all tweets con-taining the hashtag #50dollarsnot50shades were harvested between 3 February and 7 February 2015 using **Netlytic** software. A total of 8,146 tweets produced by 794 Twitter users were collected, suggesting a strong interest in the topic shortly before the release of the movie. The most commonly occurring keywords were: *women*, *boycott*, *abuse*, *violence*, *campaign*, and *donate*. This suggests that the campaign was successful in drawing attention to its primary concern, namely how women are depicted in mainstream media and what has been referred to as the "glamorizing of abusive behaviour" (Couch, 2015). One tweet stated, "Instead of rewarding Hollywood for glamorizing sexual violence, donate to a domestic abuse shelter on Valentine's Day. #50dollarsnot50shades."

Many tweets called for a boycott of the movie, suggesting that it had negative effects on society. But more importantly, as shown in Figure 3.2, Twitter activity drew attention to the important role of women's shelters, the widespread social problem of women's abuse, and the need to protect those in society who are most vulnerable. This case study shows how Facebook and Twitter are no longer neutral tools: they can serve a specific purpose, namely to create awareness of social problems and mobilize others to take action. As such, digital media can become central players in current debates around social issues.

The opposing view—that technology is value-laden—tends to equate technological development with human progress. In this view, any new experience realized through technology is seen as progress for the entire human race. Feenberg (1999) shows how the first landing on the moon is often described as a collective achievement: *we* as humans landed on the moon. This removes any sociological, cultural, and economic analysis from the technological experience and buries the political consequences that lie behind many technological developments. For example, there is usually no mention in the moon landing story about the arms race taking place between the United States and the USSR at the time, or about the funding that supported it, i.e., taxpayers' money that was used with the aim of advancing science and technology at the expense of education and health care.

Autonomous versus Human Controlled

The second dimension of Feenberg's model distinguishes between technology as exerting control and technology as controlled by humans. The concept of technical development is at the centre of this discourse. Technological autonomy is based on the idea that technological developments and inventions are guided by independent or self-serving dynamics, separate and distinguishable from societal or human influences. Although human beings are involved in the creation of technologies, supporters of **autonomous technology theories** would argue that humans have little choice in deciding how a given technology will evolve and diffuse in society. The underlying assumption of this theory is the notion that technology propels and alters the development of social structures and cultural values.

Within this view, once technologies are introduced into an environment, they will be the key factor in determining the direction of social change and progress. Once the technology is fixed within a society, the corresponding roles and actions associated with that technology become more normalized, thus limiting the input of **human agency**. For instance, the introduction of television is perceived as a catalyst in re-configuring leisure, communication, consumer, and cultural practices in the twentieth century. Supporters of the autonomous technology theory would argue that television as a technological medium became a focal point in family and social life. It changed the manner in which information was acquired and processed, and also created mass communal events through which people indirectly and simultaneously shared analogous experiences. Today, televised events such as the Super Bowl or the series finale of a popular television show, such as *M*A*S*H* or *Seinfeld*, could be considered examples of this phenomenon.

By contrast, critics of the autonomous viewpoint argue that technology is a socially constructed entity, whose meaning and use is determined by human action. Rather than being diminished by technology, human agency becomes the central ingredient in understanding and determining the role of technology within its social context. People have a choice in selecting and deciding how technologies will be used, as well as determining the value given to a particular technology. Concepts showcasing this viewpoint, such as the social construction of technology (SCOT, discussed below), centre around the belief that technology is shaped by human needs and social factors. The cultural norms and values within a social system influence the construction, diffusion, and utilization of the technological product (see Chapter 6). This reasoning can be used to suggest why certain technologies fail to diffuse in cultures or societies that are indifferent toward adopting a product or system that is incompatible with their social beliefs or structures.

Four Theories of the Technology–Society Intersection

As indicated on page 45, Figure 3.1 shows the four main theories identified by Feenberg (1999) along the two dimensions of interest previously discussed, forming four quadrants, each representing a different vision of technology's intersection with society. Each will be discussed next and concrete examples provided.

1. Determinism

Determinism is divided into two primary and opposing theoretical views: technological and social determinism. **Technological determinism** proposes that technology is the driving force in developing the structure of society and culture (see Figure 3.3). Technological determinists adhere to the notion that technology directs and shapes social interactions and systems of thought. The uses of technology are dictated by the design of the technology itself. Technological determinists view technology as an independent and autonomous entity guided by its own internal logic. In response to technological developments, society changes its institutions, modes of communication, labour practices, and cultural meanings. Moore's law is an example of the view of technological determinism. It stipulates that the prediction that "the number of transistors that could be placed on an integrated circuit would continue to double at short, regular intervals has held true ever since, although the interval soon stretched from twelve to eighteen months" (Ceruzzi, 2005, p. 584). As the speed and capacity of computers increases, humans need to adapt to and keep up with these changes. And since technology is self-directing, it is not influenced by social or cultural factors within society.

The second perspective, **social determinism**, sees factors in society as creating specific uses of technology (see Figure 3.3). Social norms, attitudes, cultural practices, and religious beliefs are perceived as directly impacting how technology is used and what its social consequences are. For

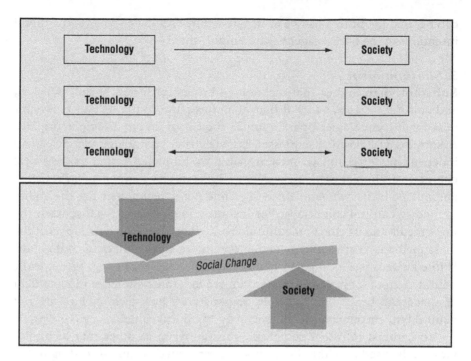

Figure 3.3 Technology and Social Change

example, research into the use of media for communicating during a relationship breakup found that norms around communication impact young people's perceptions of media adequacy. Text messaging and social media, for instance, were not perceived as adequate for transferring complex messages during a breakup, whereas in-person communication was perceived as more adequate (Gershon, 2010). (We will discuss the impact of social norms on communication during breakups in more detail in Chapter 10.) This example illustrates the social determinism view, which argues that societal or group norms will determine how a technology is utilized. To summarize, technological determinism views technology as the driving force of social change, while social determinism views social factors as affecting technological development and use.

2. Instrumentalism

Instrumentalism analyzes technology as a neutral tool or instrument, whose purpose is to fulfill users' specific tasks. Instrumentalists believe that technology can be understood as an evolutionary process in which technologies are the product of previous technological endeavours, whose rationale is to improve productivity and efficiency. Since technology is characterized as being merely a neutral tool, **instrumentalism** proposes that technologies can be used for either positive or negative purposes depending on the moral intentions of the human agents who employ them.

3. Substantivism

Substantivism argues that technology brings forth new social, political, and cultural systems, which it then structures and controls. This view supposes that technologies operate under their own inherent logic and goals. A substantivist position expresses the view that technology can act as an independent force and is uncontrollable by humans. Acting as a neutral character, technology shapes society and dictates its components. Propelled and guided by its own embedded logic and goals, technology has the ability to modify cultural conditions. For instance, in Chapter 2 we discussed the mass media and its effect on cultural production. The embedded logic of the mass media is to attract large audiences and to commodify cultural goods. While a circus is a local performance that attracts a limited, geographically bounded group of people, a movie can reach a mass audience independent of space and time. This example demonstrates how technologies are not neutral but, encompass specific social and political values.

In contrast to instrumentalism, substantivism assumes that technologies can be used for either liberating or destructive means, according to the nature of the technology itself, which establishes and controls society, rather than according to the means and goals of human actors. Human agency, then, cannot control technologies; instead, the technology's inherent logic and goals determine its use. From this perspective, the logic and goal of a weapon is to harm and perhaps even to kill. By contrast, the logic and goal of the printing press is to diffuse information. These examples show how the nature of technology predetermines how the technology will be utilized and the kinds of impact it will have on society. Substantivism gained social relevance during the Cold War, when the atomic bomb made the possibility of mass destruction very real. Atomic weapons shaped society, increasing fear and impacting people's perceptions of safety.

4. Critical Theory

Critical theory suggests that technology is the product of both technical and social factors. Technology is not simply a means of satisfying goals but a process that directs a specific mode of living and understanding. Technology is not viewed as a symbol of linear progress, rather, as an element capable of adopting different possibilities and directions depending on the social influences and values of its users. Technology must be understood, then, within the context of its use and development. When governed by a **technocracy**, technology embodies the values, social structures, and goals of **hegemonic elites**. That is, the ruling class dominates through the use of technologies that subserve their needs. By contrast, participatory democratic actions offer an alternative to technocracy through "tactical resistance to established designs [that] can impose new values on technical institutions and create a new type of modern society" (Feenberg, 1999, p. 128). Through resistance, technology can be used toward democratic aims, instead of technocratic interests reflecting the values of the social system that makes use of the tool. Chapter 11 discusses the example of counter-surveillance to illustrate the use of technology to question existing forms of domination in society and to establish new norms.

Science and Technology Studies (STS)

Science and technology studies (STS) is an interdisciplinary field concerned with the study of how scientific and technological changes intersect with society. Early STS theorists such as Ellul and Vanderburg (1964, 1981) and Mumford (1967, 1981) argued that technology was an independent force dominating society and thus requiring some form of control and delimitation (Cutcliffe & Mitcham, 2001). STS, however, has abandoned the view that technology is an autonomous force at work independently from society. It now aims to analyze technology in its unique social, local context of "complex societal influences and social constructs entailing a host of political, ethical, and general theoretical questions" (Cutcliffe & Mitcham, 2001, p. 3). This fits perfectly with the definition of technology proposed in Chapter 1. Technology in this context is conceptualized as value-laden, actively shaping and in turn being shaped by culture, politics, and social values (Cutcliffe & Mitcham, 2001). It rejects deterministic assumptions of the effect of technology and calls for **holistic approaches** that employ **qualitative methods** as a means to study technology, such as interviews, case studies, and ethnography. An example of how local context shapes technology is seen in the rise and fall of the notion of the **MySpace band**. Tófalvy (2014) employs a qualitative method that relies on case studies to describe how unknown bands, such as Job for a Cowboy, garnered overnight success as a result of their MySpace profiles. The site provided a global audience of fans with immediate access to songs, information about the band, and details on the members. Equally important to grasp is why these bands so quickly lost popularity—bringing down the entire genre and discrediting the notion of the MySpace band. The *deathcore scene* was rather unknown prior to its rapid success in the mainstream, resulting from MySpace exposure. This success, however, had a backlash, as people started to refer to these bands very dismissively. One quote states, "another shitty myspace [*sic*] band gets signed" (advocate) (Tófalvy, 2014). This suggests that the rise and fall of the genre and the role played by the social networking site MySpace can only be understood through a detailed and careful analysis of the local context, the role of a global audience, and the nuances of the industry. Table 3.1 provides a useful visual summary of key characteristics of STS approaches (Bijker et al., 1999).

There are two major challenges to applying STS to any research project (Cutcliffe & Mitcham, 2001). First, STS aims at conducting meaningful research at both the micro and macro levels. Hence, STS needs to combine individual and global levels of analysis to be able to have a real impact on society's understanding of technology as well as policy. The linking of micro- and macro-level phenomena is a key challenge to sociological inquiry in general. The second major challenge is to embrace neither a utopian (promotional enthusiasm) nor a dystopian (anti-science and technology) view but, to provide in-depth analyses, the kind of analyses that uncover the local context and cultural backgrounds of users of technology, including their motivations for adoption. We discuss two approaches within the field of STS that are representative of the field: social construction of technology (SCOT) and actor network theory (ANT).

Social Construction of Technology (SCOT)

Social construction of technology (SCOT) emerged in the 1970s and its roots are evident in the sociological theories influencing academia during this period. In particular, the humanities eschewed a top-down view of history, politics, and the arts in favour of a bottom-up approach that sought to understand the social constructs and relationships underpinning everyday life.

SCOT advocates, such as Wiebe Bijker and Trevor Pinch, do not see technology as shaping human action but instead see human action as shaping technology. Social constructivists argue that a technological object can acquire different uses and values according to the social context in which it

Table 3.1 Key Characteristics of STS Approaches

Characteristic	Description
1. Rejection of technological determinism	STS rejects the notion of technological determinism, where technology is perceived as the agent of social, cultural, political, and economic change.
2. Rejection of social determinism	STS also rejects the notion of social determinism, where the inventor of a technology alone drives technological progress without any consideration of the social system in which an invention occurs.
3. Holistic approach	STS intends to study the entire socio-technical system and not the social, political, cultural, and economic dimensions separately. That is, social factors are examined in relation to use or non-use of technology.
4. Qualitative methods	STS uses qualitative methods, such as case studies and ethnographies, to provide an in-depth examination of socio-technical systems that generate rich descriptions.

Source: Based on Bijker et al., 1999.

is placed. For example, video games can be a fun way for kids to spend their downtime, learn new skills, and enhance their self-worth through mastery of the game goals. A different use and value can be given to video games when they are offered to those same kids by a single father who needs to balance work-related demands and taking care of his younger children. In this case, the video game becomes an inexpensive babysitter that allows the father to focus on other tasks while his children are absorbed in the video game console. However, this scenario has further ramifications if the father, out of necessity, allows the child to spend many hours on the game and this then negatively affects the child's behaviour (Nierenberg, 2014; Przybylski, 2014). On the other hand, a study by Przybylski (2014) shows that children between 10 and 15 years of age who spent less than one hour a day playing were better adjusted psychologically than those who spent no time on these games. This study suggests that engaging in video games, particularly when that engagement is limited in time and scope, does not necessarily have only negative effects on psychological adjustment and well-being. Hence, the value and consequences of any technology are best understood in terms of different uses and the value assigned in the specific social context.

Scholars employ SCOT to understand technical change, the design of tools, and the technology–society relationship. Four key terms help understand the interplay among design, technology, and society: (1) the **relevant social group**, (2) **interpretive flexibility**, (3) **closure** and **stabilization**, and (4) **wider context**.

1. Relevant Social Groups

Relevant social groups are important because of their influence on the meaning attributed to an artifact (Bijker, 2009). Meaning is obtained through interacting with like-minded social groups, who share a similar opinion about a given artifact and its uses. Pinch (2009) has argued that "[i]t is the meanings given to technics . . . that provide a way of understanding successful, failed, tangential, and niche-market technologies" (p. 46). Without the necessary societal support, a new or existing technology can fail to be viewed as useful within a given group, causing both new and older products to be viewed as obsolete. An example of this is the study by Grimes (2014) that attempts to examine how the world of video games can be seen as a "heavily negotiated terrain of activity" (p. 5). Grimes's children are the relevant social group as they are users and co-shapers of the video games and play a role in how "ideal play" is conceptualized in this context. The six video games examined by Grimes are depicted in Table 3.2, including their launch dates, owners, and market sectors.

Based on her analysis of the games, Grimes (2014) identified four themes in terms of how the child player was configured and described in the six games:

Table 3.2 Six Virtual Worlds Selected for Analysis

Name	Launch Date	Population Size at Time of Study[a]	Owned By	Market Sector
BarbieGirls	April 2007	1 million	Mattel	toys, media
Club Penguin	October 2005	4 million	Disney	toys, collectible game cards, media
GalaXseeds	February 2007	60,000+	Corus Entertainment	media/TV
Magi-Nation	February 2008	unknown	Cookie Jar Group	toys, collectible game cards, media
Nicktropolis	January 2007	4 million	Nickelodeon	media/TV, toys
Toontown	June 2003	1.2 million[b]	Disney	theme park, media, toys

[a] Data on population sizes were drawn from company-published press releases and player rankings on the virtual worlds' websites.
[b] Estimate for paying members. However, Disney announced in 2008 that since its launch in 2003, over 20 million avatars have been created within Toontown.

Source: Reproduced from Grimes 2010. © 2015, SAGE Publications

1. *Easily amused*: The analysis revealed that most games had limited opportunities for interaction, customization, and communication. This seems to be in stark contrast with the games' goals of promoting interactivity and creativity.

2. *"At risk"*: Most of the games contained many safety features to restrict the content that children could see and to limit their interactions with other players. Often a predefined list of terms was provided by the game to limit interaction to these terms. This greatly restricts communication between players and players' ability to verbalize their thoughts and experiences.

3. *Nice player*: In most games, an idealized form of children's play was represented through the reinforcement of rules around appropriate behaviour. It was made clear that no bullying and no troublesome or mean behaviour would be tolerated, even though these are often a part of play and not uncommon behaviours on playgrounds.

4. *Consumer*: Most of the games involved some kind of currency that allowed players to purchase additional features or virtual items. In some cases, virtual consumption was also tied to real-world monetary exchanges.

The analysis shows play being narrowly designed around a neoromantic, consumerist ethos. The designers seem to struggle between a need to design games that are creative, imaginative, and fun, and the need to provide an environment for children that is safe, rewards kindness, encourages learning, and at the same time allows for consumerism to occur.

2. Interpretive Flexibility

Interpretive flexibility describes how artifacts are not neutral; instead, their meaning emerges in a socio-cultural context. For Pinch and Bijker, what this means is "not only that there is flexibility in how people think of or inter-pret artifacts but also that there is flexibility in how artifacts are designed" (1987, p. 40). The movie *The Gods Must Be Crazy* provides an example of interpretative flexibility. The Coca-Cola bottle creates major upheaval in the community as the bottle is repurposed for a variety of tasks, including curing snakeskin and making music, and as a mortar for food preparation. Because each community member feels that this bottle has become central to his or her work, and because there is only one bottle, the result is inevit-ably conflict and controversy. The movie makes it clear that a simple tool, such as a bottle, can be used for multiple purposes and its meaning and relevance emerge in a socio-cultural context.

3. Closure and Stabilization

As an artifact gains prominence in society, its flexibility to be interpreted for other uses decreases because the social construction of the artifact's mean-ing becomes solidified. *Closure* describes the moment in the cycle of design when the relevant social group has reached a consensus of what the tool is all about. When stabilization is reached, the tool has been assigned a very specific use and little experimentation will occur from that point onward as to what other purposes the tool could serve.

Pinch and Bijker further distinguish between **rhetorical closure** and **closure by redefinition of the problem**. Rhetorical closure occurs when a technological problem is not solved but a solution is presented by changing the language used to describe the problem and hence modify its social meaning. That is, the solution to the problem does not require a technical change to the artifact itself but, new rhetoric about safety. In closure by redefinition of the problem, again a technical problem is not solved but is instead reformulated in different terms. This shows that problems linked to technology often reflect how people interact with and make sense of these technologies.

4. Wider Context

The last term is *wider context*, which describes how "the sociocultural and polit-ical situation of a social group shapes its norms and values, which in turn influ-ence the meaning given to an artifact" (Pinch & Bijker, 1987, p. 428). Norms and values are powerful frameworks for interpreting artifacts and for under-standing their value in society. A prime example can be seen in reproductive technologies such as birth control. Even though birth control methods such as hormonal contraceptives are generally safe and effective, with widespread popularity in many parts of the world, they are rejected in some regions because they are in opposition to the culture's values and norms. (This clashing of val-ues and technology will be discussed in chapter 5 under the umbrella term **compatibility**.)

Pinch and Bijker's (1987) primary example for demonstrating the social construction of technology is that of the bicycle. Early bicycles such as the penny-farthing bicycle (also known as the high-wheeled or the ordinary bicycle) were easily recognizable because of their large, prominent front wheel and small rear wheel. These bicycles were used primarily by young men for the purposes of sport, whereas women were openly discouraged from using them. However, these early models were beset by safety issues, especially vibration and braking, which led to a redesign of the bicycle that ultimately made it more useful for all riders. For example, the introduction of smaller, air-filled tires improved safety for female and elderly cyclists. Engineers had previously viewed the air tire as a "theoretical and practical monstrosity," whereas users over time experienced its practicality and value in terms of increased speed and safety (Pinch & Bijker, 1987, p. 427).

Box 3.2 uses the case study of the electric car in France to further exemplify some of these points, and demonstrates how the development of the electric car can be examined using SCOT. The strength of this approach is that it provides a useful framework for understanding how design unfolds over time and helps identify key social factors.

Nevertheless, critics of SCOT, such as Langdon Winner, have argued that the theory lacks an understanding of "the dynamics of technological change," such as the social context, economic conditions, and structural relationships within society at the time of a particular technology's introduction

Box 3.2   The Case of the Electric Car in 1970s France

Despite its anticipation for several decades, the age of the electric car is only now arriving thanks to California-based car manufacturer Tesla. With their low fuel costs, quiet hum, and clean emissions, electric cars should be more popular than they are. Yet while hybrid vehicles (those powered by hybrid fuel cells) have made their mark on the North American automotive landscape, the emergence of the electric car has been slow. As discussed by Callon (1987), the development of the electric car is an interesting example of how the success of an emerging technology can be heavily weighted by the social factors and shifting values constructing its meaning.

Callon's (1987) work analyzed the attempt of several parties, representing science, industry, and government, to combine their knowledge to create an electric car in 1970s France. In response to social protests and spiralling fuel costs, Electricité de France (EDF) envisaged "a society of urban post-industrial consumers" who shared the notion of ushering in a "new era of public transport" driven by the cost-effective and environmentally friendly electric car (Callon, 1987, p. 85). The Compagnie Générale d'Electricité (CGE) would design the electrical components of the vehicle, such as the motor and batteries, and car manufacturer Renault would assemble the vehicle's body and structure. Problems began to arise within the process, however, when the cheap catalysts envisioned to run the vehicle became contaminated or destabilized. Furthermore, Renault started to actively critique the project based on its newly acquired electrochemical expertise and its understanding of consumer needs. Worst of all, the general public's initial enthusiasm for the electric car, with its projected better fuel performance and fewer emissions, rapidly waned in the face of rising unemployment (Callon, 1987, p. 91). Without support from relevant social groups, interest in the project died and the traditional car was once again perceived as an acceptable, and perhaps even appealing, mode of transportation.

(Winner, 2003, p. 234). Second, critics have argued that SCOT supporters spend too much time studying the development and social construction of a technology, while at the same time showing "a disregard for the social consequences of technical choice." Winner (2003) characterizes these as the **social after-effects** that result from selecting or adopting one technology over another, such as the transformation of "personal experience and social relations" (p. 237).

A third area of criticism is the way in which SCOT scholars give importance and salience to the opinions of some groups and interests over others. That is, SCOT overlooks those groups within society that have no input in approving a technology or that suffer from the social consequences of that technology's selection (Winner, 2003, p. 238). By disregarding these groups, SCOT provides only a limited perspective on how technologies are diffused and how they gain social relevance in society. Additionally, the relativist nature of the SCOT approach—in which each social group gives meaning to a technology—provides little information for determining whether one social construction is better or more valid than another (Boreham, Parker, Thompson, & Hall, 2008).

Actor Network Theory (ANT)

Actor network theory (ANT) is a sociological theory popularized in the 1980s by scholars Latour, Callon, and Law. This theory treats "everything in the world as a continuously generated effect of the webs of relations within which they are located" (Law, 2009, p. 141). Proponents of this approach examine and describe the relationships and practices undertaken by actors. Within ANT, **actors** or **actants** can emerge in a variety of forms ranging from human beings to concepts or ideas, technologies, institutions, and so forth. Rather than explain why relationships between actors occur, the theory instead examines *how* these relationships are constructed and practised—that is, ANT is based on a constructivist approach, where relationships are placed in a particular social context. A strength of this theory is its ability to examine the active processes and interconnected relationships between human and non-human actors, which is not possible in many of the other theories of technology.

At the core of understanding these relationships is the concept of the **network**. Networks consist of relationships between people, but they also comprise interactions with objects and organizations. In Latour's classification of the term, a *network* contains "resources that are concentrated in a few places" and that are connected to one another (1987, p. 180). Subsequently, the "connections transform these scattered resources into a net that may seem to extend everywhere" (Latour, 1987, p. 180).

In contrast to the contemporary usage of the word *network* to characterize the transportation of information, ANT views the role of the network as one of **transformation** (Latour, 1999). Networks are categorized by their size, concentration of resources, and fragility. Using telephone lines as an example, Latour notes that individual lines are "minute and fragile" to the point that they are not rendered on typical maps, and each line can be easily cut (Latour, 1987, p. 180). However, as a group, the telephone lines seemingly encompass a vast network, crossing geographical boundaries and functioning as a single unit. Nevertheless, if a single element of the network is fractured or disabled, the network is prone to failure. To remain strong, networks undergo a continual process of re-evaluation and redevelopment, which includes being influenced by elements from other networks. For instance, the Internet has changed the telephone network in fundamental ways.

Box 3.3 shows how Latour employed ANT to uncover the complexity of the process that led to Pasteur's discoveries. Latour (1988) suggests that the translation of the laboratory to the unfamiliar environment of the field was crucial to Louis Pasteur's success. Equipped with laboratory equipment, such as microscopes and logbooks, the Pasteurians engaged in fieldwork, learning from people such as farmers and veterinarians, in order to be able to determine which conditions and factors were leading toward diseases and their potential causalities. The results of Pasteur's trials "were to create a new object that retranslated the disease into the language of the laboratory" (Latour, 1988, p. 76).

When viewing Pasteur's triumphs through the prism of ANT, responsibility for his discoveries shifts from a single individual to the multitude of actors, human and non-human, whose respective contributions impacted the development of scientific discoveries. Thus, when studying the history of technology from a sociological perspective, we can use ANT to understand and acknowledge the roles, systems, and networks necessary in the development and promotion of new technologies.

Box 3.3   Discovering Pasteurization

French chemist and microbiologist Louis Pasteur is renowned as being one of the most important scientific minds of the nineteenth century. Innovations in microbiology attributed to Pasteur include vaccines for anthrax and rabies and the practice of sterilizing medical equipment, as well as the process that bears his name: **pasteurization**. The last, arguably Pasteur's most celebrated achievement, assisted with the elimination of disease-causing pathogens found in various foods and beverages, such as milk and cheese.

Responsibility for the success of these scientific and technical breakthroughs has long been solely accredited to Pasteur, but it is important to realize that many individuals contributed to the discovery. In the concept known as the **Great Man Theory**, history is often written and mythologized in overly simplistic terms, where great events are attributed to remarkable individuals, often men, who demonstrated intellectual or political prowess during their lifetimes. Yet such a viewpoint neglects the myriad socio-economic, political, cultural, or technical transformations that may have influenced the direction and choices that these individuals made. In the example of Pasteur, farmers, assistants, medical doctors, and collaborators helped him during his work. The focus on a single person ignores the input of all these social groups, as well as the transmission of knowledge and information from external sources necessary to the work of brilliant thinkers such as Pasteur.

Commenting on feats linked to Pasteur in particular, Bruno Latour (1988) has argued that "[i]f the whole of Europe transformed conditions of its existence at the end of the last century, we should not attribute the efficacy of this extraordinary leap forward to the genius of a single man" (p. 15). Using ANT as a guide, then, one instead can view Pasteur as an actor whose technical accomplishments were the product of a network of laboratories, logbooks, and scientific associates. Enrolling the services of likeminded individuals within the scientific community, Pasteur was equipped to translate the interests of other actors in his network, including farmers. The members of Pasteur's laboratory were then able to address the multitude of ideas and issues held by the various actors and render these concerns into a language that was usable within the setting of the laboratory in order to combat the non-human actor, that is, the microbe.

Despite ANT's merits, however, scholars have identified several weaknesses. First, a major point of criticism for the opponents and detractors of ANT is the heterogeneous nature of its actors and networks. By placing human and non-human actors on the same footing, too much emphasis is placed on the role of non-human actors, thereby reducing human actors to mere objects. This is particularly relevant when detailing the role of power in shaping, re-casting, and ending alliances between human and non-human participants (Grint & Woolgar, 1997). The role of power in defining the relationship between human and non-human participants was discussed in Chapter 2 when we examined how the nature of work, and the relation between craftspeople and their craft, drastically changed as a result of the introduction of new weaving and spinning machines in the beginnings of the industrial era. In this instance, weaving machines did not remove crafts-people from their jobs, but employers used their position of power to replace highly skilled craftspeople with a larger, less expensive, and unregulated workforce (Berg, 1994). Second, critics have also suggested that ANT fails to properly define or describe the nature of its networks: the structure of these networks can appear overly complex and abstract, making it difficult for others to understand what the networks mean. Third, critics have opined that the theory tends to acknowledge localized networks and fails to examine either the role of broader macro-level social structures or the influence of cultural practices in affecting the construction and redevelopment of a network (Walsham, 1997).

Conclusions

Simple approaches to understanding the interrelationship between technology and society have been largely refuted. Utopian and dystopian visions of technology are too simplistic and do not consider how technology has become embedded in our everyday practices. Technological determinism views the effect of technology on society as unidirectional and does not consider social factors. By contrast, social determinism assumes that social factors drive technological design, use, and consequences alone without ascribing any power or influence to technology. Not even approaches advocating soft determinism provide a satisfactory answer as to how technology and society intersect. Current understandings of technological society propose a **mutual shaping** process, where technological factors impact society and in turn societal factors impact technological design, development, implementation, use, and social consequences. In these approaches, technology is not studied as a universal force; instead, technologies are examined in unique social contexts with specific cultural, religious, and political characteristics.

Another important factor in understanding the interrelationship between technology and society is globalization. Social change occurs in a global context, as technologies diffuse across borders, cultures, and social groups. As technologies become more ubiquitous and integrated into our daily social practices, routines, and ways of being, continued critical, in-depth, and con-textualized analysis of our technological society will be necessary.

Questions for Critical Thought

1. When comparing utopian and dystopian views of technology, which one do you think has more applicability to society today? Provide a rationale for your point of view.

2. What are the main criticisms put forward against the actor network theory (ANT) approach?

3. Pinch and Bijker show how the social construction of technology (SCOT) approach can be utilized to examine the development of the bicycle. What other examples from your own life can show the usefulness of this approach for examining modern technological developments?

4. How can we study how video games influence children's learning and well-being? Are some games more suitable than others to the concept of the ideal "child player"?

Suggested Readings

Feenberg, A. (1999). *Questioning technology*. New York: Routledge. The book provides a critical analysis of the heavy reliance of society on technology and outlines key theoretical perspectives on the complex interlink of society and technology.

Tófalvy, T. (2014). "MySpace bands" and "tagging wars": Conflicts of genre, work ethic and media platforms in an extreme music scene. *First Monday, 19*(9). URL: http://firstmonday. org/ojs/index.php/fm/article/view/4354/4115. doi: http://dx.doi.org/10.5210/fm.v19i9 .4354. This article presents two cases on the music industry and its interrelation to global means of information dissemination such as MySpace.

Pinch, T., & Bijker, W.E. (1984). The social construction of facts and artifacts, or how the sociology of science and the sociology of technology might benefit each other. *Social Studies of Science, 14*, 399–441. The paper describes an integrated social constructivist approach toward the study of science and technology. From this perspective, science and artifacts are defined as social constructs.

Grimes, S.M. (2014). Configuring the child player. *Science, Technology & Human Values*. Advance online publication doi: 10.1177/0162243914550253. The article presents a study of various video games and argues that these are negotiated spaces where ideas resurface of what an imagined, ideal "child player" looks like.

Online Resources

Society for Social Studies of Science (4S)
http://4sonline.org/
> This is an international non-profit organization dedicated to the study of science, technology, and medicine, with an emphasis on how these develop and interact with their social contexts.

Computer History Museum
www.computerhistory.org/
> The world's most comprehensive institution dedicated to the history of computing and its impact on society.

With Kids and Video Games, Moderation Is Key
www.huffingtonpost.com/2014/08/07/kids-and-video-games_n_5656399.html
> This article addresses the challenges that parents confront when making decisions about how much time children should spend playing video games.

4 Gendered Technology

Learning Objectives

◎ to examine the meaning of the terms *gender* and *sexualities* and the range of conceptualizations available in the academic literature;

◎ to look at historical and contemporary theoretical and methodological approaches to the study and critique of gendered technologies;

◎ to investigate the relation between household technologies and physical and mental labour and call into question perspectives of technological determinism;

◎ to examine the role of women in the IT industry and obtain an overview of current interventions aimed at increasing gender equality in this field;

◎ to take a closer look at how the gendered body becomes reintegrated into the digital world in the form of images, discourse, media depictions, and user-generated content.

Introduction

In technology design, use, and implementation, *gender* is often invisible. It is not invisible because it is purposefully erased but simply because gender is not viewed as an important consideration. Why would tools, techniques, and even software, cellphones, and the Internet need a gendered perspective? In this chapter, we investigate the nuanced and bold ways in which gender influences technological innovation and implementation. Through a review of how key theorists of gendered technology have come to see the link between technology and gender, we open the opportunity for more mature discussions of what gender is and how it shapes the study and development of technology. In a world that embraces multiple perspectives, diversity, and gender equality, the plurality of *sexualities* in the social world also needs to be taken into account. Similar to our example of how bicycles had to be redesigned to fit the needs of female riders (see Chapter 3), we also discuss how digital technologies can be redesigned with gender in mind. Yet again, we emphasize the need to see gender not as a dichotomy, one where bodies can be placed in easily recognizable boxes, but instead as a complex interplay of biological and physiological features and interactions with the social world. We show how there is a need for both dichotomous understandings of gender—i.e., large-scale studies that examine differences between women and men—and more nuanced studies of gendered lives, as they play out in our digital world.

Talking about Gender and Technology

Erasing Gender and Sexualities from the Technology Debate

Understanding sex and gender has been a vibrant area of investigation in disciplines such as sociology, women's studies, and anthropology, to name a few. This interest in unpacking sex and gender is, however, fairly recent, having begun only in the late twentieth century. The *Oxford Dictionary of Sociology* writes that this area "was not a major concern in sociology until late in the twentieth century" (Scott & Marshall, 2005, p. 595). Before this, scholars often disregarded gender as an important subject of study, particularly in the study of technology.

The World Health Organization (WHO) defines *sex* as the biological and physiological features that define men and women, while *gender* "refers to socially constructed roles, behaviours, activities, and attributes that a given society considers appropriate for men and women" (World Health Organization [WHO], 2014). It further explains that these categories are not necessarily mutually exclusive: intersex individuals, for example, possess elements of both sexes. Despite this biological diversity, however, we tend to label people as either male or female. As Albanese (2012) points out, the difference lies in how societies and cultures treat the diversity of sexualities that exist, "making sex and sexuality political and social issues rather than mere biological facts . . ." (Chapter 10). This is why it is important to see gender and sexualities as they influence the social world, because even though gender and sex are private and personal spheres, they are also deeply social (England, 2014). We need only to scan the Web for the latest news to realize that "contemporary politics are full of contentious debates about abortion, sex education, same-sex marriage, pornography, sex work, sexual harassment, systematic rape as a weapon in wars, and female genital cutting" (England, 2014).

When we look at the study of technology with this in mind, then, we realize that often gender is absent from these discussions. Three key observations can be made:

1. Technologies are often treated as neutral objects and are designed with neither a specific gender nor a specific user in mind.
2. Technologies are perceived as impacting women and men equally, without taking into account that men's and women's bodies are different.
3. Debates around gender issues are often initiated only after the design of a tool is completed instead of encompassing all aspects of technological development, use, and implications.

There has been remarkably little critical debate around the role of gender and technology design, use, and implementation until recently. However, a vibrant area of study has emerged that tackles these questions. There is a need, though, to move away from simplistic understandings of gender as a dichotomy and open scholarly debate further to allow for a plurality of perspectives and sexualities in the social and digital world.

Theories to Understanding Gender and Sexualities in Technology

The debate around women and technology is historically grounded in discussions of women in science (Wajcman, 2013), women's household work (Oakley, 1974), and women and paid labour (Huws, 2003). Two starkly opposing views have informed our understanding of the relation between women and technology (Wajcman, 2013). The *women's liberation view* advocates that technology can liberate women by (a) supporting fertility choices; (b) easing the burden of household work; and (c) creating alternative, flexible work environments particularly suited for women. By contrast, the *women's oppression view* states that women will (a) be enslaved through these technological advances; (b) have fewer choices in general; and (c) become more reliant on the existing technologies.

How technologies are perceived as oppressive is exemplified in the debate around *reproductive technology*. Stanworth (1987) provides an overview of what kinds of technologies are commonly grouped under reproductive technology and includes birth control, foetal monitoring, and infertility programs. Central to the argument of the role of reproductive technologies in the lives of women are the assumptions about how they influence the lives of women. Generally only the positive changes that these bring to women's lives are emphasized. Wajcman (2013) stresses that most discussions view technology as solely responsible for social change in society and hence also responsible for the well-being of women. The reason advances in reproductive technology are so contested is because birth control is perceived as part of the overarching patriarchal structure, further enabling the male domination of women and their bodies. Women and their struggles for self-determination are often absent from these discussions. For instance, historian Shorter (1991) sees women as victims of their own bodies and reiterates that reproductive technologies have allowed them to become equal to men. These types of arguments tend to neglect the active role of women in shaping how technologies affect their bodies and in the collaboration of men and women when looking at, for instance, infertility programs. A study on the use of cellphones by midwives in rural Indonesia, for example, shows that technologies can be re-appropriated in the context of reproduction; here, cellphones became key to the work of midwives as they engaged with their female clients (Chib & Chen, 2011).

Along these lines, a third perspective could advocate for an active role for women in shaping technological design, development, and implementation and in appropriating technologies for their own purposes. The *women inclusion view* tries to move away from simple deterministic perspectives and instead advocates that women need to be more integrated into the technology debate not only as users, but also as active participants. This includes women taking on leadership roles in IT companies, becoming, for example, chief executive officers (CEOs) and chief information officers (CIOs). In order to more fully understand the current debate on women and IT, it is important to examine historical, theoretical, and methodological approaches. Of particular relevance is the debate around women and household technology.

Household Technology

The kinds of *household* or *domestic technology* continue to proliferate, including things like vacuum cleaners, dishwashers, and irons. This list can probably be greatly expanded and shows a large reliance on household technologies and how deeply interwoven they are in the lives of men and women, but in particular in those of women. In fact, until the 1970s, unpaid household labour was primarily the domain of women and few studies looked at the implications of this imbalance. Ann Oakley's (1974) influential book *The Sociology of Housework* shows a fundamental shift in how industrial sociology views housework by arguing that it is also work, even if unpaid. One key implication of this shift in attitude is the assertion that women's work in the home is in fact work, even if it is unpaid labour, and that this solitary form of work, even if not physically highly demanding, can be repetitive and unfulfilling. This links directly to our discussion in Chapter 7 on Marx's concept of **alienation**, the deep separation between labour and identity. Wajcman (2013) has described housework in terms of three characteristics.

1. *Privatized*: Housework is not visible and as a result is not directly compensated or acknowledged in the same way as other forms of work are. There is no final product that is celebrated by a community.
2. *Decentralized*: Unlike paid labour, which is often embedded in a hierarchical structure, housework is dependent only on the homemaker. There are no established formal roles, tasks, or deadlines, making it difficult to determine when work is complete.
3. *Labour-intensive*: Many jobs in the service sector require long hours but are not necessarily physically demanding. Housework is physically labour-intensive and also has no pre-established beginning and end.

But how do technologies play a role in domestic work? The introduction of household technology opened a new era for homemakers, both male and female, and signified a revolution in how housework was done. First, household technology was endorsed because it facilitated the work of homemakers.

This led to the term **labour saving technology,** which denoted the direct impact of technology on housework. The most significant change, though, was perceived as lying in the speed at which housework would be accomplished. Again, the assumption was that technology would diminish the physical demands on women and also expedite tasks, freeing up leisure time (this idea will be discussed further in Chapter 7). The home, once a private place, became industrialized and subsumed under the principles of **scientific management** as a result of technological change. However, a crucial study by Vanek (1974) demonstrated that despite the increased reliance on household technology by homemakers, no conclusive evidence could be found of actual savings of labour and time. Moreover, McGaw (1982) in her analysis concludes that "substantial changes in household technology left the sex, hours, efficiency, and status of the household worker essentially unaltered" (p. 814). While a shift occurred in terms of how much time was spent on various tasks, little change occurred in terms of the amount of time spent on housework overall.

How can we explain these contradictory findings about the effects of household technology on domestic work? From a technological determinism perspective, technology freed up time and reduced the amount of work women had to do at home, a welcome change. Nonetheless, technological change is never straightforward, and as Cowan (1983) has argued, the industrialization of the home occurred in a more complex way and hand in hand with other social changes. For example, the mechanization of the home consisted mainly of replacing previously physically demanding jobs with other more mechanized tasks but did not necessarily save much time (Cowan, 1983; Wajcman, 2013). But more fundamentally, there was a switch in expectations and in the division of labour. A combination of the development of the *domestic science movement* and *germ theory* increased expectations around cleanliness and tidiness, which quickly became representations of social status, happiness, and well-being (Wajcman, 2013). In addition, in the early twentieth century many households still had outside help, and the modernization of the home largely reduced the reliance on personnel. As Wajcman (2013) puts it, "[t]he split between public and private meant that the home was expected to provide a haven from the alienated, stressful technological order of the workplace and was expected to provide entertainment, emotional support, and sexual gratification" (p. 100).

To further question and understand the relation of women and men to household technology, we need to explore in more detail notions of use and competency vis-à-vis household technologies. This gap can be referred to as the *user-actor gender gap*: women are represented as users, but not as engaged actors in the process of tool development. To understand the full impact of household technologies on the division of housework, an analysis is needed of (a) men's and women's relationship to housework and (b) men's and women's relationship to technology. Wajcman (2013) states that "[c]ultural notions of masculinity stress competency in the use and repair of machines" (p. 104), while the role of women is often seen as that of users of technology. In this context, household machines further reinforce female stereotypes and also do not allow for men to take over tasks that are perceived as being in the domain of women. Thus, men repair and maintain machines but do not see themselves as users of household technologies. Even though many of the notions from the 1970s and 1980s about gender roles are changing, some evidence suggests that women, even when employed outside the home, continue to do most of the housework, whereas men are more likely to contribute to nonroutine tasks, such as those that are performed outdoors. Moreover, many same-sex couples must negotiate their relationship to household technologies, as gender roles may be less clear (Connidis & McMullin, 2002).

In your opinion, what are the latest household technologies that are making their way into the home? Do you think that cellphones can be considered household technologies? How about tablets that help in the access and organization of recipes? In Box 4.1 we discuss the movie *Her* (2013, Director: Spike Jonze), which pushes the limits in terms of what defines a household technology and how that technology impacts both the home and social relations.

Box 4.1   New Household Technologies: The Virtual Agent "Her" Speaks to a User's Emotions

Central to the making of *Her* was the idea that technology should be invisible but not non-existent. That is, in a futuristic world technology is so ubiquitous and embedded in everyday life that it fades into the background, becoming seamlessly integrated into our environments (Vanhemert, 2014). In *Her*, the main character, Theo, purchases a new operating system a female by the name of Samantha who is embedded in his cellphone and who is designed to help him with various tasks. While Samantha is charming and understanding, and challenges Theo to look at the world differently, she is not your average household technology, as she does not clean or chop veggies. She does, however, fill Theo's need for sociability and emotional connectedness, for example, by greeting him in the morning and helping him to get his day started. Samantha resembles the chatterbots and intelligent agents discussed in Chapter 1, as she calls into question the boundary between human and machine. Vanhemert (2014) speculates that we will interact with computers in the future not by sitting down to pay attention to our screens but rather by interacting with our *user interface* (UI) anywhere, at any time, through natural language.

(See "Why *Her* will dominate UI design even more than *Minority Report*," *Wired* online: www.wired.com/2014/01/will-influential-ui-design-minority-report/)

Annapurna Pictures/The Kobal Collection

The virtual avatar—Samantha—flexibly adjusts to the emotional state of her user, Theo.

The movie *Her*, as discussed in the previous box, shows how women continue to be the providers of support, emotional connectivity, and understanding—even in the form of an intelligent agent.

Gender and IT Use and Skills

How we understand gender and technology is not limited to how women use and understand household technology and the impact of these technologies on their lives. Since the introduction of the World Wide Web (WWW) in 1994 by Tim Berners Lee, there has been an intense ongoing debate about how women use, and make sense of, the Internet and related mobile technologies differently from men (Fallows, 2005; Shade, 2014).

Use of Computers and the Internet

Early research on computers consistently demonstrated that men were more likely to own and use a computer than women were (Brosnan & Lee, 1998; Durndell, Glissov, & Siann, 1995). This gap is somewhat surprising considering that in the 1980s and 1990s women were primary users of computers in the workplace. A study from 1999 by the U.S. National Center for Education Statistics showed that 56 per cent of women and 44 per cent of men used a computer at work (as cited in Fountain, 2000). Some research has documented that even in those circumstances where women were given the same access to computers as men, they tended to use them less (Kirkup, 1995; Scragg & Smith, 1998; Shashaani, 1997).

Similar trends to those found in computer ownership have also been observed in terms of access to the Internet, supporting the notion of a digital divide in terms of gender. In a study by Katz, Rice, and Aspden (2001), however, they found that this trend was quickly being reversed. Based on data stemming from national representative telephone surveys, the authors showed that until 1996 fewer women were online. After that, however, the gap started to close, as new users of the Internet tended to be female rather than male. Instrumental for clarifying the complexities of the gender gap is a study by Bimber (2000), in which he corroborated previous findings showing that a gap exists between men and women in terms of access to the Internet. Unique to his research was the finding that this difference was a result of other factors, with the most important being socio-economic differences between men and women. He suggested that eventually "this gap will narrow of its own accord, because educational and income differences between men and women are slowly shrinking" (p. 874). More recent studies on the digital divide in developed countries further support Bimber's (2000) prediction. For instance, Haight, Quan-Haase, and Corbett (2014) found that men and women in Canada were equally likely to have Internet access. These studies overall show that in the 2010s, there exists no difference in access to the Internet between men and women in developed countries (Haight et al., 2014; Ono & Zavodny, 2003).

Digital Skills

Looking at Internet access alone is not a sufficient measure of the extent to which a person engages with the digital world. A number of scholars have proposed that investigating a person's competency when online is important as well, because this shows to what extent a person can navigate different digital challenges (Haight et al., 2014; Hargittai, 2002; Witte & Mannon, 2009). Many studies now integrate measures of digital skills that aim at determining a user's ability to understand and use the Internet (Hargittai & Hsieh, 2012). These measures are important to obtain a more comprehensive understanding of what kinds of activities individuals participate in when they are online.

A 2005 Pew report found that men are much more active online and complete significantly more activities than women (Fallows, 2005). Table 4.1 shows differences between men and women across online activities. Specifically, the table shows that women are more likely to send an email, get maps or directions, look for health resources, and obtain religious information. Men, by contrast, are more likely, among other activities, to research products and services, check weather, get news, and use do-it-yourself (DIY) websites.

The results of the Pew (2005) study indicate that men completed more online activities than women, which is a surprising finding as it suggests that the alleged gender gap within prior digital divide literature, whereby

Table 4.1 Online Activities: Where Men's and Women's Use of the Internet Differs

	% of Online Men	% of Online Women	Date of PIP Survey
Activities Where Women Lead			
Send email	88	94*	Sep 05
Get maps or directions	82	87*	Feb 04
Look for health and medical info	58	74*	Dec 02
Get support for a medical issue or personal problem	50	66*	Nov 04
Get religious/spiritual info	25	34*	Nov 04
Activities Where Men Lead			
Research product/service	82*	75	Mar 05
Check weather	82*	74	Nov 04
Get news	75*	69	Mar 05
Use do-it-yourself website	60*	50	Mar 05
Check sports information	59*	27	Feb 04
Get financial info	56*	33	Nov 04
Do job-related research	54*	48	Mar 05
Download a computer program	48*	31	Jun 05
Pay bills	42*	35	Jan 05
Listen to music at website	38*	29	Jun 04
Listen to radio broadcast	38*	20	Jun 04
Rate a product, service, person	33*	28	Sep 05
Download music files	30*	20	Jun 05
Do online auction	30*	18	Mar 05
Download video files	22*	13	Jun 05
Remix content	21*	15	Jan 05
Visit adult website	21*	5	Jun 05
Trade stocks, bonds, funds	20*	6	Nov 04
Use webcams	19*	13	Mar 05
Take class for personal enrichment	15*	11	Jan 05
Pay for digital content	14*	7	Jun 04

* indicates a statistically significant difference

Source: "How Women and Men Use the Internet" Pew Research Center, Washington, DC (December 28, 2005). http://www.pewinternet.org/files/2005/12/PIP_Women_and_Men_online.pdf.

men had higher activity levels online, continues to exist (Fallows, 2005; Wasserman & Richmond-Abbott, 2005).

This gender gap is corroborated in a study of computer use by Chinese and British students. Li and Kirkup (2007) found men more likely than women to use email, spend time in chat rooms, and play computer games. Relevant to understanding differences in computer use is their finding that men showed higher levels than women of self-confidence about their computer skills. Men were also more likely than women to think that using a computer is a male activity and skill. This study suggests that gender continues to be an important factor in understanding attitudes about and use of computers. Li and Kirkup (2007) write that "[w]omen are less likely to be attracted to computer courses and to a computer-related career" (p. 302). Even though women are gaining more access to computers, their willingness to enter IT-related fields does not seem to have changed.

Women Working in IT-Related Fields

The Lack of Women in IT-Related Fields

There have been dramatic changes in employment in fields related to IT. The U.S. Department of Commerce in 1999 developed a list to describe occupations in the information technology sector and included computer scientists, computer engineers, system analysts, and computer programmers. Since this list was developed, the number of job titles has skyrocketed to include, among others, software design/development, testing/quality assurance, and knowledge management, as well as jobs in the service industry and medical fields. Not only has the range of jobs encompassing IT-related work expanded, but the number of individuals working in these fields has also grown rapidly (see Table 5.1 in Chapter 5 for the number of individuals working in computing in Silicon Valley). Even though men have traditionally occupied the majority of jobs in the IT sector, this growth also opens up opportunities for women, as Fountain (2000) indicates: "[t]he extensive reach and penetration of information technology into virtually every area of society creates enormous opportunities for women" (p. 45). Despite the rapid growth of the industry and the potential for the employment of women (Landivar, 2013), however, a consistent critique has been the lack of women working in the industry as designers, developers, CEOs, and CIOs.

What is interesting about this trend is that while there is no lack of female representation in the paid labour force, particular industries still continue to show persistent gender segregation (Erickson, Albanese, & Drakulic, 2000). This process is complex, because it often takes the form of **gender resegregation**, in which women are placed in positions perceived as more feminine and jobs that women occupy are also redefined as "women's work" (Reskin & Roos, 2009).

From the 1920s to the 1980s, secretaries were primarily women who helped with office jobs. A secretarial position was considered an excellent job with responsibilities ranging from typing letters and documents to organizing events and hosting visitors. The introduction of computing technology and networked computers not only changed the responsibilities of a secretarial job, but also created a myriad of new forms of related employment, many with less status, low pay, and long hours. For instance, many companies outsource data entry to China, India, or Taiwan, where **cybertariats** (Huws, 2003) work day and night shifts inputting information about credit card usage, insurance policies, and medical records. Cybertariats are often women, commonly working in developing countries, who are paid minimum wage for routine data-entry jobs. These types of low-wage technology jobs do not influence the design or uptake of technology; more women are needed to help provide valuable input and perspectives that can help shape the future of the IT sector.

A report by the U.S. National Center for Women and Information Technology (2014b) indicates that in 2011, 25 per cent of the computing workforce in the United States consisted of women. When one looks at leadership positions, that number drops. A 2014 report put together by the Information Technology Association of Canada (ITAC) shows that women constitute about 16 per cent of the board members of Canadian public Internet and computing technology (ICT) corporations. These figures suggest that more women are needed to increase female representation at the leadership level. Also in 2014, ITAC started a review of its own board membership and increased women's representation strategically; 32 per cent of its board members are now women. These kind of strategic moves are needed in the industry to ensure that women have an input into how design, development, and implementation of IT occurs.

The U.S. National Center for Women and Information Technology (2012) reported that in 2012 women occupied only about 20 per cent of CIO positions at Fortune 250 companies. This absence of women will likely continue in the next decade, as this gap is also present in STEM (science, technology, engineering, and math) studies at the university level (National Center for Women & Information Technology, 2014a). In 2010, women represented about 57 per cent of the undergraduate body, but only 14 per cent of women took computer science as their major (National Center for Women & Information Technology, 2014a).

Why do we see a trend toward fewer women choosing IT careers when this sector is growing and providing increasingly well-paid employment, and when the statistics for IT adoption consistently show that women are using a wide range of technologies in their daily life? Genevieve Bell, a technology analyst, stresses that women between 40 and 60 years of age are an important segment of the population, as they help shape the direction the IT field will take. She finds that these women not only are more likely to adopt new technology but are also engaging with these technologies more.

Listen to her talk at www.abc.net.au/radionational/programs/bigideas/what-does-our-technology-future-look-like3f/4003568.

The majority of sociological analyses have focused on women as users rather than active agents of change. If women are heavy users, why are they not designers as well?

The fact that women are heavy users of IT is an important trend, as it shows that women are comfortable engaging with new gadgets. At the same time, though, it is important to stress that their role should not be only as users. There are many reasons why more women are needed in the IT industry as active agents. Fountain (2000) writes, "[T]he influence of users, though important and far-reaching, is limited. Designers fashion technology more deeply, pervasively and fundamentally" (p. 47). Fountain's critique shows that it is important for women to be users of IT and to have the skills to use and understand IT, but that it is also important for women to take leadership roles as designers, developers and chief financial officers (CFOs) of IT companies. It is only through this active engagement that gender diversity will be achieved.

The big question that scholars, feminist researchers, and sociologists have been pondering is, Why is there such an absence of women from these kinds of jobs? This question is not a trivial one and has led to much debate in academic circles and policy discussions. This links directly to a larger trend in society, where women are often absent from discussions around STEM topics (science, technology, engineering and math), an area which has been targeted for greater inclusion of women. Jonathan Eisen (2012), professor at UC Davis and prominent TED speaker, was invited to the 2013 winter Q-Bio meeting in Hawaii. When he examined the list of speakers more carefully (see his blog post at http://phylogenomics.blogspot.ie/2012/09/q-bio-conference-in-hawaii-bring-your.html), he was shocked to realize that only one female speaker was attending. This of course raises the question of why women were absent from this meeting. This is not an easy question to answer, but Caperton (2012), a pseudonym used by one of the bloggers on Feministe, put together a table in the form of a BINGO, which is depicted in Figure 4.1, to open up the debate and create further awareness around the gender divide. The figure shows, in a critical way across rows and down columns, various reasons that women may not be included in an event. To address the lack of women in the IT sector, a wide range of initiatives and policies have been developed—some targeted at women in developing countries, some at high-school students, and still others at women in developed countries. A few of these initiatives and their intentions are listed in Box 4.2.

There are several complexities concerning the interventions listed in Box 4.2. Although courses like Ladies Learning Code are providing a space for women to come and learn programming skills, there is not as of yet any substantial proof that these classes help attendees achieve their goals. What kinds of approaches can help women learn IT skills without feeling marginalized?

There are other ways that the gender divide in technology could be surmounted. Mitch Resnick of the LifeLong Kindergarten group at MIT's Media Laboratory has long argued for the need to teach children to code. By introducing these skills at an early age, there is a greater chance that girls and boys alike will feel able to take on this type of learning. Resnick and his team (2014) created Scratch, a programming language that is designed

Female Conference Speaker				
B	I	N	G	O
Women just aren't interested in this field	There aren't enough qualified female speakers	We need big-name speakers, and few of those are women	It's a male-dominated field	There aren't a lot of women in C-level positons
Both women we called were booked that weekened	Both women we booked bailed at the last minute	All the women were probably busy	Female speakers are always burnt out from speaking so much	Trying to get more female speakers is sexist
The organizers just wanted to get the best speakers they could find	You can't kick out a male speaker just to fit a woman in there	FREE	You can't shoehorn in a woman where she doesn't fit	Women never volunteer to present
You have to be bold; people aren't just going to invite you to present	Women are shy	Women only ever want to talk about woman-stuff	Women need to act more like men	No one has complained about this before
Attendees want to hear from people like themselves	Well, there aren't that many female attnedees, either	We're only responding to demand	Fine, YOU tell me who they should have invited	Who? I've never heard of her.

Figure 4.1 Female Conference Speaker Bingo in STEM Research
Source: Caperton Gillett/Feministe

for children to learn to code and which has an online community that has created over 4.5 million projects since its launch in 2007. When they become part of this community, Resnick (2014) notes, children "start to think of themselves differently. They begin to see themselves as creators and designers, as people who can make things and express themselves with digital media, not just browse, chat, and play games. While many people can read digital media, Scratchers can write digital media and are thus prepared to become full participants in today's digital society." You can hear more from Resnick here in his TedX talk from 2012 at www.ted.com/talks/mitch_resnick_let_s_teach_kids_to_code#t-637536.

Box 4.2   Bringing Women into IT Jobs: Diversity of Interventions

There have been several attempts to make technology, and coding in particular, more inclusive for women.

Ladies Learning Code

The Ladies Learning Code initiative was started in Toronto, Ontario, by Heather Payne, whose goal for the organization was to "create an environment where women can come and learn beginner-friendly computer programming and other technical skills in a social and collaborative way" (Payne, quoted in Gaier, 2012). After having difficulty finding useful and approachable sources while attempting to learn how to create her own website, Payne asked the Toronto Twitter community for ideas about how to solve this problem. The idea for Ladies Learning Code came out of a brainstorming session with 80 other interested people. As of 2014, Ladies Learning Code had held 289 events in 18 Canadian cities, with over 8,000 attendees taking classes on Javascript, Photoshop, and even 3D printing. The demand for their courses runs high, and they now offer classes for various age groups.

Website: http://ladieslearningcode.com/

The ADA Initiative

The ADA Initiative was founded in 2011 by Valerie Aurora and Mary Gardiner. Named after Ada Lovelace, the world's first computer programmer, the goals of the ADA Initiative are to "support women in open technology and culture through activities such as producing codes of conduct and anti-harassment policies, advocating for gender diversity, teaching ally skills, and hosting conferences for women in open tech/culture" (ADA Initiative, 2014). By helping women to feel more comfortable at technology conferences, and to be involved in all aspects of technology, the ADA Foundation hopes to raise the numbers of women in the IT sector workforce. You can learn more about the ADA Initiative in this video of Mary Gardiner's talk at Wikimedia 2012:

Video: www.youtube.com/watch?v=oONsY48OQdc#t=786

Because of the relevance of and interest in these programs, the list of similar initiatives is rapidly growing. Many of these new programs have different intended audiences. Below is a list of some other programs that might be of interest:

Black Girls Code: www.blackgirlscode.com/

Mother Coders: www.mothercoders.org/

PyLadies: www.pyladies.com/

Resnick is not alone in these thoughts. Libraries are changing to include more hands-on learning and **makerspaces** are quickly becoming places that girls and boys can visit to pick up skills they might not get in the traditional classroom. These spaces are changing the way that people think about all types of things, from commodification to education, by providing access to technology, training, and information to all groups in society.

Technology and the Body

When it comes to the design and development of technological artifacts, the body is often erased. **Body erasure** is defined as the neglect of considerations related to the body in the design and use of technology, including a person's body shape, ethnicity, and specific gender characteristics and features. Bringing the body back into discussions of technology is relevant for three reasons.

- *Technology interacts with the body*: Technology directly interacts and integrates with the body, often becoming closely entangled with it. McLuhan eloquently stated this in 1964, saying that we become our tools and our tools become us. For him, there was a close interplay between what our bodies do and what our technologies allow our bodies to do. For McLuhan, for instance, watching television was much more than just entertainment. He saw television as deeply affecting how we process and make sense of information and compared this with how these processes occur when we interact with other media, such as books and newspapers, for instance. Even though he could not provide direct empirical evidence to support this, he understood at a basic level that our information processing varied depending on the medium, leading to his well-known saying "the medium is the message" (see also Chapter 2).
- *Not all bodies are the same*: The assumption that the body can be erased is problematic simply because not all bodies are the same. A striking example of this can be found in the development of the bicycle. Pinch and Bijker's (1987) case study of how the bicycle was invented and developed (Chapter 3) shows how bicycles were designed around the 1810s and 1820s with young men in mind for the purpose of sports. Women, who wore elaborate dresses, were discouraged from riding. Also, the bikes were designed in such a way that it was basically impossible to ride a bike while wearing typical women's clothing. It was not until the 1880s that the *safety bicycle* was invented, which changed people's attitudes toward bicycles. They were no longer seen as dangerous sport vehicles for young men only; instead, they became a mode of transportation for both men and women.

- *Technology does not determine the body*: Often assumptions of technological determinism are responsible for body erasure. In the case of reproductive technologies, the introduction of the birth control pill was seen as a major positive change for women (Wajcman, 2013). Judy Wajcman has provided a critical examination of the discourse around the positive and unilateral change that reproductive technologies provide. She writes that "[t]he real dangers for women that accompany medical and scientific advances in the sphere of reproduction are directly related to the different circumstances of women's position in society" (Wajcman, 2013, p. 74). For example, not all women can afford reproductive technologies, such as *in vitro* fertilization, 3D rendering of babies, and amniocentesis. Are these technologies, then, a further divide between affluent and marginalized women, and between developed and developing countries? This debate is ongoing and there are a plurality of feminist perspectives. The take-away message is that the effects of reproductive technology are not completely positive; they also reproduce existing inequalities of power, wealth, and marginalization. Moreover, some of these technologies may have secondary effects on women's bodies that are difficult to quantify and may be unexpected. As such, there is a call for critical analysis of how technologies affect and intersect with the human body—whether male, female, or transgendered.

In Box 4.3 we discuss the pro-ana community as a case study of a controversial online community that has brought the body back to the Internet. The Internet tends to be text-based, and as such, the body is often not present in interactions over chat or via **blogs** and Web pages. This creates an artificial neutrality in terms of who is presenting certain arguments, whose voice and viewpoints stand behind a particular debate/issue.

Box 4.3   The Pro-Ana Community: The Presentation of Self through the Digital Body

The Internet is an important information resource for young people on health-related topics, including mental health (Rasmussen Neal & Hoffman, 2011). One topic that is frequently Googled is *anorexia nervosa*, as it is of relevance to teenagers and young adults. Anorexia nervosa, an eating disorder, is a potentially life-threatening condition. While the Internet has facilitated easier access to information about the disease, this accessibility has also led to the emergence of a community, referred to as the *pro-ana community*, that promotes and supports the negative behaviours associated with anorexia nervosa. The websites that promote anorexia nervosa often

Continued

contain content (images and stories) that is disturbing to view. Therefore, no links to these websites are included in this book, but a search on the key word "pro-ana" will yield several relevant hits. Pro-ana websites, similar to celebrity gossip sites like TMZ.com, bring the female body back into the Internet by not only focusing their websites directly on the body but also by including images of individual users and of models, movie stars, and women in the media who are thin. Not surprisingly, concerns have been raised by the media, therapists, and scholars about the potential social effect of pro-ana websites on young people. Do they provide a means of social support for people who are struggling with eating disorders? Or do they further promote ideal bodies and put further pressure on women to fulfill an ideal that our society, and in particular the mass media, promotes?

Several studies have emerged in recent years with the aim of understanding this community better. A study by Norris et al. (2006) found that pro-ana websites tended to include similar elements. A key part is the inclusion of "A Letter from Ana," which is a personal letter directed at community members. The text tends to read as follows: "I expect a lot from you. You are not allowed to eat much. I will expect you to drop your caloric intake and increase your exercise." These websites also included "thinspiration" content, which consists of pictures, messages, and stories to promote the pro-ana ideals. Many websites also feature tips and tricks that help weight loss, as well as links to resources such as support groups, medical information, and other pro-ana communities.

In terms of the "neutrality of technology" debate, it is essential to consider these types of ethical questions. Censoring these types of sites is not an ideal solution vis-à-vis freedom of expression and freedom of information, of course. The reason why this topic is important and needs further attention is that "the issue of body image has been named as a central issue in third wave feminism because all women, feminist or not, 'offer heartfelt and complex emotions on the topic' (Richards 198)" (Dias, 2003, p. 32). Without supporting the ideas of pro-ana, Dias (2003) recognizes that bringing women's agency into the debate about eating disorders is central, instead of silencing women's voices and their struggles.

The pro-ana community is an example of how the body is brought back into the virtual realm. A study by Boero and Pascoe (2012) shows that boundary work in pro-ana communities is also embodiment work. Boundary work refers to the establishment of boundaries around who is a member of the pro-ana community and who is an outsider. Embodiment work describes the work done to bring discussions around the body to the forefront through the display of images, text referring to the body, and discussions around ideal body shapes. That is, the creation of rituals and the use of tools that reinforce community boundaries also help make the realness of the body a central aspect of the community. The rituals that signal who is a member of the community and who is an outsider include photo sharing, updates, and posts. The kinds of tools used to demarcate community boundaries include the use of aggression and knowledge as a means to question others' claims to belonging to the community. If a person does not have the knowledge around what it means to live with pro-anorexia then they are excluded from the community. Yeshua-Katz and Martin (2012) argue that the body serves as a means to demonstrate membership in the online community and that members seek social support from others online. Often these women get little support in their physical, everyday communities because of the stigma surrounding individuals living with anorexia nervosa, and may withhold information that they feel will not meet society's standards.

This links to what Goffman (1963) has described as the type of support that stigmatized individuals look for. This often includes "information control techniques" that encourage them to open up to a community that understands their struggles (Goffman, 1963; Yeshua-Katz & Martins, 2013). Goffman has described how stigmatized individuals will seek support from people like themselves to evade further marginalization; it is their own community of like-minded individuals that can provide social support, a sense of belonging, and understanding.

Conclusions

This chapter argues that even though gender and sexuality are deeply private and personal spheres, they closely intersect with the social world around us. This necessitates the development of innovative research methods and comprehensive theoretical frameworks that allow us to investigate how technology is gendered and how gender and sexualities interplay with technological design, development, and implementation. There is much need for further research to examine a wide range of core societal issues. The chapter also stressed that technological determinism is a framework that often simplifies complex societal processes. An example of this reductionism was discussed in the section on household technologies, which were promoted as being labour and time saving. We learned that technological change occurred simultaneously with other changes in society, including the advancement of germ theory and the domestic science movement. As a result, the promises of time saving were replaced by increases in the expectations placed on women regarding cleanliness and tidiness in the home. Hence, technologies did not have a direct impact on household work: their effect was moderated by other factors. We showed that women are often key users of a wide range of technologies and often adopt these technologies early. There is, however, a lack of women working in the IT sector and in particular in leadership positions. We examined current initiatives to bring women into IT-related work and discussed their merits and challenges. Finally, the chapter ended with a section on the body online. Much of the research tends to erase the body from discussions of the virtual. We argued that recent approaches try to bring the body back into research on virtual communities. An example of this was the body of work around the pro-ana community and their use of text, image, and video to talk about and problematize the female body.

Questions for Critical Thought

1. Why has the discussion of gender and technology only started in the late twentieth century?

2. Why has there been more progress toward gender equality in other spheres of work than in IT and its related fields?

3. What factors are responsible for the underrepresentation of women in IT work? What barriers exist for women in these fields?

4. What factors have contributed to the closing of the gap between men and women in the adoption and use of the Internet?

5. How do different sexualities represent their bodies on digital platforms? What do these differences in expression tell us about the link between body and gender?

6. What interventions do you see as most effective for helping women become more integrated into IT-related fields? Do you support gender-segregated approaches toward learning IT-related skills, such as writing computer code? Explain your position.

Suggested Readings

Carter, C., Steiner, L., & McLaughlin, L. (Eds). (2013). *The Routledge companion to media and gender.* New York: Routledge. This comprehensive volume includes contributions from scholars around the world on the topic of media and gender, including issues of production and policy-making, representation, audience engagement, and the place of gender in media studies.

Vanhemert, K. (2014). Why *Her* will dominate UI design even more than *Minority Report. Wired Magazine.* Retrieved 26 August 2014 from www.wired.com/2014/01/will-influential-ui-design-minority-report/. This *Wired Magazine* article discusses how the movie *Her* will influence user-interface design.

Frizzo-Barker, J., & Chow-White, P. A. (2012). "There's an app for that": Mediating mobile moms and connected careerists through smartphones and networked individualism. *Feminist Media Studies, 12*(4), 580–589. doi: 10.1080/14680777.2012.741876. This article discusses how the theory of networked individualism can be applied in the study of how moms and careerists use smartphones in their daily lives.

Wajcman, J. (2007). From women and technology to gendered technoscience. *Information, Communication & Society, 10*(3), 287–298. doi: 10.1080/13691180701409770. This work presents a classic exploration and critical analysis of the tensions between technology and gender.

Whitehouse, G. (2006). Women, careers and information technology: An introduction. *Labour & Industry, 16*(3), 1–6. This is a comprehensive overview of and introduction to the topic of women and IT-related work.

Online Resources

Anita Borg Institute
http://anitaborg.org/

> Founded by Dr. Anita Borg in 1997, this institute brings together women with an interest in technology. It promotes the representation of women in the IT sector and the development of technology by women. It hosts a mailing list to support women in the technology field, referred to as Systers (http://anitaborg.org/get-involved/systers/).

These Are the 11 Wealthiest Women in Tech
www.businessinsider.sg/11-wealthiest-women-in-tech-2014-7/#.U-PXIuM7t8H

> This article in *Business Insider* showcases the 11 wealthiest women in the high-tech industry, including Sheryl Sandberg, COO of Facebook. Sandberg has also written a book based on her experiences in the industry, and has signed a movie deal with Sony Pictures.

Doing IT around the World Albums
www.passionit.info/albums.php

> This website portrays the daily lives of women around the world who take part in the technology industry. The areas of technology that they engage in are varied and include software development, hardware, consulting, and knowledge management.

Girl Develop It
http://girldevelopit.com

> This website and community promotes coding, design, and development for girls and women. It is a network of city chapters in different locations in the United States and provides workshops, classes, and conferences. It also has an active Twitter account, @girldevelopit (14,000 followers in 2014), and uses the hashtag #womenintech. The website includes a list of resources to help beginners learn how to write code, including online courses on coding.

Feministe Blog
www.feministe.us/blog/

> This is one of the oldest blogs on women, women's issues, and women and technology, designed by and run by women to discuss relevant topics in the media, academia, and society at large.

5 Techno-Social Designing

Learning Objectives

◎ to look at how technology is designed and developed prior to users adopting it;

◎ to trace the emergence of technopoles and uncover their social significance in the context of modern cities and economies;

◎ to discuss the concept of the creative class and show how it is leading toward economic prosperity in post-industrial cities;

◎ to investigate the concept of research and development (R&D) and the pressures existent in the sector;

◎ to examine the inner workings and outer pressures of software development teams, in particular in the gaming industry.

Introduction

Users of technology are, for the most part, oblivious of the stages that precede the adoption and use of a technology. For instance, it took many iterations, failures, and setbacks before the cellphone gained widespread acceptance and use. Most users do not consider the creative processes that underlie technological invention and innovation because these processes do not directly affect their day-to-day use of tools. The aim of this chapter, then, is to uncover these often hidden creative processes and to examine the visions of developers, the challenges experienced in research and development (R&D), and the complex interweaving of technological development and societal factors.

In addition to examining R&D, in this chapter we introduce the term *technopole* to describe specialized cities dedicated solely to technological innovation. Silicon Valley is presented as an instance of a technopole that combines a highly educated workforce with military and economic interests. We discuss the political, social, and economic repercussions of technopoles, as well as their vulnerability in the context of fragile global markets.

The chapter continues by explaining the concept of R&D, the pressures existent in R&D teams, and the ways that innovation occurs in these teams. We then directly link R&D to economic development and review Schumpeter's classic economic model, which argues that the structure of society is directly linked to creative processes and innovations. Next, we present data that compare expenditures on R&D across nations and examine how these are linked to global economic development. The final part of the chapter examines in more detail the inner workings and the outer pressures of software development, which is one type of R&D that has come to occupy a central role in the world economy. We focus on the gaming industry in Canada—specifically in Vancouver, Toronto, and Ottawa—as an example of the kind of labour that is involved in the development and production of video games. As part of the discussion on software development, we examine how technological design can encompass social features. Social features include aspects of the design that facilitate social interaction, such as allowing users to share a news story with a friend or group of friends. For this purpose, we explain the terms *object affordance* and *social affordance* in order to better understand the complex interplay of technological design and social processes.

Technological Design and How It Intersects with Society

The study of technology tends to focus on technologies that are widely used in society without giving much consideration to the **creative processes** that take place in the design and implementation phases of those technologies. However, technological design occurs long before a technology is revealed to users. Extensive testing, developing, and prototyping take place during the design phase of a new product, which can extend over a long period of time. For example, developments of the cellphone were described as early as 1945, when J.K. Jett, the head of the U.S. **Federal Communications Commission (FCC)**, announced that AT&T had for the first time used a type of low-powered transmitter that employed high-band radio frequencies that could allow millions of users to communicate (Farley, 2005). The first cellphone was introduced in 1973 with the release of a handset that weighed approximately 2 kg (Texeira, 2012). Despite these advances, however, cellphones did not become widely used in the United States until the 1990s and did not really take off until around 2002. In 2014, cellphone penetration rates were above 100 per cent in some Asian countries; Hong Kong, for example, had 237 phones per 100 inhabitants, suggesting that each individual owns multiple devices.

What are the reasons for the general public's lack of knowledge about the field of technology design? Why do scholars not have a better understanding of how design unfolds if it often spans such a lengthy period of time? Several important factors are responsible for the lack of knowledge about this phase. We discuss three of the more central factors next.

1. *Lack of reflective processes*: Because developers of technology are primarily concerned with the day-to-day tasks at hand and are also usually pressed for time, they do not tend to reflect on how the design process unfolds and what factors are having an impact on it. When, for example, Pasteur and his team developed the pasteurization process in the nineteenth century, they were not concerned with *how* they made the discovery; indeed, they had more pressing concerns, such as developing a more effective technique for food preservation that ultimately could help prevent illness and save lives (Latour, 1988).

2. **Retro-analysis**: Most accounts and analyses of how a given technology was designed often become relevant, or have social significance, only after the fact. For instance, Bruno Latour (1988) examined the complexities of how the process of pasteurization was developed almost 200 years after Pasteur and his team discovered the technique. The majority of insights are gained through archives, memories of people involved, and any other paper trail available.

3. **Black box of design**: Many innovations occur behind closed doors as a result of competitive pressures, and hence it is difficult, or impossible, for researchers to obtain access to these developments as they unfold. This is particularly the case with research linked to the military, which often falls under the rubric "top secret." But this secrecy applies equally to innovations occurring in other industries: fears of spies are not merely a myth in R&D but often a reality. Former Google employee Paul Adams (2011) experienced the consequences of secrecy in the software development industry when he left Google to start working for Facebook and was denied authorization to publish his book *Social Circles*. For Google, this work represented a major infringement of its intellectual property, as Google+ had not been released at the time. The company feared that information contained in Adams's book would constitute a leak to the public prior to the much-anticipated release of Google+.

The three factors outlined above are linked directly to our limited understanding of how design unfolds. There is a need to develop new strategies to better examine how social factors affect technology design, production, and use. Sociologists can make an important contribution by helping us understand how individuals make sense of technology and how social factors affect design and production. Inequalities in wealth distribution, poor labour conditions, and social unrest constitute central pieces of this sociological analysis. We next examine how systems theory helps us to understand the social factors at play in technological design. Then we look at technopoles as the key centres of innovation, where products are designed and produced.

Systems Theory

In this section, we discuss the key premises of **systems theory**, a highly influential approach to the study of how technological and societal factors impact design. Systems theory examines how physical artifacts, social institutions, and social context all interact in complex ways to influence design and cause social change (Hughes, 1983). In his influential book *Networks of Power: Electrification in Western Society, 1880–1930*, Thomas P. Hughes defines *systems theory* as the study of self-regulating social and natural systems that can influence their own behaviour through feedback loops. Bánáthy (1997) defines a **system** as "a configuration of parts connected and joined together by a web of relationships" (p. 22). Hughes developed systems theory with the aim of understanding the design and development process of technologies in the context of societal forces. For him, societal forces play a key role in the design and development process because technological changes are closely linked to the goals and interests of individuals, groups, and organizations. The case study Hughes employed to illustrate the use of systems theories for the purpose of studying technology was the development of the electric power grid. His primary goal in presenting this case study was to

> explain the change in configuration of electric power systems during the half-century between 1880 and 1930. Such change can be displayed in network diagrams, but the effort to explain the change involves consideration of many fields of human activity, including the technical, the scientific, the economic, the political, and the organizational. This is because power systems are cultural artifacts. (Hughes, 1983, p. 2)

The systems approach allows researchers to simultaneously examine micro- and macro-level phenomena; for instance, design decisions made in Facebook's headquarters can be directly linked to trends unfolding in the wider society, such as the introduction of Twitter, which has posed serious competition (Kirkpatrick, 2010). Hughes (1983) suggested that three stages characterize the design and development of a technology:

1. *Technology development*: In this phase, the technology is being invented and developed. The technology slowly takes shape, with inventors and entrepreneurs working on creating a prototype or demonstrating its utility. Often other players, such as managers and financiers, may also be indirectly involved in this phase.
2. *Technology transfer*: During the technology transfer stage, innovations are transmitted from one geographic area or social group to others. In this phase, agents of change play a central role in aiding in the transfer of technological know-how from inventors to the larger public or

specific target groups (see Chapter 6 for a more in-depth discussion of this issue). Agents of change can include inventors, investors, managers, etc.—generally, individuals with a vested interest in the spread of the innovation.

3. *System growth*: Examining the growth of a system is a methodologically challenging task. A good example of this process is the development of the personal computer (PC). The PC has experienced differential growth in its various components, including random-access memory (RAM), processor (CPU), screen quality, and storage capacity (hard disk). Differential growth occurs when one component develops rapidly, leaving many other areas of development behind. For example, in the computer industry software developed rapidly, often forcing PC hardware components to keep up with the requirements in speed and capacity (Dedehayir & Mäkinen, 2008). As a result, users had to update their computer every few years so that current software programs could be run efficiently. Central to the examination of system growth is an understanding of **reverse salients** or **salience**, which is an imbalance in the growth of a system's sub-components. The concept has been widely adopted in the social and computer sciences because "the socio-technical characteristic of the concept affords flexibility" (Dedehayir, 2009, p. 586).

Hence, a key task of developers is to work around irregularities and attempt to have the system fully functional as a coherent whole. In order to be able to tackle these reverse salients, developers must first identify them as **critical problems**. Only then can potential solutions be proposed. A critical problem refers to a challenge that requires a complex solution, often bringing to bear both technological innovation and institutional or social change. An example of a reverse salient that was redefined as a critical problem is the idea of a stand-alone PC. While early developments in computing were aimed at developing powerful processors, it quickly became apparent that the PC's value lay not in its capacity as a stand-alone device but, rather, in its ability to network. This revelation required a complete rethinking of the challenges confronting developers.

In the view of science and technology studies (STS) and systems theory, design is a central topic of inquiry that needs to address political, economic, social, and cultural factors. Without an understanding of how these factors play a role in the design of technology, technological progress is reduced to a purely technical process, ignoring the fact that technology is a central component in our technological society. Next we discuss the concept of *technopole* and its close interplay with the global economy.

Technopoles: Centres of Innovation

The term **information society** has been widely used to describe a shift in the economy from a structure where production was at the centre of economic development to one where knowledge is considered a central asset (Fuchs, 2010). Several terms have been employed to describe this shift, including *post-industrial society*, *post-Fordism*, *knowledge society*, *the information revolution*, and *network society* (Bell, 1973; Castells, 1996). In this new economic model, information and knowledge become key commodities, with capital and production still being relevant but as secondary industries affiliated with the information society.

As a result of this shift, the centres of power have also shifted. Many terms have been used to describe the physical places dedicated to innovation, including *high-tech sectors*, *biotechnology*, and *tech hubs*. Castells and Hall (1994) use the term **technopole** as an umbrella concept and define technopoles as "planned developments" whose function it is "to generate the basic materials of the informational economy" (p. 1). Technopoles have been created in many parts of the world and show a certain kind of homogeneity: they are complex socio-technical systems constituting a geographical area that is made up of buildings, people, institutions, and corporations.

Castells and Hall (1994) view contemporary technopoles as arising from three interrelated processes:

1. **Information revolution**: A technological revolution built around information technologies, creating a need for the design of new digital tools, platforms, and content. As a result, a wide range of products and services are needed to sustain the information society that results. Examples include online book retailers (e.g., Amazon), online travel brokers (e.g., Expedia), and photo-sharing sites like Flickr.
2. **Globalization**: The formation of a global economy that transcends national boundaries, governments, and laws. Such a system is highly interconnected, or **interdependent**, with each single component affecting other components located in different geographic regions. A good example of this is the impact of the U.S. subprime mortgage crisis in 2007 on all aspects of the global economy, including the technology sector. On pages 90–91, we discuss Ireland as an example of a country that particularly suffered from the 2007–08 economic downturn (Kirby, 2010).
3. **Informational production**: The development of new forms of economic production centred on information. *Informational* describes an economy where "productivity and competitiveness are increasingly based on the generation of new knowledge and on the access to, and processing of,

appropriate information" (Castells & Hall, 1994, p. 3). This is a trend away from the agrarian and industrial models, where the sum of capital, labour, and raw materials created economic growth. In the new model, the outputs from science, technology, and information-related industries are the basis for economic expansion. (Rao & Scaruffi, 2010)

These three processes lead toward the creation of technopoles as centres of innovation, where new technologies are developed and tested. In these highly competitive environments, technological innovation develops from "learning by doing" instead of being based on off-the-shelf solutions (Castells & Hall, 1994). Those companies and institutions that compose the technopole have to be flexible and willing to constantly experiment with new ideas in order to remain competitive in a global market. These centres of innovation must, then, integrate seamlessly with service facilities in emerging economies, as well as with production centres often located in developing economies, "creating a synergistic interaction between design, production and utilization" (p. 5). For example, the design, testing, and prototyping of products may occur in North America, but the production process often takes place in Asia, necessitating high degrees of co-operation and coordination among different firms. In Box 5.1, we examine Silicon Valley as a model of a technopole that unites highly skilled workers, a geographic area, social networks, and public institutions with corporations that provide large sums of capital investment.

Before its contemporary inception, Silicon Valley had a historical research-oriented focus based on developments in electrical engineering at Stanford University (Rao & Scaruffi, 2010). As Castells and Hall (1994) explain, Frederick Terman, a professor of radio engineering at Stanford who later became dean of electrical engineering, was key to initiating and fomenting R&D initiatives in Silicon Valley. Terman used his influence to nurture gifted students, such as William Hewlett and David Packard, and provided them with funds to begin their own **startup companies**. Startups are newly created companies with a strong emphasis on R&D. They often rely on **venture capital firms** and **angel investors** to help them establish their operations. Angel investors are individuals who provide capital investment for initiating technology businesses and in exchange become shareholders of the company or receive some form of repayment over time. Hewlett and Packard formed HP and became one of the most well-known electronics companies in the world.

Terman also had a vision for how Stanford could encourage entrepreneurship. He separated R&D from industry by creating the **Stanford Industrial Park**, which was built on university land but worked as a loosely connected entity. Terman invited talented individuals from the burgeoning electronics industry to Stanford Industrial Park with the idea of creating a

Box 5.1

Silicon Valley: Centre of Innovation

Silicon Valley is the first and perhaps most innovative technopole in the world. The area consists of a 40-mile by 10-mile (70-kilometre by 15-kilometre) radius in the San Francisco Bay Area, reaching from Palo Alto to San Jose (Castells & Hall, 1994; Henton et al., 2011; Rao & Scaruffi, 2010).

While little technological innovation was present in the Bay Area in the 1950s, a rapid expansion occurred in the 1970s and continues to this day (Rao & Scaruffi, 2010). Table 5.1 shows a breakdown of employment in the Bay Area between 1959 and 1985. The increase in jobs in such sectors as computing—from 0 in 1959 to 56,126 in 1985—is unprecedented. We can observe similar trends in the expansion of fields such as semiconductors, with an increase from 0 jobs in 1959 to 47,069 in 1985. A recent report on Silicon Valley shows that jobs continue to be plentiful, with companies trying to recruit engineers, designers, and computer scientists (Henton et al., 2011). The same report points toward another period of rapid expansion, documenting an increase from 2009 to 2010 of 12,300 jobs in the areas of computer systems design, employment services, and computer and electronic product manufacturing (Henton et al., 2011). Companies such as Apple, Google, and Facebook continue to hire, with Google alone adding 1,900 jobs in its 2011 fiscal first quarter (Swartz, 2011).

Table 5.1 Employment Structure in Silicon Valley, 1959–1985

Employment	SIC	1959	1965	1970	1975	1980	1985
Computers	3,573	0	0	8,938	19,902	52,738	56,126
Other office machines	375*	0	0	979	1,869	2,582	2,748
Communications	366	895	5,027	7,271	10,043	19,603	29,677
Semiconductors	3,674	0	4,164	12,290	18,786	34,453	47,069
Other electronic components	367*	4,295	4,619	14,174	11,622	25,472	23,731
Missiles/parts	372	0	0	2,274	0	0	750
Instruments	38	328	1,202	2,567	14,646	24,912	19,382
Drugs	283	0	282	0	750	1,976	1,954
Software/data processing	737	0	0	0	3,887	7,813	15,368
IC labs	7,391	118	2,193	1,978	1,642	3,856	6,133
Electronic wholesale	5,065	131	693	1,107	2,092	3,703	9,179
Computer wholesale	5,086	199	243	373	620	2,005	2,807
Total high-tech employment		5,966	18,423	51,951	85,859	179,113	214,924
Total manufacturing employment		61,305	88,038	131,613	154,126	256,437	272,332

Note: *SIC Codes 357 exclusive of 3573 and 3674, respectively.

Source: U.S. Bureau of the Census—County Business Patterns.

Tall, cylindrical buildings are home to the Oracle Corporation headquarters in Silicon Valley, California.

community that fused technical research and scholarship. This is a good example of the optimization of the use of basic research to solve applied problems, as discussed in Chapter 2.

Companies in Silicon Valley also benefited from the desire for cutting-edge electronic equipment and devices by the U.S. military and its related aerospace industries. By the 1970s, Silicon Valley companies had a strong industrial basis, as well as financial and research support, from military and commercial financial backers and nearby universities (Castells & Hall, 1994). This mix of diverse and influential players led to large growth in the technology industry.

Global Technopoles

Technopoles have emerged around the globe as governments become more and more eager to capitalize on the growing technology industry. However, technopoles also bring risks to local industries (Kirby, 2002). Ireland is a prime example of an economy that showed rapid growth between 1995 and 2007, with many high-tech companies moving into the region. As a result, real estate developed quickly, jobs expanded—particularly in the high-tech industry—and the country experienced an economic boom that was nick-named the **Celtic Tiger**. Figure 5.1 shows the ratio of exports based on foreign-owned companies versus indigenous companies from 1995 to 2005. This imbalance between foreign- and indigenous-owned companies, and its heavy reliance on foreign investment, is what has made Ireland's economy vulnerable to global changes.

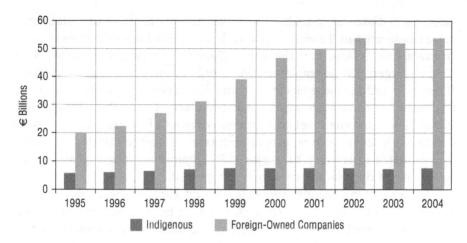

Figure 5.1 Irish Exports
Source: Forfás, Globalisation and the Knowledge Economy – the Case of Ireland, www.oecd.org/dataoecd/59/5/37563948.pdf.

In 2008, the country suddenly experienced a recession and in 2009 thousands went to the streets to protest as the situation continued to worsen (Kirby, 2010). This downturn illustrates how technopoles are vulnerable to global trends and can dissipate quickly, leaving the local community with debt, unemployment, and poor living conditions.

Technopoles and Exploitation

Technopoles influence their surroundings in varied ways; their influence on Western nations is fundamentally different than the effect they typically have on developing countries. In Western nations, technopoles tend to create vibrant and prosperous regions that bring together innovators, investors, and diverse talent; whereas developing nations become the supplier of services and goods. One example of how developing nations work hand in hand with technopoles located in Western nations is the establishment of **supplier factories**, which are mega-factories located in countries such as Mainland China, India, and, more recently, Indonesia. Supplier factories are dedicated solely to the mass production of goods for the technology industry. Many technology giants have supplier factories located along the East Coast of China, for example, in the provinces of Guangdong, Fujian, and Zhejiang. Conditions in these facilities are notoriously exploitive.

What does **exploitation** in these companies entail? A report by China Labor Watch (2011) suggests that workers are often forced to work over-time; that fire and safety risks do not meet standards as outlined in China's labour law and brand companies' social responsibility codes of conduct; and that workers receive poor compensation and are often exposed to toxic chemicals. One company that has received considerable negative media attention is Foxconn, a multinational electronics contract manufacturing company located in Taiwan. Foxconn is considered the largest electronics contractor manufacturer in the world (*Circuit Assembly*, 2009) and is among China's largest private employers. Most of Foxconn's clients are American, European, and Japanese electronics and information technology companies, manufacturing such well-known products as the iPad, Kindle, and Playstation 5. International attention was drawn to Foxconn's poor working conditions in 2011, with reports of high rates of worker suicides; the situation escalated in January 2012 when 150 employees threatened to commit suicide if working conditions were not improved.

Marx's (1996) original thinking around exploitation came from his analysis of industrial-based factories, in which he observed that the proletariat worked hard under dire conditions but obtained only a fraction of the gains made from the sale of products. The capitalists—those who own the economic means to invest in production—ultimately keep most of the earnings for themselves, refusing to share with those who produced the goods.

For Marx, a salient aspect of exploitation was alienation, a concept we will discuss in more depth in Chapter 7. Alienation results from engagement in repetitive and automated tasks that do not reflect a person's skills. Workers at supplier factories are required to repeat the same task all day long, without much variation. Further, workers may be embedded in gigantic halls or areas with hundreds of other workers but may have little to no contact with them. This leads to further feelings of alienation, depression, and loneliness.

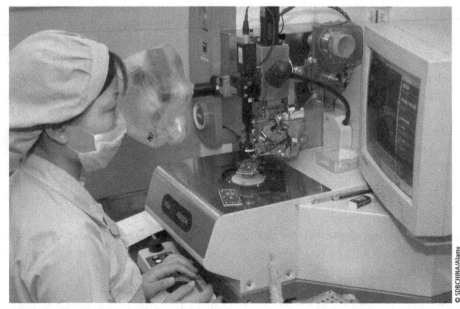

© SDBCHINA/Alamy

Chinese manufacturing in the high-tech industry.

Watchdogs and Social Responsibility

The poor working conditions in technopoles around the world have drawn considerable attention from the media. An article in *The Guardian* entitled "The woman who nearly died making your iPad" reported on how Foxconn employs "young, poor migrants from the Chinese countryside, cramming them into vast workhouses and crowded dorms, then spitting out the ones who struggle to keep up." Closing the factories is not a viable option to resolve the problem because so many workers would lose their jobs. Fuelled by this and other media reports, various independent institutions have sprung up with the aim of monitoring the working conditions in these types of factories and helping to develop solutions. One such institution is China Labor Watch (CLW), a non-government organization (NGO) based in New York City. Labour activist Li Qiang founded CLW in October 2000 to investigate and monitor workers' rights in China through the release of reports, legal action, and support of workers. The company has an excellent record of bringing cases to court and pointing the way toward needed changes in policy and regulation.

Based on Marx's work on exploitation, scholars and social activists have proposed alternative models that can help improve working conditions in these factories regardless of where they are located, whilst allowing for global capital to continue flowing into low-waged developing countries (Yu, 2008). One such model is based on notions of social responsibility: corporate social responsibility, or CSR. This entails the adoption of corporate codes of conduct to help regulate labour practices and encourage supplier factories to commit to higher standards of corporate conduct (Yu, 2008). While these corporate codes of conduct vary considerably, they tend to stress the elimination of child labour and forced labour, the benefits of collective bargaining, and stipulations against discrimination (Tsogus, 2001) Yu has identified a series of positive outcomes in the literature (2008):

- enhanced brand value and reputation;
- connections to customers and their expectations;
- positive employee morale;
- increased productivity; and
- better crisis management.

Evidence suggests that these corporate codes of conduct help companies address problems of poor labour conditions; but they only tackle the tip of the iceberg. That is, they help address some problems, but do not create real social change in terms of improving low wages or long working hours, or extending workers' rights to association (e.g., meeting to discuss labour concerns) (Yu, 2001). Further understanding is needed of how socially responsible capitalism can operate and help improve working conditions in supplier factories located in technopoles around the globe.

Despite the risks associated with the development of technopoles, governments in both developed and developing countries continue to invest heavily in the high-tech sector and to attract competitive companies through tax incentives, infrastructure, etc., in the hope of being part of the economic prosperity brought about by the informational economy. In Chapter 9 we discuss the so-called "Internet dictator's dilemma" that some nations face: on the one hand, they would like to profit from this new economy, but at the same time they want to continue controlling the information diffused to their citizens. The move toward digital societies is not just about economics, then; such a move also has social, political, and cultural consequences. This is evident in the examples of Egypt, Libya, and Tunisia, which we will discuss further in Chapter 9.

The Role of Research and Development (R&D)

In the previous section we discussed the relevance of technopoles to the economy. We focus now on the role of **research and development (R&D)** within industries, companies, and nations. No company can survive in a competitive market without R&D. Even companies that invest extensively in R&D can collapse if they do not focus on the right kind of technology. Both Kodak and Polaroid, for example, saw their business models collapse and their profits vanish as a result of inefficient R&D and the companies' slow uptake of digital photography. R&D is defined as "creative work undertaken on a systematic basis in order to increase the stock of knowledge, including knowledge of man, culture and society, and the use of this stock of knowledge to devise new applications" (OECD, 2009). The **Organisation for Economic Co-operation and Development (OECD)** includes three areas in its conceptualization of R&D and defines them as follows:

1. **Basic research**: Consists of experimental or theoretical investigation that is aimed at acquiring new understandings of the underlying foundations of phenomena and observable facts. Basic research differs from applied or experimental research in that it is not intended to lead to any particular application or use in the field.
2. **Applied research**: Also constitutes original research conducted with the aim of acquiring new knowledge. In contrast to basic research, it is intended primarily to address or solve practical problems.
3. **Experimental development**: Systematic research based on existing knowledge that aims to develop new materials or products; to propose new processes, systems and services; or to modify processes already in place.

Even though all three areas contribute to the economy and are thought to provide direct economic returns, companies tend to invest primarily in applied research and experimental development, while universities and governments tend to support basic research. These differences in focus are a direct result of the expected economic returns of the three areas of R&D. Historically, there have been many different attempts to model the link between R&D and economic development. However, most of these theories were basic, did not provide much insight into the mechanisms that linked R&D to the economy, and neglected to consider the following important questions: How does R&D yield gains? What mechanisms are in place to increase the economic returns coming from R&D?

Many scholars see Joseph Schumpeter (1883–1950), an economist and political scientist at Harvard University, as "providing the most comprehensive and provocative analysis since Marx of the economic development and social transformation of industrializing capitalism" (Elliott, 2004, p. vii).

Economic Development and the Creative Process

In his analysis of economic development, Schumpeter identified the **creative process**—defined as the development of the economy through the production process—as a central activity of economic prosperity. He then divides the creative process into three distinguishable stages: (1) invention, (2) innovation, and (3) imitation.

1. Invention

The stage of invention, which Schumpeter referred to as the **process of circular flow**, is characterized by general equilibrium because there is little change in the interrelation of economic factors. During this stage, the supply of goods is perfectly tailored to meet consumer demands, and as a result no tensions or social problems arise in the social system. This stage has no innovators, leaders, or heroes because actors are only passive observers of a well-functioning economic system.

2. Innovation

For Schumpeter, radical transformations occur during the innovation stage, bringing about a fundamentally different social system. Schumpeter further proposed four kinds of changes that occur during the innovation stage: (a) increases in salaries, (b) population growth, (c) changes in consumer tastes and choices, and (d) changes in how production occurs. While growth is an important aspect of the innovation stage, what is decisive is that change occurs not only quantitatively but also qualitatively. Schumpeter argued that even if you add "successively as many mail coaches as you please you will never get a railway thereby" (Schumpeter, 2004, p. 64, Footnote 1). Similarly, many high-tech companies have been created in the past two decades, but few of them have the profit margins, user base, and influence of Google. This led Jeff Jarvis, from City University of New York, to propose in his book

What Would Google Do? that Google simply had developed a radically different approach to packaging and offering information services to users. All the other newly created companies may be quantitatively different, but they are not fundamentally different and are lacking this element of innovativeness.

This proposal led Schumpeter to identify innovation as the single most important driver of economic prosperity, which he understood to be the "commercial or industrial application of something new—a new product, process, or method of production; a new market or source of supply; a new form of commercial, business, or financial organization" (Elliott, 2004, p. xix). The consequence of innovation is a radical transformation in the economic structure of society, which in turn disrupts social structures. Schumpeter introduced the term **creative destruction** to summarize the social, economic, and cultural consequences that innovation brings about.

Innovation, while desirable, is not easy to accomplish. Schumpeter (2004) identified three key factors that impact innovation. First, innovation is based on new ideas and processes, making it difficult to accurately predict the expected outcome and potential future revenue (Jarvis, 2009). In general, there is little information and knowledge about how processes will unfold, leading to great uncertainty. Second, because there is such a great deal of uncertainty, it is difficult for investors to predict the **return on investment (ROI)**, and hence there is apprehension about supporting the innovation (Miller, 2011). (Return on investment is the net return when the cost of investment and the gain from investment are taken into account.) Third, there is a general reluctance to accept change in society, making it difficult for innovators to convince others of the usefulness of their ideas. Even Alexander Graham Bell found it difficult at first to convince others of the usefulness of the telephone (Fischer, 1992).

These three obstacles to innovation become apparent when the **innovator-entrepreneur** is compared to the capitalist. The capitalist relies on detailed economic analyses, which show in predictable ways the revenues that will result from investment. By contrast, innovators are more heroic figures because of their willingness to take risks and their tendency to experiment with new forms of thought and action. As Elliot (2004) argues, at the centre of Schumpeter's social and economic analysis lies the figure of the innovator-entrepreneur, who through his vision drives technological change, which then will impact all aspects of society. The distinction between innovator-entrepreneur and capitalist became much more nuanced in 2011, with Google, for instance, investing approximately US$200 million in the acquisition of new startups (Miller, 2011).

3. Imitation

Schumpeter (2004) analyzed economic development and established that it does not evolve evenly but, instead, in **cyclical fluctuations**. By this, he meant that innovations occur suddenly, often in clusters. Why does economic development follow this kind of cyclical fluctuation? First, Schumpeter put forward the argument that these fluctuations are not indicators of a failure; quite the contrary, they are the normal way in which capitalist systems evolve and even prosper. Second, Schumpeter attributes the cyclical nature of the economy to the process of **imitation**. Once an innovation is diffused into society, other producers will learn about it and want to reproduce it in order to profit from its widespread popularity. This process of imitation—both in the original industry and in secondary industries—results in economic growth. For example, an innovation in the car industry will lead other car manufacturers to follow and develop similar models. At the same time, other industries will develop or improve products to support those in the automotive sector, such as better glass, roads, safety equipment, etc. Once the innovation is widespread and ceases to be new, capital investment diminishes as no additional ROI is expected. Further, "as an avalanche of consumer goods pours onto the market [there are] dampening effects on prices; rising costs and interest rates squeeze profit margins: and the economy contracts: recession" (Elliott, 2004, p. xxvii). From this standpoint, recessions are a predictable and normal part of the cycle of economic development and to be expected as innovations reach their peak.

In summary, Schumpeter's economic and social analysis suggests that innovation is at the centre of economic development and closely linked to the structure of society. From this point of view, R&D is a centrepiece of economic development, and new technologies are forces of social, political, and economic change. In the next section, we examine how nations invest in R&D as a means to spur economic prosperity.

Global R&D

Why should nations care about R&D? And why should governments invest taxpayer money in R&D if that money could be invested in social programs, education, or health care? The expenditures linked to R&D accrued by companies, institutions, and nations are an indicator of their commitment to science, technology, and innovation. Based on Schumpeter's (2004) analysis, innovation can be directly linked to economic output. The higher the investment in terms of capital, people, and infrastructure that a nation makes in R&D, the greater the economic return. The **gross domestic expenditure on R&D (GERD)** is most frequently used for the purpose of comparing the investment in innovation that occurs across nations. The GERD index takes into consideration the total expenditure (current and capital) on R&D accrued by a nation over a one-year period, including expenses by companies, research institutes, universities, and government laboratories (OECD, 2009, Science and Technology Section).

Figure 5.2 shows the top countries' expenditures in R&D as a percentage of gross domestic product[1] (GDP) for 1998 and 2007, with Sweden being the country that spends the highest amount worldwide. Currently, only data up to 2007 are available on the OECD website; however, because the OECD

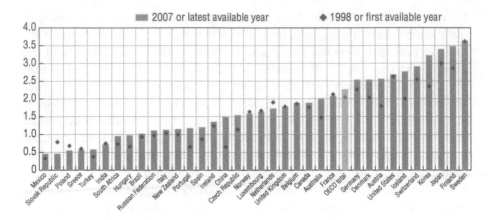

Figure 5.2 Gross Domestic Expenditure on R&D (as a Percentage of GDP)
Source: OECD (2009), "Expenditure on R&D", in OECD Factbook 2009: Economic, Environmental and Social Statistics, OECD
Publishing. http://dx.doi.org/10.1787/factbook-2009-54-en

attempts to keep its statistics updated, more recent data should be available soon (see www.oecd.org).

Important indicators of a nation's potential to innovate, in addition to the GERD, are the number of patents issued, peer-reviewed publications, and new products developed. While most nations are committed to providing support for R&D, the expenses linked to innovation need to be carefully weighed, for example against expenditures in the areas of health care, the military, and basic infrastructure. Because various groups in society have different interests, finding the right balance between economic and social interests is a challenge for most governments.

In addition to monetary investment in R&D, other initiatives have been developed to expedite and improve innovative processes. One recent global trend to encourage innovation has been to decentralize and spread R&D teams around the globe. Many large companies have adopted this approach, including Microsoft. Microsoft Research, the company's research arm, is devoted to carrying out both basic and applied research in the areas of computer science and software engineering. Instead of Microsoft Research physically being in a single location, it has three institutions in the United States (Redmond, Washington; Silicon Valley; and Cambridge, Massachusetts) and six additional international locations (Bangalore, India; Cambridge, England; Cairo, Egypt; Beijing, China; Aachen, Germany; and Herzelia, Israel) (visit Microsoft Research's website at http://research.microsoft.com to see the worldwide locations on a map). The company's researchers usually work in local teams with members who are collocated and also have some involvement in global projects.

There are, however, R&D teams in other companies that are fully integrated around the globe. The purpose of these dispersed work structures is to benefit from the diversity of cultural backgrounds, expertise, and languages that a global team provides. In addition, a key advantage is the time gap between team members who work in different time zones. This allows team members to take on different shifts in developing the product: while part of the team sleeps, another part takes over and continues development, helping reduce the time to completion considerably. These initiatives demonstrate the kinds of pressures experienced by R&D teams in a global, competitive market. For companies in the high-tech sector, managing innovation becomes a central aspect of remaining competitive.

Understanding the Social Milieu of Software Development

Software development has become a central component of R&D. The relevance of software development, and its potential to attract millions of users who will produce massive amounts of content, can be seen in the high financial value of companies such as Facebook, Twitter, Flickr, and The Huffington Post. In 2011, AOL bought The Huffington Post, an American news website and aggregated blog, for $315 million. In 2006, Google purchased YouTube for $1.65 billion, even though it had not yet made a profit. Facebook, another company that has not yet made a profit, is now valued at $100 billion (Bilton & Rusli, 2012). The high financial value of these companies shows that code is not just a string of bits but rather a tool that facilitates complex social behaviours, such as informing, sharing, and collaborating on a large scale.

Carmel and Sawyer (1998) have developed a theoretical framework that emphasizes the social milieu in which software development occurs, and they distinguish between two different types of teams: **packaged software development** and **information systems development**. Packaged software development refers to software that is produced in large quantities and can be obtained off the shelf; Microsoft's Office suites are an example. This is in contrast to information systems development, which is customized software, such as Facebook, that is designed to meet the needs and requirements of a particular group of users. Further, Carmel and Sawyer's framework distinguishes four levels of analysis that are critical for understanding the work of these teams: (1) industry, (2) tasks, (3) cultural milieu, and (4) groups (Quan-Haase, 2009). Table 5.2 summarizes the key differences between packaged software development and information systems development for each of the levels of analysis. To better understand the social milieu in which software development is embedded, we examine each level in more depth.

1. Understanding the Industry

The high-tech industry in which software development occurs is characterized by intense time-to-market pressure: companies compete to be the first to deliver software that includes the "latest" functionality at low prices (Dubé, 1998; Krishnan, 1998; Zachary, 1998). As indicated in Table 5.2,

Table 5.2 Software Development Framework

	Packaged Software Development	Information Systems Group
Industry	• Time-to-market pressures • Success measures: profit, market share	• Cost pressures • Success measures: satisfaction, acceptance
Tasks	• Staff assigned to specific tasks • User is distant and less involved in development • Process is immature • Software development is via coordination	• Staff assigned to specific projects • User is involved and provides input • Process is more mature • Task accomplishment is independent
Cultural milieu	• Entrepreneurial • Individualistic • Long work hours	• More bureaucratic • Less individualistic • More set working hours
Groups	• Less likely to have matrix structure • Involved in entire development cycle • More cohesive, motivated, jelled • Opportunities for large financial rewards • Large discrepancies in income • Small/collocated	• Matrix-managed and project-focused • People assigned to multiple projects • People work together as needed • Salary-based • Relies on formal specifications • Larger/dispersed

Source: Adapted from Carmel and Sawyer, 1998.

the time-to-market pressures are greatest for packaged software development teams because they are dependent on frequent and highly innovative releases. Currently, we observe these pressures in the growing tablet and e-book reader industry, where companies are in stark competition to acquire market share. For these companies, it is essential to acquire early market share and position themselves as a leader.

2. Understanding the Tasks

The primary task of software development teams is to write code. While all team members know how to program, each person is responsible for specific components of the software that require specialized expertise in areas including quality assurance, programming, marketing, design, and client services. In the information systems groups, people are more closely integrated with the development of the product than is the case with packaged software. When software is developed for a client, usually that client will have very specific needs that the software has to meet, while packaged software is tailored toward a large user base.

3. Understanding the Cultural Milieus

The work culture of software development teams is characterized by highly individualistic work habits (Borsook, 2000). This means that developers have no predetermined work schedule, but their schedule and tasks are constantly changing. In the lead-up to a release date, employees can work 50, 60, or even 80 hours per week, and the pressure at those times is high. Not all developers, however, have the same status within a team. The term

software cowboy describes the high-performing developer, who is a "brilliant genius, who single-handedly conceives and codes clever new systems in sweaty and sleepless weekends of nonstop programming" (Constantine, 1995, p. 48). There are always a few software cowboys in every team, who earn above-average incomes and excel in writing code and solving programming problems. To exemplify the role of these innovator-entrepreneurs in software development, Box 5.2 discusses Mark Zuckerberg as the key developer in the initial stages of the creation of Facebook.

Box 5.2 also illustrates some important aspects of the cultural milieu of software development, in which it is essential for programmers not only to excel at writing code but also to be able to anticipate users' needs. Two key terms in computer science help bridge the gap between the writing of code and

---

Box 5.2

Designing Social Networking Sites

In the early 2000s, a number of social networking sites (SNSs) emerged on the Internet, including Six Degrees, hi5, and Friendster (boyd, 2006). Despite the fact that these sites had a lot in common, small differences in the functionality of each site prompted users to migrate from one social networking site to another. Over time Facebook became one of the most popular social networking sites, with about 1.11 billion monthly active users in 2013 (Facebook, 2013). The movie *The Social Network* illustrates a number of unique characteristics of the cultural milieu of software development. Mark Zuckerberg's original intent was to create Facebook as an exclusive website for Harvard students (Kirkpatrick, 2010). He believed that Facebook would take off because it was based on Harvard's brand and supplemented the already existing social structure of *exclusivity* that is so central to Harvard's culture of fraternities and sororities.

Zuckerberg, the inventor and key developer of Facebook, comes across in the movie as a genius developer who would certainly fall under the description of a software cowboy, someone who spends long hours in front of the computer writing code (Kirkpatrick, 2010). What also becomes apparent when we analyze how Facebook's code developed is that Zuckerberg had a very good understanding of how social processes interfaced with the technological. Before the social networking site took off, he was trying to find the relevant feature that would help make Facebook more popular than other similar sites. He realized that "relationship status" was at the core of how users were interacting with the software. Although writing the code for including relationship status in the interface was straightforward, it was the social information it was intended to convey that was relevant to this group of users. This shows how the writing of code for software cannot occur in isolation from people's needs and from relevant social processes. If software is not relevant for a specific user group, then people will simply not adopt it. In other words, interface (usability) and content have to go hand in hand.

the requirements of users. *Object affordance* describes how physical objects can be designed in such a way that they facilitate behaviour (Norman, 1988). For instance, a doorknob is designed in a way that suggests that the user turn and pull it to open a door. The concept has been employed in human–computer interaction (HCI) to better understand how programs can be designed to elicit specific behaviours and facilitate the navigation of computer interfaces (Sears & Jacko, 2008). The term **social affordance** has been used to describe the "relationship between the properties of an object and the social characteristics of a group that enable particular kinds of interaction among members of that group" (Bradner, 2001; Bradner, Kellogg, & Erickson, 1999, p. 154). The term helps us understand how a simple change in the design of a tool can have social repercussions. For instance, if a Facebook user changes her status from "in a relationship" to "single," this information can trigger a series of events; for instance, friends and relatives may contact her to see what happened and how she is doing. Others will know that the relationship has terminated and provide emotional support. Yet others will interpret this as a signal that she is potentially available for new romantic relationships.

4. Understanding Team Structure

The existence of software cowboys does not preclude the team from showing high levels of co-operation and cohesion (Wysocki, 2006). Carmel (1995) labelled this type of highly cohesive working unit a **core team**. Team structures in software development vary considerably. A high level of communication and exchange between members of the team is necessary because of the interdependence of all components of the product. Moreover, consultation on design issues is also required because these affect the operability of the code.

Of particular interest are game developers because the profession "is one of ongoing struggle, from meeting production deadlines to dealing with the precarity of work from project to project" (Livermore, 2008). One central theme in this industry is the difficulty in separating work from play. Those who are employed as developers and testers of video games often think of their work as consisting of fun, making it difficult to regulate work hours and expectations. This problem is further confounded by the fact that workers in this industry are often attracted by fairly informal work settings, where it is difficult to determine when work starts and ends.

One example described in the media pinpoints these types of social problems: the spouse of a game developer, known online under the pseudonym EA Spouse (of an Electronic Arts employee in British Columbia), blogged about the poor and problematic labour practices in the industry. The blog describes in detail the long hours as well as the repercussions for family life:

> Now, it seems, is the "real" crunch, the one that the producers of this title
> so wisely prepared their team for by running them into the ground ahead of

time. The current mandatory hours are 9am to 10pm—seven days a week—with the occasional Saturday evening off for good behavior (at 6:30pm). This averages out to an eighty-five-hour work week. Complaints that these once more extended hours combined with the team's existing fatigue would result in a greater number of mistakes made and an even greater amount of wasted energy were ignored. (http://ea-spouse.livejournal.com/274.html)

Working in industries where work and play are seamlessly interwoven creates many social problems in terms of the repercussions for family life, in addition to the toll on the individual.

Conclusions

This chapter addresses the often neglected topic of technological design, showing that its complexity results from the way that design unfolds. In the past, studies of design largely disregarded the influence of social factors, instead focusing primarily on the technology as the driving force. The field has moved away from understanding design as a technologically deterministic process, and several approaches have been developed within the field of STS to investigate the mutual shaping of social and technological factors in the process of design. These approaches provide new terminology and models to analyze how design unfolds and to examine its close interlink with social, economic, cultural, and historical factors.

The chapter introduces the concept of technopoles as an umbrella term to describe centres of innovation. Technopoles such as Silicon Valley represent the engines of the information society because they comprise highly skilled workers, infrastructure, and capital investment for the purpose of designing and developing innovative products in the industry. However, not all regions of the world can afford to sustain technopoles, further increasing the gap between the haves and the have-nots. Even those regions that have developed technopoles are vulnerable to global pressures and changes in global markets, as the example of the rapid fall of the Celtic Tiger illustrates. We conclude by showing that in an information society, nations and markets are highly interdependent. Changes, even small ones, in one sector or one region can have social and economic consequences in other parts of the world.

Our analysis of GERD, the measure of investment in innovation, shows large discrepancies among nation-states. Sweden, Finland, Japan, and Korea are the largest investors in R&D in the world. Canada and the United States invest considerably in R&D and are positioned in places number 14 and 7, respectively. Mexico is the last country to be included in the chart, and many other nations are not included at all as they show almost no investment in R&D. On the one hand, there is large integration, mobility, and dependence among the key centres of innovation and world markets. On the other hand, the disparities between the haves and the have-nots, both between nations and within nations, are ever increasing. This necessitates future detailed analysis of technopoles and their social, economic, and political consequences.

Questions for Critical Thought

1. What are the key factors that have led to our lack of knowledge in the field of technology design?

2. Explain the concept of technopole by using Castells and Hall's framework. Then discuss its economic, cultural, and social impact on local communities.

3. How does Schumpeter view the link between economic development and innovation? Do you think his theory continues to be relevant in the twenty-first century?

4. What are the key premises of object and social affordances? Discuss how this framework applies to the use of Facebook.

Suggested Readings

Zackariasson, P., & Wilson, T.L. (2012). *The video game industry: Formation, present state, and future* (Vol. 24). New York: Routledge. Provides an overview of the video game industry and its economic and social intricacies.

Yu, X. (2008). Impacts of corporate code of conduct on labor standards: A case study of Reebok's athletic footwear supplier factory in China. *Journal of Business Ethics, 81*(3), 513–529. An engaging overview of the merits and problems of socially responsible capitalism.

Kirkpatrick, D. (2011). *The Facebook effect: The inside story of the company that is connecting the world.* New York: Simon & Schuster. The book recounts the story of how Facebook developed into an influential startup, and discusses the impact of Facebook on social relations, marketing, and information dissemination.

Shah, A. (2014, September 4). Apple attacked over "worsening" factory conditions in China. *PCWorld.* Retrieved 10 December 2014 from www.pcworld.com/article/2602980/apple-attacked-over-worsening-factory-conditions-in-china.html

Online Resources

China Labour Watch
http://chinalaborwatch.org/home.aspx
> CLW is a not-for-profit, non-governmental organization (NGO) that advocates for workers' rights in China by increasing the transparency of supply chains and factory labor conditions.

SourceForge
http://sourceforge.net/
> This site hosts thousands of software development projects created and developed by the community of open-source developers.

Microsoft's R&D global teams
http://research.microsoft.com/en-us/
> This site provides an overview of the location and focus of Microsoft's R&D global teams.

6 The Adoption and Diffusion of Technological Innovations

Learning Objectives

◎ to understand the process that underlies the adoption of technological innovations and the factors affecting this process;

◎ to understand the classic model of the diffusion of innovations;

◎ to examine key adopter groups, how the groups differ, and their characteristics;

◎ to investigate what social factors are most salient in the adoption of a diversity of technologies ranging from simple innovations such as boiling water to multi-media tools like the iPhone;

◎ to examine how social theory on the adoption and diffusion of technological innovations can be applied to market research.

Introduction

The study of technology typically focuses on those tools, techniques, and apparatuses that have been widely adopted in society. That is, we are most interested in technologies that are well known and have made an impact on how we live. Although less attention is paid to technological adoption and diffusion, this area of research provides insights into a set of research questions that are central to society: Why is one tool adopted over another? What tools did users reject? What processes—at the micro and macro levels—are at play during the adoption and diffusion of an **innovation**? The study of adoption and diffusion shows that technologies are not a given but are instead a result of social, cultural, political, and historical factors.

This field of study is referred to as the **diffusion of innovations**. The field has grown exponentially: in 1962 there were 405 publications in the area; by 1983 the number had increased to 3,085 (Rogers, 1983). In fact, a search conducted in 2015 for the terms *diffusion* and *innovation* on *Scholars Portal*[1] (limited to social sciences) yielded 71,410 entries, and these counts did not include the vast number of publications in related fields, such as engineering, science, and medicine. One reason for this rapid growth is the pervasiveness of technology in our society and its increasing impact on how we work, play, socialize, and communicate. We can readily see this impact when we examine the use of virtual worlds, such as *World of Warcraft* (*WoW*) or *Second Life*, where users gather for work meetings, build virtual objects for fun, fight virtual enemies, and hang out to make new friends. Scholars no longer see technology adoption and diffusion as a purely technological matter but have come to see it instead as reflecting social processes as well. This chapter will provide an overview of the key concepts, theories, and research findings in the diffusion of innovations literature and discuss them in relation to the diffusion of specific technologies, such as water boiling, the QWERTY keyboard, and the iPhone.

Technological Innovations: The Process

The most influential researcher in the diffusion of innovations literature is Everett Rogers, a rural sociologist and communication scholar. His seminal work *Diffusion of Innovations* (2003) is the second most cited book in the social sciences and provides a comprehensive overview of diffusion studies.[2] In the book, he defines an *innovation* as "an idea, practice, or object that is perceived as new by an individual or another unit of adoption. An innovation presents an individual or an organization with a new alternative or alternatives, with new means of solving problems" (Rogers, 2003, p. xx). The term *innovation* is used interchangeably with *new technology* or *technological innovation*. **Adoption** is referred to as the decision to start using an innovation for a specific goal. While adoption takes place on an individual basis or at the organizational level, *diffusion* describes the process by which, over time, an innovation becomes adopted by a social group. Hence, diffusion is a macro-level phenomenon that is structural in nature.

Early models of the diffusion of innovations tended to place the innovation itself at the centre of the diffusion process. The assumption was that an innovation that was superior to previously established technologies would quickly spread and become widely used in society. Hence, diffusion was solely a matter of technological superiority. These models, however, did not capture the complexity of how diffusion occurs; adopters need to be considered, as they are active participants in the decision-making process. These models also failed to account for the social, cultural, and political factors that affect adoption; individuals are members of social groups and the norms, beliefs, and attitudes of these groups will also shape adoption decisions.

Inventing and Copying Technology

Jared Diamond has long been interested in the evolution and history of innovations. He argues that studying the origins of technological innovations is central to understanding social change in society. When one looks at the history of tool use, for example, social groups may at first appear to be highly innovative, constantly developing creative solutions to existing problems. Based on the anthropological record, however, Diamond concludes that innovations are rarely developed locally; most innovations are taken from other social groups—this is referred to as the copying of technology. Social groups are less likely to invent new ways of dealing with problems than they are to copy existing solutions developed and tested elsewhere. Two key factors affect whether innovations are more likely to be invented locally or copied from other societies: **ease of invention** and **interconnectedness** (Diamond, 1997).

Innovations that are easy to invent are more likely to be developed locally, while innovations that are complex are usually copied. As Diamond (1997) explains, "[s]ome inventions arose straightforwardly from a handling of natural raw materials. Such inventions developed on many independent occasions in world history, at different places and times" (p. 254). Pottery is a good example of an invention that has several independent origins, probably because pottery results from the handling of a raw material, in this case clay. By contrast, the magnetic compass was invented only once in world history because of the sophistication in design and the need for integration of various domains of knowledge with technical skills. Other inventions identified by Diamond that have been invented only once in the Old World and never in the New World include the water wheel, the rotary quern, and the windmill, which suggests that the spread of most technologies is a social process where one social group learns about a new technology from another.

Geographical location plays an important role in a society's adoption of technologies. Societies located in central areas, such as medieval Islam, for example, with access to both their own inventions and those of their neighbours, were generally better equipped for and more receptive to acquiring and adopting new technologies, in contrast to more geographically isolated regions and societies, such as Tasmania. Societies that were isolated needed to rely on their own ingenuity because they could not easily borrow ideas or inventions from other social groups. Conversely, the diffusion of some technologies was principally connected to a need to retain power over rivals, as in the Maori tribes' acquisition of muskets from European traders in early-nineteenth-century New Zealand (Diamond, 1997).

While the study of technological innovations tends to focus on the spread of ideas and tools, there have been instances in history where new technologies were abandoned, a process referred to as **technological regression** (Diamond, 1997). An example of technological regression is the history of guns in Japan. Guns were first brought to the country in 1543 by Portuguese traders. Following this initial acquisition, the Japanese rapidly adopted the weapon, manufacturing their own guns and becoming one of the largest areas of gun ownership in the world. Within less than a century, however, guns completely disappeared from the island. There were three key socio-cultural factors mitigating against a complete adoption of the gun as a mechanism for war in the Japanese context: (1) customs, (2) power, and (3) politics. The Japanese warrior class, the samurai, who held great political and cultural sway, were against the weapon. The samurai weapon of choice, the sword, was a powerful "class symbol," and samurai warfare itself was centred on single combats between swordsmen. The samurai saw the gun, therefore, as an ungraceful weapon. The gun's popularity also receded because of its foreign origin, as goods and ideas produced outside Japan became increasingly despised as part of an anti-foreign backlash (Diamond, 1997).

The Classic Model of the Diffusion of Innovations

The most influential model of diffusion is that of Everett Rogers, first proposed in 1962 based on his seminal work in rural sociology on the spread of agricultural innovations. Rogers was keenly interested in how agricultural innovations found acceptance by farmers. He interviewed 200 farmers to find out what motivated them to either adopt an innovation or reject it. Unlike most of the previous work on the topic, Rogers's work focused on the social factors that influenced adoption. Based on his own work and subsequent studies in the field, he proposed a comprehensive model of the diffusion process.

For Rogers, the concepts of **uncertainty** and **information** were central to the diffusion process. Potential adopters are constantly dealing with high levels of uncertainty because they do not know whether or not the new innovation will yield the expected outcomes; hence, its adoption is coupled with risks. If they adopt and the innovation does not provide the expected personal and societal benefits, negative effects could ensue at the economic, social, environmental, and societal levels. The deployment of the atomic bomb in Hiroshima and Nagasaki during WWII is an example of a technology that had not been employed before but was tested in the context of war and yielded disastrous effects for humanity.

A more mundane example of uncertainty as described in Rogers's model of diffusion is the adoption of new hardware/software. For example, when the Apple iPad 2 was released, consumers were tempted on the one hand to buy the new device to obtain the flexibility of downloading e-books, surfing the Web, checking email, and, most importantly, being able to annotate and edit text in a flexible manner. This multi-media device also provided a wide range of entertainment capabilities, including watching movies on demand, creating a complex music library, and participating in both single and multi-player online games. Owning an iPad itself was also a powerful symbol of how tech-savvy the user was. On the other hand, there was considerable uncertainty as to whether the new application would become widely used and accepted or whether another, superior tool would be developed, making the iPad 2 obsolete shortly after its deployment. In addition, the quantity of e-books that would be available at cost-efficient prices on the iPad was still uncertain. The Nook and Kindle, in contrast, carry Project Gutenberg's 1.8 million free books in addition to 500,000 other titles they make available to their users. Potential buyers then had to ask themselves whether it was worthwhile to spend C\$599 for the iPad 2, or whether they should wait until the next **killer app** became available, or simply buy a Kindle, Nook, or Sony Reader instead. The choice also carries some risk, as users who choose a poor model (e.g., poor development, lack of apps, inferior technical support) will suffer the consequences. For example, the BlackBerry PlayBook e-reader/tablet failed to capture the attention of users because it did not seem as cutting-edge as competitor brands and eventually faded away. Research In Motion (RIM) lost about 10 per cent of stock shares and had to pay almost \$500 million to account for unsold PlayBooks, which led to businessinsider.com voting the tablet as the number one tech flop in 2011.

Information, the second key concept in Rogers's model, becomes an important resource because it reduces uncertainty and helps potential adopters make a decision about a particular technological innovation's usefulness and efficiency. Information can be obtained from multiple sources, including the technology itself, peers, the media, and individuals inside and outside one's social group. The quality and extent of the information that an adopter receives will determine the certainty with which that person can make a decision. The amount of information available also affects the time it will take an individual to decide whether to adopt or to reject.

The Main Elements of the Diffusion of Innovations

Rogers defines *diffusion* as "the process by which an innovation is communicated through certain channels over time among the members of a social system" (2003, p. 5). In this definition, four main elements become prevalent in the diffusion of innovations: (1) the innovation, (2) communication channels, (3) time, and (4) a social system. We next discuss each element in the context of Rogers's model of the diffusion of innovations.

1. The Innovation

Innovations, as defined earlier in this chapter, consist of new ideas, practices, or objects linked to technology and hence encompass all elements of our proposed definition of technology—what was referred to in Chapter 1 as material substance, knowledge, technological practice, technique, and societal complexity. Not all innovations, however, are of the same type; indeed, the nature of innovations can be classified in a number of different ways, based on their complexity, target audience, etc. Some innovations take off quickly, while others diffuse slowly. For example, blue jeans, a consumer good, took only five years to spread throughout the United States, while the use of the metric system is still not widespread in Canada even though it was introduced in 1970 and had a dedicated government agency promoting it (the Metric Commission). If Canadians are asked today about their height and weight, most will still reply in feet and pounds, respectively.

To help us distinguish among the wide range of innovations, Rogers identified five perceived characteristics of an innovation (see Figure 6.1): (1) relative advantage, (2) compatibility, (3) complexity, (4) trialability, and (5) observability. These five characteristics of innovations help us predict the speed with which an innovation spreads and help us understand how the nature of the innovation itself affects the process. Each characteristic is discussed next.

First, **relative advantage** assesses the merits of an innovation in relation to the idea, practice, or object it is to replace. If potential adopters perceive that the innovation has added value, they will be more likely to adopt it. Early models tended to focus solely on the characteristics of an innovation as a means to assess its potential for adoption within a social group. That is, the models emphasized the "objective" advantages of a technology. This simple view is now obsolete because empirical studies have demonstrated that it is the "perceived" advantage of a technology that matters. An individual's perception is strongly influenced by social factors, including the social prestige associated with the innovation, the adoption rate of others in the social group, and information about the innovation received from communication channels.

Second, **compatibility** refers to an innovation's fit with a social group's existing norms, values, and attitudes. Only in those instances where a good

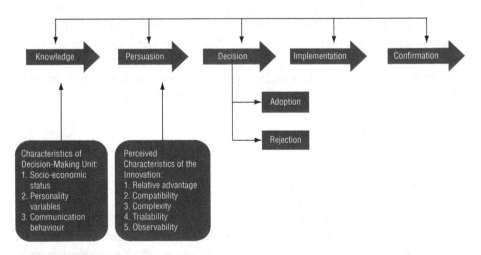

Figure 6.1 The Innovation–Decision Process
Source: Adapted from Rogers, E.M. (2003). *Diffusion of innovations* (5th ed.). New York: Free Press, p. 165.

fit exists will an innovation be adopted. For example, birth control continues to be rejected in a large number of communities across Latin America because they view birth control as inconsistent with their religious and cultural beliefs.[3]

Third, **complexity** describes the level of proficiency needed to comprehend the workings of a technology and use it with ease. People will be more likely to adopt technologies that are transparent in their function and benefits than those that are difficult to operate. Photography, for example, diffused slowly in society because people were not sure at first how cameras worked and what the consequences would be of depicting their image. Even today, in rural areas of some developing countries people refuse to be photographed because they fear that the camera could take away their soul.

Fourth, innovations that users can test prior to implementation are more likely to be adopted than those that cannot be tried. **Trialability** lets potential adopters reduce the uncertainty associated with the innovation and gather evidence about its value and associated potential risks through hands-on experience.

Last, Rogers identified the characteristic of **observability**, which refers to the visibility of the innovation itself and its benefits to other members of the social group. If others can see the innovation and how it works, they are much more likely to discuss it with each other and thereby obtain valuable information that can help them with the decision-making process.

2. Communication Channels
Central to the process of diffusion of innovations is the communication that occurs between individuals. Communication channels are the means by which the exchange of information occurs. The most commonly utilized forms of communication for the purpose of diffusing an innovation are the mass media, including television, radio, newspapers, and the Internet. While mass media are the most efficient means of reaching a large audience, they are not as effective at persuading a potential adopter as are interpersonal channels. Communication among peers is effective because peers can provide first-hand accounts about their experience with an innovation. Individuals are more likely to trust these accounts than messages coming from the mass media, which often represent the interests of vendors.

In the literature, two additional reasons have been identified for the strong influence of personal relationships in comparison to that of mass media. First, a large number of individuals are not exposed to mass media because they do not read a newspaper on a regular basis or watch news on television. Thus, personal relationships have a greater reach with this group of people, who chat more informally about technologies. Discussions with friends and family are an important component in the decision-making process. Second, individuals who are less interested in technologies are more likely to discuss an innovation informally with a friend than to obtain information from formal sources, such as newspapers or the radio. This is because they are not motivated to seek out information on technological developments on their own account. Their general involvement with technology is low and hence most of the information they obtain about a given innovation will occur accidentally through encounters with other adopters in their social circle.

3. Time

In the social sciences, time is usually a variable that is of little relevance. Most studies completely ignore time because it is a part of all phenomena and therefore does not merit much attention. Research in the diffusion of innovations, in contrast, is unique in the social sciences in terms of its emphasis on time, which is a central variable for examining when individuals first become aware of an innovation. Distinct adopter categories can be observed based on when individuals adopt a specific technology. These are described later in the chapter. Time also helps to explain an innovation's rate of adoption within a particular social system, which is measured as the number of adopters within a given time period.

4. Social System

Rogers (2003) defines the social system as "a set of interrelated units that are engaged in joint problem solving to accomplish a common goal" (p. 476). The units are individuals, groups, or organizations that are interested in acquiring information about a technological innovation in order to make a decision about whether to adopt or to reject that innovation. Examining the diffusion process within a social system is necessary because the structure of the social system as well as its values, norms, and beliefs have a major impact on the diffusion process.

The Innovation-Decision Process

After reviewing numerous adoption studies, Rogers was struck by the finding that the rate of adoption was similar across a wide range of innovations. When he plotted the frequency of adoption on a graph by time, Rogers discovered that the rate of adoption formed an S-shaped curve, which Rogers termed an **S-shaped curve of adoption**. Figure 6.2 shows how a few individuals adopt an innovation early, the majority adopt an innovation at the midpoint of the cycle, and a few adopt the innovation very late. The moment when the majority of individuals in a social group adopt an innovation is referred to as the point where the S-shaped diffusion curve takes off. It represents a critical turning point for the diffusion of any innovation because it is at this point that it has been widely adopted in society.

To determine what occurs during the adoption process, Rogers (2003) examined the innovation-decision process and identified five distinct

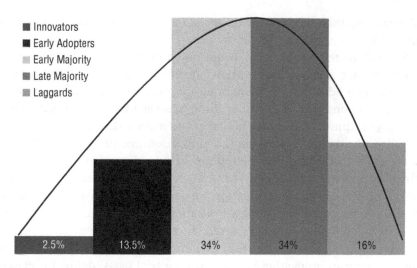

Figure 6.2 Adoption Categories
Source: Adapted from Rogers, E.M. (2003). *Diffusion of Innovations* (5th ed.). New York: Free Press, p. 247.

stages: (1) knowledge, (2) persuasion, (3) decision, (4) implementation, and (5) confirmation. Figure 6.1 (on page 110) depicts the various stages that an individual goes through when making a decision about the adoption of an innovation.

First, in the **knowledge stage** an individual learns about an innovation for the first time and obtains information about how it operates. Coleman, Katz, and Menzel (1966) found that information about an innovation was often obtained quite by accident through conversations with peers and interactions with sales personnel, and by exposure to the media. Individuals vary in terms of how receptive they are to information about technological innovations. Those individuals who have a need to solve a specific problem or who want to accomplish a particular task are more receptive to obtaining information related to their need. Hence, those individuals seek out messages that are in agreement with their interests, needs, and attitudes. The process of seeking out relevant information is referred to as selective exposure and shows how individuals may be exposed to the same information but evaluate its relevance in different ways based on their needs.

Different kinds of knowledge are relevant in the knowledge stage. **Awareness knowledge** is a term meaning the moment at which an individual becomes aware of the technology's existence and considers adopting it. From the awareness of the innovation emerges a need for **how-to knowledge**, which explains how the innovation is used properly and in what settings it can be employed beneficially. Finally, **principle knowledge** encompasses an understanding of the mechanisms that lie behind an innovation. For example, understanding the usefulness of and need for sanitizers is based on mechanisms outlined in germ theory.

Second, in the **persuasion stage** potential adopters continue to seek out information about an innovation, albeit now in a very active manner. Through such additional information, adopters develop either positive or negative emotions toward the innovation; these attitudes combined with the knowledge acquired earlier will help them to make a decision.

Third, the **decision stage** in the innovation-decision process describes the activities that lead toward adoption or rejection of an innovation. As defined earlier in this chapter, *adoption* refers to the decision to use an innovation. Rejection, by contrast, is the decision not to use a new technology. The decision-making process is often described as clear-cut: either an innovation is adopted or it is rejected. In reality, the boundaries between adoption and rejection are blurred, with many potential adopters first partially adopting an innovation by using it on a trial basis, defined previously as *trialability*.[4] Once they have tested the innovation, they make a conclusive adoption decision. When it is not possible to test the innovation first, they will seek the opinion of peers who have had first-hand experience with it. Rogers terms this *trial by others* because the opinion of other users will help inform a person's adoption decision.

Fourth, in the **implementation stage** an individual starts using the innovation. It is here that an adopter often runs into technical problems. At this stage, information seeking continues to be central as the adopter troubleshoots the encountered obstacles. If users find it difficult to solve the problems encountered, they may stop using the new technology and return to what they are familiar with. Most diffusion research has tended to focus on changing attitudes or adoption behaviours, and has placed less emphasis on implementation itself and the social consequences of adoption.

Fifth, following the implementation of a new tool, adopters continue to seek out information about the innovation to confirm that they have made the right decision by adopting the innovation. This stage is referred to as the **confirmation stage** and unfolds over a lengthy period. If information arises that disconfirms the usefulness of the innovation, adopters will either try to seek out further information or consider discontinuing use of the innovation, particularly if using the innovation has negative consequences that are confirmed by peers as well. This has been referred to as **discontinuance** and describes the rejection of an innovation after earlier use. If researchers fail to consider discontinuance, conclusions about an innovation's acceptance rates may be overestimated. Several factors impact discontinuance, including perceived characteristics of the innovation, competing innovations, evaluations of peers, and the innovation's fit with the social system's norms.

While media hype suggests that new technologies are adopted at a rapid pace, this is not the case, regardless of whether a given innovation is advantageous or not. Rogers (2003) writes, "Many technologists think that advantageous innovations will sell themselves, that the obvious benefits of a new idea will be widely realized by potential adopters, and that the innovation will therefore diffuse rapidly. Unfortunately, this is very seldom the case. Most innovations, in fact, diffuse at a surprisingly slow rate" (p. 7), as is illustrated in Box 6.1 with the example of the nondiffusion of the Dvorak keyboard.

Box 6.1   Diffusion and Adoption of the QWERTY Keyboard

Early theories of the diffusion and adoption of technologies focused on the characteristics of the technology itself as a means for understanding individuals' willingness to embrace a tool. Many examples, however, have shown that the adoption process is neither linear nor unidirectional; instead, many social factors play a role in how technologies are diffused in society. An example of **nondiffusion** is the Dvorak keyboard. The standard keyboard, which most of us use several times daily, is the QWERTY keyboard, which was invented in 1873 and is named after the letters formed on the keyboard's upper left row. The main reason for introducing the QWERTY keyboard was to slow down typists. In the late eighteenth century, typewriters consisted of type bars that had to be stroked. When typists stroked two letters quickly, they would often get caught and the machine would require repair. To avoid the rapid typing and entangling of type bars, Christopher Latham Sholes designed a keyboard that positioned the letters in such a way that it was awkward to type the most frequently used sequences, thereby slowing down typists considerably while not diminishing the machine's performance.

In 1932, August Dvorak, at the University of Washington, designed a keyboard that would speed up typing again. He created an arrangement in which the most frequently used letters—A, O, E, U, I, D, H, T, N, and S—were located across the top row of the typewriter. Moreover, the letters were arranged in such a way that the right hand, the stronger hand, would be performing more of the work, instead of the left hand, which does most of the work on the QWERTY keyboard. The QWERTY keyboard also has a number of inefficiencies in addition to its slow speed, namely fatigue, higher error rate, and disorientation on the keyboard. Despite the many advantages of the Dvorak keyboard over the standard keyboard, however, it failed to diffuse in society, even though the American National Standards Institute and the Computer and Business Equipment Manufacturers Association approved it. The main reasons for the lack of diffusion seem to be associated with existing interests on the part of the manufacturers and the sales industry, as well as the habits of typists themselves (Diamond, 1997). As Paul David (1985) has noted, Dvorak lost out to QWERTY because of factors of "technical interrelatedness, economics of scale, and quasi-irreversibility of investment," which enabled QWERTY to become "locked-in" (p. 334).

Source: Reprinted with the permission of Free Press, a Division of Simon & Schuster, Inc., from *Diffusion of Innovations 5e* by Everett M. Rogers. Copyright © 1995, 2003 by Everett M. Rogers. Copyright © 1962, 1971, 1983, by Free Press, a Division of Simon & Schuster, Inc. All rights reserved.

The persistence of the QWERTY keyboard into the twenty-first century, even though it is inferior to the Dvorak keyboard in so many ways, shows how adoption and diffusion are often unrelated to the efficiency, benefits, and utility of technologies themselves and are instead closely associated with the complexities of the social system into which they are introduced. Box 6.1 shows that many social factors play a role in the adoption and diffusion of technologies, even in developed societies. This is an important consideration because we often tend to ascribe to developing nations a lack of rational choice while assuming that individuals in developed nations make innovation decisions based on efficiency alone. The QWERTY example demonstrates that when it comes to the adoption and diffusion of innovations, many factors need to be considered simultaneously, not all of which are rational. One of the key factors affecting the diffusion of innovations is the role of change agents, which we discuss in the next section.

The Role of Change Agents

Even though **change agents** are not depicted in the model in Figure 6.1, they are instrumental in all stages of diffusion, with their most central role being to make potential users aware of a technological innovation and to provide them with information that will help them to make an informed decision about whether to adopt or to reject the innovation. Box 6.2 provides an example of how a change agent attempts to introduce an innovation into a social group. The example is of a failed diffusion campaign and highlights the challenges a change agent confronts as well as the large number of social, economic, and cultural factors that need to be considered when examining the role of change agents. Once again, we learn that the diffusion of technological innovations is not a linear, rational process where the innovations themselves are at the centre of diffusion but, instead, a complex social process taking place at many levels of analysis.

Box 6.2   The Innovation of Water Boiling as Introduced by a Change Agent

The Ministry of Health in Peru set out to introduce innovations geared toward health improvement and disease prevention in rural villages in Peru. A key innovation that the ministry was introducing as part of this program was water boiling to reduce the spread of illnesses, such as typhoid. While the innovations had clear health benefits, they failed to obtain widespread acceptance. In a village called Los Molinos in the coastal region of Peru, only 11 of the 200 families who lived there adopted the innovation.

The key sources of water in the village are a seasonal irrigation ditch, a spring, and a public well. Primarily children, and sometimes women, are given the task of fetching water. Water boiling was introduced by the local health worker, Nelida, who in this case was the change agent. The goal was to introduce homemakers in Los Molinos to the innovation of water boiling and to then persuade them to adopt water boiling as a routine behaviour to prevent the spread of disease. The program ran over a two-year period and Nelida spent considerable time with the families in the village.

Nelida organized a series of public talks given by a medical doctor to inform the villagers of the need to boil water regularly. In addition, she visited every family in the village several times to talk to them about water boiling and its advantages. She gave special attention to 21 families and visited each around 18 times. Of these 21 families, 11 adopted water boiling into their daily habits, while no other families in the village adopted water boiling. How can we understand this lack of acceptance in view of the clear benefits for the community?

A number of factors led to the demise of the campaign. First, water boiling was in opposition to cultural beliefs and local values. Hot water is given only to sick individuals in the community; healthy individuals will drink only cold water. This was incongruous with the message Nelida was attempting to convey, namely that boiled water would lead toward improved health.

A second important factor was the approach Nelida took. She worked with several women who were considered outsiders in the community. They were more open to Nelida's message and willing to adopt the new innovation because as outsiders they were seeking her approval and attention. For these women, their adoption decision had less to do with embracing germ theory and understanding the advantages of the innovation and more to do with their position as outsiders in the village's social network. By contrast, Nelida did not approach villagers who occupied central positions in the village's social network, even though they could potentially have had greater influence on the adoption process.

Third, many women in Los Molinos were suspicious of Nelida. They felt that Nelida wanted to inspect their homes to determine their cleanliness and felt their privacy was invaded by her presence—they referred to her as the "dirt inspector." These homemakers also rejected her because they felt Nelida represented the values of Peru's middle class and hence they could not easily identify with her. Rogers (2003), in his final analysis of the Los Molinos case, concludes that the change agent, in this case Nelida, "was too 'innovation-oriented' and not 'client-oriented' enough. Unable to put herself in the role of the village housewives, her attempt at persuasion failed to reach her clients because the message was not suited to their needs" (p. 5).

Source: Wellin, E. (1955). Water boiling in a Peruvian town. In B.D. Paul (Ed.), *Health, Culture and Community*. New York: Russell Sage Foundation.

The example of Los Molinos portrays change agents as central players in the diffusion of innovations process. In Los Molinos, the role played by the change agent was complex and directly linked to the socio-cultural context of the village. The change agent failed in promoting the innovation, despite its many advantages to villagers. In the next section, we continue exploring the diffusion process by looking at different adopter groups.

Classifying Adoption Categories

Research consistently shows that members of a social group adopt innovations at a different pace, with some members adopting an innovation early in the process and others adopting it much later. Early researchers realized the importance of identifying and categorizing adopter groups but could not agree on terminology and method of categorization. In 1962, as mentioned, Rogers proposed the S-shaped curve of adoption to classify adopters, and this quickly became the dominant method of categorization.

The relevance of the S-curve of adoption to classifying adopter categories becomes evident when the cumulative rate of adoption is plotted instead of the absolute frequency by time. This curve has the shape of the normal distribution, often also referred to as a bell curve, with 50 per cent of individuals adopting halfway through the adoption period. Rogers employed this bell-shaped curve as a means for categorizing adopters based on when they adopted a new innovation relative to others in the social system. Five key types of adopters were identified (see Figure 6.2 on page 113):

1. *Innovators*: These individuals constantly seek out new ideas and information, and this thirst for newness leads them to expand their social circles—which is why they are often referred to as cosmopolitans. Their role is that of importing new ideas into their social group from the boundaries; that is, they are the **gatekeepers**. Because innovations are risky, they need to be able to cope with the uncertainty associated with adopting new tools, devices, and procedures.
2. *Early adopters*: Individuals in this group play the most central role in the diffusion of innovations process. They are well respected among their social network and serve as role models. Others in their social group will come to them for advice on the usefulness of technological innovations. As a result, they have been termed **opinion leaders**: individuals whose opinions influence the attitudes and behaviours of others in the social group. Unlike innovators, who are cosmopolitans, early adopters are similar to others in their social group and have ties to people in the community.
3. *Early majority*: These are individuals who are a step ahead of the average adopter. Before adopting an innovation, they go through a careful deliberation process where they consider the pros and cons of new ideas vis-à-vis the status quo. In comparison to innovators and early adopters, they have no gatekeeping or opinion leadership role in their social group. Instead, they serve as **interconnectors**; that is, they serve as a

bridge between early and late adopters, providing relevant information about the innovation to the late adopters and often convincing them of the usefulness of the adoption.

4. *Late majority*: Members of this group adopt only after the average adopter has started using the innovation. They wait for everyone else to adopt first to reduce the uncertainty associated with adopting innovations. For these individuals, adoption occurs as a result of economic forces combined with pressure from their peers. The late majority are hesitant to adopt and skeptical of anything new; they would rather stick to the old ways of doing things.

5. *Laggards*: This group represents the traditional individuals who are the last in a social system to adopt an innovation. Laggards are often isolated or are more locally oriented and connected to others with similar traditional values. Ironically, by the time laggards adopt a technology, new innovations have often already superseded the technology in question. Hence, when laggards adopt a technology, all members of a social system have adopted the innovation, and a state of market saturation can be observed.

Socio-economic characteristics perform a crucial function in shaping individuals' ability or willingness to adopt new concepts, technologies, and innovations. Early adopters, for example, have been shown to be wealthier and better educated than the laggards. Additionally, early adopters have shown an ability to absorb abstract concepts, accept change, seek information, and be well connected with both communication channels and peers, more so than laggards. Because of their increased financial resources, early adopters are more willing and able to take on the risks associated with new innovations, such as investing in a new idea or technology that may never be diffused into the mainstream. Often members of the laggard category may be forcefully pushed to adopt the new technology. For example, technical support and updates for the operating system Microsoft Windows XP (released in 2001) were discontinued as of April 8, 2014. At the time of support expiration, millions of users worldwide were still using XP as their predominant OS, such that it still had a market share of around 27 per cent for all desktop operating systems. In China, about 50 per cent of computers were still running Windows XP, and governments were paying a significant amount of money to Microsoft to extend support. Users who continue to use XP will be susceptible to more security risks, which has served as a push to upgrade machines to the new Windows 8 operating system. Moreover, Microsoft has even offered a $100 discount to upgrade from XP, as a form of incentive payment for adopting their newest OS.

Rogers's (2003) adoption categories have important implications for how we understand the spread of new technologies in society. The five groups represent differences in how individuals in society approach new technologies and in their willingness to adopt. The categories show that innovations take time to spread, with innovators and early adopters employing new technologies first and others in society slowly following their example. Hence, time is an important factor when examining the spread of innovations, as well as the innovation-decision process. To show the applicability of the concepts, we will discuss several current examples in the remainder of the chapter.

Marketing Relations with Early Adopters

This chapter has so far discussed Rogers's classic model of the diffusion of innovations in detail. Even though the model was proposed in the 1960s, it has had a continued impact on disciplines such as sociology, communications, technology adoption studies, and science and technology studies (STS). In this section, we will examine how social theory on the adoption and diffusion of technological innovations can be applied to market research. This is a topic that is of great relevance to those developing digital tools, software, hardware, or any new technology. We will discuss a series of on-the-ground examples to illustrate the continued relevance of Rogers's classic model.

The literature on digital innovations is one area that shows extensive use of Rogers's social theories. His work has widespread acceptability and applies to many market analyses of digital artifacts. Trendsspotting.com tech analyst Taly Weiss discusses the role of innovators and early adopters in online marketing as follows: "[I]t's understanding the role they play and how they are to be approached. Getting it wrong can cost companies revenue. But getting it right can propel a product or brand to the front of the pack" (Rich, 2010). Market analysts continue to worry about how innovators and early adopters behave because they understand that having a critical mass is central to the diffusion of any technological innovation, digital or otherwise.

Laura Rich, a technology analyst from Yahoo.com, provides a compelling examination of how Apple and Google have dealt with early adopters. The case studies show that Apple neglected its early adopters, and had to quickly rethink its marketing strategy to keep this group's support. When the iPhone was released in the United States in 2007, its sticker price was US$599. Many early adopters wanted to be the first to own an iPhone and, because of the demand, had to line up at stores for hours to obtain one. For these early adopters, being the first to own an iPhone was important, and lining up was only a small hassle when considering the reward of owning the desired gadget. These are not average users of cellphones but a subset of people who feel strongly about Apple products and for whom the iPhone is more than just a cellphone. These early adopters of Apple products—who call themselves "fanboys"/"fangirls"—felt let down by Apple when only a few months later the price dropped to as little as US$399. On the Web and through traditional media, they expressed their outrage and disappointment with Apple. Steve Jobs, Apple's former CEO and one of the most influential players in the technology sector, realized the mistake Apple had made by offending their most devoted and trusted users. In a public apology he directly addressed early adopters:

> [E]ven though we are making the right decision to lower the price of iPhone, and even though the technology road is bumpy, we need to do a better job taking care of our early iPhone customers as we aggressively go after new ones with a lower price. Our early customers trusted us, and we must live up to that trust with our actions in moments like these. We want to do the right thing for our valued iPhone customers. We apologize for disappointing some of you, and we are doing our best to live up to your high expectations of Apple. (Jobs, n.d.)

How could Apple, a key leader in the sector, have disregarded its early adopters? Despite their central role in the diffusion process, early adopters work behind the scenes: they are not paid by companies, and they do not play any official role. As Figure 6.3 shows, however, they are part of the bumpy beginning that many innovations need to overcome. And despite not having a formal role, early adopters are central to the process for three main reasons. First, the work of early adopters is done most of the time through their personal connections with family, friends, neighbours, and co-workers. It is in this mentor role that their influence on the adoption process plays itself out. Second, they often disseminate the information about an innovation by showing strong endorsement. For example, early iPhone adopters used their devices in public spaces, attracting the attention of other potential adopters, thereby indirectly contributing to publicity by creating product awareness as well as endorsement. Third, early adopters have gone through the innovation-decision stages. They can then share information they have gathered about the product and the attitude they have developed with potential adopters.

Another great case study of how a new media product has diffused with the help of early adopters is the mainstreaming of YouTube—in terms of both its consumer base as well as its producer base. YouTube gained popularity as a result of early adopters' forwarding links to YouTube videos via email and instant messaging. These early adopters would often send mass emails to friends, making them aware of new, meaningful, bizarre, or comical videos.

Two YouTube videos were instrumental in the spread of the service into mainstream: "Lazy Sunday" and "Numa Numa." In December 2005, early adopters started forwarding the link to a *Saturday Night Live* sketch titled "Lazy Sunday"; it quickly went viral, introducing many people to YouTube

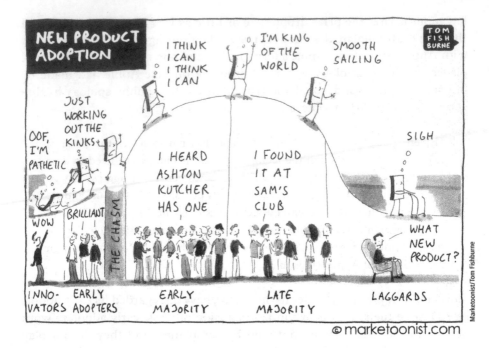

Figure 6.3 "Marketoonist" Tom Fishburne's Humorous Twist on the S-Shaped Adoption Curve

for the first time. The video featured Chris Parnell and Andy Samberg dancing and singing a farcical hip-hop song about cannabis. A second video that was instrumental in making YouTube mainstream and encouraging users to become content producers was "Numa Numa," which shows Gary Brolsma performing the song "Dragostea Din Tei" by the Moldovan band O-Zone. The original "Numa Numa" video has been seen 700,000,000 times worldwide—the second-most-viewed viral video after the video of the *Star Wars* kid, which shows Ghyslain Raza swinging a golf-ball retriever (BBC, 2006). These videos brought much-needed exposure to YouTube, showing new users the ease with which YouTube could be accessed and hinting at the ease with which this group might in turn create and share their own YouTube videos. As of 2015, YouTube had slightly more than 1 billion unique users, representing about one out of three Internet users globally.

In this section, we have looked at how Rogers's classical model of the diffusion of innovations has been applied to market analysis. Analysts pay a lot of attention to their early adopters because they realize that having a critical mass (i.e., enough people who support the product or idea in question) is central for the adoption of any innovation, and in particular for the adoption of digital tools and Web 2.0 sites and services. Not paying careful attention to early adopters can backfire and cause companies to lose their most valued customers, as the example of Apple demonstrated. Early adopters play a number of key roles in the diffusion process by creating product awareness, endorsing the product, and spreading the message via word of mouth, which often happens online on Facebook, Twitter, and Flickr.

Conclusions

This chapter provides an overview of methods and processes affecting technological diffusion in both historical and contemporary terms. The value placed on newly acquired ideas, practices, and objects, which Rogers defined as innovations, can differ radically between societies, spatial areas, and historical eras. Those who see a tool's distinctive benefit may consider adopting, borrowing, or re-calibrating this technology to the specifications of their social, economic, or cultural needs. However, acceptance is not a given. Considerations such as uncertainty, utility, cultural adaptability, and economic resources guide this decision-making process, as described in Rogers's model of the innovation-decision process. Ultimately, members of a social group may reject a technology or alter their perceptions of its usefulness, resulting in the abandonment of an object or idea in spite of its benefits—which is described as technological regression.

In a high-tech society, modern consumers, organizations, and governments are faced with similar concerns, questions, doubts, and analyses. For every technological success, there have been notorious failures. Portable electronic devices, such as the iPhone 6 or Samsung Galaxy, have become radically integrated into society, bringing with them a new colloquial language and set of expectations for managing, organizing, and conducting one's personal and professional life. In contrast, many recent technologies—e.g., DIVX discs, the Apple Newton, and the Segway—have been rejected primarily because of factors such as cost, perceived lack of usefulness, or incompatibility with other accepted technologies. Similarly, as with the Dvorak keyboard, there are examples of contemporary technologies, such as HD DVDs, that were unable to diffuse within society because of the increased acceptance and industry support for Blu-ray, a competing technology.

As our world rapidly changes, we must understand the social processes underlying technological diffusion. The existence of technological divides among adopter categories provides evidence that the rapid disposal of aging technologies in favour of new-fangled gadgets may not always be the best course of action.

Questions for Critical Thought

1. How are the concepts of uncertainty and information linked in the innovation-decision process?

2. Define the process of technological regression and discuss what sociological variables have an impact on it.

3. Using QWERTY as an example, discuss the concept of nondiffusion. What are the types of socio-economic or cultural variables that can underpin nondiffusion?

4. Discuss the role of change agents in the innovation-decision process. What factors must change agents consider when introducing an innovation?

5. Compare and contrast innovators and early adopters. Which of the two adopter categories is more important for the diffusion of innovations, and why?

6. What makes Rogers's diffusion of innovations model so relevant for the study of social media? Discuss the use of Facebook as an example.

Suggested Readings

Choia, H., Kimb, S.-H., & Lee, J. (2010). Role of network structure and network effects in diffusion of innovations. *Industrial Marketing Management, 39*(1), 170–177. Investigates why an innovation sometimes diffuses throughout society, while at other times it diffuses only to sub-groups.

Diamond, J.M. (2005). *Guns, germs, and steel: The fates of human societies.* New York: Norton. Diamond's award-winning book analyzes the various structures, values, networks, and properties that have shaped the acceptance and adoption of new technologies and ideas throughout human history.

Martin, K., & Quan-Haase, A. (2011). Seeking knowledge: The role of social networks in the adoption of ebooks by historians. In C. Johnson, P. McKenzie, & S. Stevenson (Eds.), *Proceedings of the Canadian Association of Information Science, 48*(1), 1-10. Retrieved from www.cais-acsi.ca/proceedings/2011/91_Martin_Quan-Haase.pdf. This paper examines how e-books are diffusing among scholars of history

Rich, L. (2010, March 15). Shiny new things: Ad age insights. *AdAge.* Retrieved from http://adage.com/images/bin/pdf/shiny_new_things.pdf. In her essay, Rich examines the influence of early digital adopters in contemporary society and the types of factors they ascribe to their decision-making process in choosing whether or not to adopt a new device.

Rogers, E.M. (2003). *Diffusion of innovations* (5th ed.). New York: Free Press. Rogers's classic work investigates the processes that define and characterize the adoption or rejection of innovations.

Online Resources

Apple WWDC 2010 Video
https://www.youtube.com/watch?v=z__jxoczNWc
> Former Apple CEO Steve Jobs introduces the iPhone 4 at the Worldwide Developers Conference on 7 June 2010, in San Francisco, California.

International Communication Association (ICA)
www-rcf.usc.edu/~ica/
> The ICA is an organization linking communications researchers, and includes mass communication as one of its 17 principal divisions. This group also publishes several journals, such as the *Journal of Communication.*

7   The Labour of Technology

Learning Objectives

◎   to examine the role technology has played historically in the division of labour and resulting labour struggles;

◎   to become familiar with key labour theories of the twentieth century, including scientific management and Fordism, and understand their social implications for society;

◎   to analyze the relationship between technology and the emergence of immaterial labour;

◎   to critically examine how information and communication technologies (ICTs) are changing organizational structures from hierarchical information flows to networked organizations;

◎   to obtain an overview of contemporary approaches to the understanding of the complexities of digital labour, the link between labour and play, and the emergence of makerspaces.

Introduction

The goal of this chapter is to elucidate the ways in which technology and work intersect. We discuss changes that have occurred in the nature of work processes as a result of technological advancements, focusing in particular on deskilling and immaterial and digital labour. Additionally, we examine how information and communications technologies (ICTs) are facilitating the development of new organizational structures—often covered under the umbrella term **networked organization**. Workers are now located globally and connected to their managers 24/7 via mobile phones, pagers, and the Internet. How does this hyperconnectivity affect workers' private spheres, well-being, and mental health? Finally, the chapter reviews how Web 2.0 technologies facilitate new forms of production based on the principles of collaboration, sharing, and open source. Makerspaces are also a new phenomenon in that they allow the public to get involved in making technology and thereby exploring the black box of design, discussed in Chapter 5. The discussion in this chapter makes it clear that technology is not a neutral mediator in conflicts arising from changes in work conditions. On the contrary, technology becomes an active force that shapes and influences the nature of work itself, working conditions, and the structure of society as a whole.

Luddites: The Early Struggles with Technology

We have observed that during the early stages of the Industrial Revolution (1760–1840), the application of technology caused a shift in the roles and working conditions of labourers, particularly in the textile and agriculture industries. In the textile industry, machines were introduced to simplify and speed up weaving processes. This allowed employers to hire non-skilled workers at lower wages, leading to an increase in unemployment among highly skilled craftspeople (Berg, 1994). To protest against **deskilling**, some workers took action against what they saw as unjust changes and angrily revolted against the machines that they held responsible for the decline in their status and livelihood. The term **machine breaking** describes workers' destruction of technology as a way of demonstrating their frustration with economic, social, and work changes related to industrialization (Hobsbawn, 1952). These acts were centrally coordinated, as the machines were viewed as threats to standards of living, employment, wages, and working conditions (Dinwiddy, 1979; Hobsbawn, 1952).

Key to understanding these social upheavals and the act of machine breaking are the **Luddites**. According to Binfield (2004), "Luddites sought to put an end to the manufacturers' use of certain types of machinery" (p. 3). Specifically, they targeted machines that would lower production costs through decreased wages or work hours. The group reached its political height around 1812, when machinery was becoming more widespread in factories. The Luddites utilized guerrilla tactics, often attacking or even killing the owners of machinery and threatening local officials who collaborated with employers (Binfield, 2004).

The term *Luddites* is connected to Ned Ludd, the semi-mythical, fictitious leader of the movement. According to folklore, **Ned Ludd** was a weaver who was whipped by his master and responded by destroying a knitting frame (Sale, 1995). This rebellious act was viewed as a symbol of the empowering of workers through aggressive behaviour against technology. Luddism faded in part because of the strict penal consequences given to those engaged in machine breaking, such as deportation to the then penal colony of Australia for a period of 7 to 14 years (Jones, 2006; Sale, 1995). The term **Neo-Luddism** is often used in the digital era by advocates of technology to describe in negative terms those individuals who are opposed to or who question technological developments. It is important to realize that similar trends of deskilling continue to exist, as digital technologies become ubiquitous and create new labour conditions. For instance, news bloggers often directly compete with the work of professional journalists and media experts by making content available for free or for a minimal fee. By contrast, professional journalists are often in regulated employment that includes benefits (e.g., vacation), specified working hours, and a set of expected tasks. This shift toward precarious labour will be discussed in more detail later in this chapter.

Technology and the Division of Labour

A central question of this book is whether technology is the central actor leading to social change, merely a tool for specific social, political, economic, and cultural purposes, or an integral, inseparable part of daily life. This question also frames our discussion about the intersection of technology and labour. We discuss in the following section how two trends in the early 1900s, scientific management and Fordism, are further continuations of this process of deskilling by technology through the division of labour. These two trends also illustrate how technology ceases to be merely a tool but instead becomes seamlessly integrated into the social and economic system of production.

Since the late nineteenth century, scientific management has emerged as a prevalent theory of work behaviour and management. Pioneered by American mechanical engineer Frederick Winslow Taylor and thus often referred to as **Taylorism**, scientific management aims to increase worker efficiency through the application of the scientific method to the understanding of labour. Its core principles are based on the idea that work processes can be systematically studied and, based on this knowledge, standardized in ways that make them more efficient and less prone to error.

Having closely observed industrial production at a number of manufacturing firms in the United States, Taylor (2003) deplored the inefficiency he saw, arguing that production could be increased significantly if it were under a better form of management. For Taylor, "the best management is a true science, resting upon clearly defined laws, rules, and principles" (2003, p. 119). Thus, he developed a system of scientific management which he believed would allow industrialists to minimize waste and maximize output. Taylor advised that an expanded and more involved management oversee the production process. Managers were to rationally and systematically organize the workplace, define specific and clear responsibilities for workers, monitor all work closely, and reward employees based on productivity. An important responsibility of managers was conducting time studies, which consisted of first recording a worker's movements in detail, then breaking the task down into smaller segments, and finally reassembling these segments with the aim of increasing productivity. In this way, management takes over "the burden of gathering all of the traditional knowledge which in the past has been possessed by the workmen and then of classifying, tabulating, and reducing this knowledge to rules, laws, and formulae" (Braverman, 1974, p. 112). This process often resulted in a division of labour where each worker was given a very specific task to complete for each item produced.

Scientific management radically streamlined work processes, leading to the development of mass production techniques by, for example, eliminating wasted time by optimizing workers' motions. As industrialists realized its potential, Taylor's system, or elements of it, was implemented around the world (Nelson, 1992). From the standpoint of business owners, scientific management dramatically helped to cut expenses and consequently increase profits. In many instances, productivity drastically improved, and companies were able to produce more products and sell them at potentially lower prices.

At the same time, however, the implementation of scientific management principles had a number of negative and wide-ranging consequences for work environments. Though Taylor (2003) had optimistically supposed that his ideas would benefit both employers and employees, in practice they tended to be much less favourable to the workers—or even detrimental to their working conditions. First, the standardization that was involved in streamlining production brought about further deskilling because it enabled the hiring of inexpensive, unskilled labourers (Braverman, 1974), to which workers reacted with resentment and opposition. Second, instead of workers becoming further specialized in their trade, scientific management resulted in the division of labour, thereby alienating workers from their craft (Pruijit, 1997). Third, workers lost control over their work as management imposed standardized production processes. They had less freedom to use their own discretion, and tensions between the working and managerial classes increased. Finally, the work often became very monotonous; workers felt disconnected as tasks became increasingly routine, standardized, and ultimately meaningless. All these factors together led to what Marx has referred to as alienation (*Entfremdung* in German), which describes the gap between workers' crafts and their actual work (Ollman, 1976). As the mid-twentieth century neared, scientific management became stigmatized in many academic circles, as scholars criticized the theory for its dehumanization of workers and neglect of social aspects of work and the workplace. Box 7.1 discusses a series of related studies, the Hawthorne Experiments, which suggest the need for a greater emphasis on the social dimensions of work.

Even though mechanization itself was less of a concern to Taylor's scientific management, its principles laid the foundation for the integration of technology in the management of work. Whereas Taylorism required control from management to guarantee that workers performed tasks with maximum efficiency, **Fordism** took the principles outlined in the scientific method a step further by introducing technology as a means to mechanizing, standardizing, and expediting work processes. At the Ford Motor Company, a system was developed where tasks were not only systematically divided to maximize efficiency but were, in addition, mechanically paced through an

Box 7.1   The Hawthorne Experiments

The Hawthorne Experiments were a group of research studies conducted between 1924 and 1932 at the Western Electric Company's Hawthorne plant in Chicago. Though their initial purpose was to find methods of increasing productivity through improvements to physical working conditions and remuneration (Pennock, 1930), the researchers concluded that social aspects of work had a much greater impact on worker efficiency (Carey, 1967, p. 404). It was less the physical changes themselves and more the perception among workers that they were receiving special treatment and attention from a concerned management that led to increased morale and productivity (Roethlisberger & Dickson, 2003). The studies proved very influential, and though their methods and conclusions have received considerable criticism (see, for example, Carey, 1967), they laid the foundation for the development of human relations management theory (Sonnenfeld, 1985).

assembly line, where each worker was responsible for a single, repetitive task. The first successfully mass-produced consumer good was Ford's Model T in 1908, which epitomized the coming of a new social and economic era with the introduction of a **moving assembly line** at the manufacturing facility in Highland Park, Michigan.

The moving assembly line quickly revolutionized production, increasing productivity tenfold and reducing prices dramatically (Hounshell, 1985). Edwards (1979) describes how the assembly line "functions as a system of technical control, which means that the entire production process, or large segments of it, are based on a technology which regulates the working pace and controls the labor process" (pp. 112–113).

Not only did technological advancements impact on work processes as they took place at Ford Motor Company and factories around the world, but they also led to major social change. The prices of consumer goods decreased considerably as a result of the mass production of goods, creating a larger consumer base. In addition, central to Ford's economic model was the notion that workers could become consumers of the goods they produced if their wages were increased (Sward, 1948). This led to a cycle of production and consumption that would further feed into the **mass consumption** of goods. Hence, the term **mass production** has come to describe more than just the mechanization of the process of production; it also describes the "interrelated technical, social, and political elements that sustain a unique model of social and economic organization based on the mass consumption of standardized goods" (Lewchuk, 2005).

This section discussed scientific management and Fordism as two means of production that were made possible through technological advances. Not only did technology replace workers, but when the assembly line is considered, technology dictated the pace and nature of work processes. These two means of production show how in these factories technology becomes more than an external actor: it becomes part of the social and economic system of production. As a continuation of this discussion, the next section demonstrates how technology continued to affect society in the late twentieth century by creating new work structures referred to as networked organizations.

The Networked Organization

Most organizations follow a formal structure or hierarchy to describe work roles and the functions associated with these roles. In these organizational structures, power is distributed from the top down to the bottom levels of the hierarchy. Organizations that follow such a structure are referred to as **hierarchical organizations** and are the most prevalent form of management, in particular among large businesses. These organizations use an **organizational chart** to depict employees' roles, which often includes lengthy descriptions of work functions and reporting relationships, indicating who reports to whom. Figure 7.1 depicts the 2009 organizational chart of the **Wikimedia Foundation**, which operates **Wikipedia**, among other wiki projects. At the top of the hierarchy in Figure 7.1 are the executive and deputy directors, who manage and coordinate the technology, the programs, and the finance divisions.

The widespread use of the Internet and related information and communication technologies (ICTs) has transformed how people work and, more importantly, communicate in organizations. Arguments about the nature of these transformations range from subtle changes in the speed, volume, and ways in which people communicate, to more radical changes consisting of a shift in how power is distributed, how decision making takes place, and how information flows (Bonabeau, 2009; Jarvenpaa & Ives, 1994). The term *networked organization* or network-centric organization is used to describe these new forms of work (Oberg & Walgenbach, 2008; Quan-Haase & Wellman, 2006). Networked organizations tend to have several unique features. Three key features include the following:

1. *Paperless work*: There is a trend toward the paperless office, where information and data are collected, stored, and managed in digital form (Sellen & Harper, 2002).
2. *Virtual teams*: These are teams that are located in different countries or continents that work on a project for specific periods of time, but never meet face-to-face. Once the project is completed, they are either assigned to a new project or they switch to a different job.

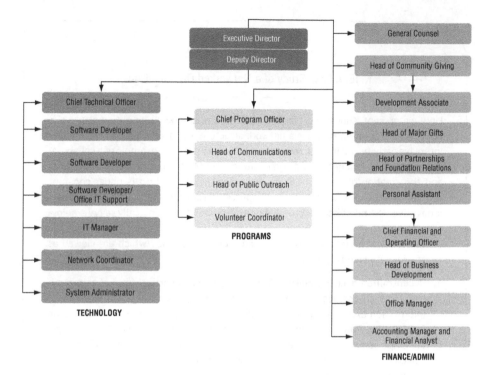

Figure 7.1 Wikimedia's Organizational Chart
Source: Wikipedia.org.

3. *Mobile reach*: The use of mobile technologies to facilitate communication. Smartphones, such as the BlackBerry and iPhone, have blurred the work–home boundary by providing flexibility, mobility, and constant accessibility to employees.

In addition to the changes that have taken place in terms of the use of technology, we can also observe changes in the **social structure** of these organizations. Box 7.2 presents a case study to illustrate the key characteristics of networked organizations. It is important to not only consider the pros of working in a networked organization but also to critically examine the cons of these new work structures, in particular in terms of surveillance practices, 24/7 availability, and changes in productivity.

Even though the concept of the networked organization has become popular, the results regarding the effects of ICTs on organizations are inconclusive (Markus & Robey, 1988). Certain kinds of effects, such as speed of communication and increased volume of messages, are apparent within most organizations (Oberg & Walgenbach, 2008; Sproull & Kiesler, 1991). With regard to changes in organizational structure, the results show that the effect of technology, as we have mentioned before, is not unidirectional and does not occur in predictable ways. ICTs have been found to both

Box 7.2   KME: A Case Study of a Networked Organization

Here we present Knowledge Management Enterprises (KME) as a case study of a high-tech corporation that has a network structure. Its involvement in knowledge-intensive activity and its high reliance on ICTs make it a good example of a collaborative community in a networked organization. For KME, the exchange of information and the creation of new knowledge are essential, as the firm is under constant competitive pressure to develop and improve its services and products. To remain innovative, KME relies heavily on collaboration among technologically savvy employees using ICTs.

KME shows the following three structural characteristics, which are viewed as central for networked organizations:

1. **Decentralized decision-making**: The company has a vertical form of communication, which enables workers rather than management to be at the centre of information exchanges (Bonabeau, 2009; Castells, 1996; Monge & Contractor, 1997, 2003). Bonabeau suggests that in these new forms of work, "many people are empowered to make their own independent decisions" (2009, p. 49) as they can collaborate in real time using various technologies for data gathering, editing, and dissemination.

2. **Local virtualities**: Even though KME employees are collocated, they tend to communicate via digital media, creating dense networks of exchange (Quan-Haase, 2009; Quan-Haase, Cothrel, & Wellman, 2005). The observation that people are no longer interacting visibly in public spaces does not necessarily reflect isolation, but it does show that not all interactions take place in person.

3. **Bridging connections**: At the company, digital means of communication facilitate external communications that bridge organizational boundaries, allowing for the creation of sparsely knit, boundary-spanning structures (Quan-Haase & Wellman, 2008; Sproull & Kiesler, 1991).

centralize and decentralize decision making, and to have no effect when one was expected (Barrett, Grant, & Wailes, 2006; Franz, Roby, & Koeblitz, 1986). For example, in her study of a team of scientists, Roehrs (1998) found that ICTs did not help in making peripheral actors more central in the information network. In this group, technology supported existing work relations and hierarchical structures, but it did not change in either positive or negative ways how people were connected to each other.

An important ethical consideration when examining networked organizations and their heavy reliance on technology is the social and health consequences from an always-on society. To what extent is being "technologically tethered" to our jobs beneficial (Murray and Rostis, 2007)?

Wireless technologies keep us always connected to our work, family, and friends 24/7, keeping us in a seemingly constant state of busyness—we are in a hyperconnected, hyper-digitized society (Quan-Haase & Wellman, 2006). When your employer provides you with a company cellphone and pays for your phone bills, these are often accompanied by occupational expectations around the clock. As a result of this fast pace and sense of over-connectivity, people often report feeling overwhelmed, exhausted, fragmented, and drained. Chesley (2014) has noted that individuals experience more distress when they have to take their work home with them and it overlaps with their personal lives. She found that work-related technology often facilitates interruptions and multitasking, which increase both perceived productivity and stress. When using such technologies at home for work purposes, employees reported more distress partly as a result of increased hours. This is alarming when considering how common taking work home has become in recent years. Based on a report from 2010, about 8 to 9 per cent of U.S. workers said they brought their work home with them (Eldridge & Wulff Pabilonia, 2010). This kind of alienation was captured in Brigid Schulte's new book *Overwhelmed* (2014), where she describes her busy life, constantly rushing from one thing to another. As a reporter for the *Washington Post*, Schulte has many work obligations and tight deadlines; at the same time, she is a mother and wants to be fully involved in her children's life. She is clearly not alone in her time angst; rather, this is a reflection of Nowotny's (1994) assertion 20 years earlier that modern citizens struggle to find time for themselves and as a result often feel rushed, unsatisfied, and perhaps even unproductive despite their never-ending busyness. Furthermore, work that follows you home is often unpaid and can set a precedent of perpetual accessibility in that your boss assumes you are available whenever needed. Moreover, cellphones can also reinforce a stigma of unproductivity when workers use them on the job, as employers often assume that workers are engaging in private matters via their devices while at work. However, Chesley (2014) also found that personal technology use at work has been linked to more effective stress management, as technologies often connect us to resources of social support or provide us with ways to temporarily mentally escape the pressures on the job. The key appears to be a balance of technology use at home and at work.

In conclusion, the analyses of how ICTs lead to organizational change show that this is a complex social process in which many cultural, organizational, and social factors need consideration. ICTs have not only shaped the structure of organizations but have also led to the creation of a new type of worker, one that moves away from industrial-based labour to immaterial labour.

The Immaterial Labour of Technology

Autonomous Marxism, also known as autonomism, is a political movement as well as a theoretical perspective that originated from 1960s Italian

Marxist ideology. Antonio Negri, Paolo Virno, and others later developed it into a variant of Marxist social theory with an emphasis on workers' ability to self-organize with the aim of creating changes in the workplace and throughout society at large. The term *autonome* has Greek roots and refers to living within society, following one's own rules.

One of the key thinkers of the autonomous movement was Lazzarato (1996), whose major contribution to social theory was to recognize the social and work changes taking place in certain sectors of the economy. He observed that since the 1960s, new forms of labour had been emerging that could no longer be classified as industrial based but, rather, existed around the outputs of the industrial era. These changes in labour resulted from new developments within the production system. With the new systems of production in place, the market was inundated with inexpensive consumer goods. Once most Americans owned a Model T, for example, Ford Motor Company saw demand stall. It was at this point that producers realized that an important part of the production cycle was to create **markets** for their products. For example, General Motors, on the advice of Alfred Sloan, developed five lines of cars—Chevrolet, Pontiac, Oldsmobile, Buick, and Cadillac—that increased in price, reflecting the owners' economic and social status; this was referred to as the *ladder of success*. As a result, an entire industry emerged around marketing, which includes branding a product, developing an advertisement campaign, and finding consumer or niche markets. Lazzarato (1996) employed the term **immaterial labour** to describe the industries that support industrial work and encompass "the labor that produces the informational and cultural content of the commodity" (p. 133). Lazzarato (1996) further distinguished between two kinds of immaterial labour.

The first kind of immaterial labour describes labour that does not entail manual labour. Lazzarato (1996) observed that in addition to the work being done in factories, an increasing number of workers were being employed to perform information-related tasks. The shift consisted of these new workers focusing on "selling" rather than "manufacturing" products. The term **white-collar worker** was introduced to describe these professionals or educated workers. The work they perform is "immediately collective, and we might say that it exists only in the form of networks and flows" (p. 136). And the move away from manufacturing toward a service or information economy is often described as **post-Fordist** or **post-industrial**.

Bell (1973) characterized this kind of post-industrial society as consisting of three core elements: (1) an increase in services over manufacturing; (2) a dominance of science-based industries; and (3) the creation of a new social class—the **technical** or **technocratic elite**—who have expertise in the technical areas. Later, with the technology boom of the 1990s, Richard Florida introduced the term *the creative class* to describe workers in the high-tech sector (Florida, 2001; Reese, Faist, & Sands, 2010). He sees these workers as central for the economic development of post-industrial cities in North America because they are usually educated, creative, open to new ideas, and have higher-than-average incomes.

The second kind of immaterial labour describes the activities and processes that are necessary to shape culture, fashion, tastes, consumer behaviours, and public opinion. Marketing firms, such as the Kaplan Thaler Group, became a part of North American culture through their clever and pervasive branding approach. For example, in 1999 only 10 per cent of Americans were aware of the Aflac brand, an insurance company. With a series of commercials featuring the "Aflac Duck," the Kaplan Thaler Group increased Aflac's brand awareness to 94 per cent and sales grew by 55 per cent. Now the Aflac Duck has become a part of American popular culture. The marketing strategy that the Kaplan Thaler Group used is comprehensive and includes, in addition to traditional television and radio advertisements, social media presence via a Facebook page, a Twitter account, and YouTube videos, demonstrating a huge change in the strategy used to sell products to consumers.

In the industrial era, technology radically transformed the nature and pace of work. By contrast, in the post-industrial society, technology had a much more pervasive effect on work itself, creating a radically new form of work. Immaterial labour directly exists in relation to technology, which helps in creating, transmitting, repackaging, and diffusing information about products on a global scale (Dyer-Witheford, 2001). The aim is no longer to produce new merchandise but to create a savvy marketing strategy around a product, which is aimed at promoting and selling it. It was not technology alone that created these changes, though: the social and political landscape was such that it allowed for these social transformations to occur. In the next section, we will discuss the value of user-generated content and resulting unpaid immaterial labour as it takes place in Web 2.0 environments.

The Value of User-Generated Content and Unwaged Immaterial Labour

Immaterial labour is also reflected in the type of work that users in **Web 2.0** environments perform. Web 2.0 developed as an alternative form of communicating on the Web; instead of information being static, Web 2.0 offers a range of features that facilitate, among other things, interactivity, collaboration, and feedback.

At the centre of Web 2.0 is the concept of **user-generated content**, or **UGC**, which characterizes a shift from content being centrally produced and distributed to a model where it is created, produced, and edited by **end-users**. The value of user-generated content is in most cases not associated with a price tag because those who produce content are not paid. In contrast to immaterial labour that takes place in the context of paid work, users of social media who generate content, such as users of Flickr or Twitter, do not get paid. They are motivated to participate because they are a part of a shared, collaborative community (Bell, 1973; Bruns, 2008). The affective relationships that are formed in the context of the community are central to continued participation. There are also personal gains to be made through membership. Members of the community can become central figures with strong reputations for their expertise through such functions as code development, community coordination, or administrative service.

Box 7.3 discusses Facebook as an example of a service that relies on Web 2.0 immaterial labour.

Box 7.3   Facebook as Web 2.0 Immaterial Labour

Facebook is a good example of a Web 2.0 application that is based on immaterial labour. In 2010, there were 500 million worldwide users of Facebook, of which Canada had the highest penetration rate. As of 2015, there were 1.44 billion monthly active users (Facebook, 2015), with over 19 million Canadians—more than half of the national population—checking their pages each month. According to Jordan Banks, the managing director of Facebook Canada (Oliveira, 2013), daily Facebook usage by Canadians is about 13 per cent above the average worldwide: "One of the things is the percentage of monthly users that come back daily. Sixty-one per cent is pretty much the global average; in the U.S. that number is somewhere around 70 per cent and in Canada it's 74 per cent."

Young Canadians use Facebook more than any other communication technology, including email, texting, and cellphones, and have an average of 190 Facebook friends in comparison to 130 for the rest of the world (Moretti, 2010). Facebook as a corporation provides the infrastructure for users to add personal information. In turn, users generate content daily for other users by adding pictures, writing on friends' walls, adding comments to posts, rating posts, and linking to internal and external information. While most users would not consider this work but, rather, art, pleasure, fun, and leisure time, this investment of time and content constitutes revenue for Facebook. In July 2014, Facebook was valued at about US$192 billion—a disproportionate amount for a social networking tool that facilitates social exchanges. Its value becomes quickly apparent when we examine the capital invested into Facebook. For example, Microsoft invested a total of US$240 million for a slim 1.6 per cent stake (Stone, 2007).

What are the assets that give Facebook such high value? The most valued asset is the revenues gained through direct advertisement to users. Users are exposed to a series of advertisements, often tagged as "sponsored," simply by logging on to the service. A recent study found that Canadians are interacting frequently with brands that have a presence on social media sites. Of the estimated 19 million Canadians on Facebook in 2014, nearly 2.5 million are fans of the Tim Hortons Facebook profile. Interestingly, a recent report found that in 2012 fast food restaurants placed a total of six billion ads on Facebook, which added up to 19 per cent of their online advertising campaigns. Two companies—Dunkin' Donuts and Wendy's—went so far as to place more than half of their online ads on Facebook (Harris et al., 2013). And Starbucks reached 35 million Facebook likes and 4.2 million Twitter followers, making it the most popular fast food brand (Harris et al., 2013). This represents a drastic increase in the reliance on social media for advertising brands or specific products and shows the increasing relevance of social media as a means to reach out to consumers.

Second, Facebook has a strong influence on consumers because their users can recommend products to their friends directly. Sheryl Sandberg (as quoted in Moretti, 2010), who is Facebook's chief operating officer, asserted that "[a] recommendation by a friend is the best kind of marketing," showing the power of peer-to-peer recommendations. The third value of Facebook is that it allows third parties, such as marketing companies, to better understand users and consumers through their interactions with the content. Facebook provides data on users' opinions about content and their likes and dislikes of advertisements, companies, and products. This is very much the kind of information that would be difficult for marketers to obtain from such large numbers of individuals. About 50 per cent of Canadians spent no less than an hour on Facebook every day updating their profiles, posting on friends' walls, and adding content. To some extent, Facebook users are "working" while on social network sites by providing important information for marketers about product trends, consumer preferences and opinions, and the value of products.

The labour that takes place in Web 2.0 environments is unique because it is unpaid. People who actively participate in these environments contribute because they feel personally involved. As Sundén (2003) argued, people **write themselves into being** on social media and express, through their digital footprint, their identity, their social webs, and their daily activities. Profiles become extensions of people's identities (Hogan & Quan-Haase, 2010). In this context, users' expression of self becomes closely interlinked with, or almost inseparable from, their digital labour.

The Role of the Prosumer

ICTs have not only changed the nature of labour; they have also profoundly modified the relationship among the consumer, the producer, and the product. The first to acknowledge this change was Alvin Toffler (1970, 1980), who introduced the concept of **prosumer** or produser in the 1980s to describe the merging of *producer* and *consumer*. Consumers become active in the production process by performing tasks that used to be delegated to producers. Many do-it-yourself (DIY) kits are available that allow consumers to be empowered and independent from producers. For example, the IKEA model of putting furniture together oneself without the help of a service person, sometimes accompanied by high levels of frustration and low levels of success, puts this process into the hands of consumers.

Following Toffler, in 2006 Don Tapscott and Anthony Williams introduced the idea of *prosumption* by combining the words *production* and *consumption*. **Prosumption** describes new modes of production where customers play a central role in the design, development, and use of the end product (Tapscott & Williams, 2006). An example is *Second Life*, a virtual world in which its users are given a great degree of freedom to shape the product by creating their own avatars and building digital artifacts in a 3D environment. In prosumption business models, corporations will often provide only the infrastructure, and prosumers will be in charge of producing content. In these cases, prosumers not only are co-producers but often also drive the creation of the product because there would be no product without their active participation.

Produsage is a term coined by Axel Bruns (2008) and is a modification to the concept of prosumption. Bruns uses the term *produsage* to describe the shift in the mode of production that is characteristic of the labour taking place within Web 2.0 environments. This new model blurs the line between producers and consumers and empowers users as they take control over the production and the distribution of content. In the produsage model, the end goal is the creation of an **information commons** (Hippel, 2005), which provides the social structure for supporting the core activities of the community, such as sharing, collaborating, negotiating, and developing. This information commons—an amalgamation of nodes consisting of content, users, and producers—then ultimately allows the information to continue to be relevant and up-to-date in the context of the community. Any online platform in which people actively collaborate to generate content can be considered an information commons, including Wikipedia, Facebook, and Flickr.

Most of the labour performed by produsage communities is offered for free, without expectation of a wage, benefits, or any other kind of return. This kind of work differs fundamentally from the kind of work done by waged immaterial labourers in corporate environments, as discussed in the section earlier in the chapter. Involvement in produsage communities is motivated by an interest in the content itself, by the affective relations that develop among participants in a produsage project, and by the satisfaction of creating a product that will serve the community.

There are exceptions, however, as with Amazon's Mechanical Turk (see www.mturk.com/mturk/welcome), which pays participants for performing small problem-oriented tasks. Here, a global workforce comes together to perform any digital task necessary, from responding to surveys, to analyzing marketing strategies, to providing suggestions for slogans. Mechanical Turk pays its employees per task and facilitates access to a global, diverse, and on-demand workforce that has no contracts, no benefits, no job security, no boss, and no structure.

Preconditions of Produsage

Central to our understanding of collective action and hence collaborative content production is the coming together of technical possibilities, social organization, and collective features. To understand the processes better, Bruns (2008) has created a model of produsage by describing four preconditions and four key principles of distributed and collaborative content production.

Table 7.1 outlines the four preconditions, and shows how, in an ideal online community, ownership is shared and all members have equal opportunities to contribute.

Key Principles of Produsage

Once the preconditions outlined in Table 7.1 are in place, open, participatory communities can form to produce content collaboratively. Bruns (2008) proposes four key principles that are characteristic of different produsage projects. Not all principles are present in all produsage projects, but at least some of them need to be in place for such projects to be successful. The four key principles are highlighted in Table 7.2.

Table 7.1 Preconditions of Bruns's Model of Produsage

Preconditions of Produsage	Key Features
1. Probabilistic, not directed, problem solving	• Problems are not solved from the top down, as in traditional bureaucratic organizations. This leads to what Bauwens (2005) has described as **holoptism**, an open concept to problem solving, where all members of the group have equal insight into all components of the problem. • All members are volunteers. • No centralized decision-making occurs. • Problems get solved when they are identified as relevant by the community. • All work relentlessly to find solutions.
2. Equipotentiality, not hierarchy	• In **equipotentiality**, all members have the ability and possibility of contributing equally to the end result. • Participation is all inclusive, and members provide expertise on any aspect of the project.
3. Granular, not composite tasks	• When projects require little administration and have independent tasks, project completion goes faster when many people work simultaneously.
4. Shared, not owned content	• Information flows freely and is shared, distributed, and re-used in a fair manner among members. • Each member represents an equal node in the network. • Data are shared by both providing and consuming resources.

Table 7.2 Principles of Bruns's Model of Produsage

Principles of Produsage	Key Features
1. Open participation, communal evaluation	• The idea or contribution is proposed, then evaluated by the community. • Evaluation by multiple community members leads toward a better outcome. • Communities are highly inclusive and heterogeneous.
2. Fluid heterarchy, ad hoc meritocracy	• Communities are based on input and expertise. • Individual participation occurs when needed and when expertise aligns to a project. • Individuals or small teams can make decisions regarding projects without top-down approval.
3. Unfinished artifacts, continuing process	• The fluid nature of the organization naturally leads to projects that do not yield finished end projects. • Projects remain works-in-progress, with members continuing to improve the product.
4. Common property, individual rewards	• Content created by the community is then available to all members, regardless of their participation in the project. • Projects that grow out of or expand upon the original are encouraged. • Community-based copyright standards have been created to guarantee intellectual property rights.

Bruns (2008) proposed the four preconditions and the four key principles as a means to analyze work and work structures as they take place in digital environments.

It is important to also note the roots of some of these concepts. The concept of ad hoc meritocracy comes from the work of Alvin Toffler (1970), who described the coming of **adhocracy** as a new form of organization. In adhocracy, individuals or teams are assembled as they are needed to solve narrowly defined, short-term problems instead of having permanently assigned roles and functions based on organizational charts, as described in the earlier section on the networked organization. In the context of produsage, these ad hoc teams are also based on the reputation that participants build as leaders and as experts in the community; hence, participation and relevance are based on merit.

While produsage communities do not follow strict hierarchies, they still require some form of regulation to operate. Regulations are particularly important to solve disputes among contributors. For example, in Wikipedia it is common for individuals or groups to emerge with divergent views on sensitive or controversial topics. When Michael Jackson died on 25 June 2009, his Wikipedia page was being constantly updated (about 100–200 changes per day). A battle emerged between those who revered him and wanted to portray him in the best possible light and those who were critical of him and wanted to emphasize the accusations of child molestation. To help the Wikipedia community to function smoothly, a comprehensive list of rules has been developed that users need to follow if they do not want to be banned from participation. There are a number of ways in which disputes among participants can be solved. For example, participants can discuss their differences "through comments and annotations 'in the margins,' and by the repeated overwriting of existing passages in a shared effort to arrive at a better representation of communally held values and ideas" (Bruns, 2008, p. 27). As well, people may look at the history of individual entries and participants' past contributions to determine the evolution of the content. The most fundamental principle guiding participation in Wikipedia is the **neutral point of view (NPOV)**, which expects participants to represent in each article "fairly, proportionately, and as far as possible without bias, all significant views that have been published by reliable sources" (Wikipedia, 2011). Hence, a combination of community- and technology-based processes provides the necessary context for produsage communities to function.

When we examine the extreme case of unfinished artifacts, it is central to look at software that is referred to as **perpetual beta**. This is software released to users under the understanding that it is incomplete and in a state of improvement. The main rationale for releasing software before its completion is to receive feedback from users as the product is being developed and to alter the website or service to reflect some of the suggestions made by users.[1] Figure 7.2 shows the key characteristics of projects that work with perpetual

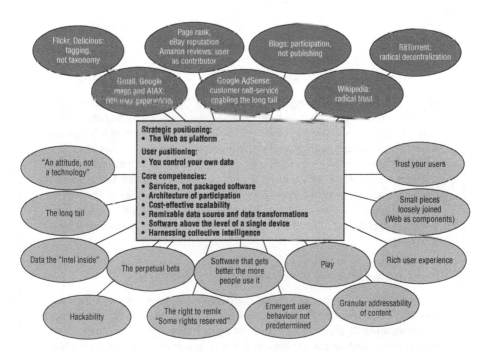

Figure 7.2 Characteristics of Perpetual Beta

Source: Tim O'Reilly, "What Is Web 2.0?," http://oreilly.com/pub/a/web2/archive/what-is-web-20.html?page=1. © 2005 O'Reilly Media, Inc. All rights reserved. Used with permission.

beta releases. O'Reilly (2005), who coined the term *Web 2.0*, argues that it also makes sense to continually release new versions and develop the software in the open because software is in a constant state of change; as a result, setting a release deadline only compromises the product's quality.

Makerspaces: The DIY Community Gone Viral

The Internet and the use of ICTs have also lent themselves well to another type of community: makers. The maker community is a **subculture** of do-it-yourselfers who work together on various projects, often involving new and upcoming technologies. **Makerspaces**, also called hackerspaces or fab labs, are the meeting places of these communities and usually include workbenches and desk space, and tools for woodworking, metal working, and electronics (Anderson, 2012). There is often a nominal monthly fee to belong to a makerspace, which grants you round-the-clock access not only to the space but also to the tools that have either been contributed by other community members or purchased with members' dues. Some of the most common technologies found in makerspaces are laser-cutters and **3D printers**, whose changing role in society is discussed in Box 7.4.

Box 7.4   3D Printing and Its Social Implications

3D printers are one technology that has the potential to change people's buying and selling habits. By enabling people to design, duplicate, and create objects that they would previously have purchased, the 3D printing revolution could change consumerism. 3D printers work by an additive process, placing small layers of material (often ABS plastic, a low-cost engineering plastic that is easy to machine fabricate) down until the entire object is recreated from a single digital file. Often found in makerspaces, and becoming common in both public and academic libraries, 3D printers let people to print everything from that missing IKEA screw to jewellery, and even human body parts. This short video demonstrates how to print a digital file on a 3D printer:

> How does 3D printing work?:
> www.youtube.com/watch?v=dnlVrLqrEI8

Of course, with any new technology there are ethical questions that arise, safety concerns that emerge, and lessons to be learned. One of the main debates that has arisen regarding 3D printing is the ability of a user to create potentially harmful and illegal objects, such as guns, in the comfort of their own home. When a U.S. citizen first uploaded to the Web the instructions for printing a gun, known as the Liberator, with a 3D printer in 2013, the U.S. government was quick to remove the files, but not before they had been downloaded more than 100,000 times (Greenburg, 2014). Questions regarding the ethics of using 3D printers to fabricate guns, in the larger context of gun laws and restrictions in Canada, were raised when the Liberator gun was replicated in the Critical Making Lab at the University of Toronto. An article from *The Toronto Star*, available at www.thestar.com/news/gta/2013/07/03/u_of_t_labs_3d_printer_gun_raises_disturbing_questions.html, discusses how anyone can now print a gun and how this may affect existing regulations around gun ownership.

3D printing also has a positive side: it drastically reduces **technological waste**. ABS plastic, and other materials that are used in these printers, can be melted down and re-used to make other objects. Old toys, household goods, and even milk jugs can be melted down and made into filament for 3D printers, bringing new meaning to the phrase "everything old is new again" (Gilpin, 2014). Another plus is convenience—for example, imagine going camping and being able to print any object you may have forgotten.

3D printing is one technology that is often found in makerspaces, but recently more regular consumers have started purchasing the technology as well. As a result of having to maintain various cutting-edge technologies, makerspaces are expensive to run, and the various projects that take place within them can also prove to be costly. One solution to this problem has been the development of online **crowdfunding** platforms such as **KickStarter**. Chris Anderson (2012) notes three ways that crowdfunding platforms provide solutions for makers: (1) they move the revenue stream for a project forward in time, by turning sales into pre-sales, (2) they turn the customer base into a community through a sense of participation in a project and word-of-mouth about its successes; and (3) they complete market research on an idea or concept for the makers before they have invested in bringing the project to its completion. The makerspace community would not exist in the same capacity if it were not for the Internet and various social media applications. Makers come together and participate in maker faires, **hack-a-thons,** and coding conferences both online and offline to support each other in building, creating, destroying, and rebuilding. Information on these gatherings is posted and distributed online. In a well-known TED Talk (link below), *Make Magazine* founder Dale Dougherty explains the details and social benefits of makerspaces.

"We Are Makers"
www.ted.com/talks/dale_dougherty_we_are_makers

Conclusions

This chapter has shown that the relationship between technology and work is not at all straightforward. The introduction of mechanized technologies during the Industrial Revolution alienated labourers from their work. Prior to industrialization, tools had been a part of craftsmanship, and had been used as extensions of the human body. Industrialization brought about radical change by directly substituting human labour with machinery, as well as skilled workers with cheap labour. With scientific management, the process of deskilling continued with further standardization and division of labour. Fordism not only took deskilling to the next level but introduced technology as a means of controlling work processes. Under these conditions, workers no longer had agency over their work; instead, they became simply a cog in the wheel.

Yet in post-industrial societies, technology is no longer a substitute for the worker but a vehicle that allows individuals to apply information-based skills in order to develop, produce, and enhance their labour. The advent of immaterial labour represented a turning point, where instead of further deskilling workers, technology created labour around the creation, transmission, diffusion, and repackaging of information. Yet again this has led to both positive and negative changes in workers' daily routines.

In Web 2.0 environments, we see new forms of digital labour emerge through participation in produsage projects. These new forms of work are in stark opposition to hierarchical forms of organizations in that they emphasize collaboration, sharing of resources, and increased communication. Technological advances have reshaped the nature of work as well as the conditions and relations within these environments. Nonetheless, we learn that ICTs can change social structures in organizations toward networked forms of work. In many corporations, however, ICTs have only become integrated into work routines without necessarily fundamentally changing hierarchical communication structures.

The introduction of technologies into the workplace has eliminated traditional professions yet has also created new vocations. Information technologies in particular can also become an integral component of modern collaborative work, which connect a new generation of globalized workers and information-hungry consumers in order that they may embark on new projects and situations. Indeed, within our twenty-first-century information society, communities themselves have taken on an increasingly participative role in determining the effectiveness and applicability of technology. A good example of this is the creation of makerspaces, digital and physical places where people of all ages come together to explore, design, and literally make objects. This leads to close interactions of the digital global sphere with the local and the emergence of materiality as an important dimension of technological design. As we shall discuss in later chapters, the conditions upon which the success of a technology rests often reside within the socio-economic and cultural dynamics inherent within a community.

Questions for Critical Thought

1. Explain the concept of Neo-Luddism and trace its roots to the Luddite movement in Industrial Revolution—era England.

2. Using Flickr as an example, discuss how the concept of immaterial labour helps explain Web 2.0 applications.

3. Explain how the concept of the networked organization contrasts with hierarchical forms of work. Do you think that some level of organizational structure is still needed in organizations for the purpose of coordination? Explain.

4. Is it possible to manage and control the immaterial labour performed by workers in the twenty-first century in a similar manner as the labour performed by industrial workers was controlled in the nineteenth and twentieth centuries?

Suggested Readings

Anderson, C. (2012). *Makers: The new industrial revolution*. New York: Crown Business. This book, written by the editor of *Wired* Magazine, explains the new revolution that open-source design and 3Dprinting has brought about.

Brown, B., & Quan-Haase, A. (2013). "A workers' inquiry 2.0": An ethnographic method for the study of produsage in social media contexts. *TripleC, 10*(2). Retrieved from www.triple-c.se/. A new method for the study of immaterial labour in Web 2.0 environments is outlined and its merits discussed.

Bruns, A. (2008). *Blogs, Wikipedia, Second Life, and beyond: From production to produsage*. New York: Peter Lang. The author discusses the term *produsage* in great detail and presents current practices of produsage.

Dyer-Witheford, N. (2001). Empire, immaterial labor, the new combinations, and the global worker. *Rethinking Marxism, 13*(3/4), 70—80. This article addresses the complexity of immaterial labour and its relation to the global worker.

Shirky, C. (2008). *Here comes everybody: The power of organizing without organizations*. New York: Penguin Press. This book shows how the Internet has changed the publishing industry by allowing consumers to be active producers, in a similar manner as the printing press did in the fifteenth century.

Tappscott, D., & Williams, A.D. (2006). *Wikinomics: How mass collaboration changes everything*. New York: Portfolio. This book explains how new forms of virtual collaboration are a powerful means of working together.

Online Resources

The Fibreculture Journal
http://fibreculturejournal.org/
This journal publishes cutting-edge research on digital media, networks, and transdisciplinary critique.

The Foundation for P2P Alternatives
http://p2pfoundation.net/

> The mandate of the foundation is to obtain a better understanding of the social impact of peer-to-peer technology and thought.

Mashable
http://mashable.com/

> The site provides up-to-date information on the technology industry.

Mute Magazine
www.metamute.org/

> The key topics of Mute Magazine are culture, arts, and politics as they take place online.

Produsage
http://produsage.org/

> This resource is maintained by Axel Bruns and provides a general overview of the theory of produsage.

Technology and Inequality

Learning Objectives

◎ to discuss how differences in technology ownership and know-how lead to social, economic, and cultural inequality;

◎ to critically examine how the phenomenon of the digital divide has transformed from a problem solely of access to one linked to digital skills and social media adoption;

◎ to understand the global digital divide and the micro- and macro-level barriers that exist in developing nations with regard to access to and use of technology;

◎ to rethink the meaning of the term *technology transfer* as it applies to developing nations;

◎ to question the usefulness of the digital divide framework in the context of policy by reviewing critical perspectives.

Introduction

In this chapter, we address issues of inequality as they play out in technological use, implementation, and impact. Understanding technological inequality is of great importance to researchers, policy-makers, and politicians because technology provides educational, political, and economic advantages, creating power imbalances and, potentially, conflict among social groups. This chapter specifically examines digital inequality as a pressing issue of our times: what are the social consequences for those disconnected from the Internet? While researchers agree on the importance of studying the digital divide, much controversy still surrounds its definition (Epstein, Nisbet, & Gillespie, 2011; Stevenson, 2009; Vehovar, Sicherl, Husing, & Donicar, 2009). This chapter covers the historical developments of the digital divide concept, examines the complexity of its measurement, and considers its relevance to policy in Canada and the United States. A key argument is that the use of digital technologies not only reflects access but also reveals differences in skill level. Many individuals, despite having access to digital technologies, cannot take full advantage of the resources available to them online because they do not know how to navigate and evaluate the endless number of resources available. We also take a closer look at recent arguments that the digital divide extends to the use of social media sites. These sites provide individuals with a means of staying up to date with the news, connecting with their social networks, and accessing valuable information and cultural resources. What happens to those individuals who do not have access to social media or do not fully comprehend its relevance in society?

We also cover the *global digital divide*, which describes the gap in *access* to and use of the Internet that exists between **developing** and **developed nations**. Many developing nations, such as Somalia, continue to struggle in their effort to become digital, having to overcome numerous barriers of access, skill, and infrastructure. Nonetheless, penetration rates have increased in these nations in an unexpected way; surprisingly, individuals often gain access to the Internet not through computers but through cellphones. We discuss China as a prime example of a **newly industrializing nation** that has struggled to join the **information society** and in the process has developed an ambivalent relationship with the Internet. There are currently 618 million Internet users in China according to the China Internet Network Information Center (2014), and this represents less than half of the country's population. This means that there are a further 618 million or so Chinese citizens who could potentially go online in the next decade. The Chinese example shows how the impact of the Internet on society is complex and cannot be limited to a single sphere. The chapter ends with a critical reflection on and a series of conclusions about our current state of knowledge regarding the Internet's role in creating social change.

The Digital Divide

The **digital divide** describes discrepancies between social groups in access to, use of, and empowerment by networked computers and other digital tools. Initially, policy-makers and scholars used the term to describe the gap in ownership of stand-alone personal computers that existed among various social groups. However, with the rapid expansion in the networking of computers in the 1990s, the term *digital divide* came to denote access to digital resources primarily via computers but also via cellphones, **phablets**, laptops, and tablets (Epstein et al., 2011; Stevenson, 2009; Vehovar et al., 2009). The term gained particular prominence when, in a 1996 speech, U.S. president Bill Clinton and U.S. vice president Al Gore used the term to emphasize the social and technological challenges presented to America in the **information age**, where a gap would emerge between the **haves** and **have-nots**. Closing the digital divide turned into a key political target within the North American policy framework (Epstein et al., 2011).

Issues of the digital divide have been phrased in terms of how the Internet provides opportunities to overcome or exacerbate existing inequalities. Norris (2001) writes about how "digital networks have the potential to broaden and enhance access to information and communications for remote rural areas and poorer neighbourhoods, to strengthen the process of democratization under transitional regimes, and to ameliorate the endemic problems of poverty in the developing world" (p. 6). Consequently, questions regarding the digital divide are of major concern to all citizens because the economic, cultural, and social possibilities of individuals and nations can depend on people's ability to leverage digital technologies and participate in the information age. Also important to consider and critically assess are the early studies of the digital divide and their focus on access. These studies show how the debate around the digital divide has changed over time as well as the kinds of challenges early users of the Web needed to overcome, including high costs for computers and modems.

Early Studies of Penetration Rates

Early studies of the digital divide were primarily concerned with issues surrounding access. Key to examining **access** has been an assessment of the Internet's **penetration rate** in various social groups. Two U.S. surveys conducted in 1995 and 1998 by the **National Telecommunications and Information Administration** (NTIA) pointed out alarming differences in Internet penetration rates based on age, gender, education, rural/urban regions, single-/dual-parent households, ethnicity, and income (Epstein et al., 2011). The results show that inequalities existent in society are reflected in Internet usage, with those online being primarily white, younger males with higher socio-economic status living in urban areas.

The U.S. debate was mirrored in Canada, where a number of surveys were conducted in the mid-1990s to assess the extent to which Canadians were connected. A Statistics Canada report investigated in more detail the effect of income on connectivity (Dickinson & Sciadas, 1996). A comparison of 1994 and 1995 household penetration rates for various *information and communication technologies* (ICTs) shows two trends: (1) telephone and cable both have reached high penetration rates and these are stable; and (2) an increase can be observed in the availability of computers and modems. In 1994, 99 per cent of Canadian households had a telephone, 74 per cent had cable, 25 per cent had a computer, and only 8 per cent had a modem.[1] By contrast, in the 1995 data 99 per cent had telephones, 73 per cent had cable, 29 per cent owned a computer, and 12 per cent had a modem. While there is a demonstrated increase in computer and modem ownership within the one-year period, it remains unclear what social groups are adopting these technologies and which are falling behind.

For this purpose, the penetration rates for ICTs were calculated separately for each **income quartile** (see Table 8.1). Four income quartiles were examined in the study: (1) less than C$21,398; (2) C$21,398–C$39,949; (3) C$39,950–C$63,034; and (4) above C$63,034. Table 8.1 shows that for telephone and cable penetration rates little to no differences can be observed between the high- and low-income quartiles. By contrast, income

Table 8.1 Penetration Rates and Income, 1995

	Income Quartiles				
	Bottom	**Second**	**Third**	**Top**	**All**
	<$21,398	$21,398–$39,949	$39,950–$63,034	>$63,034	%
Telephone	96	99	99	99	98
Cable	64	70	77	82	73
Computer	12	20	32	50	29
Modem*	5	7	14	22	12

* Average annual rates compounded

Source: Dickinson, P. & Sciadas, G. (1996). *Access to the Information Highway.* Statistics Canada Report. Retrieved from www. statcan.gc.ca/pub/63f0002x/63f0002x1996009-eng.pdf. Reproduced and distributed on an "as is" basis with the permission of Statistics Canada.

is strongly associated with both computer and modem penetration rates. In the highest income quartile—those who earn more than C$63,034 a year—computer and modem ownership were 50 per cent and 22 per cent, respectively. Individuals in the lowest income quartile—those who make less than C$21,398 a year—report much lower percentages of computer and modem ownership: 12 per cent and 5 per cent, respectively. Dickinson and Sciadas (1996) raise the issue of inequality: "As penetration rates rise, households that can least afford their own terminals will make up a larger proportion of the 'have-nots'" (p. 6). We conclude that in the 1990s affordability was one of the main constraints to household ownership of a computer and modem.

In the Statistics Canada report discussed above (1996), similar gaps were found along other key socio-economic variables. For example, when the head of the household was employed, computer ownership was 38 per cent, while only 21 per cent and 13 per cent of those unemployed or out of the labour force, respectively, reported owning a computer. Households where the head had a university degree were six times as likely to own a computer as households where the head had less than a grade 9 education. Stark differences in penetration rate are also observed between rural and urban areas: 22 per cent and 6 per cent of rural residents owned a computer and modem, respectively, while 30 per cent and 13 per cent of urban residents owned a computer and modem, respectively.

What conclusions can we draw based on early analyses of Internet penetration rates in Canada and the United States? First, access to the Internet reflects existing inequalities in society, with income, employment, education, ethnicity, rural/urban location, and age all affecting adoption patterns. This is not surprising, as economic resources are required to purchase a computer and to connect to the Web via an Internet service provider (ISP). Also, education and age play a role because users need skills to utilize a computer and navigate the Internet. This was particularly the case in the early 1990s when graphical Web browsers, such as Chrome, Safari, and Explorer, did not yet exist to facilitate the navigation and retrieval of content. Second, the gap in access may exacerbate existing inequalities by putting the "have-nots" at a disadvantage over the "haves" in terms of information, connectivity, and skills. Since these early studies of the digital divide, a number of changes have occurred. Of particular relevance have been initiatives specifically aimed at decreasing digital inequality.

Closing the Digital Divide

The large discrepancies in access to the Internet brought the issue of the digital divide into public consciousness and triggered new policies targeted at increasing digital inclusion. What kinds of interventions were devised to address issues of the digital divide? Programs were created not only by governments but in parallel by non-profit organizations and private funding agencies. One of the government-led interventions in Canada was the Canadian Advanced Network and Research for Industry and Education, or CANARIE. Founded in 1993 and based in Ottawa, CANARIE (2010) is a fibre-optic and satellite data network that "facilitates leading-edge research and big science across Canada and around the world." CANARIE's networking capabilities allow researchers to collaboratively analyze data that can lead to discoveries in the realms of education, health sciences, and technology. Box 8.1 shows an example of a U.S.-based government initiative that worked closely with schools and libraries.

Box 8.1   E-Rate

In the United States, **E-Rate** was established in 1997 to provide schools and libraries with affordable access to the Internet. E-Rate is the abbreviation for the Schools and Libraries Program of the Universal Service Fund, which is administered under the direction of the Federal Communications Commission (FCC). E-Rate is built on the concept that "technology has great power to enhance education" (Federal Communications Commission [FCC], 2004).[2] The program is designed chiefly to assist American schools and libraries in acquiring telecommunications equipment and services. E-Rate has been effective in providing Internet access in public classrooms and in libraries. Indeed, the number of public classrooms with Internet access increased from 14 per cent in 1996 to 95 per cent in 2005 (Education and Library Networks Coalition, 2007). E-Rate provides discounts of 20 to 90 per cent to schools and libraries, depending on poverty levels. However, E-Rate does not cover expenditures such as hardware, software, or staff training (Puma, Chaplin, & Pape, 2000). The program has spent a total of US$19 billion on discount services since its inception.

Box 8.1 shows the range of initiatives developed in the U.S. with the aim of closing the digital divide. Despite the good intentions of such initiatives, the digital divide is a complex problem that cannot easily be solved with the provision of infrastructure, computing resources, and funds. What is the effectiveness of these initiatives and can they effect real social change? Have penetration rates increased along the lines of inequality?

While the gap in access to the Internet has shrunk considerably since the mid-1990s, scholars have identified disparities among users in terms of the types of access they have to the Web (dial-up, broadband, or wireless), their knowledge and skills when online, and the variation in online activities they perform (Vehovar et al., 2009). Mossberger, Tolbert, and Stansbury write that "[i]f some individuals cannot use computer technology, then all the access in the world will do no good. Further, if people cannot find the assistance they need to use the technology, then access alone does little to alleviate the problem" (2003, p. 39). Hence, access to the Internet may be less of a concern over time in Canada and the United States, but differences among Internet users in terms of their skill level continue to be problematic. As a result, alternative definitions of the digital divide have been proposed that better reflect the complexity of the concept. These definitions look at the digital divide beyond penetration rates and examine it in terms of the kinds of benefits obtained from Internet use.

One alternative definition is the one proposed by Mossberger, Tolbert, and Stansbury (2003), where the authors identify four central components of the digital divide: (1) the access divide, (2) the skills divide, (3) the economic opportunity divide, and (4) the democratic divide. We discuss each dimension next and how it affects individuals' lives and their opportunity to leverage resources.

The Access Divide

The access divide examines whether or not a person has access to the Internet and the type of access as well as the location and frequency of use. In the early days of the Internet, having a dial-up connection provided access to a wealth of information. This is no longer the case because the Internet has evolved from a primarily text-based information repository to a multi-media immersive environment. Dial-up does not adequately support Web pages with images, video, and/or voice, making it excruciatingly difficult and frustrating for people with dial-up access to take full advantage. According to a 2008 Pew report, 55 per cent of Americans at that time had a broadband Internet connection at home, a 25 per cent increase over 2005, when broadband connection was less than 30 per cent. By October 2010, it had increased again to nearly 70 per cent, according to the National Telecommunications and Information Administration (2011), suggesting that the digital divide in terms of access to broadband is slowly narrowing in the United States.

Still, in 2008, as many as 10 per cent of American users had dial-up Internet connections (Horrigan, 2008), based mostly on affordability and broadband availability. When asked why they would not give up their dial-up connection, 35 per cent reported that price was the key reason for continued use, 19 per cent indicated that nothing would make them switch to broadband, and 10 per cent said that broadband was not available where they lived. A more recent Pew report shows that 65 per cent of Americans have broadband at home and only 3 per cent continue to rely on dial-up. Hence, affordability and the rural/urban divide continue to be barriers to equal access to broadband in the United States.

The situation is similar in Canada: data from the 2009 *Canadian Internet Use Survey*, referred to as the CIUS, show that Internet penetration continues to grow steadily in this country. In 1994, 8 per cent of Canadians were online. That number increased to 12 per cent in 1995, 68 per cent in 2005, 73 per cent in 2007, and 84 per cent in 2012 (The Canadian Press, 2013). More detailed analyses of Canadian data reveal that the increase in penetration rates of ICTs comes primarily from middle-class users as well as younger generations. Haight, Quan-Haase, and Corbett (2014) investigated data from the 2010 CIUS and found that discrepancies in access to the Internet in Canada are still impacted by a number of key demographic variables. The study found that individuals with household incomes between $41,000 and $65,000 are more than twice as likely to have Internet access as those with incomes below $25,000. This likelihood increases to about 5.4 times for Canadians who make more than $100,000 per year. Individuals who have less education are less likely to have access to the Internet. Being a university graduate makes one 3.56 times as likely to use the Internet as those with only a high school education, while those without high school educations are about 67 per cent less likely to use the Internet. Current students, either in high school or in post-secondary institutions, are 4.63 times as likely to use the Internet as the high school education group. The study suggests that age also continues to be a significant predictor of Internet access in Canada such that the older you are, the less likely you are to be online. A study examining the reasons and rationales for the aging population's slow adoption of ICTs shows that this group often perceives technology as more suitable to the lifestyle and skill set of younger individuals (Quan-Haase, Martin, & Schreuers, 2014).

Another key challenge to Canadians' Internet use is the country's geography, specifically its low population density in relation to its geographic size. As a result, commercial carriers have limited economic incentives for connecting rural or remote areas. In their analysis of Chapleau, a rural Northern Ontario community, Collins and Wellman (2010) discuss how rural Canada is unique in terms of Internet adoption in at least two ways. For one, there is little infrastructure available in these areas in terms of broadband connectivity; without high-speed Internet, it is difficult for residents to access images and videos online. Second, and most importantly, "[t]he Chapleau experience did not reflect rural Internet users becoming the same as urban and suburban Internet users" (p. 1363). That is, rural and urban Internet users are dissimilar in terms of how they make use of the Internet in that rural users tend to integrate it into their own social practices and daily habits. To some extent, then, it becomes an Internet that serves rural lifestyles. Living in a rural area is associated with being 49 per cent less likely to access the Internet than those who live in urban areas.

Canada's diverse cultural population also presents challenges to closing the digital divide; for example, more than half of Torontonians (1,237,720) in 2013 were foreign born, up from 48 per cent in 1996 (City of Toronto, 2006). Haight et al. (2014) found that recent immigrants in general were 68 per cent less likely to be online than those individuals born in Canada (or earlier immigrants). In the Canadian context, it is also relevant to discuss the challenges encountered by First Nations individuals. Broadband is employed by First Nations people to deliver services and connect globally, "[b]ut outside of major centres, many First Nations remain underserved" (First Mile, n.d.) Often this is linked to a lack of infrastructure to provide broadband or a lack of equipment and high costs. To improve connectivity, different strategies have been proposed to increase First Nations people's inclusion in the networked society. According to McMahon (2014), the **First Mile project** is an approach that focuses on "ways that public policies, regulations, and other supports enable user communities to generate and sustain their own networked digital infrastructures" (p. 4). Coalitions have been formed between indigenous groups across Canada in order to influence the policies and regulations governing their digital infrastructures, which has contributed to a form of digital self-determination for indigenous communities. For more information on the First Mile project visit http://firstmile.ca.

In sum, the divide between haves and have-nots has not been completely closed: the gap continues to exist along the lines of income, education, age, rural/urban location, and immigrant status. There are also other key aspects that are often disregarded in the debate in addition to access. In the next section, we examine some of these factors, including knowledge levels and skills.

The Skills Divide

The **skills divide** can be examined in terms of **technical competence** and **information literacy**. Technical competence includes knowledge about how to use computers, whereas information literacy refers to the ability to seek out information, evaluate it, and use it for specific purposes, such as finding a job, solving a problem, or dealing with health-related concerns.

In Canada and the United States, attempts to close skills-based gaps in the digital divide occurred early on through the establishment of community-based

Figure 8.1 First Mile Project: Resources and Networking

training programs. In Canada, the **Community Access Program (CAP)**, a government initiative administered through Industry Canada beginning in 1994, was aimed at providing Canadians with affordable access and the necessary skills to use the Internet in primarily rural areas (Cullen, 2001). These skills included basic computer and Internet skills, from elementary Web design to advice about online education (Cullen, 2001). In Canada and the United States, libraries in particular have played a central role in terms of providing computer skills to users (Bertot, Jaeger, McClure, Wright, & Jensen, 2009). Hargittai and Hsieh (2010) suggested that digital skills can be adequately measured by noting an individual's Internet knowledge—that is, their understanding of Internet-related key terms. Box 8.2 illustrates their measure.

Haight et al. (2014) further proposed that an individual's level of online activity, namely how many activities they perform on the Internet, could serve as a proxy for Internet knowledge and digital skills. The reasoning for this measure is that the more ways one can meaningfully interact with the Internet, the more knowledge one likely possesses about the medium. The evidence contained in the study by Haight et al. (2014) shows there is a divide in terms of levels of online activity among demographic variables in Canada. Income is a predictor of online activities: individuals with household incomes between $41,000 and $65,000 performed 0.48 more activities on a 0 to 23

Box 8.2   Measuring Digital Skills

A series of validated measures have been developed to measure a person's digital skills. One such measure was developed by Hargittai and consists of 27 terms with which a person has to indicate whether or not he or she is familiar. To measure your own level of digital literacy, complete the set of items below and count how many times your answer is "Yes."

Term	Yes/No	Term	Yes/No
Reload		Frames	
Advanced Search		Podcasting	
Favorites		Web Feeds	
Bookmark		Torrent	
Spyware		BCC (on email)	
Preference Setting		Bookmarklet	
Blog		Wiki	
Firewall		Cache	
PDF		Widget	
JPG		Phishing	
Tagging		Malware	
Weblog		Social Bookmarking	
Newsgroup		RSS	
Tabbed Browsing		Total = (sum of yes answers)	of 27

scale than those earning below $25,000, while this number increased to 1.4 times for those with incomes above $100,000. Having less than a high school education is associated with performing fewer activities than those with a high school education. Being a current student, either high school or post-secondary, or having a university education is associated with engaging in 1.86 and 2.78 online activities compared to the high school–educated individuals, respectively. This study also found that men perform more activities online than women, urban residents do more online than their rural counterparts, and recent immigrants engage in more online activities than Canadian born or earlier immigrants. Finally, it was shown that age is negatively associated with the level of online activity, with younger Canadians engaging in more activities online. Funding to the CAP initiative was cut in 2012, but CIUS data suggest there is a need for policy and programs to help older Canadians increase their digital skills.

The Economic Opportunity Divide and the Democratic Divide

The **economic opportunity divide** reflects the advantages provided by access to digital technologies, such as finding a job, obtaining health information, and being able to take an online course. The **democratic divide** describes the use of the Internet for political engagement, such as obtaining information about political candidates or parties, being able to make donations to political entities, and communicating with government, for example, over email.

Linked to differences in income and education are variations in people's ability to navigate the Internet and find relevant information. Hargittai (2002) concludes that

> [m]erely offering people a network-connected machine will not ensure that they can use the medium to meet their needs because they may not be able to maximally take advantage of all that the Web has to offer. Policy decisions that aim to reduce inequalities in access to and use of information technologies must take into consideration the necessary investment in training and support as well. (Conclusion section, para. 2)

As the Web continues to develop and applications become more varied, the divide based on access, skills, economic opportunity, and engagement in a democratic discourse is becoming a more pressing policy issue.

The Social Media Divide

An important aspect often neglected in writings about the digital divide and its social implications is the continuously changing nature of the Internet (Haight et al., 2014; Quan-Haase & Wellman, 2004). The Pew Research Center reports increasing adoption of **social networking sites** (SNSs) by all age groups: 57 per cent of all American adults and 73 per cent in the 12 to 17 age group are users (Pew Research Center, 2013). Of those who used a social networking site, the Pew Center reports that 64 per cent visited it daily in 2014 compared to 51 per cent in 2010. Heavy social networking site usage has been widely criticized and time spent on a social networking site has been described as wasted (*Time Magazine*, 2014), but engagement on social networking sites is not just about having fun. Rather, recent evidence suggests that it is tied to positive outcomes ranging from identity management to informational access and the creation of social and cultural capital (Ellison, Steinfield, & Lampe, 2006).

For Pierre Bourdieu, a renowned French theorist, social and cultural capital form the very foundation of social life and determine social relations among individuals. **Social capital** is understood by Bourdieu (1973) as the resources, both actual and potential, available through a person's social networks. **Cultural capital** describes the sum of intangible social assets that allow an individual to claim membership in specific social groups (Bourdieu, 1973). Cultural capital allows individuals to show credibility and belong to social groups. Examples include formal education, knowledge of the arts, and understandings of appropriate behaviour and norms. The growing evidence linking social media use and forms of non-economic capital suggests that examining differences in the adoption and use of social media are critical for studies of the digital divide (Haight, Quan-Haase, & Corbett, 2014; Hargittai & Hsieh, 2010).

The social media divide is the gap that exists between users of social networking sites along key demographic variables, such as gender, income, and education. Haight et al. (2014) conducted one of the first studies of the social media divide and found that for Canadians, education was a central predictor of social networking site adoption. Canadians with lower levels of education were more likely to be users of social networking sites in comparison to those with a high school education. Current students (high school and post-secondary) were by far the most likely adopters of social networking sites: 87 per cent usage compared to 48 per cent for those with less than a high school education. Furthermore, women were more likely to adopt social media than men: women were 58 per cent more likely to use Facebook, Twitter, or Instagram than men. These findings corroborate those of a study conducted by Hargittai and Hsieh (2010) of first-year high school students living in the United States. The authors found that 90 per cent of girls and 86 per cent of boys utilized a social networking sites; the 4 per cent difference was statistically significant. This divide has important ramifications in terms of social capital enhancement. Considering that social networks are an important source of instrumental and emotional support, those who do not use social media are without another tool that can help facilitate social network growth and maintenance.

The Pew Research Center (Smith, 2014) published six new facts about Facebook adoption in North America. To get a sense of how Facebook users interact with the system, we discuss each of the six facts next:

1. Some users dislike certain aspects of Facebook. For instance, some users indicate that their number one dislike is the oversharing of information that they feel should remain private. **Oversharing** makes them uncomfortable. They also stated that others sharing photos of them and content about them without their prior and explicit consent is another key reason for disliking how the site works. Surprisingly, Americans did not report a negative attitude toward the **fear of missing out** (or "FOMO") phenomenon. They reported that it did not cause them any anxiety to view posts about activities and events that they themselves were not involved in.

2. Women and men often have varying reasons for why they use Facebook – but everything starts with sharing and laughs. Table 8.2 shows differences between men and women in their use of social networking sites. Women are more likely to engage in a wide range of activities, such as looking at videos and photos, sharing information, and helping Facebook friends.

3. Half of all adult Facebook users have more than 200 friends in their network. The size of a person's Facebook network varies considerably by age, with younger users having larger networks than older users. The median number of Facebook friends for 18- to 29-year-old users was 300, whereas the median number of friends for users aged 65 and above was 30.

4. Twelve per cent of Facebook users say that someone has asked them to **"unfriend"** another person in their network. Requests to unfriend someone come from other friends in 35 per cent of cases; 23 per cent come from current spouses, and 12 per cent come from former spouses or romantic partners.

5. Facebook users "like" their friends' content and comment on photos relatively frequently, but most don't change their own status that often. Of those who use Facebook, 44 per cent "like" at least once a day content posted by their friends, and 31 per cent comment on their Facebook friends' photos on a daily basis.

6. Half of Internet users who do not use Facebook themselves live with someone who does. Even though not all Internet users are avid contributors to Facebook, half know someone who is and can update them on what is going on within the site.

Table 8.2 Facebook Use, Men versus Women

Percentage of male/female Facebook users who cite the following as "major reasons" why they use Facebook	Men	Women
Women are <u>more likely than men</u> to cite these as major reasons for using Facebook:		
Seeing photos or videos	39	54
Sharing with many people at once	42	50
Seeing entertaining or funny posts	35	43
Learning about ways to help others	25	35
Receiving support from people in your network	16	29
Men and women are <u>equally likely</u> to cite these as major reasons for using Facebook:		
Receiving updates or comments	39	39
Keeping up with news and current events	31	31
Getting feedback on content you have posted	16	17

Source: "Reasons for Facebook use, men vs. women," in Smith, Aaron (2014). "6 new facts about Facebook." Pew Research Center. 3 February 2014. www.pewresearch.org/fact-tank/2014/02/03/6-new-facts-about-facebook/

The Global Digital Divide

The term **global digital divide** was coined to describe the differences in access to and use of the Internet among nations and regions of the world. Most analysis of the digital divide focuses on disparities within Western nations. An equally pressing concern is, however, the inequality in access to technology between nations. These disparities in access are thought to have major social and economic consequences for nations and their development. The problem is often perceived as one of centre and periphery, where developing countries control the flow of information (Fuchs, 2008). In 2001, the North American dominance in terms of Internet use was reflected in usage statistics that showed that as much as 60 per cent of the online population was North American (ACNielsen, 2001, as cited in Chen, Boase, & Wellman, 2002). Statistics collected by the United Nations demonstrate that North America, Europe, and Australia have the highest levels of computer penetration, with 49 per cent[3] to 89 per cent, which is in stark contrast to the 0 per cent to 5 per cent levels found in some of the poorest regions of the world, including Africa, Central America, and Asia. The low levels of computer usage and Internet penetration in these nations undermine their efforts to improve their citizens' quality of life and increase their participation in the global economy.

Developing countries continue to struggle in their efforts to become digital, having to overcome numerous barriers that exist at both the micro and macro levels. The most salient ones include the following:

1. *Lack of infrastructure*: The developing world is lacking in terms of hardware, software, and Internet connectivity. This is particularly true for rural areas.
2. *Economic barriers*: The cost of computers is one major deterrent for many in the developing world. This cost is coupled with the monthly payment to ISPs that is necessary for Web access.
3. *Illiteracy*: Many parts of the developing world continue to have high levels of illiteracy.
4. *Poor computing skills*: Even if individuals have literacy skills, they may have no previous experience with keyboards or computers.
5. *Lack of support*: It may be difficult to find others who have had past experiences with computers and the Internet to help them troubleshoot computing problems with hardware, software, and Internet navigation.
6. *Cultural barriers*: Often, norms and customs are not in agreement with or do not facilitate the use of information and communication technologies (ICTs).

Nonetheless, the composition of Internet users has changed considerably since the early inception of the Web, with a large proportion of Asians,

Europeans, and South Americans now being avid users. To address the gap between developed and developing countries, the two-phase World Summit on the Information Society (WSIS) was held in 2003 and 2005 by the United Nations with the aim of establishing programs that could target those nations lagging behind. The **International Telecommunications Union (ITU)** published a comprehensive report in 2007 examining the digital divide in 181 economies. Sadly, the global digital divide is still a reality and will not dissipate any time soon. As previously mentioned, the barriers to access are numerous and often directly linked to key factors of inequality: poverty, illiteracy, infrastructure, and political/social realities. While ICTs hold much promise, Gurstein points out that they can have a positive impact only if coupled with appropriate socio-economic policy. It is also important to keep in mind that "rather than closing the divide for the sake of it, the more sensible goal is to determine how best to use technology to promote bottom-up development" ("The Real Digital Divide," 2005). **Information and communication technologies for development (ICT4D)** aims to use ICTs directly to reduce poverty and improve health care, education, and

Box 8.3   Closing the Global Digital Divide: One Laptop per Child

One Laptop per Child (OLPC) is a U.S. non-profit organization whose mandate is to "create educational opportunities for the world's poorest children by providing each child with a rugged, low-cost, low-power, connected laptop with content and software" (One Laptop per Child, 2010b). The idea behind OLPC is to empower the world's least-advantaged children by involving them in their own education and increasing their connectivity to others.

Nicholas Negroponte, the former head of MIT's Media Lab, established OLPC in 2002 following a trip to Cambodia. There, Negroponte witnessed first-hand the effect of providing children and their families with connected technologies. Understanding that two billion children in the developing world have little or no access to formal education, Negroponte aimed to use new technologies, particularly cost- and energy-efficient computers, to assist in the education of disadvantaged children by providing increased access to resources and tools available through digital sources (One Laptop per Child, 2010a).

Beginning in 2005 with a prototype featuring a yellow hand crank used to power the computer, known as the green machine, OLPC soon began to gain support of organizations such as the **United Nations Development Programme (UNDP)**. By November 2006, OLPC had developed its first **XO laptop** using a basic version of Linux's Fedora operating system and an interface known as Sugar.

Despite the OLPC's good intentions, the program has been heavily criticized. Kraemer, Dedrick, and Sharma suggested that "expecting a laptop to cause such

Continued

revolutionary change showed a degree of naiveté, even for an organization with the best intentions and smartest people" (2009, p. 71). While OLPC presented the XO as a method for helping to close the digital divide, African critics have argued that the scheme tries to impress Westernized ideas of education and progress onto regions where necessities such as clean water, formal education, and health-care programs are of far greater importance (Smith, 2005).

The low cost of the XO laptop should make it affordable for a large segment of the population. However, some have argued that purchasing the device is not so straightforward because OLPC has not taken into account the additional costs associated with the technology in terms of software upgrades and licences, training, technical support, maintenance, and replacement of broken or malfunctioning computers (Kraemer et al., 2009). Critics have also argued that rather than providing a low-cost alternative to traditional laptops, OLPC instead should have spurred PC manufacturers to mass-produce small, cheap, and low-quality netbooks that were highly dependent on the same manufacturers for repairs. In response, companies such as Microsoft started producing affordable versions of their software, and offering them to developing countries and OLPC target markets, such as Nigeria and Libya (Kraemer et al., 2009).

Designed with good intentions, OLPC's program serves as a paradigm of the types of technological and social issues affecting developing countries. In spite of its seemingly minimal startup costs, OLPC's concept overlooked the type of unique cultural, political, and socio-economic conditions facing poorer countries. By viewing ideas of the digital divide through a Westernized lens, OLPC failed to understand the concerns of local environments, particularly in regions where basic nutritional, health, and educational needs trump the purchase and diffusion of digital technologies. Additionally, once OLPC's ambitious program became a competitive threat to traditional industry powerhouses, the originality of their mission became subsumed and overtaken by corporations with greater resources, reputations, and reaches in global markets.

work conditions. Box 8.3 discusses the One Laptop per Child initiative as an ICT4D example that has had an impact on some of the poorest regions of the world.

The social and economic consequences of the digital divide continue to be the subject of much debate. Chen, Boase, and Wellman argue that

these inequalities may increase as the Internet becomes more central to global life: from keeping in contact with migrant kin, to acquiring information, to engaging in farm-to-market commerce. Hence, rather than socially including marginal people and countries, the embedding of the Internet in everyday life can enhance and deepen power relations underlying existing inequalities. (2002, pp. 80–81)

China's Move toward Digitization: A Unique Example

The People's Republic of China, or China for short, is a unique case in terms of the diffusion of the Internet for a number of reasons. First, China has seen incredible growth in its information and communications sector—both for personal use as well as business. Second, China has a population of more than one billion, or about 20 per cent of the world's entire population, making it one of the largest countries in the world. Hence, even if only a small proportion of its population is online, this actually represents a large amount of both Internet traffic and, more importantly, Internet content. According to the China Internet Network Information Center (2014), there are currently 618 million users and this represents less than half of the country's population, as we mentioned on page 148.

Third, China is the world's fastest growing economy with a nominal gross domestic product (GDP) of US$4.99 trillion in 2009 according to China's National Bureau of Statistics, making it the third largest in the world after the United States and Japan (Batson, 2010). It is, thus, an important player in the telecommunications sector—as both a consumer and a producer of products and services. On 19 September 2014, China's largest e-commerce company, Alibaba, went public on the New York Stock Exchange (NYSE), leading to the largest initial public offering (IPO) to date (BBC, 2014). At a price of about $92 per share, the company raised 25 billion dollars, thereby surpassing the record set in 2010 by China's Agricultural Bank with 22 billion dollars raised. What do these numbers really mean? The fact that a Chinese e-commerce site is worth more than Facebook, eBay, and Amazon together signals that the fastest growing market is now in Asia and not North America. It also signals that economic transactions will likely increase exponentially in Asia in comparison to the North American market. Simply looking at the numbers, this makes sense: China has about twice the number of people online as does North America, and this number is set to double in the next decade (Zickuhr, 2013).

Fourth, China's governmental policy has been to promote digitization, while at the same time limiting access to content. Indeed, China has been criticized for its **Internet censorship**, which is enforced through laws, regulations, and repression of citizens. These four examples are just some of the many reasons why China is a unique case in terms of Internet diffusion.

The China Internet Network Information Center (CNNIC) has played an important role in documenting China's digital divide over the past decade and in pointing toward important social and economic trends. A 2006 survey based on telephone sampling found that 123 million users are online, of which 41 per cent are female and 59 per cent are male; by 2013 that number had increased to 618 million. In comparison to other developing countries, the penetration rate in China is fairly high, although still much lower than in OECD countries. The majority of users are young (see Table 8.3): almost

Table 8.3 Internet Users in China by Age

Under 18	18–24	25–30	31–35	36–40	41–50	51–60	Over 60
15%	39%	18%	10%	7%	7%	2%	0.8%

Source: China Internet Network Information Centre, 18th Statistical Survey Report on the Internet Development in China (Bejing: CINIC, 2006), p. 9.

40 per cent of users are between 18 and 24 years of age. Fewer than 1 per cent of users are in the 60-plus age group. However, insufficient broadband infrastructure in many remote locations and high charges for Internet access are exacerbating the digital divide in China (Flew, 2008).

As Chinese people embrace the Internet and information flows more freely through China's networks, the government remains ambivalent about joining the information society. (See the discussion on the Internet dictator's dilemma in Chapter 9.) On the one hand, China wants to be a key player in the high-tech sector and benefit from the economic advantages provided by e-commerce, networking, and online services. On the other hand, it understands that the Internet's array of communication capabilities, decentralized nature, and ease of access to information can potentially undermine the Chinese Communist Party's rule. In June 2014, the Chinese government started a comprehensive campaign to further tighten national and international security (Bradsher & Mozur, 2014). On a day-to-day basis, this means difficulties with sending and receiving emails, limited access to Internet resources, such as Web pages, PDFs, and news, and restricted use of services. For instance, Twitter and Facebook were already censored, but now companies such as Line and Kakao Talk, which operate in Asia, are also censored. The censorship has been referred to as **China's Great Firewall** and impacts worker productivity, e-commerce, and social contact among friends and family (Goldsmith & Wu, 2006).

Critical Perspectives of the Digital Divide

There is no doubt that the digital divide is a central problem of our times, as it is inextricably intertwined with existing inequalities (Stevenson, 2009). Yet the digital divide concept has also become a tool used by developed nations to impose standards of industrialization on developing countries. Gurstein (2007) provides a thoughtful critique of the digital divide concept and points out four difficulties with research in the area:

1. A large majority of the studies of the digital divide document only the existence of a divide and fail to outline ways of addressing the problem.
2. Most analyses of the digital divide suggest that access alone is a solution to the problem without addressing the larger socio-economic issues that

developing countries are struggling with, such as health care, education, and wealth disparities.

3. For Gurstein, the debate is ignoring "the underlying reasons for the impacts of the DD [digital divide] such as on-going trends towards increasing social and economic polarization—with the well-off getting better off and those behind falling even further behind as they find themselves unable to take advantage of ICT opportunities" (2007, p. 45). Providing access will certainly have a social impact on communities, but whether or not access will provide the economic, social, cultural, and educational advantage that lies at the heart of inequality remains unclear. Can access close gaps in inequality?

4. Access needs to be accompanied by training, means of production and distribution, and an economic model of return. Without a more comprehensive plan of development, access will provide little positive return in countries where illiteracy prevails, basic needs are not met, and social unrest continues to exist.

Gurstein's (2007) central point is that the debate surrounding the digital divide should not obscure prevailing inequalities in society, which cannot easily be resolved through technology alone. Similarly, Stevenson (2009) argues that the digital divide is often used as a discursive resource to benefit governments, information capital, and public service professionals. Epstein, Nisbet, and Gillespie (2011) examined how the various definitions of the digital divide had an impact on policy. They found that framing the digital divide as a problem of access emphasized the provision of adequate infrastructure, largely neglecting more fundamental problems of information literacy.

By contrast, framing the problem in terms of skills moves responsibility for the digital divide from governments to citizens, who are perceived as needing to take action in order to obtain the necessary proficiency to access Web resources. This shows that how the digital divide is defined and framed has important repercussions for policy initiatives, as the skills perspective may "diminish the public's call for public policies or collective efforts to address the problem," leading people to assume that it is the responsibility of individuals and educational institutions (Epstein et al., 2011, p. 101).

Conclusions

What conclusions can we draw about our current state of knowledge regarding the Internet's role in creating social change? This chapter has provided an analysis of the various attributes and characteristics that define and shape the digital divide. In an era in which the Internet is ubiquitous in everyday life, many would perceive the digital divide to be a relic of the recent past. Yet despite the rapid consumption and adoption of ICTs, digital inequality remains a pressing issue for both developed and developing nations. The digital divide can no longer simply be correlated with one's ability to access the Internet or own a computer. Rather, the digital divide can be attributed to a lack of digital skills to competently use the Internet or to the inability to seek out information necessary for being an active participant in contemporary politics or culture. Notably, many contemporary scholars and social theorists now view the digital divide in its many overt and distinct forms. These include, but are not limited to, geographical, economic, educational, social, cultural, and technical spheres. In addition, recent arguments suggest that it is necessary to look also at discrepancies in the use of social networking sites, as these are important sources of social and cultural capital.

The closing of the digital divide is not simply solved, nor is it predicated on supplying marginalized groups with affordable or donated computer hardware and software. It is a project that primarily requires an understanding of the socio-economic factors defining the digital divide, as well as the unique local conditions affecting millions of people who are unfamiliar with the omnipresent and continued experiences of using information technologies as an integral component of everyday life. This issue has both short- and long-term implications, affecting how information is used, manipulated, consumed, and distributed.

Questions for Critical Thought

1. What are the key limitations of early examinations of the digital divide?

2. What are the central barriers to overcoming the digital divide in the developing world?

3. What are the unique challenges that China confronts as it moves into the information society?

4. Provide an in-depth critique of the digital divide concept. In your considerations, address the concept's strengths and weaknesses.

Suggested Readings

Epstein, D., Nisbet, E.C., & Gillespie, T. (2011). Who's responsible for the digital divide? Public perceptions and policy implications. *The Information Society, 27*(2), 92–104. An investigation into the effects of different digital divide discourses on public perception of responsibility.

Haight, M., Quan-Haase, A., & Corbett, B. (2014). Revisiting the digital divide in Canada: The impact of demographic factors on access to the Internet, level of online activity, and social networking site usage. *Information, Communication & Society, 17*(4), 503–519. Examining access to the Internet, level of online activity, and social networking site usage in the Canadian context, the authors rely on data from the Canadian Internet Use Survey (CIUS), which is based on a national representative sample.

Hermida, A. (2014). *Tell everyone: Why we share and why it matters*. Toronto: Doubleday Canada. An engaging read about who is participating in social media and how news and information are disseminated on the Internet.

Witte, J.C., & Mannon, S.E. (2010). *The Internet and social inequalities*. New York: Routledge. Using sociological principles, this book investigates how use of the Internet reflects and assists in shaping contemporary social inequalities.

Online Resources

First Mile
http://firstmile.ca/
http://meeting.knet.ca/mp19/

First Mile is a meeting place to obtain knowledge about community-driven technology adoption and use. The site contains many resources as well as access to MyKnet, a free online social networking site based in Northern Ontario.

United Nations Science and Technology for Development Network (StDev)
http://stdev.unctad.org/themes/ict/docs.html/

The website contains reports from around the world about the current state of the digital divide as well as information on recent conferences addressing concerns around the issue.

"China clamps down on Web"
www.nytimes.com/2014/09/22/business/international/china-clamps-down-on-web-pinching-companies like-google.html?_r=0

This article by *New York Times* correspondents K. Bradsher and P. Mozur describes the current policy of the Chinese government vis-à-vis Internet use and censorship.

Community in the Network Society

Learning Objectives

◎ to investigate "the community question" and its link to industrialization;

◎ to provide an overview of the social capital concept and its relevance to community;

◎ to discuss and critically examine how the Internet has increased or decreased the social capital available in communities;

◎ to contrast Durkheim's concepts of mechanical and organic solidarity and to show how these apply to current conceptualizations of a network society;

◎ to re-examine the concept of the public sphere in light of widespread use of information and communication technologies for the support of protests and social movements, in particular looking at the use of social media and cellphones.

Introduction

In this chapter, we examine technology's impact on how societies are structured. The chapter starts with a brief overview of definitions of *community* and introduces two key theoretical concepts as proposed by Ferdinand Tönnies that help readers to better understand the basic structuring of society—*Gesellschaft* and *Gemeinschaft*. What follows is a critical examination of the debate over how communities, and our concept of what constitutes them, have changed as a result of industrialization, urbanization, and globalization by comparing three different, prevalent perspectives: community lost, community saved, and community liberated. The chapter also further discusses Pierre Bourdieu's concept of *social capital*, which was first introduced in Chapter 8, to better explain how resources are transferred and mobilized within communities. We review two types of social capital—private and public—and argue that each contributes in a unique way to the wellbeing of communities. Next, we discuss theorizing by Robert Putnam suggesting that social capital is in decline, and we consider the consequences. For Putnam, technologies, for example television and the Internet, are a key factor in affecting the decline and compromising democratic debate.

The chapter also considers the impact of the Internet on community and presents various competing perspectives. On the one hand, early analysts such as Howard Rheingold characterized the Internet as a utopian place, where new communities of organic solidarity could be formed without constraints of space and time. On the other hand, skeptics, such as Norman H. Nie, saw the Internet as another technology that would draw people away from family and friends and alienate them from society. We contrast and critically examine the utopian and dystopian views, arguing that we need to develop new perspectives to better understand how the Internet has affected social structure. Based on a discussion of the Durkheimian notion of organic solidarity, Lee Rainie's and Barry Wellman's (2012) concept of the *triple revolution* is discussed in detail and their theory of networked individualism presented as an alternative viewpoint. The chapter concludes with a discussion of how the Internet has affected our understanding of the public sphere. As part of this discussion, we take an in-depth look at the events that unfolded in Egypt in February 2011 and analyze the role that social media played in initiating, supporting, and helping to organize these social movements and protests.

What Is Community?

We can study communities from a number of different perspectives. Traditionally, researchers have studied communities in terms of location; that is, a community is a group of people who live in a bounded geographic area. However, we can also study community in terms of smaller social units that come together because of shared interests, work, religion, etc. By contrast, some very broad definitions include all of society as community.

Ferdinand Tönnies (1957/1963) was the first to study the fundamentals of community and proposed the distinction between **Gemeinschaft** and **Gesellschaft**. *Gemeinschaft* is generally translated from German as "community" and refers to a cohesive social entity that is united by a pre-existing bond. *Gemeinschaft*-based affiliations are ends in and of themselves and do not directly serve a utilitarian purpose even though benefits can be obtained from the association. Family ties are a perfect example of a form of *Gemeinschaft* that connects people in tightly knit groups. By contrast, *Gesellschaft* is translated as "society" or "association," describing the coexistence of individuals who are self-serving units and come together because of an overarching goal. In *Gesellschaft*-based associations, people are only loosely connected through bonds that are often goal-oriented. The **nation-state** is an example of *Gesellschaft* because its members are grouped together as a result of sharing the same geographic boundaries and national identity.

Gemeinschaft and *Gesellschaft* represent ideal types or archetypes of social relationships; that is, most social groups cannot be categorized into either pure *Gemeinschaft* or *Gesellschaft* but tend to have elements resembling one or the other. Tönnies (1957/1963) shows through his analysis of social life that both forms of social organization—*Gemeinschaft* and *Gesellschaft*—can coexist at a single point in history as each describes a different aspect of social organization. Individuals live in narrowly defined groups based on kinship, location, and affiliation (e.g., religion), but at the same time can be part of larger social structures that attain goals (e.g., nation-states, jurisdictions).

Gemeinschaft is often used to represent the ideal type of society, one where people are closely connected, share an identity, and engage in reciprocity. This contrasts with *Gesellschaft*, which is perceived as an inferior form of social organization because members are alienated, there is little willingness for co-operation and collaboration, and people live segregated from one another. Next, we focus our discussion on how industrialization, urbanization, and bureaucratization have affected community.

Community's Link to Industrialization

Barry Wellman has used the term **"the community question"** to summarize the debate around how community has changed over time and the role played by technology. He argues that this is a pressing issue because it links micro- and macro-level analysis in that it addresses "the problem of the structural integration of a social system and the interpersonal means by which its members have access to scarce resources" (Wellman, 1979, p. 1201). The central question has been whether communities are declining or thriving and how this impacts the flow of essential resources such as social and economic support, current information, and the exchange of goods and services. Wellman (1979) distinguishes among three theoretical views: (1) community-lost, (2) community-saved, and (3) community-liberated.

Community-Lost

Analysts who belong to the **community-lost view** have painted a bleak picture of the state of community in Western societies. They see industrialization as the cause of a decline in community, resulting from long work hours that leave little time for other activities. For instance, women have moved in large numbers into the workforce with increasingly long work hours, and this has changed how socialization takes place in the home and neighbourhood (Costa & Kahn, 2001). Urbanization, in conjunction with urban sprawl, creates isolation and a general lack of public spaces, further reducing opportunities for socialization. New modes of transportation and communication have emerged that support distant interactions, removing people from their immediate vicinities and, ultimately, creating loose-knit communities.

At the centre of the community-lost argument is the comparison between contemporary urban living and pastoral community. Supporters of the community-lost perspective see pastoral community as composed primarily of local social interactions in closely bounded groups. In these communities, people are primarily involved with fellow members of the few groups to which they belong: at home, in the neighbourhood, or at work. These networks are fairly homogenous, with members sharing a common geography, identity, and belief system, as well as common social ties. In part, people idealize pastoral community by portraying it as a simple but happy way of life. In this view, the constraints placed on identity formation and self-expression through shared norms and beliefs are disregarded.

Community-Saved

The **community-saved view** was developed in opposition to the community-lost view. This perspective focuses on how friendship and family networks continue to dominate as forms of social organization even in heavily industrialized societies. Part of the argument is that a move is taking place where loosely bounded networks often increase their level of connectivity, leading to close-knit clusters similar to those found in the pre-industrial era. The evidence has consistently shown that close-knit groups continue to exist, in particular within poorer neighbourhoods, where people need to rely on one another for emotional, economic, and social support (Espinoza, 1999). Hence, despite the social changes taking place as a result of industrialization, urbanization, and modernization, there is some evidence supporting the idea of community-saved.

The community-lost and community-saved views, however, have several limitations and therefore require some rethinking. Wellman (1979) has criticized the community-saved view because of its narrow focus on documenting the continued existence of pre-industrialized forms of community without giving much consideration to the changes that have occurred in the structure of society since the Industrial Revolution. In addition, Wellman criticizes both community-lost and community-saved views because of their disregard of the social networks that develop and form outside geographic boundaries:

> Thus the basic Community Question, dealing with the structure and use of primary ties, has been confounded in both the Lost and Saved arguments with questions about the persistence of solidary sentiments and territorial cohesiveness. But, whereas the Lost argument laments their demise, the Saved argument praises their persistence. (p. 1206)

Wellman's comment shows that the community-lost view tends to focus on the loss of geographically bound ties without giving much consideration to social ties formed outside the core groups of the neighbourhood and family. By contrast, the community-saved view tends to disregard changes that have occurred in the structuring of society as a result of modernization by emphasizing the continued existence of geographically bounded ties.

Community-Liberated

A third perspective is depicted in the **community-liberated view**, where the central argument is that community life is not lost but has undergone radical transformations. In this view, communities continue to exist in society but with new dimensions. Instead of socialization taking place within narrowly defined geographic boundaries, people socialize outside of local neighbourhoods and family ties (Guest & Wierzbicki, 1999; Rainie & Wellman, 2012; Wellman & Frank, 2001). Indeed, while immediate neighbours may not know each other or may not socialize as frequently as those in the pastoral communities of the eighteenth century, socialization does continue with friends and family who live at a distance (Fischer, 1992; Mok, Wellman, & Carrasco, 2010).

The car and the telephone facilitate the formation of these new social structures, where emphasis is placed on establishing and maintaining unbounded networks. While in-person visits continue to be the primary form of socializing, the telephone occupies a unique role in that it promotes distant communication (Wellman & Wortley, 1990).

The community-liberated view provides unique insights into the structuring of society and the link between micro- and macro-level developments. Clearly, industrialization, urbanization, and bureaucracy have left their marks on society. What is relevant, then, is to understand what the nature of community is in the context of modern life.

Social Capital and Its Relevance to Community

To further explore the nature of community in the context of modern life, this section focuses on social capital. Definitions of **social capital** abound. Pierre Bourdieu (1977/1998) describes it as the accumulated actual and potential resources to which individuals have access through their membership in groups and connections to networks. That is, these relations provide a collectively shared kind of capital consisting of credentials that allow them to exchange favours, credits, and resources. Social capital, thus, is the sum of valuable resources that can be obtained through the relationships actors have with friends and relatives and the **social networks** that these relationships form (Wellman & Berkowitz, 1988). The focus in the social capital perspective, then, is no longer only on the formation of community but also on how members of a community manage their resources. These resources are of greatest importance when building a healthy community because, according to Putnam (2000), "[a] growing body of literature suggests that where trust and social nets flourish, individuals, firms, neighborhoods, and even nations prosper" (p. 319). In communities, where social capital is high, trust among individuals is high, as is reciprocity. That is, people give without expecting immediate returns, in turn creating an atmosphere of mutuality.

Therefore, we must understand the concept of social capital and its role as a building block in holding societies together.

We can view the benefits derived from social capital as either private or public effects. Private effects are benefits brought to individuals through their ties, while public effects are all those positive characteristics of living in densely knit and reciprocal communities. For example, a person finding a job with the help of a friend reaps the benefits of private effects, whereas feeling safe at night on the streets because neighbours are watching out for each other is an illustration of the advantages accrued through public effects.

TV and the Decline of Social Capital in the United States

A major concern has been a decline in social capital in the United States, which can have serious implications for community, solidarity, and ultimately the vitality of a democratic society (Putnam, 2000). To document the decline, Robert Putnam examines the extent to which Americans were involved in a number of social behaviours, including whether or not they (1) attended church services, (2) visited relatives, (3) gave or attended a dinner party, (4) attended a sports event, and (5) visited neighbours. Using U.S. General Social Survey (GSS) data, Putnam demonstrates that people are less engaged in their community now than they were in the 1960s and 1970s. For instance, Figure 9.1 shows a steady decline in informal socializing, that is, visiting friends, attending celebrations, visiting bars, and participating in informal conversations.

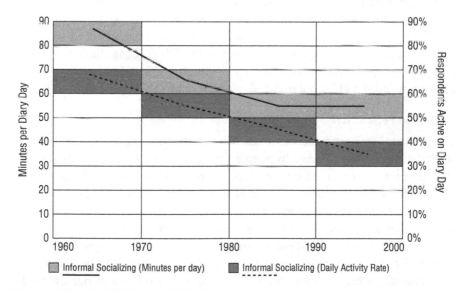

Figure 9.1 Informal Socializing, 1965–1995
Source: Adapted from Putnam, R.D. (2000). *Bowling Alone: The Collapse and Revival of American Community.* New York: Simon and Schuster, p. 109.

Each social or community activity can be seen as an opportunity to increase private and public social capital. Through these interactions, a person can learn about job opportunities and discover information about the community. Therefore, the social capital obtained through formal as well as informal relations is relevant for the prosperity of individual members as well as for the community as a whole.

For Putnam (2000), technology has directly contributed to this decline. He argues that with industrialization came increased participation in more individualistic activities, such as watching television. The move toward individualized activities has had an enormous impact on how people socialize and participate in their communities. Entertainment tends to occur more within the home, reducing opportunities for socialization, for meeting neighbours, and for getting involved in community activities. Putnam (2000) further argues that watching television is a passive form of entertainment that does not involve chatting, debating, or interacting. In addition, television has an absorptive effect that even reduces social exchanges among family members in the home, further contributing to the demise of social capital (Steiner, 1963). Although television has indeed had a considerable effect on socialization, scholars see the impact of the Internet as more pronounced and transformational.

Revisiting Community in the Internet Era

What impact has the Internet had on community? Has the Internet strengthened community and increased social capital? Or has it further isolated individuals and decreased community involvement? Since the 1990s, there has been an ongoing debate about how the Internet has affected socialization, communication, and civic participation. We discuss three competing perspectives previously proposed by Wellman, Quan-Haase, Witte, and Hampton (2001): (1) utopian, (2) dystopian, and (3) supplement.

1. Utopian Perspective

In the **utopian perspective of the Internet**, analysts see the Internet as stimulating positive change in people's lives. According to this perspective, the Internet has changed our concept of community because it spans geographic boundaries and connects individuals across time and space. As well, digital media are perceived as leading to the formation of new forms of community that allow people with common interests to meet.

Rheingold defines **online communities** as "social aggregations that emerge from the Net when enough people carry on those public discussions long enough, with sufficient human feeling, to form webs of personal relationships in cyberspace" (2000, p. xx). Rheingold based his definition on his own experience in a virtual community called the **WELL** (Whole Earth

'Lectronic Link), which started in the 1980s and had a large following in the San Francisco Bay Area. The online community formed a close-knit social network that provided members with friendship, social and emotional support, information, and a digital space for discussion.

From a utopian point of view, the Internet has a positive effect on many social realms, including e-democracy, e-learning, and e-health. In stark opposition to the utopians is the dystopian perspective, which we discuss next.

2. Dystopian Perspective

The key argument of the **dystopian perspective of the Internet** is that the Internet draws people away from their immediate, local environments, potentially alienating them from social engagement and civic participation. Theorists continue to raise concerns about how technology is making us lonelier. Early theorists focused on the Internet's anonymous nature, the numerous possibilities for deception, and the rather shallow relationships that are formed online. Dystopians argue that in-person communication is richer and more fulfilling, and provides interactivity, whereas text-based exchanges online are alienating. Putnam (2000) argued that online interactions, like television viewing, can be immersive, taking people away from their immediate in-person contacts. Another concern Putnam raised was the negative influence that global connections could have on local community. He also feared that the Internet could have detrimental effects on the public sphere as people moved to the Internet for entertainment and socializing and away from public spaces (Putnam, 2000).

One key argument has stated that mobile devices further alienate individuals from their community and public spaces. When individuals are in public spaces, like parks, plazas, and malls, they tend to focus on and interact with their devices instead of paying attention to their surroundings. While much speculation has arisen about these negative effects, little evidence exists to show whether social change has occurred and, if so, the nature of this change. In a recent study, Hampton, Goulet, and Albanesius (2014) examined how mobile technologies influence the way in which individuals interact with one another in public spaces such as parks, malls, and libraries. They used digital cameras and laptops to record human interaction in these public spaces. The study followed the approach taken by renowned sociologist William H. Whyte half a century ago: using film, photography, and detailed note taking, Whyte documented people's behaviour in different public spaces in New York City.

Hampton et al. (2014) found that people's use of cellphones in public spaces was much lower than expected. On the steps of the Metropolitan Museum of Art (Met) in NYC, for example, only 3 per cent of individuals were seen using their devices. When individuals did use their cellphones or tablets, they were alone. They also observed that individuals who were in

In New York City's Bryant Park, cellphone users can now take advantage of solar-powered charging stations like this one.

groups rarely used cellphones. This indicates that cellphone use fills gaps between face-to-face communications and does not necessarily replace it. The study provides concrete evidence against the dystopian perspective. It suggests that mobile technologies have aided in connecting individuals across space and time but have not taken people away from interacting in groups and hanging out in public spaces. Technology seems to be a way for individuals to maintain social ties even when they are alone in a public space: they can participate in social media (e.g., check Facebook pages), answer emails, and coordinate meetings and gatherings on the go. The study further suggests that the widespread impression of high cellphone use in public spaces can actually be attributed to the observation that lone persons are both more likely to use cellphones and to linger in a given area, unwittingly making themselves into indicators of obnoxious technological immersion in public.

3. Supplement Perspective

The utopian and dystopian perspectives both provide rather simplistic views of the impact of the Internet on the structuring of society. Perhaps these perspectives have given too much weight to the Internet in terms of its ability to radically transform the nature of community. While the Internet can provide the means for increased interaction and community involvement, it can also isolate individuals and increase the risk of harm. To better understand how the Internet has affected society, we need to consider a number of mediating factors:

- a user's previous experience with the Internet;
- a user's personal characteristics (e.g., age, gender, and personality);
- the existence of prior forms of community, whether online or offline; and
- the type of Internet use (e.g., surfing, gaming, emailing, or chatting).

Only by carefully analyzing these factors will we be able to better understand how the Internet impacts society.

Overall, the evidence suggests that the Internet provides an important and central means of communication. However, as a medium it *adds* to other forms of communication rather than replacing them. This third perspective has been termed the **supplement argument of the Internet** (Wellman et al., 2001). Box 9.1 reviews a study that provides evidence in support of the supplement argument.

Box 9.1   Social Capital in the Internet Era

Evidence suggests that the Internet neither decreases nor increases social capital. A number of large-scale studies have demonstrated that with an increased reliance on the Internet for socialization and communication, the use of other media does not decrease (Howard, Rainie, & Jones, 2002). This line of thinking has been referred to as the supplement argument (Wellman et al., 2001).

In a study of U.S. and Canadian Internet users, it was found that email had become an important means of keeping in touch with friends and family (Wellman et al., 2001). However, as the amount of email sent and received increased, face-to-face interactions and phone calls did not decrease. This strongly suggests that email supports existing social networks but does not replace telephone and in-person communication. Indeed, Table 9.1 shows that people continue to use the telephone the most for contact with friends and family regardless of geographic proximity. This is followed by email for friends both near and far.

In contrast, face-to-face meetings continue to be used more frequently than email exchanges for communicating with family members who live nearby. People use email to keep in touch with family who live far away because of distance constraints. Interestingly, individuals who have little social contact via telephone or in person are also unlikely to use email for socializing. Similarly, people who visit and telephone frequently also email frequently, suggesting that those who already have established communication patterns carry these seamlessly over to the Internet.

Continued

Table 9.1 Social Contact with Friends and Family, Near and Far

	Phone (Days/Year)	F2F (Days/Year)	Email (Days/Year)	Letters (Days/Year)
Friends Near	126	92	118	9
Family Near	114	58	49	7
Friends Far	25	10	85	8
Family Far	43	10	72	10

F2F = face-to-face

Source: Huysman, M., and Wulf, V. (Eds.). Social Capital and Information Technology, Figure 9.1, Social Contact with Friends and Family, Near and Far, ©2004 Massachusetts Institute of Technology, by permission of the MIT Press.

The data show that the Internet has joined the telephone and in-person communication as a main means of staying in touch—but one that can be more convenient and affordable. The Internet offers a new array of communication possibilities, including real-time communication via chat, Twitter, Facebook, and blogs (Klemens, 2010). Clearly, this affords new possibilities in terms of the ease in connecting geographically dispersed people and organizations bonded by shared interests (Quan-Haase & Wellman, 2004). In sum, the capabilities of the Internet add to and supplement interactions with other media rather than replacing them. Not all pre-established social behaviours have been revolutionized; people continue to visit friends and family in person and to talk on the phone.

The evidence so far suggests two trends emerging in how the Internet has affected community, social networks, and communication: (1) the "rich get richer" hypothesis and (2) networked individualism.

The "Rich Get Richer" Hypothesis

The **"rich get richer" hypothesis** argues that the Internet does not have the same effect on all users; instead, for those users who are already socially involved and who have existing social support, the Internet will further strengthen and expand these networks (Kraut, Kiesler, Boneva, Cummings, Helgeson, & Crawford, 2002; Tufekci, 2010). In other words, the Internet will benefit these people because it will provide an additional medium to keep in touch. Kraut et al. argue that "[t]hose who already have social support can use the Internet to reinforce ties with those in their support networks. [T]hese groups would gain more social involvement and well-being from using the Internet than those who are introverted or have limited networks" (2002, p. 58). Furthermore, the "rich get richer" hypothesis predicts that those who already have large networks can use the Internet both to maintain these networks more efficiently and to continue increasing their network size.

Ellison et al. (2006) investigated the link between the use of Facebook, a platform that is specifically geared toward not only supporting existing ties but also increasing an individual's social network size, and social capital. The authors investigated two forms of social capital: bonding and bridging. **Bonding social capital** describes connections with strong ties, those individuals with whom one shares an intimate bond. **Bridging social capital** indicates linkages with weak ties, people one associates with but who are not close. Not surprisingly, individuals who engage with their Facebook networks and use the site frequently show greater levels of both bonding and bridging social capital. This suggests that Facebook use facilitates the building of social capital online, which then translates into the mobilization of resources both online and offline.

Networked Individualism

The networked individualism argument provides twenty-first-century context for the Durkheimian notion of organic solidarity. In the *Division of Labor in Society* (1893/1960), Durkheim describes an early form of society with few divisions, where people come together based on what he referred to as **mechanical solidarity**. This form of solidarity is based on shared understandings around social roles and reveals a cohesive social structure, with a strong collective conscious. The notion of a **collective conscious** was introduced by Durkheim to describe "shared beliefs, ideas and moral attitudes which operate as a unifying force within society" (*Collins Dictionary*, 2000). Durkheim contrasts mechanical solidarity with **organic solidarity**, which describes a society in which individuals occupy specialized social roles that evolve around labour, social status, and other defining variables. Organic solidarity consists of multiple partial networks that exchange resources and goods. More importantly, in an organic solidarity the role of the collective conscience diminishes; this liberates individuals to develop their own identities free from shared beliefs and oppressing norms.

To further this debate, Rainie and Wellman (2012) base their arguments on Castell's (1996) notion of the networked society, and strongly argue against dystopian views favouring the "death of community." By providing evidence that relations integrate in-person, Internet, and mobile means of connection, Rainie and Wellman (2012) have argued that a **"triple revolution"** is taking place, as shown by the following:

1. the long-term turn away from being bound up in solidary groups to manoeuvring among social networks;
2. the proliferation of the personalized Internet as a powerful means to communicate and acquire information with fewer distance constraints; and
3. the even more rapid spread of mobile devices such as cellphones and tablets for always-accessible communication and information.

This, they contend, has led to "networked individualism," where people are well connected but no longer as clustered in kinship groups, workplaces, and village-like neighbourhoods.

Networked individualism indicates a society that has moved away from a model where people are embedded in groups, what Tönnies called *Gemeinschaft* and Durkheim referred to as *mechanical solidarity*, to more loosely connected networks, that is, a society that looks like Tönnies's *Gesellschaft* and Durkheim's *organic solidarity* (Rainie & Wellman, 2012; Wellman, 2001). Individuals no longer feel a strong commitment to groups but instead tend to build and maintain their own personalized networks (Rainie & Wellman, 2012). Barry Wellman (2001) writes that "[t]his is a time for individuals and their networks, not for groups. The all-embracing collectivity (Parsons 1951; Braga and Menosky 1999) has become a fragmented, personalized network. Autonomy, opportunity, and uncertainty rule today's community game" (p. 248).

Social media facilitate a networked structure of interaction because they allow each person to maintain his or her individualized social network. For example, Facebook allows each user to add friends, family, and acquaintances without any restraints of group affiliation. While networks in digital space may overlap, they are still distinct enough that they arguably represent a social structure where people move over time between various groups and networks, instead of being a member of a single network. This is a fundamental shift in the structure and functioning of society.

How Is Technology Transforming the Public Sphere?

To what extent is technology eroding the existence of the **public sphere**? The public sphere is essential for democracy because it provides "a discursive space in which individuals and groups congregate to discuss matters of mutual interest and, where possible, to reach a common judgment. Public spheres are discursive sites where society deliberates about normative standards and even develops new frameworks for expressing and evaluating social reality" (Hauser, 1998, p. 86). Habermas (1962/1989) developed the notion of the public sphere based on a historical analysis of the social processes underlying the creation, flourishing, and collapse of the **bourgeois public sphere** of eighteenth-century Central Europe. Three areas compose the bourgeois sphere of debate:

1. *Status*: For public debates to be open, opinions need to be voiced regardless of a person's status.
2. ***Domain of common concern***: The issues addressed in the public sphere need to be of relevance to a larger social group and not restricted to the interests of small, influential groups.

3. *Inclusivity*: The issues discussed must be open and accessible to everyone in terms of their content. That is, cliques or closed groups do not represent the public sphere.

While public spaces—such as plazas, parks, and centres—were at the heart of the public sphere in the past, an increasing reliance on technology means that these places have become less relevant. Urbanization, industrialization, and the spread of suburbs have all contributed to the erosion of the public sphere. Recent debate has focused on how the introduction of new digital technologies will further transform the public sphere.

Theories of the Demise of the Public Sphere

Sunstein (2001) has warned about the problems that arise from using technology to access information. While the advantage of technology is that it allows people to filter information and customize their selections, at the same time this limits people's exposure. Because users tend to visit websites that are very specialized and often geared toward specific audiences, the element of randomness is often eliminated. This reduces people's exposure to a variety of views and perspectives, and potentially creates a biased world view. For Sunstein (2001), digital technologies can lead to a reduction of information in the public sphere, thereby creating a new form of society, which he terms Republic.com, because these tools make it easier to filter, personalize, and customize content. The analysis by Sunstein suggests that digital technologies are a contributing factor in the demise of the public sphere. Instead of connecting citizens and facilitating conversation, debate, the flow of information, and the organization of political and social movements, digital technologies are contributing to narrow perspectives and are further isolating citizens.

To describe how debates take place in the public sphere, Habermas (1984/2001) introduced the notion of the **ideal speech situation**, in which implied rules structure the debate, allowing all individuals equal and unbiased opportunity to voice their opinion. At the centre of the ideal speech situation is the lack of any kind of coercion that could influence participants' willingness to voice an opinion. Noelle-Neumann (1974) builds on the concept of the ideal speech situation and proposes her theory of the **spiral of silence**. In this view, participants of the public sphere are willing to share their opinions if they perceive that these are in accordance with those of the majority. That is, if most people think that stigmatization is no longer a major concern to society, then people will agree with and voice this opinion. People whose opinion is in the minority (i.e., who believe that stigmatization continues to be of central relevance to society) will tend to refrain from expressing it in public. The Internet and social media in particular have been seen as an alternative means of engaging in public discourse, one that is more open to a plurality of opinions. In Box 9.2, we discuss findings from

Box 9.2   Social Media and the Spiral of Silence

A study by the Pew Research Center investigated the extent to which social media platforms facilitate democratic debate and aid in the creation of a new digital public sphere. The Pew conducted a survey of 1,801 adults in the United States and asked them about Edward Snowden's 2013 revelations of widespread government surveillance of cellphone and email records. The key findings indicate that people were more willing to discuss the Snowden–National Security Agency (NSA) story in person than on social media like Facebook and Twitter. (As will be discussed in more detail in Chapter 11, Edward Snowden, a former employee and ex–NSA contractor, leaked thousands of classified documents to the media. This story sparked a major debate not only in the United States but around the world, about the surveillance practices of intelligence services and citizens' rights to privacy.) The survey also found that those who were not willing to discuss the story in person were also not willing to discuss it on social media. That is, social media did not provide an alternative discussion platform for individuals who were reluctant to share their opinions with others. Finally, people were a lot more willing to share their views about the Snowden–NSA story, both in person and on social media, like Facebook, if they thought their audience agreed with them. This study provides direct support for the spiral of silence theory and shows that it extends to the Internet.

a 2014 Pew study that portrays a different picture, one where social media do not, in fact, provide that much-hoped-for forum for democratic debate.

The results presented in Box 9.2 show that Americans were more likely to discuss the Snowden–NSA case in person rather than on social media. As many as 86 per cent of Americans indicated that they would discuss the case with a friend or family member, but only 42 per cent indicated that they would voice their opinions on a social media site. Hence, for the average American, the Internet does not function as an alternative digital public sphere, nor is it deemed to be more suited for democratic debate than in-person interactions. Next, we explore a different angle of the debate about how the Internet affects the public sphere.

Third Places

Another important element of the public sphere is the notion of the **third place**. For Oldenburg (1999), the home is the first place, where family and friends come together. Work is the second place, where people spend a lot of their time and have a distinct set of co-workers and friends. Third places are coffee houses, taverns, restaurants, bars, libraries, and other locations that people visit routinely. These places ground people in the neighbourhood and community and allow them to interact and develop a sense of place. Third places are important locations for public opinion to form and for civil society to thrive. For example, a critical third place in eighteenth-century Europe was the enlightenment salon, which served as a venue for philosophical and academic conversation, as well as relevant social commentary and political analysis among citizens (Goodman, 1989).

How do digital technologies impact the role of third places in our technological society? Putnam (2000) argues that television has pulled people away from third places, with entertainment now taking place within the walls of the home. From his viewpoint, the Internet will have similar effects, immersing people in a world of information that has little overlap with their local community.

It is true that the data show fewer people engaging in local organizations, attending church, and participating in politics, as discussed earlier; however, digital technologies are in fact playing a *different* role in creating third places and rebuilding the public sphere. Digital technologies seem to be filling the gap left by traditional third places by providing alternative spaces to hang out, meet people, exchange ideas, debate social and political topics, and post and exchange information. While television seemed to contribute to the erosion of the public sphere (Putnam, 2000), the Internet as a medium provides much greater capacity for citizen engagement. (See the discussion of produsage in Chapter 7.)

The Internet as a Tool of Political Engagement

Indeed, the Internet is not only a source of entertainment but also a tool for political engagement and a place for civil society to emerge. The interactive nature of digital communication allows users to engage with material in a different manner than what TV affords. Not only can debate arise online, but community can form around political, social, and economic issues of concern to citizens. We will discuss this in Box 9.3, where we consider the recent uprising in the Middle East and the role social media has played in this particular social movement.

A key issue has been the role of the Internet both before and during the uprising (Howard, 2011). The Western media have been quick to conclude that this revolution was caused by social media, as the term "Twitter Revolution" suggests. However, analysts have cautioned people about making conjectures about how social media affected the process. Indeed, Zuckerman writes about how other factors have been central in leading up to the uprising: ". . . [A]ny attempt to credit a massive political shift to a single factor—technological, economic, or otherwise—is simply untrue. Tunisians took to the streets due to decades of frustration, not in reaction to a WikiLeaks cable, a denial-of-service attack, or a Facebook update" (2011).

Even though for Zuckerman social media is not the single factor in creating social change, he acknowledges that social media played an intrinsic

Box 9.3   Social Media in the Middle East

Social media has taken off in the Middle East with a large increase in users (Social Bakers, 2011). For example, protests in the Arab region started not in the streets but with short tweets on Twitter and posts on Facebook. The recent uprisings in Tunisia and Egypt have been labelled a **Twitter Revolution** because the Internet provided a platform to organize, mobilize, and voice opinions. In an eerily accurate prediction of the soon-to-take-place Twitter Revolution, Philip Howard, in his book *The Digital Origins of Dictatorship and Democracy* (2011), titled the prologue "Revolution in the Middle East Will Be Digitized." Howard's prescience shows how ICTs have become an integral part of political and social debate in the Middle East, adding to traditional forms of exchange taking place in coffee and tea shops, in taverns, on the streets, and in markets.

As the tension on the streets of Cairo increased, the government felt pressure to act quickly to evade a digital revolution. Its strategy was to shut down the Internet in an attempt to freeze the masses and stop them from organizing and going to the streets. This shutdown has been referred to as the use of the **Internet kill switch** and has opened a debate about the possibility of governments using their power and legislation to shut down the Web. The Egyptian government correctly recognized the power of social media to influence people to protest. The movement was not a small group of people in isolation rallying for change but, rather, the digital sphere mobilizing for social and political transformations. While the government identified the role of social media in initiating the protests, it made a mistake in thinking that flipping the Internet kill switch would stop the protests. The government not only cut citizens off from current national and international information about how the events were unfolding but also halted the protesters' ability to communicate and organize. In addition, the government cut off citizens from their cellphones, which meant no calls, no texting, and no Web access. Egypt was basically a zone of zero information and connectivity. That is, no emails, Facebook posts, or tweets could be received or sent from Egypt, effectively preventing citizens from communicating with one another and from exchanging news with the rest of the world. Surprisingly, this isola-

role in how the protests unfolded: "[A]s we learn more about the events of the past few weeks, we'll discover that online media did play a role in helping Tunisians learn about the actions their fellow citizens were taking and in making the decision to mobilize" (2011). Some analysts argue that social media were particularly critical in enabling protest leaders to mobilize; these leaders are referred to as **digital revolutionaries**. Wael Ghonim, who is a Google executive and played a role in the early stages of the uprising, saw great value in social media, saying, "[T]he revolution started on Facebook," and "[I]f you want to liberate a society just give them the Internet" (MacKinnon, 2011). The Arab Spring movement used social media extensively to voice opinions, exchange information, and organize during the early stages of the

tion did not stop the movement but, gave it further momentum. Now that people were cut off from all telecommunications, they went to the streets to express their anger and discontent about what they felt was an abuse of power on the part of their government. As a result, this change in government strategy infused a social movement with renewed strength and focus.

Furthermore, Twitter has been banned in many other countries in the Middle East and Europe either temporarily or for longer periods of time, including Iran (Shaheed, 2014), Turkey (BBC, 2014), and China (Bamman, O'Connor, & Smith, 2012). In 2014, news service France 24 reported that Turkish citizens were bypassing the Twitter ban in that country by learning how to change their DNS numbers and IP addresses and by using VPNs (virtual private networks). Interestingly, the instructions were spread by the use of graffiti—by people physically writing Google's public DNS numbers on walls and other surfaces all over Istanbul.

Anti-Mubarak protester holding a sign praising Facebook for helping to organize the 2011 protest in Tahrir Square, Cairo, Egypt.

protests. Figure 9.2 depicts the number of followers of Ghonim's Twitter account as the events unfolded. We observe a stark increase between 6 and 11 February 2011 from about 20,000 followers to as many as 80,000.

Srinivasan (2011) argues that we cannot deny the impact the Internet is having on politics. He writes, "With four billion mobile phone users and 30% of the world's population with basic Internet access, it's absurd to dispute the implications of these technologies on social, political, and economic life" (2011). Even individuals who are not connected are nonetheless affected by the technological changes. The Internet in and of itself is not a political tool; as Table 9.2 shows, people can use social media for many different reasons. What is unique about social media, however, is their

Total followers:

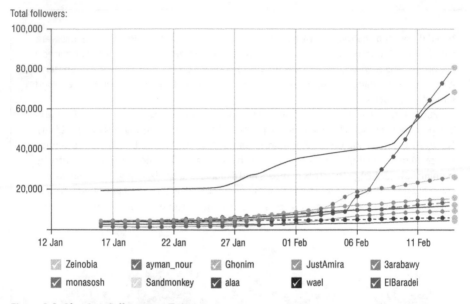

Figure 9.2 Ghonim's Followers on Twitter
Source: Tufekci, Z. Can "Leaderless revolutions" stay leaderless: Preferential attachment, iron laws and networks, *Technosociology* blog, 14 February 2011. Retrieved from http://technosociology.org/?p=366.

Table 9.2 The Uses of Social Media

Medium	Personal Use	Use for Activists
YouTube	Cute videos of your cats	Videos of trade union protests
Flickr	Cute photos of your cats	Subversive photos unblocked by firewalls
Google	Overlay your cute cat photos on a map of your neighbourhood	Overlay of prisons, land ownership in your country
Twitter	Real-time updates on your cats being cute	Real-time updates on whether activists are free or imprisoned
Blogger	Links to aspects of your cats' online presence	Online newsrooms reporting on activist activities

Source: Based on Zuckerman, E. The cute cat theory talk at ETech, *My Heart's in Accra* blog, 8 March 2009.

ability to connect people in real time in an organic and networked structure, which requires little centralization and command. New ICTs, "such as the internet and mobile phones, have had clear roles in both starting new democratic processes in some countries and in entrenching them in others" (Howard, 2011, p. 3).

The term **digital public sphere** describes the new forms of association that are developed online and the possibilities that they provide for citizens to organize and mobilize. Some of the central changes that have occurred as a result of the digitization of the public sphere according to Gripsrud, Moe, and Splichal (2010) are as follows:

1. Changes and processes occur on a global scale.
2. Various media converge and blur.
3. The commercialization of the media.

Hillary Rodham Clinton, in her February 2011 speech entitled "Internet Rights and Wrongs: Choices and Challenges in a Networked World," portrayed the Internet as the public sphere of the twenty-first century: "The Internet has become *the* public space of the 21st century. The world's town square, classroom, marketplace, coffeehouse and nightclub. We all shape and are shaped by what happens there. All two billion of us and counting" (2011, emphasis in original).

Clinton has also addressed the challenge the Internet poses as both an open space for debate and a source of economic growth. This challenge, often referred to as the **Internet dictator's dilemma**, creates enormous pressures on oppressive regimes. At the core of the problem is that non-democratic countries wish to take part in the digital economy through e-commerce, e-health, e-education, and other areas, while simultaneously controlling citizens' Internet use and censoring content. Clinton has pointed out that these regimes "will face a dictator's dilemma, and will have to choose between letting the walls fall or paying the price to keep them standing" (2011).

As Day and Schuler have noted, the "increasing communication and collaboration between social movements, civil society and community networks does . . . possess the potential for an emerging counter-culture" (2006, p. 20). Many of these initiatives are created and organized from the bottom up, through the use of a range of participatory tools that empower the community (Day & Schuler, 2006). These communities are diverse and vary in purpose: "[t]hey are not like organisational structures—the boundaries of which can be identified, quantified and measured—communities are messy, hard to pin down and problematic" (Day & Schuler, 2006, p. 27). Our discussion of the digital public sphere concludes with a comment by Srinivanas: "Even if new technologies can serve both democratic and repressive purposes, no one disputes their continued growth as the economic, social, political, and cultural substrate of our times" (2011, n.p.).

Conclusions

Community is in constant flux. As social, technological, and economic change take place, community and its forms of expression also shift. While much of the debate around the concept of community has focused on how much it has changed from the early pastoral community of the eighteenth century to our current high-tech society, this comparison does not really address the more important issue of what the current forms of community are. As people change their communicating and socializing patterns, new theories and measurements of community need to develop as well.

Early writings emphasized either the Internet's negative or its positive impact on social structure. The utopian perspective saw new communities of solidarity forming online without constraints of space and time. By contrast, the dystopian perspective emphasized potential negative effects of text-based communications that did not afford the rich contextual forms of exchange made possible in person. Both perspectives tend to provide a limited understanding of the impact of the Internet on the structuring of society. The Internet is blending into the rhythms of everyday life, supporting mundane activities such as banking, surfing for information, planning vacations, etc., as well as creating a sphere for new forms of socialization. Facebook and Twitter provide new platforms for staying in touch with large numbers of people from various spheres of a person's life, ranging from family, close friends, and acquaintances to co-workers and co-activists. These tools are changing the structure of society—people are no longer embedded in narrowly defined, local clusters, but instead tend to socialize with a heterogeneous, global social network. These networks are characterized by constant change as people shift locations, interests, and jobs. This new form of structure has been referred to as networked individualism because each person has his or her own unique network of family, friends, co-workers, and acquaintances. Overall, the evidence suggests that industrialization, urbanization, bureaucracy, and the digital media did not destroy community but instead have transformed its structure, composition, attitudes, and communication practices.

The public sphere is also undergoing transformations as a result of digital technologies, which provide alternative means of voicing, sharing, and debating opinions. Despite these new opportunities, the use of social media also creates new challenges. For example, in many countries, using Facebook as a means to express dissenting and alternative opinions about controversial topics circumvents censorship and oppression. From this, new challenges emerge as Facebook and other social media need to provide secure environments where dissidents can express their views without jeopardizing their safety (MacKinnon, 2011). Social media is still in its infancy and as its use becomes more integrated into society, both opportunities and challenges will arise.

Questions for Critical Thought

1. Does the Internet resemble a social structure similar to *Gemeinschaft* or *Gesellschaft*?

2. Provide an overview of the evidence that suggests the Internet is neither increasing nor decreasing social capital.

3. In comparison with in-person discussions, does social media provide its users with an opportunity to engage in open debate? Explain your response.

4. Discuss the role of social media (Twitter, Facebook, and YouTube) in the recent uprisings in Tunisia and Egypt.

Suggested Readings

Hampton, K., Rainie, L., Lu, W., Dwyer, M., Shin, I., & Purcell, K. (2014, August 26). Social media and the 'spiral of silence.' Retrieved October 20, 2014, from www.pewinternet. org/2014/08/26/social-media-and-the-spiral-of-silence/. This report describes the extent to which Americans voice a plurality of opinions on social media in comparison to in-person debate.

Howard, P.N. (2011). *The digital origins of dictatorship and democracy: Information technology and political Islam*. Oxford, England: Oxford University Press. An insightful book on the changes taking place in the Middle East and the role of information technology.

Putnam, R.D. (2000). *Bowling alone: The collapse and revival of American community*. New York: Simon and Schuster. The author argues that social capital is decreasing in America and shows how technology is linked to this decline.

Wellman, B., Quan-Haase, A., Witte, J., & Hampton, K. (2001). Does the Internet increase, decrease, or supplement social capital? Social networks, participation, and community commitment. *American Behavioral Scientist, 45*(3), 437–456. This article is a classic and presents data on the impact of the Internet on social capital.

Online Resources

Digital_nation: Life on the virtual frontier
www.pbs.org/wgbh/pages/frontline/digitalnation/etc/synopsis.html
> This outstanding PBS website for the program *Frontline* features PBS documentaries and interviews that examine what it is like to live in a digital world.

My Heart's in Accra
www.ethanzuckerman.com/blog
> An insightful blog maintained by Ethan Zuckerman, a senior researcher at the Berkman Center for Internet & Society.

"Technology is not driving us apart after all"
www.nytimes.com/2014/01/19/magazine/technology-is-not-driving-us-apart-after-all. html?_r=0
> This article from the *New York Times* addresses the fears that technologies, specifically mobile technologies, are destroying community and disconnecting individuals.

Decode: The NSA files
www.theguardian.com/us-news/the-nsa-files
> This site from *The Guardian* contains a series of interviews and reports on the nature and consequences of the Snowden–NSA case.

Technology-Mediated Social Relationships

Learning Objectives

◎ to provide a historical overview of the development of mediated communication and its role in societal change, with a focus on the Toronto School of Communication;

◎ to discuss how the introduction of the telephone helped redraw social boundaries and shift our understanding of private space;

◎ to closely examine current understandings of the term *friends* in the context of social media and how they contrast with sociological theory on what friendship is;

◎ to investigate how the Internet has affected the formation, maintenance, and dissolution of romantic relationships;

◎ to explore the concept of virtual mourning and how it shifts our understanding of death.

Introduction

In this chapter, we briefly outline the early beginnings of mediated communication and investigate the kinds of social change that have come about since their introduction. This includes an overview of the theories proposed by scholars belonging to the Toronto School of Communication, who have provided an in-depth and critical analysis of the influence of early forms of mediated communication on society. Then the chapter reviews modern trends in mediated communication and shows the complexities of crafting a virtual self that is visible and open to scrutiny by a large, networked audience. It follows with a discussion of the complex ways in which these trends affect interaction and the formation of social relationships. While most discourse focuses on the benefits of mediated communication, scholars have also warned about the potential negative effects on people's social life. We ask the following questions: Do technologies allow us to maintain strong, rewarding, and supporting relationships? Do technologies help us maintain relationships at a distance? The chapter then focuses on how social media have redefined our notion of friendship and examines the implications of these changes for social networking. This leads to an analysis of romance on the Internet, investigating how people form and terminate romantic relations using social media. Finally, the chapter ends by exploring the concept of virtual mourning and how people are renegotiating the meaning of death. Overall, we will critically discuss how technology transforms the social world around us, sometimes incrementally and in barely perceptible ways but other times drastically.

Early Beginnings of Mediated Communication

The study of how mediated communication becomes integrated into daily life and impacts society has a long tradition, starting with the early investigations from the **Toronto School of Communication**, which was a loosely connected network of scholars at the University of Toronto. Key intellectuals of the school include Eric A. Havelock, Walter J. Ong, Harold A. Innis, and Marshall McLuhan. We will briefly discuss some of the most central theories and ideas put forward by these scholars. Note that the intellectual contributions of McLuhan to our understanding of mediated communication were discussed in Chapter 2.

Eric A. Havelock

Havelock's work consisted of historical research and investigated the early methods of communication, in particular the effects of literacy. Havelock's theorizing was instrumental in stressing the political, social, and cultural changes brought about by the move from **oral societies** to **literate societies** (Crowley & Heyer, 2011). In oral societies, memory is used as the primary means for recording historical events and transmitting knowledge and traditions. In literate societies, by contrast, the written word becomes the authoritative means of recording and storing information (Havelock, 1963). Early forms of writing are complex and varied. Early **hieroglyphs** are depictions of actual objects and later hieroglyphs represent sounds, providing a more flexible system of representation (Crowley & Heyer, 2011). In the case of Egyptian tombs, written texts were meant to be permanent and hence were often inscribed in stone. As a result, **epigraphy**—the study of the history and social circumstances of written information preserved on hard materials—emerged to provide unique insights into the social structure of these ancient civilizations. A common use of writing was to document religious rituals and prayers. For Havelock, the move to literacy in Greek culture led to two fundamental shifts:

1. **Content of thought**: In oral societies, the focus is on action, either internally or externally motivated, and on the thoughts accompanying these actions—sorrow, happiness, or contentment. By contrast, writing brings with it more abstract and propositional content (Halverson, 1992), modifying consciousness and thought processes. Havelock sees Plato as the first to express the change in the content of thought brought about by literacy, through his dialectic forms of deliberation.

2. **Organization of thought**: This is perhaps the most fundamental dif-
    ference observed in the shift from an oral to a literate society and con-
    sists of changes in how main ideas and subordinate ideas are linked to
    one another. Havelock argues that in an oral society, ideas are connected
    in an associative manner, while in a literate society they are organized to
    put forth a main idea to which all subordinate ideas are logically linked.

Havelock influenced many scholars in the fields of communication, sociology, and literary studies. His work, however, has received strong criticism
from academics because of its lack of rigour, limited empirical evidence, and
inappropriate methodology (Halverson, 1992). In addition, critics claim that
Havelock did not have a full understanding of the ancient texts on which his
main arguments were based, thus limiting the validity of his findings.

Walter J. Ong

Ong (1991) continued in Havelock's footsteps, investigating social change
resulting from electronic media, such as television, the telephone, and radio.
His key intellectual contribution was to move away from a simple dichotomy between the written and the oral. He argued that different notions of
orality could exist, some of which are directly linked to *print culture*. Print
culture then is understood as a complex system including written documents, social practices emerging around written documents, and oral forms
of exchange. Ong distinguishes between **primary** and **secondary orality**
to understand communication. He argues that secondary orality represents
a form of **post-typography** because in it oral communication is dominant
over the written word. For him, secondary orality describes a second verbal
era that integrates elements from both oral and literate societies; that is, it
exists in the context of and makes reference to print culture. This form "has
striking resemblance to the old in its participatory mystique, its fostering of
a communal sense, its concentration on the present moment, and even its
use of formulas" (Ong, 1991, pp. 133–134). In oral societies individuals are
immersed in *polychronic time*; that is, multiple events occur at once without
sequence. Ong makes it clear that despite the resemblance between oral societies and secondary orality, the latter is more deliberate and self-conscious,
directly linked to writing and print culture. An example of this would be a
CNN news report (oral form of delivery) that makes reference to an event
that occurred on Twitter (print culture).

Harold Innis

An equivalent line of thinking emerged in the writings of Innis (1951), who
emphasized the structural changes resulting from literacy. Central to his
theorizing is the concept of **media bias**, which refers to the transforming
power of media in human affairs. He distinguishes between forms of com-

munication that have a **time bias** versus those that have a **space bias**. Time bias describes oral societies in which there is an emphasis on community building. In these societies, change occurs slowly because the only transfer of culture, information, and knowledge is through oral means. Hence, memory and memorization played a crucial role in the transmission of information over time, increasing the sheer amount and redundancy of information. By contrast, literate societies have a space bias that favours imperialism and commerce because writing allows for the easy dissemination of ideas and information over vast distances. Innis describes ancient Greece as an example of an oral society with a time bias that supports community and is averse to change. Innis contrasts ancient Greece with the Roman Empire, which for him had a space bias, as the Romans focused on expanding their influence throughout Europe, Africa, and the Middle East. For this purpose, written documents were important as they allowed for messages, updated rulings, and other types of information to be conveyed throughout the empire. Other examples of space-binding media include print, radio, television, and digital media because they reach a wide range of people and overcome space constraints. This links to McLuhan's writings on the global village—a concept that denotes the overcoming of spatial and time barriers leading to a more compressed world—which were discussed in Chapter 2.

The Toronto School of Communication provided many early insights into how media become integrated into society, as well as their transformative nature. Nonetheless, the group only scratched the surface in terms of the many interrelationships that exist between prevalent modes of communication and the structuring of society. Another critique of these early writers is that they tend to examine communication from a standpoint of technological determinism, assuming that technology has a strong and unidirectional impact on society instead of thinking of the relationship as a coming together of technological and societal trends. In the next sections, we examine first how the telephone slowly became adopted in North American society and then look at the effects of the Internet on forming, maintaining, and ending social relationships.

North America Calling: The Impact of the Telephone on Social Relationships

Much innovation occurred in the realm of telecommunications in the eighteenth century, leading first to the invention of the telegraph, a device that for a long time was the main means of transmitting printed information by wire or radio wave over long distances. The telegraph was followed by the introduction of the telephone, which slowly, albeit drastically, shaped the way people communicated with one another. The telephone has undergone many transformations since Alexander Graham Bell developed the first prototype (Klemens, 2010).

The initial model allowed only for the transmission of sounds: speech could not be discerned. Around 1910, the **party line** (or shared line) was introduced, making the telephone more user-friendly and affordable. **Automatic dialing** was introduced in the 1920s, resulting in a complete shift in how telephones were used because there was no longer the need for operators to relay calls. While telephones have become normalized in society and are being substituted with cellphones, their introduction was tumultuous.

Claude S. Fischer (1992b) writes about the resistance to the telephone on the part of diverse social groups and the ways in which the telephone fundamentally changed American society. For him, this transformation occurred through a mutual shaping process between the technology and social actors: "[a]s much as people adapt their lives to the changed circumstances created by a new technology, they also adapt that technology to their lives" (Fischer, 1992b, p. 5). Hence, the impact of the telephone was not radical; instead, people came to rely on the telephone gradually, over time, as the technology became embedded in existing social norms and practices, eventually functioning as an additional form of communication to in-person exchanges.

One social change that the telephone brought about was the rewriting of social boundaries set out by class, race, and status (Marvin, 1988). The telephone created different forms of **social accessibility**, where people who were previously inaccessible, such as public figures, could suddenly be reached directly and instantly. As the technology has evolved, however, people have gained more control over how they can be reached and by whom. For instance, the introduction of call display to screen calls and the use of answering machines to record messages afford more flexibility and social control. One study by Quan-Haase and Collins (2008) looks at instant messaging, such as MSN Messenger or Facebook chat, and demonstrates how the evolution of digital forms of communication can provide better control over social accessibility. They concluded that people have more control with instant messaging than with the telephone because the user can determine when to log on the system, when to log out, whom to ignore, and with whom to communicate. Megan, one of the participants in the study, explains how it works: "Usually [IM] goes right away to 'away.' Because it keeps the people who are just bored and need somebody to talk to from talking to me, 'cause then they know that I'm away. But if it's something important, then they'll talk anyway." This shows how features in the technology provide users with more control over their social accessibility.

The telephone also opened up previously sheltered social realms, such as the home: "Home was the protected place, carefully shielded from the world and its dangerous influences. New communications technologies were suspect precisely to the extent that they lessened the family's control over what was admitted within its walls" (Marvin, 1988, p. 76). Despite people's initial apprehension, the telephone became widely adopted in Western societies and has had widespread social consequences. Nonetheless, the telephone was just the beginning of the close link between telecommunications and society. The Internet as a medium would diffuse much more rapidly, and its effects would be more profound and all-encompassing.

Penetration of Mediated Communication: The Impact of the Internet on Social Relationships

The Internet as a form of communication has come to occupy a predominant role in our society. Figure 10.1 shows how penetration rates have changed in the United States from 2000 to 2014. While there are some minor peaks in the data, the trend is for an increase in Internet use among all age groups. Adults 65 and older are still the slowest to adopt the Internet as a communication tool; they are particularly slow in the adoption of social media (Haight, et al., 2014). This group of users is often referred to as **digital immigrants** because they came to the Internet late in life and have been generally slow and apprehensive in adopting novel forms of communication (Prensky, 2001). In the 18- to 29-year-old age group, an impressive 97 per cent of Americans were Internet users in 2014. This group is usually referred to as **digital natives** because they have grown up with the Internet and are unfamiliar with a pre-Internet time (Palfrey & Gasser, 2008; Prensky, 2001). In addition, the data show that 63 per cent of teens go online every day, of which 36 per cent go online several times a day and 27 per cent go online about once a day.

Since 2005, we have observed a shift in how people use media for communication. Email and instant messaging—even though they continue to be used for specific purposes—have been largely displaced by social media for

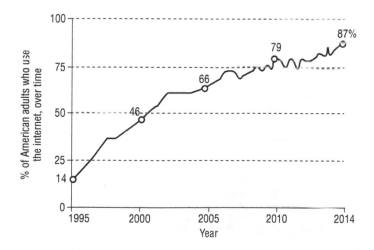

Figure 10.1 Internet Use in America, 1995–2014
Source: "Internet use, 1995–2014" Pew Research Center, Washington, DC (February, 2014) http://www.pewinternet. org/2014/02/27/part-1-how-the-internet-has-woven-itself-into-american-life/.

the purpose of communication among peers (Quan-Haase & Young, 2010). Among Americans 18 and older, 72 per cent use a social networking site. This number increases to 89 per cent in the 18- to 29-year age range (Brenner & Smith, 2013). Figure 10.2 shows that only 22 per cent of Internet users in the United States do not use a social media site (Duggan & Smith, 2013). The study also shows that 36 per cent have adopted one site and as many as 42 per cent have adopted two or more sites. For 84 per cent of Americans, Facebook continues to be their number one social networking site of choice (Duggan & Smith, 2013), while only 8 per cent use LinkedIn, 4 per cent use Pinterest, and 2 per cent indicate that Instagram or Twitter is their main social net-working site. And Americans are not the only ones to embrace Facebook as their social networking site of choice: Canadians have also embraced it in large numbers and are among the greatest users of Facebook worldwide (Oliveira, 2014). The head of Facebook Canada, Jordan Banks, stated that there are 19 million Canadians who use Facebook at least once a month and 14 million who are daily users. These numbers indicate that about half of Canadians are on Facebook on a daily basis (Oliveira, 2014).

Social media have revolutionized the communication landscape, becoming an integral part of how we interact with others and disseminate information. We next examine how these tools become integrated into our daily lives by covering four central topics including how we present ourselves online, form friendships, negotiate relations with romantic partners, and mourn loved ones.

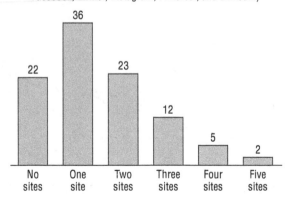

% of Internet users who use the following number of social networking sites (sites measured include Facebook, Twitter, Instagram, Pinterest, and LinkedIn)

Pew Research Center's Internet Project August Tracking Survey, August 07–September 16, 2013. N = 1,445 Internet users ages 18+. Interviews were conducted in English and Spanish and on landline and cellphones. The margin of error for results based on all Internet users is +/–2.9 percentage points.

Figure 10.2 Number of Social Media Sites Used in the United States
Source: "Number of social media sites used" Pew Research Center, Washington, DC (December, 2013) http://www.pewinternet.org/2014/02/27/part-1-how-the-internet-has-woven-itself-into-american-life/.

How Has Technology Affected Our Relationships?

We do not usually think of social phenomena, such as friendship, family ties, and romance, in terms of technology. Technology, however, does play a significant role in the creation, maintenance, and dissolution of social relations.

1. Presentation of the Self Online

Our digital lives also include an element of self-presentation. But what is the self? The *self* is often defined as containing information such as one's name, how one perceives oneself, one's likes and dislikes, one's personal beliefs and values, and other aspects that are important to who one is as a person (Sedikides & Spencer, 2011). These attributes are not perceived as stable, but rather as changing over time depending on new life experiences that are integrated into the self (Anthis, 2002; Marcia, 1966; McCrae & Costa, 1990). The notion of a single self has been dismissed by Coser (1975), who has shown that individuals have multiple selves that are displayed in different social roles and networks. That is, different attributes and behaviours come to light when a person interacts with their peers than when they interact with their professional network at work. For Higgins (1987), the self can be divided into three core components:

1. an actual self determined by a person's attributes;
2. an ideal self based on how a person wants to be perceived; and
3. an "ought to be" self that expresses a person's moral expectations.

It is through these three core components that a person's behaviours and attitudes are shaped. But how does the self operate in virtual space? Often the acronym **IRL**, meaning **"in real life,"** is used to denote people, events, and actions that exist offline. Given this difference between the two spaces, is the **virtual self** different from the real life self? Is the online self simply a replica of one's offline self? Or is it a newly crafted self?

Sherry Turkle (1995) argued that the Internet allows for identity exploration of and experimentation with variations of the self. That is, one can explore aspects of the self in a safe environment without feeling judged by a normative society. This may be particularly important for young people who are in the process of developing their identity. In her seminal book *The Second Self* (1984), Turkle discusses identity play on the Internet and writes about the effects technology has on our social and psychological lives. Using interviews with hackers she finds that her interviewees' participation in online communities fills a void in their personal lives and fulfills a need for escape from daily routines.

For Sundén (2003), the crafting of the self online is more complex than its offline counterpart. She introduces the concept of **writing oneself into being** to emphasize the active engagement that goes into digital self-presentation. This concept stresses the importance of selecting what to include in a profile, how much information is shared, and who will constitute the digital audience. This is not a random act, as Hogan (2010) points out: this is a process of **data curation**, where users act like curators of exhibits or museums, carefully selecting pictures, information, and artifacts that are all strategically positioned to craft a unique self. For Goffman (1959) this distinction was central as it emphasized agency. Goffman referred to the presentation of self in private space as a person's **backstage** and the public expression of self as the **frontstage**. This is important for understanding users' decisions as to what to post. For users social media is their frontstage and it is there that they accordingly present their most desirable elements of the self.

boyd (2006) expands Sundén's concept of writing oneself into being and explains how users also engage in **writing community into being**. This occurs through making friendship connections explicit and thereby providing credibility to a user's profile. Because the connections via social networking sites represent an extension of our offline social networks, this greatly limits the extent of self-idealization and provides a reality check for content posted. At the same time, Mehdizadeh (2010) argues that on social media individuals have some freedom to customize their profile and can engage in identity play, in particular on sites where they are anonymous. Aboujaoude (2012) has shown that some individuals go as far as to display a completely distinct "e-identity," one that has little to no resemblance to their offline selves. In some cases, the e-identity has a greater tendency to show deviant behaviour through online flaming, harassment, and personal attacks. This is referred to as the **disinhibition effect** (Suler, 2004) and results from a lack of interpersonal cues and limited enforcement of social norms. Box 10.1 discusses cyber-bullying as an example of the damaging effects of anti-social online behaviour on young people's lives.

Young people cannot effectively resolve problems of cyber-bullying on their own; they need support from key social groups and figures, including parents. In a study of how parents of victims of cyber-bullying cope and support their children, Canadian criminologist Ryan Broll (2014) found that this was very difficult for parents. Often they struggled to find a balance between their children's desire for freedom and independence when online and their simultaneous need for protection and parent intervention. What complicated matters was that parents often were overwhelmed by the technology itself; this prevented them from supporting their kids' engagement in crafting an online identity and connecting to a digital audience. For Broll (2014) this problem can only be addressed by helping parents connect to teachers, the police force, social workers, and other partners. He refers to this approach as a **network of security partners** who come together to inform, advise, and collaborate with one another in ensuring young people's safety online.

Box 10.1   Cyber-bullying: The Case of Amanda Todd

Adolescents confront new struggles growing up in a digitally mediated world. This becomes apparent when we look at the phenomenon of cyber-bullying. Cyber-bullying is commonly defined as intentionally and frequently repeated actions with the aim of harming another Internet user (Tokunaga, 2010). Often cyber-bullying is viewed as an extension of traditional forms of bullying that take place in the school-yard and include physical or verbal abuse. Some writers, though, see cyber-bullying as being inherently more difficult to escape, more damaging for the victims, and more pervasive.

A frame from Amanda Todd's YouTube post.

A case of cyber-bullying demonstrating the irreversible consequences of these malicious cyber attacks is that of Amanda Todd, a fifteen-year-old from British Columbia, Canada. On 10 October 2012, Amanda Todd was found dead. Her resolution to take her own life was directly linked to her distressing experiences online. When suicide results from attacks on a person on the Internet, it is termed **cyber bullicide**. Some insight can be gained into her struggles from a YouTube video she posted prior to her death (see www.youtube.com/watch?v=ej7afkypUsc). The photo above shows how in the video, using flashcards, she tells a story of being black-mailed and bullied online, of desperation, fear, and a sense of helplessness (Wolak, Mitchell, & Finkelhor, 2007). This feeling of having nowhere to hide is directly linked to the fact that digital technologies are pervasive in young people's lives (boyd, 2014). Sociological researchers need to understand what motivates perpetrators to engage in cyber-bullying, how to support victims, and what kinds of impacts these struggles have on personal development and youth socialization.

2. Rethinking Friendship on Social Media

What does friendship mean on social media? When we can accumulate hundreds of friends on Facebook, this changes the meaning of the word. Traditionally, **friendship** reflected an informal association without distinct boundaries. Unlike work and family ties, friendships are voluntary in nature, and the content of the friendship is determined, negotiated, and established by the two parties involved and can change over time (Fischer, 1982). There is no single meaning of *friendship* as it is culturally determined and based on social norms. Nonetheless, there is an understanding that friendship relations are strong, based on trust, and provide emotional, economic, and social support (Granovetter, 1973).[1]

On social networking sites, people send others friendship requests to connect them to their profile, a process called **friending** (boyd, 2006). An assumption people made in the past was that the list of people on Facebook directly reflected a person's IRL social network and hence was a reflection of a person's circle of close friends. This is not the case, however. Research has shown that users link their social networking site profile to a fairly disparate mix of people instead of it being a direct reflection of one's network of close friends only (boyd, 2006). Users often add people they have met only once or who are friends of friends.

The reason friendship acquires a different meaning in social media becomes evident when we focus on the features of the technology itself: social networking sites introduce novel constraints and possibilities, creating fundamentally different norms around friendship formation and maintenance (Baym, 2010).

To provide a more systematic framework of the influence of technology on friendship, boyd (2006)—in her research based on users of **Friendster** and **MySpace**—identified four different features of social networking sites that affect friendship formation:

1. **Persistence**: Data posted on profiles and walls of social networking sites remain indefinitely archived on these sites and can be retrieved in the future.
2. **Searchability**: This is a key feature of digital data because it facilitates finding information about others.
3. **Replicability**: This feature refers to capabilities provided online to reproduce content (text, pictures, and videos) and insert it in other contexts. Users can post content effortlessly from one medium to another or from one conversation into another.
4. **Invisible audience**: Determining the identity of a recipient or reader of a post is not easy, and thus tailoring messages toward specific audiences is also difficult.

These four characteristics of social media are important in terms of understanding the meaning of friendship online. On Facebook, for example, people can see who someone else's friends are; this puts pressure on peers to have a similar number of friends, to have similar kinds of friends (status, gender, diversity), or to have specific individuals as friends as well. This transparency, which was lacking before the introduction of social networking sites, can create tension, change social norms around what friendship means, and create expectations around friendship formation. That same transparency can also help activate **latent ties**, which in turn can provide useful information, social support in difficult times, and companionship when away from home (Quan-Haase & Young, 2010). The term *latent ties* describes the process whereby "adding any network-based means of communication—whether a new IRC channel, a social support group, a Webboard or email listserv—lays the groundwork for connectivity between formerly unconnected others" (Haythornthwaite, 2005, p. 136). Latent ties refer to relationships that have yet to be formally developed but have had the foundation set for friendship formation through the networking power of technology. Therefore, features of communication technologies shape how friendships form and develop online.

To what extent does the Internet facilitate the formation of new relationships? While most users of Facebook have large networks of about 338 connections on average (Smith, 2014), these relationships are rarely initiated online. While early research suggested that computer-mediated communication would facilitate the formation of new social ties, accruing evidence shows that such communication is used primarily for maintaining existing social ties (Ellison, Steinfield, & Lampe, 2007; Katz & Rice, 2002). New relationships would mean meeting total strangers online and getting to know them well through the Internet. While new relationships do form online, as in the example of Eva Markvoort, whom we will discuss later in this chapter, the majority of online exchanges occur between friends, family, co-workers, and classmates. In sum, most people we "friend" on social networking sites are people we have met before in person or people who are friends of friends. In fact, for the large part, social networking sites are a representation of our offline social networks, which limits the extent of self-idealization.

3. Romance Online

Understanding social media also includes understanding how it has changed the nature of romantic relationships—how they start as well as how they end. People use social media, first of all, to screen potential romantic partners by searching Google and visiting their online profile. In addition to providing verifying information on potential romantic partners, social media can also move the relationship forward more quickly, as text messaging, posts on walls, and Twitter tweets can fill the communication gap that might otherwise occur in between in-person meetings (McGinn, 2011).

Tufekci (2007) found that about 60 per cent of university students reported their romantic status and their sexual orientation on their social network profile. While students indicate that they are concerned about strangers accessing their profile, they also see such availability as advantageous: potential romantic partners can learn about each others' interests, meet friends of friends, and find out about a person's unique personality through wall posts, reports of past activities, and pictures. In part, the social network profile provides a glimpse into someone else's past and present life. This also serves a purpose when meeting potential partners online.

Online dating is now a fairly widespread social practice. Smith and Duggan (2013) report that 11 per cent of American adults have created a profile on one of the popular dating sites, such as PlentyOfFish (POF), Match.com, and eHarmony; 42 per cent of Americans know someone who engages in online dating; and 29 per cent are aware of someone who developed a long-term relationship following online dating. Some consider online dating as less serious and more prone to deception, but evidence from the Pew (Smith & Duggan, 2013) study shows that online dating in 23 per cent of cases leads to a serious long-term relationship or even marriage.

Romantic relationships also originate from active participation in online communities or video games. Huynh, Lim, and Skoric (2013) looked at massively multiplayer online games (MMOs or MMOGs), and noted that such games "have blurred the play/life boundary, transforming themselves from a site of pure play to a site for romantic relationship formation and maintenance" (pp. 251–252). In their study, they found that in-game romances did not remain in the virtual; they often translated into offline relationships. To those playing the MMOs, romantic interactions were a part of their constructed reality (Huynh et al., 2013). This shows that dedicated dating sites are not the only online venues for meeting romantic partners; rather, there are many different avenues for the creation and expression of romantic relationships.

Not only does the Internet play a role in the formation of new romantic relations, it has also become an important part of maintaining long-term relationships. For instance, couples who are in a long-term relationship will often post their relationship status on Facebook: a study by Young and Quan-Haase (2009) found that 60 per cent of males and 65 per cent of females posted their current status. The relationship status on Facebook functions as a social signal, legitimizing the seriousness of the relationship and assuring the partner that things are progressing well (Mod, 2010). In a study by Mod (2010), those individuals who had updated their Facebook relationship status were more likely to experience happiness and satisfaction in their relationship rather than jealousy based on their partner's online behaviours. For married couples, posting frequent dyadic profile pictures and statuses strengthened the relationship and increased satisfaction (Saslow, Muide, Impett, and Dublin, 2013). A Pew (Lenhart & Duggan, 2014) report showed that the Internet has had a "major impact" on about 10 per cent of romantic relationships, with 74 per cent of individuals reporting that the influence was largely positive, because of the possibilities of obtaining advice and social support.

Even though many reports about the role the Internet plays in romantic relations are positive, most problematic behaviour is associated with break-ups. The phenomenon known as **breakup 2.0** is complex because it involves the initiator and non-initiator of the breakup, the social network that is serving as an audience of the breakup, and the digital footprints available on social media sites. Box 10.2 showcases a study of the problematic online behaviours that emerge during the dissolution of a romantic relationship.

Box 10.2   Breakup 2.0

Ending romantic relationships has never been easy. In her book *Breakup 2.0.*, Gershon (2010) was intrigued by how social media and mobile technology have affected the formation and dissolution of romantic relationships. In her investigation, she found that young people are confused about the role that mediated communication should play in the breakup.

Gershon based her study on 72 interviews and 472 questionnaires primarily with university students. She discovered that people believe that the medium chosen to communicate the breakup is pivotal. Some media are evaluated as more serious than others and hence are more suited for ending a relationship. For most participants in the study, face-to-face communication was the medium of choice for breaking up with someone, and they considered using other media to be highly inappropriate.

In addition, Gershon identified problematic breakup practices unique to social media: changing one's relationship status on Facebook, rereading and overanalyzing emails and wall posts, stalking online, and deciding to "defriend" an ex from Facebook.

Lukacs and Quan-Haase (2015) have also noted other ways that breakups have been complicated by social media. Facebook has increased the amount of distress for parties involved in breakups due to salient digital reminders of their relationship, including pictures together, posts and messages, status updates, and other digital memorabilia. What also complicates the breakup is that social media creates another layer of interpreted communication with the ex-partner. Any information posted by the ex can be interpreted in multiple ways, some of which can be hurtful. In Lukacs and Quan-Haase's (2015) study, respondents reported that accessibility to

Continued

the ex's behaviours often promotes **cyberstalking** or interpersonal electronic surveil-lance (IES). IES is defined as the use of information and communication technologies to gain awareness of and monitor another user's online and/or offline behaviours (Tokunaga, 2011). Furthermore, distress resulting from the breakup has prompted coping strategies in the digital age that are directly related to social media. Quan-Haase, Nevin, and Lukacs (2014) proposed a typology of coping strategies on Facebook comprising 23 common post-breakup behaviours, including the removal of digital traces, limiting online communication with the ex-partner, and preventa-tive measures against ex-partner antagonism. The choice of coping strategies was informed by both prior learning from past experiences with breakups and vicarious learning from others' experiences.

Box 10.2 shows how social media have made the process of break-ing up more difficult. As a relationship unfolds, it leaves a digital trace on Facebook (Hogan & Quan-Haase, 2010), which can trigger memories of the romance even after its dissolution. van Dijck (2007) points toward the existing relationship among material culture, technology, and memory, arguing that objects mediate memory and represent a person's identity in a specific moment in time. In the same way in which people fill shoeboxes with personal items, social media become repositories of our past relation-ships. These digital traces can make it difficult to move on and leave previ-ous relationships behind.

In the context of romantic relationships, the use of media follows exist-ing social norms, often established over time within specific user groups. Gershon (2010) identifies three key concepts to explain how people adopt social media in their daily communication practices:

1. The term **media ideologies** describes the beliefs users form about com-puter-mediated communication and the perceived meaning assigned to the various forms of communication. For example, many univer-sity students perceive email as a formal medium because it resembles a letter.
2. **Idioms of practice** refers to how groups of people agree to use different media. This occurs through shared experience.
3. **Second order communication** conveys the formality and nature of a medium. For instance, texting is usually perceived as informal because of its brevity and lack of interactivity.

These conventions about how and when to use a specific medium are rel-evant social norms that help guide behaviour. The social norms that have emerged on the Internet regarding communication are referred to as **net-iquette**. Gershon (2010) argues that social media are not intrinsically formal or informal but that social groups establish norms about which media they see as appropriate for what kinds of messages and social circumstances. Breaking up via texting is perceived as completely inappropriate because texting is an informal medium that provides little opportunity for feedback and engagement. Nonetheless, this practice is becoming more prevalent as young people adopt cellphones as their primary means of communication.

4. Virtual Mourning

An important part of our culture is expressing our sympathies to friends and family who have lost a loved one. When someone dies, family and community come together to celebrate the lost life and to provide each other with emotional support and comfort. We are observing a change in how mourning occurs in the age of widespread social media use (Hogan & Quan-Haase, 2010).

Even though virtual communities in which members build strong social connections have existed since the 1980s (Rheingold, 1993), these were in the minority (Castells, 2001). Rather, in early Net culture the emphasis was on exchanging information and collaborating, as the Web was primarily the domain of academics, geeks, and the military. What we are currently witnessing is a move toward the **domestication** and **mainstreaming of the Web** as more people become users of social media and integrate it into their daily lives (Hogan & Quan-Haase, 2010). That is, people are now using the Internet not only as a source of information but as a means to socialize and to maintain existing relationships.

A consequence of this shift is the use of social media to deal with the loss experienced when a loved one dies. In this context, the Internet can be described as a *thanatechnology*, which Sofka (1997) defines as "technological mechanisms such as interactive videodiscs and computer programs that are used to access information or aid in learning about thanatology topics" (Sofka, 1997, p. 553). Thanatechnologies play an important role in society as they help people cope with the death of a family member, friend, or other member of the community.

With millions of individuals creating profiles on social media sites, a unique Net culture has inevitably evolved to deal with loss. Within this Net culture, we are observing two different kinds of mourning:

1. *Virtual mourning*: When a family member, friend, or classmate dies, people come together online to commemorate, mourn, sympathize, and provide emotional, social, and economic support.
2. *Virtual stranger loss*: This constitutes the online mourning of people who are strangers; that is, the mourning of people one has never met.

Virtual Mourning

Virtual mourning is becoming a common phenomenon. As long as a deceased user's profile continues to be updated through posts on walls, pictures, and status updates, the illusion persists that content and user are one entity. Hogan and Quan-Haase (2010) point out that "when the submitter dies, and the profile lives on, we can see this distinction all too clearly. Death has become the ultimate arbiter of this difference between the data that persists and the individual that does not" (p. 311).

Carroll and Landry (2010) discuss the persistent online presence of deceased individuals, known personally by those left behind, and how their MySpace and Facebook pages are transformed into memorial pages and sites of grieving. In their study, the researchers identify four activities that take place on social networking sites after loss.

The first activity is the creation of a narrative of the dead person's life. People tell stories about the deceased to cope with the loss. This engagement with the person's life history is a collaborative process, in which family and friends often reflect upon and negotiate the person's various and divergent portrayals.

The second activity is the posting of short, simple notes on a person's wall to publicly express feelings of loss and solidarity, which allows the community to share their feelings with others and join in the act of memorializing and coping with grief—for example, "RIP" or "I miss you." Following is another example from Carroll and Landry:

> i miss you adam, i wish you could come back but since you can't, i wanted to say that i love you very much, we all miss you, ♥courtney (posted 9 April 2007, http://profile.myspace.com/index.dfm?useaction=user.viewprofile&friendID =175255389)

A third activity is to praise the deceased and highlight their virtues, merits, and accomplishments. A fourth includes addressing the deceased directly by asking them for guidance, comfort, and understanding. This act shows how powerful profiles are in continuing to represent the deceased and in providing some form of comfort for those left behind. The engagement in these four activities brings the community closer together, and the profile of the deceased provides a central space for family and friends near and far to congregate, to share their memories, and to express their feelings of loss.

Virtual Stranger Loss

A second, and very different, form of mourning that is observed on the Internet is related to virtual stranger loss, where users mourn the loss of someone they have never actually met. In order to better understand virtual stranger loss, this section discusses first how strong relationships can be formed online with individuals we have never met in person; it then shows how the loss of those individuals can affect us emotionally. Two examples are discussed in this section: first, the life and sudden death of Canadian Eva Markvoort, and then the unexpected death of pop singer Michael Jackson.

People often underestimate the power of the Internet for forming social connections, even with strangers. Nonetheless, online relationships are as real as any other relationship we form. How can we understand why people feel so strongly for others they have only met online? How does the medium change the dynamics of friendship, community, and social support? Without the Internet, the struggle of someone such as Eva Markvoort (see Box 10.3) would have taken place privately. Traditional media, such as radio or television, would have perhaps provided a short documentary on her journey, which would have been broadcast without allowing the audience any significant intimate engagement with her. In the context of traditional media, it would have been difficult for an individual to directly respond to a story like Markvoort's and to get in touch with her.

Box 10.3   65_RedRoses: The Community around Eva Markvoort

Eva Markvoort, a 23-year-old Canadian from British Columbia, lived with cystic fibrosis (CF), a deadly disease that affects the lungs and digestive system and significantly shortens sufferers' lifespans. While undergoing treatment and waiting for a double lung transplant, Markvoort created a blog on **LiveJournal** about her experience under the name 65_RedRoses. The blog started on 15 July 2006:

> I need somewhere to vent. To let go and not always be motivating and inspiring. I need somewhere to let my fears go unleashed . . . I'm hoping to find someone else who knows what it's like to climb the stairs and not be able to breathe and hate the fact that you know your body needs a couple of weeks in the hospital. Someone else who is sick and tired of being sick and tired. Who appreciates the days when skipping and running is possible because those days are farer [sic] and fewer between.

The blog gave Markvoort a venue in which to reflect on her own struggle with CF and to communicate to a world out there on the Web about her journey. She probably never imagined the impact it—and she—would have on people's lives. Her vibrant personality and the tragic nature of her story, however, created an outpouring of support, friendship, love, and understanding. As Markvoort's health went through ups and downs, her online community provided her with comfort, reassurance, and strength. Through her blog entries, Eva touched the lives of many people who either had previous experiences with CF or who felt moved by her story and connected to her. She also got to closely know some of her online followers. Two girls whom she connected with were also suffering from CF, and by sharing their day-to-day experiences with the illness, the three became close friends. The community that formed

Continued

around Markvoort was very powerful because it was based on a shared experience and it became for her a vital source of emotional support.

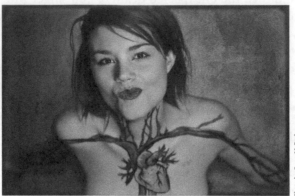

Eva Markvoort as 65_RedRoses.

A key distinguishing feature of new media is **interactivity**, which describes users' ability to provide content in response to a source or a communication partner (Ha & James, 1998). Hence, the Internet has removed a layer between the sender of a message and the receiver, allowing for a direct and high level of involvement from a larger audience. This gives audience members more control over content and its use than traditional media does. Blogs often feature a "comment and reply" function, and many of Markvoort's blog entries have comments from readers who left messages for her, to which she in turn responded. Markvoort was also able to communicate with people she met online via video chat (Skype), which allows communication partners to talk to each other in real time as well as to see each other.

With the domestication and mainstreaming of the Internet, loss, illness, and suffering have also inevitably become a part of being online. The Internet serves as a space for friends, family, and the larger community to come together and express their feelings and thoughts. It is a unique platform that overcomes barriers of time and space and, as Eva Markvoort's story demonstrates, allows those with similar life experiences to connect and provide each other with friendship and support.

A completely different kind of mourning was expressed online with the death of the "King of Pop," Michael Jackson, on 25 June 2010. When people found out about his death through traditional media, they went online to confirm the news, to find out more information surrounding the events, to look up biographical data and pictures, and to read about the reactions of the Jackson family to the event. This move toward the Internet, and toward social media in particular, was unprecedented, leading to the slowing down of the Internet as a whole and the crashing of numerous websites due to the increased Web traffic.

The kind of mourning that is expressed when celebrities die is referred to as **para-social grieving** (Sanderson & Cheong, 2010), which denotes the loss of an individual whom the mourner did not know personally. The sense of relationship with the celebrity is based on repeated exposure through the mass media, a relationship referred to as **para-social interaction** because it does not include in-person interaction. Horton and Wohl (1956) described this phenomenon as first occurring on the radio, where listeners would form very strong and intimate bonds with individuals they had never met but knew only from a radio show. While these bonds are perceived as being very personal and real, they are in fact mediated by technology and are one-sided.

A study of the development of para-social grieving on Facebook, TMZ. com, and Twitter after Jackson's death showed that all the stages of grief identified in previous research by Kubler-Ross (1965) also apply to the online environment, but in a different temporal order: (1) acceptance, (2) denial, (3) anger, (4) bargaining, and finally (5) depression (Sanderson & Cheong, 2010). People first demonstrated shock after finding out that the singer had died. This was followed by disbelief, which often led people to seek out more information about the events on celebrity gossip websites or news sites. The denial phase was followed by anger and bargaining, resulting from not understanding how Jackson could have died at such a young age, and in light of his forthcoming world tour. The final stage of grief in the online environment was feelings of depression and sadness resulting from the realization that Jackson was indeed gone.

The virtual mourning that occurs on social media sites after the death of loved ones or high-profile individuals is a new phenomenon that was not possible in traditional media. Through formal obituaries, traditional media would play a key role in providing information about the death of celebrities and key public figures, but the audience would not have been able to express and share publicly its emotions, opinions, and reactions. Social media changes the dynamics, providing audiences on a global scale with powerful ways to express their mourning, to negotiate the meaning of a celebrity or public figure's death, and to undergo the phases of dealing with loss.

Conclusions

This chapter provides an overview of how technology mediates the formation and dissolution of social relationships. The first systematic analyses were conducted by the Toronto School of Communication, whose members investigated the history and social circumstances of oral and written communication. The central contribution of the Toronto School of Communication was to demonstrate the importance of studying media in relation to society. Previous scholarship had neglected to understand the role that media play in shaping social, economic, and cultural factors. With the introduction of the telegraph and the telephone, new opportunities emerged for mediating social relationships and questioning existing social boundaries. Both tools greatly facilitated the transmission of information over long distances and across social spheres. For instance, the telephone led to the redrawing of pre-established geographical and social boundaries. The home, which was previously considered a sheltered and secluded social space, suddenly became open and easily accessible.

With the introduction of the Internet, there has been another shift in how people communicate and maintain social relationships at work, home, and school. The move toward the large-scale adoption of digital technologies helps users to stay connected 24/7 from any location. This ubiquity is possible through the widespread adoption of mobile technologies in combination with social media applications. And this move toward using social media for connectivity is certainly driven by young people. As part of this trend, new social phenomena emerge online around topics such as crafting of the virtual self, online friendship, romance, and death. The chapter discussed how "friending" is affected by a mix of social processes and technological affordances. Technology facilitates greater transparency about the nature of our social networks. This, however, creates new complexities in how we navigate our social spaces. As more people flock toward digital technologies, we are witnessing a move toward the domestication and mainstreaming of the Web (Hogan & Quan-Haase, 2010). That is, the Internet has become of relevance to many spheres of daily life: it is actually a central part of daily routines and practices ranging from reading the news, to staying in touch with friends and family, to breaking up.

Questions for Critical Thought

1. How did the introduction of the telephone change the boundaries of the home in American society?

2. Discuss the relevance of age in current adoption patterns of social networking sites. What key factors determine these trends?

3. Discuss the complex link between a person's **online persona** on a social networking site, such as Facebook, and the self. To what extent is the online persona a true reflection of the self?

4. Relationships formed online are often dismissed as shallow and unimportant. Discuss what makes online relationships meaningful.

Suggested Readings

boyd, d. (2014). *It's complicated: The social lives of networked teens*. New Haven: Yale University Press. This book is available for free at www.danah.org/books/ItsComplicated.pdf. It contains a deep understanding of teen digital life, including chapters on identity, privacy, addiction, bullying, and inequality.

Jewkes, Y. (Ed.). (2003). *Dot.cons: Crime, deviance and identity on the Internet*. Portland, OR: Willan Publishing. This volume of thoughtful essays focuses on online deviance, including such topics as crime regulation, prostitution, hacking, and identity theft. It critically examines how the Internet as an anonymous platform facilitates an ever-increasing number of fringe behaviours, making it difficult to evaluate what is and what is not criminal.

Gershon, I. (2010). *The breakup 2.0: Disconnecting over new media*. Ithaca, NY: Cornell University Press. The book shows how the dissolution of romantic relationships has changed in the context of Web 2.0 technologies and in particular social media, such as Facebook and MySpace.

Quan-Haase, A., & Hogan, B. (2010). Persistence and change in social media. Two special issues of the *Bulletin of Science, Technology and Society*, *30*(5 & 6), 309–315. This special double issue compiles 13 articles on current trends in social media.

Online Resources

Amanda Todd YouTube video
https://www.youtube.com/watch?v=ej7afkypUsc

In this YouTube video, posted by Amanda Todd, she uses flashcards to tell her story of being blackmailed and bullied online, of desperation, fear, and a sense of helplessness.

Pew Internet and American Life Project
www.pewinternet.org

The Pew is an American non-profit organization that conducts empirical research on how Americans use the Internet and the impact it has on their lives. The website is comprehensive, including reports, press releases, and statistics. Of particular relevance is their data on the connectedness of Millennials: www.pewinternet.org/Reports/2012/Hyperconnected-lives.aspx.

Kid Power
www.kidpower.org/library/article/cyber-bullying/?gclid=CKz4ooSmrMECFdRaMgodKAwArw

This is one of many websites that are geared toward providing emotional support to children and youth who are targets of cyber-bullying.

65_RedRoses: The Life of Eva Markvoort
http://65redroses.com/film/about-the-film/

This superb CBC documentary (with Force Four Entertainment) follows Eva Markvoort's brave struggle with cystic fibrosis (CF) and the mark she left on her online community. The site also includes a link to Markvoort's live blog and her memorial ceremony online.

The Surveillance Society

Learning Objectives

◎ to define *surveillance* as a multifaceted term with great relevance to the information society;

◎ to examine Foucault's analysis of power relations in society and to provide an overview of the concept and architecture of the Panopticon and its means of control;

◎ to discuss how personal information circulates in social media environments like Facebook and the ways in which this circulation is changing our understanding of private and public space;

◎ to provide an analysis of cybersecurity and its implications for everyday life;

◎ to present models of counter-surveillance and sousveillance as a means of personal resistance.

Introduction

The goal of this chapter is to define the multifaceted term *surveillance* by contrasting different perspectives available in the literature. On the one hand, transparency and the availability of information are often perceived as beneficial to society. It is argued that transparency diminishes misunderstandings, prevents deviant or criminal behaviour, and increases productivity. On the other hand, the term often also has a negative connotation implying the eradication of privacy, the diminishing of individual rights, and unnecessary obsession with data. These varied perspectives are discussed and examples provided.

The concept of surveillance has received considerable attention in society since the late eighteenth century, when British philosopher Jeremy Bentham envisioned what he called the Panopticon, an ideal form of prison consisting of a building that would allow for complete surveillance of inmates by a single guard. Originally, scholars thought of surveillance as a social process alone, and they viewed it as being only indirectly linked to technology. Recent technological developments, however, have given the term "surveillance" a completely different meaning: changes in not only the practices but also the very nature of surveillance have greatly reduced individuals' privacy rights and have taken the controversy around the recording of data, unauthorized monitoring, and data mining mechanisms to new heights. Surveillance as it occurs in social media has also been under increasing scrutiny because in these environments everybody is watching everybody else: for example, a person's Facebook profile and news feed can provide extensive information on the whereabouts of a user and the activities in which he or she engages. We discuss Facebook as an example of how people modify their behaviour as a result of being monitored by peers, family, and unknown audiences. Finally, the chapter ends with a discussion of innovative methods of counter-surveillance and sousveillance that aim at increasing awareness of the pervasiveness of these surveillance and data recording practices in our society and provide means for personal resistance.

Defining and Understanding Surveillance

The term **surveillance** originates in the French language and means "watching over." Observing the lives of other people and their behaviours, appearance, and social relationships is a naturally occurring social phenomenon. Innocuous and unobtrusive observing often occurs at coffee shops, for example, when one sits at a table and leisurely watches passersby. Most of us have probably engaged in this kind of behaviour at some point or another. Similarly, since the inception of social media tools, peers spend hours scanning through friends' photos, wall posts, and status updates. For the most part, this behaviour is desirable and welcomed, but it can also be perceived as a bit odd if no interaction takes place. The term **creeping** has been introduced to describe this pervasive behaviour, which is sometimes compared to stalking offline. In this context, the term *surveillance* takes on a rather negative connotation.

Most often, analysts link the term to the use of observation as a tool for exerting power and control, as often occurs in totalitarian regimes. Other related terms include *spying, supervision,* and *superintendence.* The *Oxford English Dictionary* (2011) provides a definition of surveillance: "Watch or guard kept over a person, etc., esp. over a suspected person, a prisoner, or the like; often, spying, supervision; less commonly, supervision for the purpose of direction or control, superintendence."

Countries around the world have institutions whose mandate it is to gather intelligence to support national and international security. The **U.S. National Security Agency's** (**NSA**) mandate is to administer the collection, processing, and analyzing of "data for foreign intelligence and counter-intelligence purposes to support national and departmental missions" (NSA, 2014). It consists of two branches: (a) The **Information Assurance mission** (**IA**) and (b) the **Signals Intelligence mission** (**SIGINT**). The IA prevents foreign nations from gaining access to sensitive or classified national security information, while the role of SIGINT is to collect, process, and disseminate intelligence information from foreign nations for purposes of intelligence and counterintelligence and also to support military operations. Network Warfare operations also fall under the mission of SIGINT, with the aim of defeating terrorists in the United States and abroad. The NSA has come under close scrutiny with the release in June 2013 of thousands of files documenting its surveillance practices in the United States and around the world. Since then, our understanding of surveillance, as a society, has changed drastically. Box 11.1 shows the societal impact that this case has had on current debates about privacy rights, data management, and mining, and the unprecedented capabilities afforded by networked technologies.

Box 11.1   Edward Snowden Leaks U.S. Spy Program

To the embarrassment of the Central Intelligence Agency (CIA), Edward Snowden, a former contractor for the NSA, leaked to the media highly confidential information on the surveillance practices employed by the United States government. Snowden had worked for the CIA and was also a counterintelligence trainer for the Defense Intelligence Agency (DIA). He later continued working for the NSA as a contractor, first for Dell and later for Booz Allen Hamilton. During this time, he acquired many classified documents and disclosed them to the media. Even though it was widely known that the FBI and CIA engage in a wide range of operations to gather information on potential threats to security, foreign states, and suspicious activities of their own citizens, the Snowden files provided direct evidence of these behaviours. But more importantly, the files revealed the extent of these practices; that is, NSA surveillance was targeting not only Internet activity but also cellphone data. More shocking still was that data were being collected from ordinary American citizens. As reported by the BBC, the Snowden report revealed "the secret court order directing telecommunications company Verizon to hand over all its telephone data to the NSA on an 'ongoing daily basis.'" Put together, that would be a lot of information on Americans.

A central question has been what is the purpose of recording and storing *all* telephone, cellphone data, and Internet activities? The Snowden case demonstrates that obtaining users' data is easy and cheap, and as a result it is advantageous for spy agencies to simply gather the massive amounts of data that flow through their networks. Secondly, because it is difficult to predict where threats come from, gathering all data is a convenient means for determining, through key word searches and data mining techniques, where these may originate. This clearly points toward a distinct approach to surveillance, one that is filled with paranoia and sees a need to monitor all Internet transactions for potential danger.

More information is available: BBC. (2014, January 17). Edward Snowden: Leaks that exposed U.S. spy programme. Retrieved 22 October 2014, from www.bbc.com/news/world-us-canada-23123964

Box 11.1 reveals the extent to which surveillance is a daily part of living and engaging in a digital society, perhaps unknown to most users. The Snowden case demonstrates the important role played by the NSA in overseeing all Internet operations. The Snowden case also demonstrates why surveillance is increasingly becoming a contested and highly polarized issue in society, affecting not only Americans, but citizens and leaders around the world.

Three Perspectives that Influence Our Understanding of Surveillance

The terms associated with surveillance and their varied meanings show how academics have approached the topic from different directions. In addition to the various definitions that exist, Lyon and Zureik (1996) have identified three main perspectives that influence our understanding of what surveillance is: (1) **capitalism,** (2) **rationalization,** and (3) power. We discuss each perspective next to show its historical relevance to our current understanding of the term.

1. Capitalism

The first big shift in surveillance occurred during the time of industrialization. New forms of capitalist production in industrial-era England accompanied the desire to increase productivity, which resulted in new forms of control (Lyon & Zureik, 1996). For Karl Marx, "the work of directing, superintending and adjusting becomes one of the functions of capital, from the moment that the labour under the control of capital, becomes cooperative" (K. Marx, 1996, p. 217). Surveillance here takes on two roles: one as an internal component of production and another as a means of **discipline** (Foucault, 1995). The role of directing and supervising, originally occupied by controllers, was later substituted with machinery. As a result, the assembly line became an efficient means of control that did not require any human intervention. Similarly, the introduction of clock-in cards and the design of offices as open cubicles were all part of a process of seamlessly embedding monitoring practices into the workplace. An open cubicle will exert means of control on work behaviour—including times of arrival and departure, work habits, regulations of breaks, and appropriate use of work time.

The study of surveillance from the capitalist viewpoint provides two advantages (Lyon & Zureik, 1996). First, it allows for an analysis based on **political economic theory,** where economic factors are the primary motivators for implementing monitoring practices, techniques, and tools. Second, this kind of analysis also "makes possible a critical stance in which systematic inequalities are exposed and a critique is made of major organizations and ideologies that perpetuate the system" (Lyon & Zureik, 1996, p. 6). Workers here have no flexibility and their individuality is erased through mechanisms of control and power.

Criticism of the perspective stresses its rather narrow focus and points out two weaknesses (Lyon & Zureik, 1996). First, the idea that all surveillance is motivated by economic factors is limiting, considering that people engage in surveillance for social reasons as well. For instance, after a breakup, individuals often are obsessed with the behaviours of their former partners (Quan-Haase, Nevin, & Lukacs, 2014). In this example, the reasons for frequently checking an ex's Facebook updates are linked to the social relations among individuals. The second weakness of the capitalist perspective is that the idea that surveillance is in and of itself negative reflects a simplified view of social processes. For example, users of social media provide detailed information about their whereabouts, their recent activities, and their current feelings. When friends, acquaintances, and even strangers spend time looking at this collage of information, they engage in surveillance. This is not necessarily a negative form of surveillance; rather, it is often welcomed by users. In general, then, the capitalist view of surveillance provides a good understanding of the economic meaning of surveillance in the context of work, but does not fully explain surveillance as it occurs in other social contexts.

2. Rationalization

The second big shift in surveillance is associated with changes in how society operates. Weber's (1920/2003) concepts of **rationalization** and **bureaucratization** are closely linked with the concepts and practices of surveillance. Rationalization describes a fundamental shift in the functioning of society: instead of behaviour relying on kinship ties, tradition, and informal affiliations, it now relies on rules based on **rational choice**. According to Weber (also see Kim, 2008), there are three factors that play a key role in this shift: (1) knowledge, (2) growing impersonality, and (3) enhanced control.

1. *Knowledge*: Knowledge is seen as the basis for rational choice. Rational choice requires an understanding of cause and effect as well as a weighing of various outcomes. Weber referred to this process as **intellectualization** because instead of relying on superstitious or mystical beliefs, decisions are based on modern scientific and technological knowledge.
2. *Growing impersonality*: Objectification occurs as part of rationalization, reflecting the Puritan's austere work and life ethic. Individuals, with their unique stories, are incorporated in a rational system, in which there is no consideration of personal concerns or matters.
3. *Enhanced control*: Most important for our current discussion, Weber saw rationalization as increasing control in social and work life. This increased control is a result of the Puritan ethic of self-discipline and self-control, which Weber referred to as **innerworldly asceticism**. Rationalization leads through institutionalization toward greater bureaucratic administration, legal formalism, and industrial capitalism.

Weber (1920/2003) introduced the notion of the **iron cage** to provide an analysis of how nation-states, institutions, and modern organizations exercise power and control over their citizens, members, and workers, respectively. For Weber, there are two sides of the iron cage. On the one hand, rationalization increases an individual's freedom because it leads toward greater transparency in terms of how individuals can achieve their goals. We discussed this in the introduction when making reference to the notion that "more information is always better than less information," as this creates transparency and allows for supervision. On the other hand, the iron cage seriously hampers human agency by narrowing down the possibilities and actions of individuals in a completely institutionalized system of rules (Kim, 2008). Weber writes that "[n]o one knows who will live in this cage in the future . . ." as these individuals will be "[s]pecialists without spirit, sensualists without heart; this nullity imagines that it has attained a level of civilization never before achieved" (1920/2003, p. 182). In a completely open society, we become restricted in our behaviours, attitudes, and opinions as everything is known to everyone, making it difficult to deviate from the societal norms and imposed standards. That is, we all become prisoners of the iron cage.

The Weberian perspective on surveillance has been criticized for its focus on technological change (Lyon & Zureik, 1996). Critics argue that this perspective sees technologies of rationalization, such as the assembly line, as the driving force of control. For example, computers at work allow for further and more invasive forms of surveillance by documenting workers' activities, potentially recording every keystroke. As Lyon and Zureik (1996) point out, the Weberian perspective provides an analysis of the social system itself and not directly of the means, whether technological, social, or institutional, by which rationalization and bureaucratization are put in place.

3. Power
The third approach associated with surveillance is based on Foucault's (1995) work on disciplinary practices. For Foucault, power is an inherent part of all social relationships and social systems. As a result, social control becomes a central feature of modern societies. Foucault's analysis of prisons represents perhaps the most compelling and influential theoretical work on surveillance. To explore his ideas in more depth, the following section presents the concept of the Panopticon and how it relates to control in modern societies.

Foucault's Analysis of Power Relations in Society

To understand the social meaning of surveillance and the role technologies play in distributing and enforcing power, it is essential to examine first the concept of the **Panopticon**. In his analysis of how society treats, labels, and punishes crimes, Foucault (1995) traces the historical development of power relations in society. He argues that these forms of punishment do not only apply to prisons, as in the Panopticon, but have become the standard means of control for our entire society (Gutting, 2010). For Foucault (1995), "[d]iscipline 'makes' individuals; it is the specific technique of a power that regards individuals both as objects and as instruments of its exercise" (p. 170). That is, individuals follow pre-established norms based on expectations that if they deviate, they will fall prey to a system of discipline. Thus, fear and uncertainty play an important role in how society operates.

Foucault's analysis starts by tracing the history of punishment: in the Middle Ages punishment occurred as a public act of degradation, where the church and king penalized criminals in the public eye using torture and death by decapitation, burning, and starvation. Foucault refers to this as **punishment-as-spectacle** because the audience is as much part of the impartment of discipline as are the bearers of justice. In the eighteenth century, however, the methods of punishment to deal with disobedience changed radically. The population started questioning these shocking and violent approaches, and the justice system replaced them with more "subtle" but equally powerful forms of subjugation. Foucault (1995) writes that "justice as a result no longer takes public responsibility for the violence that is bound up with its practice" (p. 9) but instead moves sentencing into the courtroom and the practice of punishment into a private, secluded space. Discipline is moved away from the public eye; it becomes invisible.

At the centre of Foucault's (1995) analysis of disciplinary action are three primary forms of control: (1) the examination, (2) normalizing judgment, and (3) hierarchical observation. The **examination** places individuals in a "field of documentation" (Gutting, 2010). Documents are records of various spheres of an individual's life and can serve as sources of power that help evaluate the individual (e.g., academic records) or control an individual (e.g., criminal record). These records allow those in control to "formulate categories, averages, and norms that are in turn a basis for knowledge" (Gutting, 2010) and evaluation. The information gathered on the individual can then be used to examine that person as a single case in the context of socially established norms and values, such as a university's required minimum admission averages.

A central concern of modern disciplinary control is determining the extent to which people fall into specific categories and meet expected standards. Behaviour that does not meet the set standard would be considered **deviant behaviour** and could require disciplinary action. **Normalizing judgment** can establish whether an individual meets society's set standards or falls into the category of abnormal. Society has developed standards for many aspects of life. For instance, Canada has educational standards for core subjects for each grade and sets expectations as to what children should learn and when.[1] The introduction of standards marks a radical shift in how discipline is accomplished by establishing precise norms ("normalization"). In the older judicial system, single actions were judged in terms of whether or not they were permissible by law; this older system excluded a judgment about "normality" or "abnormality" (Gutting, 2010).

The most relevant of these forms for our present discussion is **hierarchical observation**, which describes how control over people can be achieved simply through surveillance. Observation occurs in a "network of gazes" that are laid out following a hierarchical structure, with data being conveyed from lower to higher levels. For Foucault (1995), implementing hierarchical observation requires a new form of construction in which buildings allow for "articulated" and "detailed" control. Control is articulated because the physical outline embodies the hierarchical nature of the observation. Moreover, such control is detailed in that the observer has a full view of the actions of those being observed. Basically, power relations are laid out in the design or shape of the architecture, as in the Panopticon, which we discuss next.

The Panopticon as a Means of Surveillance

The use of intricate systems of surveillance as a form of punishment started as early as 1780. Foucault (1995) utilizes Bentham's Panopticon as an example to show how, in the design of buildings, power can be embedded in surveillance mechanisms. The illustration on page 220 shows how, in Bentham's design of a prison, a tower is located at the centre. The tower is surrounded by disconnected cells, and each cell houses a single individual, who is securely locked away. The arrangement is such that the supervisor, from a central point, can observe prisoners at all times without being noticed because all cells open toward the centre and the tower has visibility over all cells surrounding it. Hence, there is absolute transparency in terms of what the inmates are doing. By contrast, the lighting is set up in such a way that the inmates cannot see the interior of the tower. Moreover, they cannot even determine if anyone is in the tower at any given time. For Foucault, Bentham's model follows two principles: the **visibility of power** and the **unverifiability of power**. It is the combination of power being visible and unverifiable that is so effective in establishing discipline.

The social consequence of this architecture is that prisoners cannot determine whether or not they are being watched. The Panopticon places the individual in a position where "[h]e is seen, but he does not see; he is the object of information, never a subject in communication" (Foucault, 1995, p. 200). This uncertainty creates a new form of control in which the supervisor is no longer needed, as his or her presence or absence cannot be determined; rather, the inmate exercises control over his or her own behaviour as a result of the uncertainty of potentially being watched. Foucault (1995) describes this process of control as the **automatization of power**, showing

© topham Picturepoint/GetStock.com

Jeremy Bentham's Panopticon (after the original drawing of 1791).

[how] the surveillance is permanent in its effect, even if it is discontinuous in its action; that the perfection of power should tend to render its actual exercise unnecessary; that this architectural apparatus should be a machine for creating and sustaining a power relation independent of the person who exercises it; in short, that the inmates should be caught up in a power situation of which they are themselves the bearers. (p. 201)

In these kinds of environments, individuals need to engage in complete self-censorship and regulation. From this standpoint, the ideal form of discipline would "make it possible for a single gaze to see everything constantly" (Foucault, 1995, p. 173). This form of discipline is based on what Foucault (1995) describes as "automatic and disindividualized power relations," where no one single observant is watching and no one person is responsible for the power imbalances. Rather, it is the architecture, location, and embedded power relations that create the sense of absolute control and constant surveillance. To some extent, this is similar to the metaphor of **Big Brother,** which became pervasive in the twentieth century to explain state control. Box 11.2 describes the reality TV show ***Big Brother*** as a case study of how surveillance can be embedded in technology, and how TV and the Internet have made inverse forms of surveillance possible.

The reality TV show *Big Brother* exemplifies a new form of surveillance that does not share many elements with traditional forms of surveillance. Nonetheless, the show's setup does have a noteworthy resemblance to the

Box 11.2   Big Brother: The Act of Being Watched

Reality TV has completely shifted the social meaning of surveillance. While traditional forms of surveillance stress the involuntary nature of the act of being watched by a single observer, in the context of reality TV, the Orwellian notion of Big Brother becomes reformulated (Andrejevic, 2004). In the past, a clear distinction was maintained between those who create media products and those who consume them (Andrejevic, 2004). In that model, audiences were passive recipients of information and had limited input into the development and production of content. Reality TV has shifted the locus of power, and audiences are now also active participants—as they are selected and become "actors" in the show, these participants, and all audience members, feel empowered through direct involvement in the production process. Perhaps we can even argue that the actors of these shows *are* the content. Hence, reality TV reinvents the meaning given to surveillance because surveillance becomes yet another form of entertainment.

The reality series *Big Brother* debuted in 1999 in the Netherlands, and since has become a success in at least 60 other countries. During the first U.S. summer season, about 10 million viewers followed the show. The show revolves around the lives of 10 participants who live together in a house for the duration of the show. In the house, ironically, participants have no access to media (TV, radio, Internet); hence, they have only minimal contact with the outside world. The idea is that participants will return to basics—engaging primarily in face-to-face contact with their fellow housemates. Every week, viewers (or, in the U.S. version, housemates) vote to have one of the housemates evicted, causing that participant to lose the opportunity to win the big prize.

---

architecture of the Panopticon. In *Big Brother*, cameras and microphones are located in every room, even bathrooms, behind one-way mirrors, providing a view into housemates' daily activities from different angles. Housemates are aware of the cameras, but they cannot see them. Like residents of the Panopticon, they know they are being monitored, but they cannot predict when. Moreover, because the footage gathered is heavily edited and cut, the housemates do not know which of their activities will be made public; as a result, they have the sense of always potentially being on display. This resembles the power relations described in Foucault's discussion of the automatization of power, and also leads to a blurring of the self with capital means of production (Hearn, 2006).

While institutions and often buildings themselves were set up to support various forms of surveillance, until fairly recently technology played only a minor role in enforcement. However, advances in digital technologies, as discussed in Box 11.1, have given rise to fundamentally different modes of data collection, storage, and retrieval. We discuss next the new modes of surveillance arising from the information revolution and contrast them with traditional forms.

Technology's Role in the New Surveillance

Information technology has made our lives more open to the public than ever before. Digital tools can easily collect, store, and retrieve personal information. Gary T. Marx (2007) identifies three distinct approaches to describing the changes in surveillance as a result of the information revolution and its associated technologies: (1) functional, (2) revolutionary, and (3) cultural.

1. *Functional view*: Societies, in order to operate effectively, require some element of security and safety. To achieve these goals, personal information needs to be collected and stored. From the functional view, the transformations in surveillance are only of degree, not of kind.
2. *Revolutionary view*: The revolutionary view argues that technologies have led to a radical transformation in the very nature of surveillance and that basic privacy rights have been jeopardized. This is a rather pessimistic and deterministic view of the impact of information technology on surveillance.
3. *Cultural view*: This view also sees information technology as radically changing society. But instead of advocating for a deterministic view, the cultural view argues that social and cultural factors moderate how information technology impacts surveillance. This view, then, sees counter-surveillance in combination with new privacy laws, norms, and values as leading toward a balance between disclosure and protection of personal data.

Although we can debate whether or not these technological changes should be labelled "fundamental" and "revolutionary" or "continuous" and "expected," there is no doubt that technological developments have created radically different surveillance practices. In addition, changes have occurred in our basic understanding of what surveillance is.

As Marx (2007) indicates, traditional definitions of surveillance may be restricted in their applicability to the new modes of surveillance that have emerged as a result of the information revolution. Traditional definitions tend to emphasize close observation of a "suspected person" (see, for example, the definition we discussed previously on page 213). By contrast, new surveillance is not limited to single individuals or suspects, and physical distance does not restrict one's ability to observe. In this sense, the definition needs to be broadened to accurately capture the nature of modern surveillance practices. Marx (2007) suggests that **new surveillance** can be defined as "the use of technical means to extract or create personal data" (p. 85). To differentiate between traditional forms of surveillance and the modern types of surveillance, Marx, as illustrated in Table 11.1, contrasts the two along key dimensions.

While traditional forms of surveillance would often include informants or spies and wiretapping of telephone lines, new types of surveillance include hidden cameras in banks or stores, keystroke monitoring by employers, and audio scanners that pick up cellular phone frequencies. According to Marx's chart (Table 11.1), even something as seemingly routine as posting a funny status update on Facebook has elements of the new surveillance. This is because peers as well as third parties (e.g., marketing companies) connected to the Facebook site can easily track, observe, and record that status update. In fact, even status updates that users have started typing but never post are tracked by the company (Woollaston, 2013). For instance, Table 11.1 shows that in traditional surveillance, data reside with the collector—it stays local—whereas with the new surveillance, data are shared among companies, third parties, and institutions. The data collector in traditional surveillance was a person or even an animal; in the new surveillance it is a machine, often collecting information remotely.

There is some controversy regarding the extent to which the use of personal data on social network sites represents a form of surveillance. We can examine this issue from the viewpoint of the three perspectives outlined on pages 215 to 217. First, from a functional viewpoint, we could argue that this form of surveillance is harmless since third-party companies are primarily interested in aggregate data and will use this information for the purpose of developing and marketing better products, which will benefit consumers in the long run (Young & Quan-Haase, 2013). These third-party companies are not interested in individual behaviours, opinions, or attitudes but, rather, in trends and patterns revealed in anonymous answers by masses of people.

Second, from a revolutionary viewpoint, we can take a more critical stance, arguing that most Facebook users involuntarily grant third-party access to their personal information by not being fully aware of their ability to change privacy settings, by deciding not to change them, or by not fully understanding them. The Privacy Commissioner of Canada criticized Facebook not only for having incomprehensible privacy rules but also for having rules that do not comply with Canadian law (Privacy Commissioner of Canada, 2009). Facebook's privacy rules came under scrutiny by the Privacy Commissioner of Canada because they were longer than the U.S. Constitution itself. Navigating this complexity of rules is not made easier by Facebook's "Help Center," which is meant to assist users and is more than 45,000 words long. As a result, users need to constantly balance the need to

Table 11.1 Dimensions of New and Old Surveillance

Dimension	A: Traditional Surveillance	B: The New Surveillance
Senses	Unaided senses	Extends senses
Visibility (of the actual collection, who does it, where, on whose behalf)	Visible	Less visible or invisible
Consent	Lower proportion involuntary	Higher proportion
Cost (per unit of data)	Expensive	Inexpensive
Location of data collectors/ analyzers	On scene	Remote
Data collector	Human, animal	Machine (wholly or partly automated)
Data resides	With the collector, stays local	With third parties, often migrates
Timing	Single point or intermittent	Continuous (omnipresent)
Time period	Present	Past, present, future
Data availability	Frequent time lags	Real time availability
Comprehensiveness	Single measure	Multiple measures
Form	Single media (likely or narrative or numerical)	Multiple media (including video and/or audio)
Data merging	Discrete non-combinable data (whether because of different format or location)	Easy to combine visual, auditory, text, numerical data
Data communication	More difficult to send, receive	Easier to send, receive

Source: Adapted from Marx, G. T. (2007). What's new about the "new surveillance"? Classifying for change and continuity. In S.P. Hier & J. Greenberg (Eds), *The surveillance studies reader.* Maidenhead: Open University Press, pp. 83–94. Table 6.1, p. 87. Used by permission of Gary T. Marx.

disclose personal information to connect with their family, friends, and co-workers with the need to protect themselves against privacy threats. In this light, we can see how Facebook can be considered an example of the new surveillance and of how pervasive surveillance truly is in our information society.

Finally, from a cultural standpoint, we can argue that new laws are being put in place and new cultural practices are developing to guard users from privacy threats. For instance, in Canada the Privacy Commissioner demanded that Facebook change its privacy settings and make its options more transparent to allow users to make informed choices (Privacy Commissioner of Canada, 2009). Facebook was also forced into revising its privacy rules, both shortening and simplifying these. The increased transparency should give users a better understanding of how their settings affect the kind of personal data that third-party companies and other users are able to access.

However, it is not always clear to what extent personal information garnered through surveillance is being used, especially in the area of government surveillance of its citizens. As noted by Stedmon (2011), "as surveillance technologies become ubiquitous, the potential to monitor locations from distant control centres (possibly even from control centres abroad) means that gaps in spatial knowledge and lack of local knowledge could impact on many aspects of successful surveillance and public safety" (p. 533).

Digital Surveillance

The Internet is an information juggernaut, collecting a wide range of data on its users. The term *digital surveillance* refers not only to observation via the Internet but also to the collection of data via digital networks, tools, and devices. Some of the data collected are considered to be more personal and private than other types. Search engines track users' online search behaviour through search and toolbar logs—the logged data are referred to as the **search history**. The primary purpose of tracking this behaviour is to provide users with better search results as well as to display customized ads. For example, a user sends an email to a friend about a roofing problem and shortly afterwards, ads for roofing companies are "coincidentally" displayed on that person's search page or email provider. Some users do not consider these kinds of data to be personal and private, while others do not approve of search engines logging their search history.

There are times, however, when users are asked to share more personal information. For example, when people subscribe to a new service on a website, in addition to choosing a username and password, they are often asked to provide more detailed information about themselves, including age, gender, location, etc. Even though these data are considered personal and private, most users willingly disclose this information in order to gain access to the service (Greenberg, 2008) despite concerns about their privacy potentially being compromised. Users view it as a minimal requirement in order to take advantage of a service offered online.

A Pew survey shows that 43 per cent of Internet users know that search engines track their online search behaviour, while the remaining 57 per cent do not (Fallows, 2005). Most users, 55 per cent, disapprove of their online search behaviour being tracked, while 37 per cent do not mind. Most users disapproved of websites displaying advertisements based on their search history and Web behaviour, which is interesting given that the majority of search engines rely heavily on this information. Overall, the findings suggest that people are moderately concerned about the collection of personal information online and how this information is being used by companies. At the same time, many users do not fully understand the privacy implications of the tools they use, as demonstrated by the general lack of knowledge of how search engines operate (Pew, 2014).

How can we explain users' willingness to disclose personal information despite their privacy concerns? One perspective argues that online users are not fully aware of their vulnerability to privacy threats because they follow the "nothing to hide, nothing to fear" rule (G. Marx, 1996; Viseu, Clement, & Aspinall, 2004). According to work by Viseu, Clement, and Aspinall (2004), for most users, online privacy is not a concern as they do not think privacy violation will affect them directly. Privacy becomes a concern only when it has been lost or breached. That is, until they have a negative experience, users do not feel compelled to change their behaviours and protect their privacy.

A second reason many people voluntarily disclose information online is to craft an online presence. Studies on information revelation have consistently shown that users of social network sites reveal considerable amounts of personal information on their profiles, which consist of a number of common elements: the profile itself, status updates, pictures, and connections. This trend toward more disclosure of personal information has been defined in the literature as **information revelation** (Gross & Acquisti, 2005). Box 11.3 discusses a study of the information revelation behaviours of Canadian undergraduate students that shows no gender differences. Students of both sexes seem willing to disclose a wide range of types of information, including their location, birth date, and email address.

The media has warned of the potential dangers of providing too much information, or the wrong kinds of information, online. Students have also expressed some concerns about the potential misuse of their personal data; these concerns include a stranger finding out their address, their schedule, their sexual orientation, the name of their romantic partner, and their current political views (Gross & Acquisti, 2005).

Some theorists claim that interactive and digital media have led to the end of privacy, as "the increased use of electronic communications has been matched by the development of ever more sophisticated tools of surveillance" (Chesterman, 2011, p. 3). According to a study by Madden et al. (2013), the amount of disclosure on social media has been increasing since 2006, with significantly more individuals posting photos of themselves, their school, their city, and their email address. It is interesting to note that 20 per cent of teens posted their cellphone number in 2013 versus only 2 per cent in 2006. The popularity of selfies has also increased the number of photos shared on these sites. Such research demonstrates that individuals may be getting more comfortable with digital technologies and are becoming less apprehensive of negative privacy consequences.

Defining Privacy

What does privacy mean for the average Internet user? There is no single definition of **privacy** because it is a fluid and far-reaching concept (Young,

Box 11.3   Information Revelation on Facebook

The need to belong and be an active participant in one's online community has led many young people to disclose personal information on social network sites. In a study of Facebook undergraduate users, Young and Quan-Haase (2009) found high levels of information revelation. Figure 11.1 shows the information indicated on respondents' profiles by gender. As many as 99 per cent of users reported using their actual name in their profile (first and last name). Nearly two-thirds of respondents indicated their sexual orientation, relationship status, and interests (such as favourite books, movies, and activities). Other personal information that most people provided included their school name (97 per cent), email address (83 per cent), birth date (92 per cent), and the city or town in which they currently lived (80 per cent); almost all respondents reported posting an image of themselves (99 per cent) and photos of their friends (96 per cent). By contrast, few respondents reported disclosing their physical address (8 per cent), their cellphone number (10 per cent), or their IM screen name (16 per cent), thereby limiting the likelihood of individuals contacting or locating them outside of Facebook. For the most part, the data show that there was very little difference in terms of the types of information that female and male respondents included on their profiles.

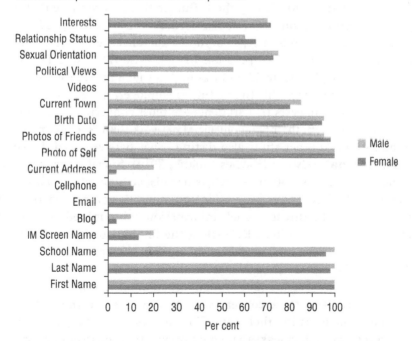

Figure 11.1 Information Provided on Profile by Gender
Source: Young, A.L. & Quan-Haase, A. (2013). Privacy protection strategies on Facebook: The Internet privacy paradox revisited. *Information, Communication & Society, 16*(4), 479–500. Copyright © 2008, SAGE Publications

Continued

> Students in the study reported that they were motivated to disclose information in order to engage with friends online. They saw their profiles as signals that reveal aspects of their personality and allow users to establish common ground and write their community into being (boyd, 2006). Young and Quan-Haase (2009) describe the importance of revealing information on Facebook for young people this way: it "seems to serve a social purpose increasing students' opportunities for social interaction and participation, as well as for the maintenance and formation of relationships" (p. 272).

2008). Westin (2003), however, defines information privacy as "the claim of an individual to determine what information about himself or herself should be known to others . . . when such information will be obtained and what uses will be made of it by others" (p. 431). This definition has pragmatic implications because it gives individuals control over how their personal information is used by other parties, including governments and corporations.

An important distinction made in the literature is between immediate and future privacy threats. Immediate threats are defined as those that result shortly after disclosing personal information on social network sites, including sexual predators and identity theft. Future threats are those that occur long after the information has been disclosed. A study of undergraduate students' privacy examined four types of future audiences: employer, romantic partner, government, and corporation (Tufekci, 2007). Table 11.2 shows that students thought the likelihood was higher that a future romantic partner would look at their profile than a future employer, the government, or a corporation. This suggests that students are most concerned about privacy breaches coming from their personal social network than from an institution or organization. Another study also distinguishes between **social privacy** and **institutional privacy** (Raynes-Goldie, 2010). Social privacy refers to the concern that known others—such as friends, acquaintances, and family members—will discover our personal information. By contrast, institutional privacy refers to the threat of one's information being mined and used by governments or corporations. Paralleling the findings by Tufekci, users in the study by Raynes-Goldie reported being much more concerned about the loss of social privacy than they were about the loss of institutional privacy. The study by Tufekci (2007) highlighted another important finding: men were more likely to be concerned than women about the government or a corporation accessing their data. This suggests that men show greater apprehension about data leaks that could breach their institutional privacy.

Institutional privacy concerns have become increasingly salient in recent years, especially in the wake of the 2013 Edward Snowden case, discussed in Box 11.1. Snowden's actions have since simultaneously branded him a hero

Table 11.2 Gender Differences in Mean Levels of Perceived Likelihood of Being Found by Future Audiences

				t Test Statistics		
	Total	**Male**	**Female**	***t***	***df***	***p***
Employer	2.90	2.90	3.10	−0.018	232	.986
Romantic partner	3.62	3.48	3.73	−1.404	232	.162
Government**	2.63	2.91	2.41	3.007	232	.003
Corporation*	2.55	2.76	2.39	2.264	232	.024

Note: Response options were: 1 = *never thought about it*, 2 = *not likely at all*, 3 = *a little likely*, 4 = *somewhat likely*, and 5= *very likely.* * p < .05 two-tailed. **p < .01 two-tailed.

Source: Tufekci, Z. (2007). Can you see me now? Audience and disclosure regulation in online social network sites. *Bulletin of Science, Technology & Society*, 28(1), 20–36, Table 11. Copyright © 2008, SAGE Publications

and a traitor depending on what perspective is taken, and opened up the debate as to whether online privacy should be a fundamental human right or whether national security should take priority over privacy. Debates about online privacy have been supplemented by an increased flow of information surrounding institutional surveillance programs by **hacktivist groups** like **Anonymous** and websites like **WikiLeaks**, whose slogan is "We open governments." Hacktivist groups are described by Singer and Friedman (2014) as ranging from single individuals to loosely linked networks of people who gather around a target or idea to tightly organized groups. Anonymous is known as a decentralized group that does not follow directives but instead operates on ideas (Singer & Friedman, 2014). Dismissing the relevance of the group Anonymous to how the Internet operates would be a great mistake, something that security expert Aaron Barr of security firm HG Gary Federal learned the hard way. In 2011, he announced that his firm had infiltrated the group, and, shortly afterward, Anonymous hacked his website, making a mockery of HG Gary Federal and calling into question its ability to provide secure networks. They also took control of his Twitter account and posted his social security number and home address. This case shows how hacktivists can influence individuals' lives, commerce, and politics.

There are several reasons why people are concerned about digital privacy threats.[2] First, digital content can easily be copied and forwarded online (boyd, 2007; Tufekci, 2007). Second, people worry about the persistence and searchability of the content, which, while making that content accessible to family, friends, and acquaintances, also allows access by strangers who have no connection with the author (Hogan & Quan-Haase, 2010; Young, 2008). Third, information taken out of context can be interpreted in different ways, potentially leading to misinterpretations and misunderstandings. Fourth, often there is a clashing of different cultures, understandings, values, and norms when personal information is moved from one social setting to another (Barnes, 2006).

Taken together, the findings on users' behaviour on social network sites are puzzling. On the one hand, users report high levels of concern about the potential immediate or future misuse of their personal data. On the other hand, people continue to disclose large amounts of personal information, including pictures, information on friends, their whereabouts, etc. This contradictory behaviour has been termed the **privacy paradox** (Barnes, 2006).

Another paradox that emerges in social media is the nature of surveillance itself. Surveillance on social media is not about one person doing the observing and another person being observed, as in traditional surveillance; instead, surveillance on social media is about everyone being both object and subject at the same time. Tufekci (2007) has referred to this as peer monitoring because in most cases it is not strangers or spies who are watching and observing our behaviours; in social media, it is our family, friends, and acquaintances who are keeping a close eye on our every move.

Counter-surveillance as a Means of Personal Resistance

In an effort to counter the pervasiveness and invasiveness of surveillance in our society, models of **counter-surveillance** have been proposed. Counter-surveillance is both a theoretical perspective and a global *social movement* (Corrigall-Brown, 2011). Social movements are defined as large, often informal, groups or organizations whose aim is to create awareness about a political or social issue. Individuals who advocate for counter-surveillance will often engage in practices that put the status quo into question and make surveillance practices visible, particularly those practiced by the state, private security, public police, and commercial enterprises. In this section, we discuss two forms of counter-surveillance: (1) sousveillance and (2) digital privacy protection strategies.

Sousveillance

Mann, Nolan, and Wellman (2003) have described sousveillance as a form of counter-surveillance that empowers those subjected to institutional, state, or corporate surveillance practices. In this approach, individuals use mobile technologies or wearable computers to record the experience of being watched. A subset of sousveillance practices are referred to as **inverse surveillance** and consist of recording, monitoring, analyzing, and questioning surveillance technologies and their proponents, and also recording how surveillance takes place by authority figures, such as police officers, guards, and border patrols. Around the globe, many groups have formed to participate in the sousveillance social movement. For instance, those engaged in inverse surveillance tactics in New York City noted as much as a 40 per cent increase in the numbers of video security cameras after the September

11 events (Mann et al., 2003). The pervasiveness of surveillance can also be observed in many other cities, such as Chicago; London, England; and even Toronto.

Sousveillance entails **reflectionism,** a perspective that proposes using technology as a mirror to question and confront the ubiquity of surveillance practices in our modern society. The aim of reflectionism is to engage people in critical debate about how surveillance is occurring, thereby creating greater transparency. Reflectionism, according to Mann et al. (2003), utilizes a method known as **inquiry-in-performance;** that is, knowledge is gained through interacting with technologies in real-life contexts, with the following two aims:

1. uncovering the Panopticon and undercutting its primacy and privilege; and
2. relocating the relationship of the surveillance society within a more traditional notion of observability (p. 333).

The process of reflectionism is closely linked with *detournement,* a concept introduced by Rogers (1994) to describe the tactic of using those very same tools that are employed to control us as a means to provoke the social controllers and make them aware of the imbalance of power. Reflectionism "extends the concept of detournement by using the tools against the organization, holding a mirror up to the establishment, and creating a symmetrical self-bureaucratization of the wearer" (Mann et al., 2003, p. 333). Anti-surveillance groups use various aspects of reflectionism to make the public aware of the ubiquity of surveillance tools and their infringement on private and public life. Huey, Walby, and Doyle (2006) report that counter-surveillance practices against police forces, known as **Cop Watch** groups, have emerged. The main goal of Cop Watch groups is to promote awareness of police brutality against marginalized populations, monitor police activity, and report police misconduct and unnecessary brutality. Forms of counter-surveillance thus play an important role in society to raise awareness around and question current surveillance practices and the activities of public and private police.

Privacy Protection Strategies

The second form of counter-surveillance, digital privacy protection strategies, occurs at a micro level, with people protecting themselves against potential threats to their privacy. As we mentioned earlier, the privacy paradox theory states that people tend to disclose large amounts of personal information online even though they express concerns about potential privacy risks. Evidence, however, suggests that people are not as naive and oblivious to threats as suggested in the privacy paradox theory.

A study of undergraduate students shows that they engage in a wide range of strategies to mitigate threats and are constantly managing their personal information online (Young & Quan-Haase, 2013). Table 11.3 shows the means and standard deviations for a series of questions and answers related to Facebook users' privacy protection strategies. The results show that the most frequently used privacy protection strategy (strategy 1) was to exchange private Facebook messages to restrict others' access to content perceived as confidential. This strategy was followed by strategy 2: changing the default privacy settings on Facebook to restrict who can see what profile elements. Another frequently used strategy (strategy 3) is to refuse to include personal information in order to prevent unknown others from gaining access. Interestingly, few participants have provided fake or inaccurate information on Facebook (strategy 8). Students do not falsify information because their friends would question the validity of the information and wonder about its meaning; refer back to the discussion in Chapter 10 on the presentation of the online self.

How common are privacy protection strategies? Rainie et al. (2013) found that 86 per cent of their sample of Internet users admitted to intentionally implementing strategies for maintaining anonymity on the Internet, and 55 per cent used such strategies for hiding from specific parties—other people, government agencies, or specific organizations. Of those strategies,

Table 11.3 Privacy Protection Strategies Used by Facebook Users

Individual Items and Scale	Mean	Standard Deviation
1: I have sent private email messages within Facebook instead of posting messages to a friend's wall to restrict others from reading the message.	4.72	0.68
2: I have changed the default privacy settings activated by Facebook.	4.33	1.25
3: I have excluded personal information on Facebook to restrict people I don't know from gaining information about me.	4.08	1.17
4: I have untagged myself from images and/or videos posted by my contacts.	3.85	1.55
5: I have deleted messages posted to my Facebook wall to restrict others from viewing/reading the message.	3.64	1.55
6: Certain contacts on my Facebook site have access only to my limited profile.	3.47	1.70
7: I have blocked former contacts from contacting me and accessing my Facebook profile.	2.91	1.71
8: I have provided fake or inaccurate information on Facebook to restrict people I don't know from gaining information about me.	1.66	1.03

Note: Items were evaluated on a 5-point Likert scale ranging from 1 = "strongly disagree" to 5 = "strongly agree."

Source: Young, A.L. & Quan-Haase, A. (2013). Privacy protection strategies on Facebook: The Internet privacy paradox revisited. *Information, Communication & Society, 16*(4), 479–500. Copyright © 2013 Routledge

the most common ways to mask their digital activities were to clear cookies and browsing history (64 per cent), delete or edit previously posted content (41 per cent), and set their Web browser to disable cookies (41 per cent). A sizable population employs more drastic options, like using a public computer for browsing (18 per cent) and encrypting emails (14 per cent). Such findings demonstrate that there are many available mechanisms for more effectively hiding one's digital footprint.

These privacy protection strategies are a way for users to balance the need to provide personal information on social media, with the purpose of actively engaging with their online social networks—consisting of family, friends, and acquaintances—with the need to protect their personal data and restrict who has access to the content. Some examples of tools used by users to protect their privacy online include proxy servers, search engines that actively delete a user's browsing history and tracking cookies, such as duckduckgo.com, and Internet browser software, such as **Tor**, which encrypts the information that is transferred between a sender node and a destination node. Users have also requested their data from companies such as Facebook. In a case often referred to as *Europe vs. Facebook*, users were granted the right to obtain access at any given time from companies about the data they hold on a single user. The case spawned a website also known as Europe versus Facebook (see http://europe-v-facebook.org/EN/Get_your_Data_/get_your_data_.html), which states that "[b]y sending an access request you get an idea about the use of your personal data by Facebook. It also shows Facebook that users care about their data and privacy" (Figure 11.2).

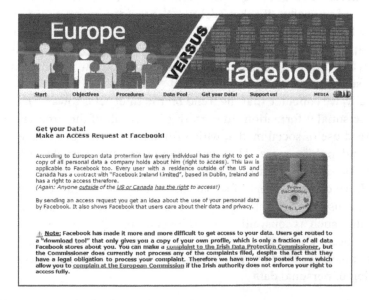

Figure 11.2 Europe vs. Facebook Case: Get Your Data
Source: Europe versus Facebook. http://europe-v-facebook.org/EN/Get_your_Data_/get_your_data_.html

Government agencies have become increasingly uncomfortable with the use of such tools (e.g., encryption technology) by ordinary citizens because they make it more difficult to collect data for purposes of national defense and security. Recent reports (BBC, 2014; CNET, 2014) have suggested that the NSA has been specifically targeting individuals who have used the Tor network, while the Russian government has allegedly offered a $110,000 prize for the person who cracks the identities of Tor users.

Conclusions

This chapter covered the complex topic of surveillance and compared traditional types with new modes of surveillance. Modern societies provide citizens of nation-states with many rights and opportunities. At the same time, these social systems are based on conventions of rationality, standardization, norms, and discipline that impose many restrictions on an individual's freedom. An additional complexity in these social systems is the role of technology in facilitating surveillance and imposing control mechanisms. Constant surveillance exposes vulnerabilities in individuals and may lead to a dystopic "Big Brother" world, where public and private life are closely monitored. We must recognize the pitfalls of technological determinism because surveillance technology alone does not determine how society defines and respects privacy.

Another central conclusion to draw from this chapter is that surveillance can take many forms. Reality TV has changed consumers' attitudes toward surveillance because in this context it is not perceived as a threat. The view of everyday life that reality TV provides is one that is not only welcome but that takes the shape of a spectacle, a form of entertainment. Surveillance—and the "ordinary" life that it allows viewers to glimpse—becomes a commodity that can be marketed just like any other commercial good or service.

Finally, we conclude that the trend on the Internet is toward *more* disclosure of personal information. In part, this is a result of the proliferation and widespread use of social media, which further blurs the boundary between private and public space. However, people are not completely oblivious to the risks associated with making so many aspects of their private lives public. Indeed, many users of social media employ a series of strategies to protect themselves against privacy threats, including strategies of counter-surveillance such as sousveillance and inverse surveillance. These strategies empower users and suggest that social norms, policies, and values shape how technologies affect privacy, creating a balance between disclosure and protection of personal data.

Questions for Critical Thought

1. Discuss the three factors—knowledge, growing impersonality, and enhanced control—that have played a role in the shift toward a Weberian society of rationalization and bureaucracy.

2. Define Foucault's concept of hierarchical observation and show how it plays out in the structure of the Panopticon.

3. Gary T. Marx puts forward three views as to how technology is changing society, namely functional, revolutionary, and cultural. Provide support for one of these views using Facebook as an example.

4. Describe the phenomenon of the privacy paradox in digital media as analysts have described it. How can we best explain users' paradoxical behaviour?

Suggested Readings

Hartzog, W., & Selinger, E. (2014, September 1). Two reasons why extreme social surveillance doesn't replace privacy. *Forbes*. Retrieved 22 October 2014 from www.forbes.com/sites/privacynotice/2014/09/01/two-reasons-why-extreme-social-surveillance-doesnt-replace-privacy/. The authors discuss the tensions between privacy and social surveillance and provide concrete examples to show the need for privacy in a digital society.

Foucault, M. (1977). *Discipline and punish: The birth of the prison*. New York: Pantheon. Through an analysis of prisons, this classic provides an in-depth historical study of the changes that have occurred in how society exerts control and enforces disciplinary action.

Chesterman, S. (2011). *One nation under surveillance: A new social contract to defend freedom without sacrificing liberty*. Oxford, England: Oxford University Press. This book provides an overview of the history of surveillance and gives many current examples.

Singer, P.W., & Friedman, A. (2014). *Cybersecurity and cyberwar: What everyone needs to know*. New York: Oxford University Press. The authors provide a deep and thorough analysis of the cybersecurity and cyberwar landscape through presentations and discussions of theories and case studies.

Young, A.L., & Quan-Haase, A. (2013). Privacy protection strategies on Facebook: The Internet privacy paradox revisited. *Information, Communication & Society, 16*(4), 479–500. This empirically-based article studies the privacy protection strategies that young people employ to guard their personal information while at the same time actively participating in social media through posts, engagement, and updates.

Online Resources

Edward Snowden: Here's how we take back the Internet
https://www.youtube.com/watch?v=yVwAodrjZMY

In this TED talk, Edward Snowden talks about the leak of top secret files and the consequences for how we think about surveillance in modern society.

Europe versus Facebook

http://europe-v-facebook.org/EN/Get_your_Data_/get_your_data_.html

> This site allows users to request their data from Facebook.

Surveillance Studies Centre, Queen's University

www.sscqueens.org/

> This website contains useful information about projects and research in the area of surveillance.

State of Surveillance: Police, Privacy and Technology

https://www.youtube.com/watch?v=6VkKeM-OK6g

> This documentary provides an interesting overview of the recent developments in crime fighting tools and their implications for civil liberties.

12 Ethical Dimensions of Technology

Learning Objectives

◎ to summarize and evaluate the three central themes of the book;

◎ to examine the ethical and moral dimensions of our technological society, including the idea of the neutrality of technology;

◎ to think critically about the metaphors of technology as destiny and technology as progress;

◎ to stress the materiality of technological production, use, and disuse and its effect on developing countries;

◎ to examine the social and health consequences of overload resulting from overreliance on mobile devices, app addiction, and an inability to disconnect.

Introduction

In the previous chapters we discussed the many ways in which technology and society intersect. The primary goal of this final chapter is to summarize the three key themes that run through the book. The first theme stresses that the study of technology needs to be approached from a socio-technical viewpoint. The second theme posits that technology and innovation are closely interwoven with economics and that this has consequences for our understanding of inequality and discrimination based on race, class, and gender. The final theme emphasizes that social change goes hand in hand with technological developments. These three themes inform how we approach and understand the study of technological change and its complex interlink to trends unfolding in society.

The second goal of this concluding chapter is to discuss some of the ethical and moral dimensions that humans encounter as they engage with technology. Some of the central themes include the neutrality of technology, technology as human destiny, and technology as progress. Moreover, most discussions of technology are theoretical in nature and disregard the materiality of technology: the labour and natural resources that go into the production of such devices as cellphones, tablets, and game consoles. We take a critical stance toward the cycle of mass production by looking at electronic waste; the aim of this critical engagement is to make visible the materiality of technology and its implications for society. Where do our technologies go when they are replaced? Through this discussion, the chapter empha-sizes the unexpected consequences of technology with which society needs to come to terms. The chapter ends with an investigation of overload, the sense of not being able to manage the many demands and expectations put forth by our multiple and diverse spheres of life. While technology is often celebrated as the harbinger of flexibility and mobility, its ubiquity has also led to increased levels of stress, which have consequences for physical and mental health. Ironically, new technologies, such as Pip and NoPhone, have been developed to help individuals reduce their stress levels and cope with their addiction to cellphones and apps.

The Book's Three Central Themes

The book covers a wide range of technologies, their uses, and social impli-cations. Nonetheless, we can identify three themes as most central in our analysis of society and technology. We discuss each theme next and draw some conclusions.

1. The Socio-technical Approach

Why is a socio-technical approach to the study of technology useful? What insights do we gain? Early conceptualizations tended to focus on technol-ogy as a material substance, disregarding the social nature of technological invention, implementation, and use (Feist et al., 2010). As society relies more heavily on technology, it is inevitable that we need a better under-standing of the link between the social and technological dimensions. The first attempt to examine this link was through the conceptual framework of technological determinism (Feenberg, 1999), which argues that technology is the single most important precursor of social change. This framework has been heavily criticized because it does not account for the complexity of the relationship; it assumes, instead, that technology alone can exert change.

Recent conceptualizations have taken a socio-technical approach in which the social and technological are closely interwoven and mutually influence each other, a relationship that has been referred to as a mutual shaping process (Bijker, 2009; Bijker et al., 1999). In such an approach, technological, political, economic, cultural, and social factors are integrated to explain how social change occurs. That is, social change is no longer examined as a single dimension; rather, it is viewed as a coming-together of different societal factors in a seamless web. An example of this was the widespread adoption by women of household technologies in the 1950s and 1960s. Household technologies did not become popular only because of their utility in the home. At the same time, changes were taking place in terms of the expectations of household cleanliness (i.e., germ theory and household science), increased incomes in middle-class families, lower prices for consumer goods, and the notion that mass-produced goods served as status symbols (Wajcman, 2013). These factors together prompted the diffusion of household technologies in North America and Europe.

Despite the strengths of a socio-technical approach for understanding how technology and society intersect, some limitations remain. First, the socio-technical approach does not explicitly delineate a select set of variables that need to be examined. The approach is rather vague in determining what factors are most central in a socio-technical analysis. Second, the approach does not state what mechanisms underlie the relationship between technology and society. It is unclear as yet exactly how these two forces come together and mutually shape each other. Finally, little detail is provided as to how a socio-technical approach should uncover the mechanisms underlying the mutual shaping process. While a wide range of methods have been proposed for the study of the socio-technical, there is still uncertainty as to the best way to approach such an investigation. These shortcomings suggest that much more work is needed to fill in the existing gaps in the socio-technical approach.

2. Technological Inequality

A central question investigated in this book is how technology and inequality are linked. Karl Marx (1970) was the first scholar to highlight how industrialization and capitalism were closely connected with social transformations. Several developments—the Industrial Revolution, Taylorism, and Fordism—have all contributed to changes in labour processes, such as deskilling, mass production, and the moving assembly line. Schumpeter (2004) later developed the Marxist theory further by arguing that innovation was the driver of economic development because it created new markets and sources of revenue.

Based on Schumpeter's analysis, we can conclude that technological inequality occurs at three levels. First, the gap between those involved in innovation and those involved in the work force continues to grow. Bill Gates, Sheryl Sandberg, and more recently Mark Zuckerberg are prime examples of this widening economic gap. Second, the difference in society between the haves and have-nots often plays out in terms of technological savviness. Those who lack technological skills are finding it increasingly difficult to join the workforce (McMullin, 2011), which creates further divides along educational levels, socio-economic status, and age, with older generations often not being able to find new employment as a result of their low levels of technological know-how. Third, a global divide exists between those nations that invent, produce, and distribute new technology and those that continue to fall behind. As will be discussed later in this chapter, developing countries are often recipients of electronic waste rather than adopters of electronic goods. This imbalance most severely impacts vulnerable people in these societies, such as children, the poor, and the elderly.

Box 12.1 demonstrates how technological inequality is closely inter-linked to economic interests. A recent debate has sprung up in the U.S. and worldwide around the concept of **net neutrality.**

A central conclusion of this book, then, is that science and technology are key parts of the economy and that investing in R&D leads to social and economic advantages. Nonetheless, the example of Ireland—the Celtic Tiger, as described in Chapter 5—demonstrates that innovation is not easily achieved. Investment in R&D also creates vulnerabilities that are difficult to manage in an increasingly interconnected, global economy. Technological inequality is perhaps the single most important challenge of the twenty-first century. How do we distribute wealth and power? What role will technologies—such as the Internet and cellphones—play in the struggle for democracy and wealth?

Box 12.1   Net Neutrality and Economic Interests

Internet Service Providers (ISPs) have been eager to work with large companies to provide services that grant preferential access to data. According to Cheng et al. (2011), "the status quo of prohibiting broadband service providers from charging websites for preferential access to their customers—the bedrock principle of net neutrality (NN)—is under fierce debate." Net neutrality is integral to how the Internet functions, as all packages (messages and data flows) are treated equally under that premise. If net neutrality were lost, a select group of customers would get preferential treatment, as data would travel at different, pre-determined speeds on the net. This phenomenon was observed during the 2014 World Cup in Brazil. Individuals who subscribed to different content providers were able to receive the signal and watch the game milliseconds earlier. While this may not seem of great relevance, when it comes to celebrating a goal, a few seconds can make a big difference both in the sense of global community and in terms of the notion of equality. Net neutrality and its consequences for the Internet are being fiercely discussed. The U.S. government said that it will unequivocally support policy in favour of net neutrality and not open the door to differential treatment of content on the Web. Net neutrality is probably one of the most contested issues in North America. In the wake of concerns that some Internet service providers may have more control in terms of how data travel via their cables, and thus potentially giving preferential treatment to some customers, the Federal Communications Commission (FCC) received an unprecedented number of comments on the topic—3.7 million in total—via its website, www. fcc.gov/comments (NPR, 2014). Over 99 per cent of those comments were in favour of net neutrality.

How can entire nations keep up with the information revolution? As technology continues to evolve and widely diffuse throughout society, it will become more essential to address these questions.

3. Social Change

While there is no single definition of **social change**, it is often described as a major change of structured social action or social structure taking place in a society, community, or social group (Weinstein, 2010). Researchers have identified a number of dimensions of social change, including space (micro, meso, macro), time (short-, medium-, long-term), speed (slow, incremental, evolutionary versus fast, fundamental, revolutionary), direction (forward or backward), content (socio-cultural, psychological, sociological, organizational, anthropological, economic, and so forth), and impact (peaceful versus violent) (Servaes, 1999).

In the context of technologically induced social change, analysts often assume that these changes are negative, short-term, revolutionary, and peaceful. For instance, the introduction of machinery in the weaving industry resulted in job losses and was the start of a trend toward deskilling that continues to affect workers in an information-based economy. Nonetheless, the term *social change* does not preclude positive change in the context of development or **information and communication technology for development (ICT4D)**. In those instances where technology is a positive force, it is used as an additional resource that facilitates the economic, cultural, and social development of social groups.

Social change does not always occur in predictable ways, and does not have the same implications for all members in society. As Servaes notes, "[t]he new traditions of discourse are characterized by a turn toward local communities as targets for research and debate, on the one hand, and the search for an understanding of the complex relationships between globalization and localization, on the other hand" (2010). As a result, the link between technology and social change is one that can only be examined in the context of specific social groups. This kind of analysis requires an indepth understanding of multiple factors, including economic, social, cultural, and historical, that affect these groups. And even within bounded social groups, social change can occur differently for distinct social actors.

Ethical and Moral Dimensions of Our Technological Society

1. Neutrality of Technology

A central concern in the debate about how technology intersects with society is the **neutrality of technology argument**. The proponents of this argument believe that technology is impartial because it lacks a set of moral values and direction. Within this model, technology is not an agent with moral choices but a passive object used to meet human needs and goals. This debate links directly to the definition provided in Chapter 1, where technology is equal to material substance. That is, technology is viewed as merely a means to an end. Consequently, technology itself is inherently neither good nor bad. However, what humans can exploit or accomplish with a given technology can fall into either category.

The value-neutral perspective suggests that since it is humans, and not technological artifacts, that possess a system of ethical, moral, and social values, technologies are placed into a moral equation only as a result of human use. Yet under what circumstances can technology accurately be described as being neutral? Swedish philosopher Sundström (1998) has described three instances in which technology could be deemed as being value neutral:

1. *Multiple uses of tools*: The first argument is based on the notion that if a technology has multiple and ambiguous uses, value is assigned to that artifact only by humans through the possible uses of the device. Hence, the application or purpose of an artifact is not limited to a singular function; rather, a number of purposes may exist for a single artifact.
2. *Uncontextualized tool*: The second argument relies on the notion that value is assigned to an object only when a value-laden being, such as a human, opts to assign a certain set of values to the device through applied practice. Therefore, if a tool or technique is not used in practice by human beings, it will contain no value properties, because of "the neutrality *before* action and the neutrality of *inaction*" (p. 42).
3. *Tool as science*: The final argument is that since technology is the product of science, which is inherently neutral, technology should also be perceived as being value neutral.

As technology becomes further entrenched in modern life, the notion of technological neutrality comes increasingly under critical scrutiny. Much of the philosophical and scholarly debate over the neutrality of technology has centred on ideas of origin and design. Critics such as Feenberg (1991) have proposed that technology cannot be referred to as neutral because it is imbued with the values present in the particular culture or civilization from which it originated. Box 12.2 describes the development and worldwide deployment of the AK-47 rifle to illustrate how tool invention and use are closely interlinked with societal norms, values, and events.

Box 12.2 demonstrates the complexity of the neutrality debate. The AK-47 was originally built to defend Russia against the Germans. No one ever imagined that it would change the face of warfare for the worse. For Green, "[t]o argue that any technology is neutral is to ignore the social and cultural circumstances in which the technology was developed, and the

Box 12.2   AK-47: Questioning Neutrality

The AK-47 rifle is the most widely used weapon worldwide. From Arctic battlefields to the jungles of Latin America and the deserts of the Middle East, the AK-47 is known for its rugged reliability, durability, and simplicity (Kahaner, 2007). The AK-47 consists of only eight pieces and can be quickly assembled in 60 seconds. As a result, it can be easily mass produced, is cheap to manufacture, and is easy to operate. Additionally, the AK-47 is reliable in inhospitable conditions, is lightweight, and is effective as a killing machine. During the Cold War, these attributes made the AK-47 and its variants[1] the weapons of choice for the Soviet Union, the Eastern Bloc, and numerous armed revolutionaries in Latin America, Africa, and Southeast Asia.

Regarding the neutrality of technology, it can be said that the AK-47 is the number one actor in warfare today. From its inception, its aim was to kill. Despite this horrific mission, the social reality behind its existence is much more complex. Its designer, Mikhail Kalashnikov, was a Russian soldier injured by German gunfire during World War II. With the Soviet military eager to develop an assault rifle for fighting against the German army, competitions were developed for the design and manufacture of a reliable assault rifle capable of withstanding the freezing climate and muddy conditions of the Eastern front (Snezhurov, 2011). Following several modifications, the Soviet military successfully tested and adopted Kalashnikov's rifle in the late 1940s.

For Kalashnikov, the invention of the AK-47 was about the defence of an entire nation against the Germans, who were brutal and systematic in warfare. The AK-47 was designed to influence the war and help combat the German troops. While the AK-47 was not deployed during World War II, from the standpoint of the Russians and Kalashnikov himself the deployment of the AK-47 seemed like a necessary, and perhaps the only, means to combat the enemy.[2]

However, taken out of this social and historical context, the weapon becomes a source of sorrow, death, and never-ending wars. The ramifications of Kalashnikov's invention can be related to the traits that made it so popular. During the Cold War, many countries that did not receive military aid from the United States instead purchased weapons from the Soviet Union. Following the collapse of the Soviet Union, many of these weapons were sold on the black market to drug cartels, terrorist organizations, and other insurgent groups. Approximately 50 million to 80 million AK-47s exist, many of which are counterfeited (Naim & Myers, 2005); the extensive supply has drastically reduced the cost of these weapons.[3]

Additionally, the ease with which the weapon can be operated has made it easy for child soldiers in conflict zones such as Sierra Leone to be instructed about its use. Figure 12.1 shows the extent to which this simple but enormously devastating weapon has expanded across all continents and regions of the world, leaving a profound social and political impact. The involvement of children in war makes the use of the AK-47 particularly contentious. Kalashnikov later opined that people should "blame the Nazi Germans for making me become a gun designer. I always wanted to

Continued

construct agriculture machinery" (Roberts, 2007). This shows how the perception of a technology can radically change depending on the social context in which it is employed (Connolly, 2002).

original users of the AK

the operators with new versions of AK

countries producing/ releasing their own variants

Figure 12.1 Geographical Spread of the Kalashnikov

policy and regulatory regimes under which that technology is deployed" (2002, p. 5). The social context in which a technology is developed does not have to match the context in which the technology is later utilized. Rather, technology is a reflection of the values, goals, and norms of the society that uses it. Technology is not neutral because it embodies the power struggles between social groups and the societal goals that these groups pursue.

Pacey (1983) furthers this argument by noting that while a basic machine removed from its point of origin may appear at first glance to be culturally neutral, "the web of human activities surrounding the machine," including its symbolic status and uses, quickly negate its neutrality (p. 3). Viewing technology as an instrument open to human use and operating on a blank slate also overlooks the reality that the design and subsequent construction of any given technology can be carried out "in such a way that it produces a set of consequences logically and temporally *prior* to any of its professed uses" (Winner, 1999, p. 32).

2. Technology as Human Destiny

The metaphor of destiny in relation to technology is a powerful mode of approaching humanity's relationship to the world. During the Victorian era, the concept of destiny in relation to technology was heavily linked to the idea of progress. Inspired by Judeo-Christian historicism and Westernized interpretations of civilization, the Victorian belief in linear progress was thought to be evidenced through technology. Following the carnage of the First World War, faith in linear progress quickly evaporated. Factors such as the destructive consequences of the atomic age at Hiroshima and Nagasaki and the general increasing entrenchment of technology into the fabric of society greatly shaped the intellectual response to and surrounding discourse about humanity's technological destiny.

Jonas (2003) argued that if in the era of Napoleon, destiny was achieved through politics, "we may well say today, 'Technology is destiny'" (p. 14). Jonas divides technology into two distinct and separate spheres: **traditional technologies** and **modern technologies**. Traditional technologies have stationary and passive characteristics representing "a possession [and] a set of implements and skills," while modern technologies are an active "process [and] a dynamic thrust" (Jonas, 2003, p. 14). This is similar to Heidegger's (2010) comparison of traditional and modern technologies as seen through a hydroelectric plant on the River Rhine, which, unlike the windmills of yesteryear, transforms, controls, and manipulates natural matter in highly artificial ways. To confront the restless impulses of modern technology, Jonas argues for ethical responsibility due to "the central place it now occupies in human purpose" (1984, p. 9).

The relationship among technology, progress, and destiny also caught the interest of Canadian communication scholar George P. Grant. A fervent Canadian nationalist and philosopher, Grant's (1986) technological outlook was greatly shaped by the willingness of then Prime Minister Lester B. Pearson and the Liberal Party to acquiesce to American requests to accept nuclear-capable warheads. Grant's broad definition of *technology* encompasses instruments and knowledge through which technology is an ontology, or mode of being connected to the nature of existence. He argues in favour of a view where technology is regarded as our "civilisational destiny" (p. 22), resulting in a view of destiny as an imposed mode of being, in which technology engulfs every aspect of society. The metaphor of destiny as portrayed by Grant suggests that human destiny is closely linked to technological change. To some extent it also suggests that technology is an inevitable and central part of humanity.

For Grant (2002), "faith in progress through technology" is such an ingrained and permanent component of North American life that "[t]he loss of this faith for the North American is equivalent to the loss of himself and the knowledge of how to live" (p. 400). He also believed that technological destiny directly shapes how we represent and make sense of the world around us and of ourselves. Grant (1986) is critical of the close interweaving of human subsistence and technology because as human reliance on technology increases, so consequently does the need to find technological solutions to correct and handle technological problems. As technology becomes woven into the very fabric of human existence—material, cultural, economic, and social—humans will find it increasingly difficult to detach themselves from technology and comprehend its dangers. The more our destiny is one with technology, the more difficult it is for us to step back and take a critical standpoint.

Destiny is a central part of Heidegger's inquiry, which he describes as a "direction, which at best may be said to set a framework and provide a set of conditions" (Ihde, 2010, p. 38) for an eventual purpose or end. For Heidegger (2010), human destiny is not fully determined but rather is closely linked to human agency and choice. Modern technology endangers this freedom by concealing the full reality of its true nature. Deluded into believing they are masters of technology, humans may be unaware of this problem and misinterpret or ignore the dangers and risks associated with technology. When humans fail to be concerned about technology and do not question its hidden intentions, Heidegger (2010) says, the fear is that humans will simply become objects of technology. This is an interesting point, as it represents a reversal: technology is not an object that humans employ; instead, humans are themselves objects, part of a technological system.

Heidegger (2010) offers a solution to the problem: not to reject technology outright but to detach ourselves from it and extensively question its purpose and role in society—what he refers to as the essence of technology. This critical lens directly reflects his call toward viewing technology as an activity, rather than a series of artifacts designed for human means (Verbeek, 2005). Thus, Heidegger supports the argument that "modern technology is not destiny imposed upon humanity, but [is] rather a manifestation of the effort by humanity to gain a measure of control over the forces of nature" (Zimmerman, 1990, p. 251).

Criticisms of Heidegger's outlook toward destiny have come principally from scholars, such as Feenberg, who have rejected the fatalism of Heidegger's approach. The critics point toward two problems with Heidegger's view. First, technology is neither always nor only negative for humanity. Technology can improve the human condition in all realms. Second, the view of faith in technology is simplistic and denies human agency. Critiquing the works of Heidegger, Feenberg (1999) argues that his viewpoint produces conclusions in which "technology rigidifies into destiny . . . and the prospects for reform are narrowed to adjustments on the boundaries of the technical sphere" (p. 14). As a result, he says, Heidegger's approach allows minimal space for the development of alternative technological practices, which perhaps take into account the moral and ethical dimensions of technological use. Additional criticisms of Heidegger's philosophy of technology have been connected to his abstract language and his nostalgia for a *pastoral era* (Verbeek, 2005). Heidegger's (2010) distinction between traditional and modern technologies is useful for understanding his nostalgia. He advocates in favour of traditional technologies, which in his view do not interfere with human nature. He rejects the use, and related social, political, moral, and ethical consequences, of modern technologies because he sees them as disturbing the natural equilibrium existent in nature.

The progressive betterment of humanity through technology has an appealing utopian sentiment, yet, as philosophers such as Grant and Heidegger have argued, perhaps such an ideal is also potentially fraught with naivety. If technology is a core function of humanity's destiny, to what extent is humankind able to extract itself from the force of technology? Additionally, to what degree should humans initiate a collective inquiry into the potential dangers, risks, and consequences (expected and unexpected) of a technology before its implementation?

Technological development, then, does not always move forward; rather, instances exist where a technology is abandoned for alternative and safer choices. In effect, human agency and societal attitudes can shape how a specific technology is used and whether or not it is discontinued.

3. Technology as Progress

Guiding our understanding of technology is the assumption that it leads to progress. This idea emerged in the seventeenth and eighteenth centuries, particularly in Europe and North America, where technology was enabling radical economic, workplace, social, and cultural change. Technology assured "liberation and enrichment on the basis of the conquest of nature which was to be accomplished through the new natural sciences" (Borgmann, 1984, p. 216). Advances in the natural sciences allowed new technologies to be developed, and these created possibilities for how people could travel, work, and spend their leisure time. An example is the creation of the railroad industry, which connected remote locations, thereby allowing for travel and hence the rapid transfer of ideas, goods, and people.

This notion of technology as progress is still deeply rooted in Western culture and continues to impact how we perceive, use, and evaluate technology. People view technology as a social and economic force and "[t]he dominance of particular technologies is often used to mark the 'progress' of modern western societies" (Hill, 1989, p. 33). These technologies become such markers of the times that we actually describe society in terms of the dominant technologies—for example, the industrial era, the atomic age, and the information society. In this view, then, technological inventions represent an improvement on previously existing technologies (Street, 1992), and progress can be achieved only if we continue to develop new technologies: without innovation, society stagnates.

Baudrillard (2005) describes technologies as objects whose value is developed through our perception of their functional or symbolic worth. In his reflections on how technology and progress are linked, he contends that "technological society thrives on a tenacious myth, the myth of uninterrupted technical progress accompanied by a continuing moral 'backwardness' of man relative thereto" (p. 133). His notion of **moral backwardness** is essential for understanding the position of individuals, vis-à-vis technology, as inferior entities who do not question the nature of their social system. Moreover, for him technological advancement does not represent progress but, is characterized by a **model of regressiveness**. In his view, technological progress and failure are put at the forefront of debates, serving as a distraction from more critical engagement with technology. Hence, technology is regressive because of this myopic view that fails to question the present production system with its inequalities, power relations, and injustices.

Baudrillard's (2005) theory uses the term **gizmo** to describe technologies that do not have a clear purpose in society. He describes how a gizmo is "always an indeterminate term with, in addition, the pejorative connotation of 'the thing without a name' . . . [I]t suggests a vague and limitless functionality" (p. 123). Gizmos "serve to reinforce the belief that for every need there is a possible mechanical answer" and that "every practical (and even psychological) problem may be foreseen, forestalled, [and] resolved in advance by means of a technical object that is rational and adapted—perfectly adapted" (p. 125). Indeed, from a Westernized viewpoint, we can relate "the measure of civilization" to the abundance and complexity of available technologies (Street, 1992).

Additionally, this perspective stresses that technology is an enabler, giving people the means to fulfill their needs and wants, and it supports the idea of **technological utopianism**, in which society uses technology to create and maintain an idealized societal form (Segal, 1985). Supporters of technological utopianism have "made technological progress equivalent to progress itself rather than merely a means to progress, and they [have] modeled their utopia after the machines and structures that made such technological progress probable" (pp. 74–75).

The view of technology as progress is rather myopic, as we discussed in Chapter 3, because it does not take into account the social consequences of technology. Simply put, progress is not a one-dimensional concept; technology and its use are embedded in the daily reality of people's everyday lives. Moreover, the metaphor of technology as progress leads us to a set of key ethical, moral, political, and social questions:

1. Is technological change always necessary?
2. Does technological advancement improve humanity?
3. Are there unaccounted-for consequences of technology that are not always apparent?
4. Does the technology-as-progress paradigm reflect capitalist notions of society?

These questions require careful consideration. They point toward implicit notions of how technology and society intersect. From this perspective, it is only through technological progress that society can solve its fundamental economic, social, health, and ethical problems. Technology, then, is no longer an option; rather, it is human fate because it is the only means through which humans can build a better world (Francis, 2009). As a result, people take technology for granted and no longer engage in questioning technology (Feenberg, 1999). Nevertheless, some oppose this viewpoint because, for them, technological change "threatens established ways of life" and therefore they see such change as a regressive force (Street, 1992, pp. 20–21). We must continue to explore these questions as technology becomes ever more pervasive and ubiquitous in society.

Electronic Waste

The ethical debates around technology need to go beyond issues of adoption and use. As discussed earlier in this chapter, it is central to gain knowledge of how the social and technological intersect. But it is also important to consider the ethical implications of what happens to our gadgets when they are broken, obsolete, or simply no longer fashionable. Most users do not think about their gadgets/electronics after they have discarded them, but many materials that compose electronics are either toxic or nondegradable. This waste is often exported to other countries, such as China, that are poorly equipped to deal with toxic materials. This creates enormous ethical challenges that are not sufficiently taken into account by the countries where the waste originates.

Electronic waste, also called e-waste or waste of electric and electronic equipment (WEEE), refers to scrapped electric or electronic devices. It comprises a wide range of discarded household and commercial technologies, including computers, cellphones, televisions, and batteries. Trends such as globalization, development, population growth, and declining retail prices have caused a steady rise in the amount of electronic waste produced annually. As electric and electronic devices are manufactured more cheaply and sold at lower cost to the consumer, these goods become more disposable, and people opt to purchase new devices instead of having old ones repaired or upgraded. Moreover, rapid technological advances encourage consumers to replace outmoded or obsolete technologies frequently.

At least 20 million tons of household electronic waste is produced globally every year (Zoeteman, Krikke, & Venselaar, 2010), and recent estimates of total WEEE production worldwide suggest that the figure is closer to 40 million to 50 million tons (Khan, Lodhi, Akhtar, & Khokar, 2014). While much of this is reused, refurbished, or recycled, much is also dumped in landfills or incinerated. Of special concern are the millions of tons of electronic waste exported from developed countries to China, India, and other developing nations (Terazono & Yoshida, 2013; Zoeteman et al., 2010). It is often children and vulnerable populations whose job it is to take electronics apart, sort them, and redistribute them for recycling. This work is not only labour inten-sive but is conducted under poor conditions, often in open dump sites, with-out proper protective gear (e.g., masks or gloves). Many of these countries do not have the resources available or policies in place to properly handle large amounts of electronic and toxic waste; consequently, hazardous substances contained in the discarded technologies are left to contaminate terrestrial and marine ecosystems. Canadian photographer Edward Burtynsky has cre-ated a movie entitled *Manufactured Landscapes*, which uses his photos to show the changes that result from industrial work and manufacturing waste in China. The photography and the movie are a social analysis of how land-scapes shape people's lives and how our heavy reliance on electronics has left a permanent mark on both the landscape of China and its people.

Electric and electronic devices contain many materials that are poten-tially harmful to humans and other organisms, including brominated flame retardants, heavy metals such as lead, cadmium, and mercury, and radioactive substances such as the isotope of americium used in some smoke detectors (Goosey, 2009). These cause little harm when recycled or discarded using the proper procedures but can otherwise pose serious environmental and health risks. Decisions concerning the disposal of electronic waste thus have an important ethical component. Though WEEE remains a serious problem,

Ghanaians working in a large electronic waste dump in Agbogbloshie, a suburb of Accra, Ghana.
Source: "Agbogbloshie" by Marlenenapoli—Own work. Licensed under CC0 via Wikimedia Commons—http://commons.wikimedia
.org/wiki/File:Agbogbloshie.JPG#/media/File:Agbogbloshie.JPG

potential solutions have been raised and in many cases implemented. For example, restrictions on the kinds of materials that may be used in electronics manufacturing limit the number of toxic substances in technologies that will eventually be thrown away (Goosey, 2009). High-level recovery systems ensure that more devices are reused and refurbished (Zoeteman et al., 2010). International co-operation in developing agreements and policies to facilitate ethical and sustainable disposal of WEEE will also necessarily play a role in mitigating the dangers of electronic waste (Khan et al., 2014).

An innovative way of increasing awareness of the issues surrounding electronic waste is the Technotrash project. Its website, technotrash.org, invites individuals to participate with the following message:

> We are soliciting personal histories of technological use, disuse, and disposal. Send us your stories and photos, and help raise awareness about the social and environmental impacts of our personal technologies and media practices.

The site features original stories about how people interact with their devices and the material footprints that these devices leave behind. Projects like this are a stepping stone toward greater awareness and the development of initiatives to ethically address the problem of electronic waste.

A Society of Overload

Have we reached a society of overload? What does a society of overload look like? And how can we address problems resulting from overreliance on technology? These are not easy questions to answer. For example, what to some may seem excessive reliance on technology may simply seem to others like normal, everyday use. Pew data (2014) reveal an interesting picture of the discrepancies in usage of social media sites in the United States. Thirty-six per cent of social media users employ a single platform to interact with their social networks. But as many as 42 per cent use multiple platforms, for example combining Facebook with Instagram or Twitter. This demonstrates how varied adoption and use of technology can be. There also exist variations in how this usage is interpreted. The social norms that a society develops around technology use are critical in how that use is evaluated and what meaning it is given. For instance, going on a date and constantly checking updates on a cellphone may be perceived as rude, while engaging in the same behaviour when going out for dinner with friends may be seen as normal and even expected. That is, social norms specific to a local or social group arise that dictate what is perceived as acceptable and what is deemed improper, and these vary considerably from one social context to another.

One central theme of this book has been that technology alone does not lead to social change; rather, change involves a coming together of multiple factors. When we look at how and why our technologies lead to feelings of being overwhelmed, a complex picture emerges. We obtain some insights into what makes life more demanding from Brigid Schulte's new book *Overwhelmed* (2014), discussed in Chapter 7, in which she describes her busy life, constantly rushing from one thing to another. She is constantly juggling different demands, trying to give her best, and integrating technology to be available to her family and to meet work demands, which, as a reporter for the *Washington Post*, are high. She describes how she manages a busy schedule in an interview on NPR: www.npr.org/2014/03/11/288596888/not-enough-hours-in-the-day-we-all-feel-a-little-overwhelmed.   Schulte's hectic lifestyle is common among North American parents and there are many factors, among which technology is a central one, that together create this sense of overload.

One important factor is the widespread use of mobile technologies that tether us to our work, family, and friends 24/7. We have, as a society, now reached unprecedented levels of connectivity not only with more people through interactions with weak and strong ties, but also with more diverse networks consisting of faraway contacts, virtual communities, and contacts and social groups (e.g., "fandoms") on various social media platforms. Hence, people increasingly need to juggle different spheres of life—work, family, social circles, and activities—while playing a different set of social roles in each. Sociological theory has described these changes in how we interact with our surroundings as part of social practices common in postmodernity; according to Harvey (2000) and Thrift (1996), what has taken place is a **time–space compression** resulting from heavy reliance on technology that allows for interactions and the flow of information to occur at a faster pace and without constraints of distance. The smartphone is an excellent example of a technology that facilitates both time and space compression, as we can, through various apps, connect with our contacts instantly anywhere in the world. The time–space compression concept describes how our societal practices, social norms, and expectations change the qualities of and interactions between time and space. As a result of these changes we see greater integration of different parts of the world, leading toward globalization.

Technology alone, however, is not responsible for overload. Women have moved since the 1960s into the work force and this trend has created enormous time pressures, changed social roles in the home, and put more demands on families. Couples now share household responsibilities, and as such there is, somewhat ironically, less time for either the home or work. Schulte's feeling of being overwhelmed and exhausted is clearly shared by many parents. But it is also a reflection of a more fundamental shift in society: modern citizens struggle to find time for themselves and as a result often feel rushed, unsatisfied, and perhaps even unproductive despite their never-ending busyness (Nowotny, 1994).

Another trend resulting from our fast-paced information society is what is referred to as **information overload**. Information overload describes the inability to effectively make decisions because of too much information. In some cases, more information is not necessarily better; rather, it freezes a person and impedes rational decision making. In a digital society, where we are constantly both accessing and sharing information, we can quickly feel overwhelmed with the sheer amount of information available (Booth, 2014).

Central to these changes is what scholars are referring to as the commodification of free time. In this view, exploitation took place under Fordism at the workplace, but workers were given complete autonomy in determining their leisure time. That is, leisure time was a discrete unit that was unpaid and therefore free of labour. Through the availability of information and communication gadgets, however, this clear division of the workplace and leisure time has collapsed. Worse still, time for leisure in our current networked, technology-driven information society appears to be shrinking rather than expanding: time is split among household demands (e.g., child care, house cleaning, shopping, cooking) and work-related tasks. If there is an emergency at work or a pressing deadline, multitasking can be a good way to fulfill demands in multiple spheres. An example of this occurs when a parent is at home taking care of her children and receives a text message from work indicating that her input is required on an important project. Rather than having to quickly arrange child care and go into the office, she turns on her computer or makes a phone call and completes the work-related task from home. In this case, technology is advantageous both for the workplace (the team gets the information they need to complete the project) and the parent (who doesn't have to sacrifice time with her children). But it also adds to the stress level of working parents by blurring the boundary between work and home. Gardiner (2014) describes this shift from an industrial society to one in which the boundaries between work and home have become porous:

> In the contemporary setting, however, capital instigates a far-reaching process of "deterritorialization", wherein formerly discrete activities and social spheres are integrated into the demands and rhythms of production itself. Capitalism now produces not only the conditions of the workplace, but the general social relations in which workers live and raise their families. Hence, the contemporary worker is involved in production not only as a labouring body but as a much broader "social subject", which far exceeds the hours they spend in the workplace itself. (pp. 34–35)

Life occurs at a much more rapid pace as information travels instantaneously through social media on a global scale, and daily rhythms are faster with people being able to coordinate with multiple networks in real time (Agger, 2004; Giddens, 2013). The concept of **deterritorialization** describes how in a networked society we observe collisions of social spheres and social roles.

A central question that needs further investigation, then, is whether or not technologies are helping us manage time more efficiently (i.e., our schedules and assignments), or if they are only exacerbating our feelings of busyness and our stress levels. While being always on and available may be good for business productivity, it can take a toll on family relations and potentially lead to stress.

One interesting finding is that people tend to underestimate how much time they spend on various activities. It is particularly difficult to determine how much time we spend online, for example, searching for information, reading the news, or checking our social media accounts. *Time Magazine* developed a calculator (http://time.com/6107/how-much-time-have-you-wasted-on-facebook/) to allow users to determine how much time they have spent on Facebook since they joined the site. The app also tells a user the number of updates they have posted. Most users of Facebook are surprised when they realize they have spent hundreds of days on Facebook, as the following Facebook post indicates: "497 days . . . a little sickening to say the least" (ShortStack, 2014).

Determining how much time one spends on social media sites is a first step toward more effective time management. Ironically, some of the latest and most popular gadgets available on the market are geared toward managing and reducing technology-induced stress. Box 12.3 discusses two of these.

Box 12.3   The Latest De-stressor Technologies

As the pace of life continues to accelerate and the number of apps available incrementally increases, people's stress levels also continue to rise. Stress may seem like a passing state of mind, not to be taken too seriously, but the World Health Organization (WHO) reports that it costs the U.S. economy alone US$300 billion a year. In Britain, about 10.4 million days a year are lost due to stress-related absences by employees. Stress can also be linked to problems like depression, anxiety disorders, and insomnia.

The most recent gadget to help individuals regulate their stress is called the Pip, a biosensor device that users hold between the thumb and forefinger. The device measures sweat, electrodermal activity, and other physiological measures usually associated with high stress levels. It will then send a signal to its user when stress is detected. This helps people to recognize stress and engage in relaxing activities such as going for a walk, meditating, or doing yoga, to bring stress levels down again.

The second gadget is the NoPhone, a simple piece of rectangular-shaped plastic aimed at replacing a cellphone. Touted as "a technology-free alternative to constant hand-to-phone contact that allows you to stay connected with the real world," the gadget looks and feels like a smartphone but is not connected to the Internet. Originally conceived as a "satirical security blanket" meant to challenge society's addiction to mobile phones, the idea was developed by Van Gould, Ingmar Larsen, and Ben Langeveld, who were tired of trying to socialize with friends who were constantly checking their cellphones. Their NoPhone campaign has already raised $18,316 on Kickstarter toward the development of the product.

Box 12.3 describes different gadgets geared toward reducing stress induced by heavy reliance on technology. As we have discussed, this dependence comes at a price, namely increased stress, which has consequences for both physical and mental health.

Conclusions

In contemporary society, technologies and technological systems are embedded in the functions of our daily lives. Our interactions with these devices have become almost second nature—to the point that we think nothing of the interplay between ourselves and mechanisms as seemingly mundane as toasters, coffee makers, televisions, and computers. Since the beginning of the Industrial Revolution, people have viewed the escalation and sophistication of technologies as a mark of progress at both a technical and a social level. These devices have increasingly become more complex in their design and functionality.

Some consider technologies to be merely neutral—passive tools and techniques humans use to fulfill specific goals or needs. Others have strongly argued that the view of technologies as neutral entities is unrealistic and does not take into account the social, political, and cultural values and intentions of the creators of particular technologies.

For theorists such as Martin Heidegger, a key to understanding the problems of technology in the past was to be found in our ability to remove ourselves from technological objects and systems; to stand back and question technology's role in society. But is this even possible in modern society? Certainly, most people do not question the role and purpose of a technology unless that technology personally affects them in a profound manner.

For example, the raw emotion brought on by a school shooting or a nuclear disaster is often a powerful catalyst that spurs an examination of the technologies involved.

There are a myriad of ethical questions that result from our reliance on technology. These range in nature from the ethical use of tools within specific social groups to the ethical implications of our technological waste. As technology becomes further entrenched in the modus operandi of our twenty-first-century existence, humans must examine the short- and long-term effects of our relationship to technology. We do not call for a rejection or an abandonment of technology but rather for a measured evaluation of technology in order to maintain a healthy social, economic, and political relationship between ourselves and technology. As technologies continue to evolve, they present new and unknown challenges that require careful consideration and scholarly investigation.

Questions for Critical Thought

1. Discuss the key arguments in favour of and against the neutrality of technology.

2. What are the problems underlying the metaphor of technology as progress?

3. Is it possible to critically examine technology if it is an intrinsic part of humanity's destiny? Provide three arguments to support your viewpoint.

Suggested Readings

Baudrillard, J. (2005) *The system of objects*. New York: Verso Press. An important philosophical work in understanding the value placed on objects within contemporary society.

Crary, J. (2013). *24/7: Late capitalism and the ends of sleep*. London, England: Verso. This critique of late capitalist societies points out that social and natural rhythms have become subsumed under the machine-like structure of a society in which people are expected to be available all day, every day.

The New York Times (2014). Net neutrality. *New York Times*. Retrieved from http://topics.nytimes.com/top/reference/timestopics/subjects/n/net_neutrality/index.html. *The New York Times* has a series of articles and videos on the topic of net neutrality, including interviews with U.S. President Barack Obama on the topic.

Schulte, B. (2014). *Overwhelmed: Work, love and play when no one has the time*. Toronto: Harper Collins. Schulte offers a funny and revelatory view of the multi-faceted stresses that are tearing our lives apart, and concrete suggestions for how to find peace and well-being in the midst of it all.

Online Resources

UNESCO's Ethics of Science and Technology Programme
http://en.unesco.org/themes/ethics-science-and-technology
> Created with the establishment of the World Commission on the Ethics of Scientific Knowledge and Technology (COMEST), this site documents UNESCO's attempt to create a dialogue for understanding science and technology within an ethical framework.

Centre for Ethics and Technology
www.ethicsandtechnology.eu/
> Based in the Netherlands, the 3TU. Centre for Ethics and Technology is a research-oriented collaboration by three Dutch universities dedicated to the study of ethics in science and technology. The site contains a publication database, areas of research, and a list of key members.

Time Magazine's Facebook Calculator
http://time.com/6107/how-much-time-have-you-wasted-on-facebook
> This website allows individuals to estimate how much time they have spent on Facebook since they joined the site through examining the number of updates and other forms of engagement a user has logged.

Glossary

access When an individual has a means to connect to the Internet, either through a computer or another digital tool. A number of different means of accessing the Internet exist, including Ethernet, dial-up, and wireless (WiFi).

actant A non-human actor who engages in relationships with human and non-human actors.

actor A person or entity bearing the capacity to (inter)act independently within society. The term *agent* is analogous.

actor network In the context of ANT, this is the sum of actors and their complex Web of interconnections.

actor network theory (ANT) A sociological theory popularized in the 1980s by scholars Latour, Callon, and Law, which examines relationships between actors and envisions the world as a series of continuous and related webs.

adhocracy Where individuals or teams are assembled as they are needed to solve narrowly defined, short-term problems instead of having permanently assigned roles and functions based on organizational charts.

adoption (or **technological adoption**) The decision to use an innovation in order to facilitate the achievement of specific goals.

agrarian societies these are social groups whose livelihood is primarily sustained through agricultural means.

Agricultural Revolution (or **Agrarian Revolution**) The shift from a Paleolithic diet to a period based on cultivated foods.

algorithm A problem-solving method used in mathematics and computer science expressed in the form of a series of instructions.

alienation A term used to describe the feelings among workers who, due to the standardization of their craft, begin to experience disconnection with and apathy toward their work duties.

angel investors Individuals who provide capital investment for initiating technology businesses and in exchange become shareholders of the company or receive some form of repayment over time.

Anonymous A network of individuals who come together for a purpose or goal. They often share similar ideas and use the Internet to make their views known.

armed drones Aircraft that have no human pilot, they are unmanned combat aerial vehicles (UCAV) and usually armed.

artifact An archaeological term describing any object used, constructed, or modified by a human.

artificial intelligence (AI) A branch of computer science dedicated to designing machines capable of resembling or outperforming human intelligence.

augmentation The ability to supplement the physical human body by connecting it to digital components with computational capabilities.

automatic dialing A form of telephone technology developed in the 1920s enabling users to automatically connect to other customers without having to go through a third party.

automatization of power Foucault's term to describe how surveillance can be used as a means to enforce self-control.

autonomous The capability of a technology to independently act within a selected environment. Within this view, technology is guided by its own internal logic, which directs and shapes social interactions and systems of thought.

autonomous Marxism Also known as autonomism, this branch of Marxist theory emphasizes workers' ability to self-organize with the aim of creating changes in the workplace and throughout society at large.

autonomous technology theories Philosophical or sociological approaches based on the belief that humans have little choice in deciding how a technology will evolve and diffuse in society. Technological determinism is an example of an autonomous technology theory.

awareness knowledge Attained through awareness of the existence of a particular technology or innovation.

backstage The elements of an individual's identity that are not revealed to the public but, rather, remain private.

basic research Scientific inquiry aimed at the development of knowledge about the world.

Big Brother A fictional character in George Orwell's novel *Nineteen Eighty-Four*. Big Brother, the dictator of the totalitarian state of Oceania, has come to represent control and surveillance for the purpose of maintaining power.

Big Brother A reality-TV show that has been broadcast in about 70 countries. Participants live in a house with minimal technology, and one of the housemates gets booted off the show every week.

black box of design A term used to describe how the unfolding of technological invention and development is difficult to observe.

blogs Originally referred to as Web logs, a blog is a type of website or a portion of a website that typically contains personal or informal views, media, and commentaries, which are displayed in reverse-chronological order.

body erasure The neglect of considerations related to the body in the design and use of technology.

bonding social capital Connections to those individuals in our networks that we feel close with, facilitating the exchange of resources.

bourgeois public sphere A term coined by Habermas for the public spaces of debate that existed historically in the late eighteenth and early nineteenth centuries in European coffee houses and other public spaces.

breakup 2.0 The dissolution of a romantic relationship and the role played by Web 2.0 technologies, such as Facebook, Twitter, and Flickr, during and after the dissolution.

bridging connections External relationships or communications for the purpose of bridging organizational boundaries to assist in the creation of boundary-spanning structures.

bridging social capital Connections to individuals that we are not close to, but that we know and can rely on for the exchange of resources.

bureaucratization A social system that allows organizations—both public and private—to achieve their goals through the implementation of rules, norms, and values.

capitalism An economic system where the means of production are privately owned.

cellular network A radio network consisting of cells, which are served by individual transmitter towers, or cell sites.

Celtic Tiger A nickname used to describe Ireland as it showed rapid economic development linked to information technology.

change agents Individuals who make potential users aware of an innovation and assist in providing information designed to help make informed decisions about the adoption of an innovation.

chatterbots Computer programs designed to simulate a conversation with human participants through textual or aural means. See also *intelligent agents*.

China's Great Firewall The technological and social mechanisms utilized by the Chinese government to control the flow of information via digital networks in mainland China.

C-Leg A prosthetic knee-joint system, using hydraulic components, that is able to adjust itself to the changing speed and walking conditions of its user.

closure Occurs when a social group has finalized experimenting with a new

tool, as no new meanings or uses are ascribed to this artifact.

closure by redefinition of the problem When the meaning of an artifact is established by rethinking the original problem instead of making changes to the artifact itself; for instance, in terms of its function or appearance.

collective conscious the social norms, social roles, and expectations that bound people together in societies characterized by organic solidarity.

Community Access Program (CAP) A Canadian government initiative, administered through Industry Canada, aimed at providing Internet access and skills for rural Canadians.

community-liberated view Where community life is not lost but has changed with people socializing outside their local neighbourhoods and their immediate family ties.

community-lost view Sees industrialization as responsible for a decline in the prosperity of community.

"community question" Addresses issues around how community has changed over time.

community-saved view Where friendship and family ties continue to exist and form close-knit clusters similar to those found in the pre-industrial era.

compatibility The extent to which an innovation fits with a social group's existing norms, values, and attitudes.

complexity A characteristic in the model of adoption that describes the level of proficiency people need in order to understand how a particular technology works.

confirmation stage The period in which potential adopters continue to seek out information about an innovation in order to ascertain whether or not they have made the right decision.

content of thought The changing manner in which humans were portrayed as a result of the shift from an oral to a literate culture.

cool media A term used by McLuhan to describe forms of media that require greater effort on the part of the viewer to understand the content and determine meaning.

Cop Watch Social groups primarily in the United States and Canada that see their mission as observing and documenting the activities of the public police to prevent misconduct and unnecessary force.

core team A cohesive group of programmers who work closely together to develop a software product.

counter-surveillance An umbrella term used to denote any form of resistance against surveillance, and includes ways of evading surveillance by the state, increasing awareness of state surveillance, and acts against the mainstream forms of surveillance.

creative destruction A term Schumpeter uses to summarize the social, economic, and cultural transformations that occur as a result of innovations.

creative processes The term Schumpeter uses to describe the design, development, and implementation of new technologies.

creeping The act of looking at others' profiles, wall posts, and pictures on social network sites, such as Facebook.

critical problems In the context of system theory, these are complex problems that require socio-technical solutions.

crowdfunding The practice of raising money from a large number of individuals for a proposed idea, project or other pursuit, most commonly through websites dedicated to supporting crowdfunding initiatives.

cultural capital These are resources and status attained through our education, knowledge of culture, and understandings around social norms. A person's cultural capital defines their belonging to specific social groups (including class), and allows them to make claims around identity.

cyber bullicide Acts of bullying as they occur in cyberspace.

cyberstalking Following obsessively the activities of a person on the Internet, via, for example, social media.

cybertariats Presented by Huws as individuals who are employed in basic data entry jobs for minimum wage.

cyborg A being or entity containing both artificial and biological components that are seamlessly connected.

cyclical fluctuations Schumpeter's term to describe changes in the economy resulting from innovations appearing simultaneously in clusters, instead of being spread over a longer period of time.

data curation Derived from the idea of curating an art exhibit, the term describes how content posted online is also subjected to careful decision making and not randomly put together.

debriefing Informing participants of a study what the intended purpose of the study was. Of particular relevance if any form of deception was part of the study.

decentralized decision making A process that allows workers rather than management to be at the forefront of decision making and information exchange.

decision stage A period featuring the activities that lead toward the adoption or rejection of an innovation.

dehumanization A concept frequently featured in the work of Ellul that refers to the manner in which technology has engulfed every level of society and human existence at the latter's expense.

democratic divide Describes the differences in political engagement of those who have access to the Internet and those who do not.

deskilling The elimination, reduction, or downgrading of skilled labour because of the introduction of technologies within the workplace.

deterritorialization A situation that arises when social spheres blend, and activities that were separated before by time and space become more closely integrated.

developed country (or **nation**) A term used to describe a nation with a high level of social, technical, industrial, material, and economic development. A list of developed countries can be found in the *International Monetary Fund's World Economic Outlook Report*, April 2010.

developing country (or **nation**) Nations with a low level of material well-being and lacking a high level of social, technical, industrial, material, and economic development. The term is not to be confused with *Third World countries*, which historically has a very different meaning.

deviant behaviour Behaviour deemed unacceptable when judged against the established norms of a society.

Diderot's *Encyclopédie* The first encyclopaedia dedicated to the documentation of craft and technique.

diffusion of innovations The study of the adoption and spread of technological innovations in society, or segments of society, over time.

digital divide Describes discrepancies between social groups in access to, use of, and empowerment by networked computers and other digital tools, such as cellphones, PDAs, and MP3s. The term also can encompass differences in skill level and knowledge about digital artifacts.

digital immigrants The generation that did not grow up with the Internet and only started using digital technologies in their adult years.

digital natives A term used to describe people born during or after the development of digital technologies who have correspondingly grown up with a knowledge and familiarity of digital technologies.

digital public sphere Public spaces formed online to help citizens organize and mobilize.

digital revolutionaries Protest leaders who use the Internet as a tool to organize protests and inform and mobilize citizens.

discipline A central concept in Foucault's analysis of power. He describes discipline as the technique used against individuals to exercise power as well as the actual instruments used to enforce it.

discontinuance The rejection of a technology or innovation after initial adoption and previous use.

disinhibition effect Internet users often engage in behaviours online that they would not show offline; this is believed to be related to the fact that a lack of feedback, limited social cues, and no eye contact disinhibits behaviours.

domain of common concern The idea that in the public sphere discussions should center around topics that are of interest and relevance to a wide range of individuals.

domestication of the Web The use of personal computer and Web-based applications for everyday personal, social, or leisure purposes and interactions.

dystopian perspective of technology The belief that technology has a destructive or negative influence on society. This can include the re-organization or changing of social or labour practices through the imposition of technology.

dystopian perspective of the Internet Predicts negative social consequences as a result of Internet use, in particular the weakening of social relations and communities.

ease of invention Describes the extent to which an innovation can be easily discovered on the basis of existing knowledge. Some inventions are difficult to discover because they require not only complex knowledge in an area but also the combination of knowledge from distinct areas.

economic opportunity divide Reflects beliefs and attitudes that individuals have about the advantages provided by access, such as finding a job, obtaining health information, and being able to take an online course.

Electronic waste (WEEE) The electronic components that need to be disposed of after a device has been thrown out.

emotional contagion The transmission of emotions from one person to another.

end-users Individuals who access websites or social media applications. Depending on their level of engagement, individuals may also supply, modify, or critique content within a Web 2.0 environment.

Enlightenment An intellectual movement that started in Europe in the late seventeenth and eighteenth centuries and embraced individual thinking over tradition and custom. It questioned in particular religious beliefs and promoted the advancement of knowledge through the scientific method.

epigraphy The study of the history and social circumstances of written information that has been preserved on hard materials.

equipotentiality A core component of produsage projects that highlights the ability of all participating members to contribute to the end result.

E-Rate A program officially known as the Schools and Libraries Program of the Universal Service Fund, which was established under the U.S. Federal Communications Commission (FCC). The aim is to make affordable Internet access possible for schools and libraries in the United States.

evolutionary model of technological development An idea proposed by George Basalla, which suggests that new technologies arise from earlier sources, rather than from mere ingenuity.

examination The process whereby information on individuals is recorded in documents, which serve the purpose of control as well as the establishment of norms.

exploitation The unbalanced relation between labour and profits, where the proletariat's work is taken advantage of as they obtain only a fraction of the gains made from the sale of the products they manufacture.

Facebook A popular social networking site, where people can create a profile and link to other users.

fear of missing out (FOMO) The notion of missing important information that results from information overload. Of particular relevance to social media sites, where updates occur frequently.

Federal Communications Commission (FCC) An agency of the U.S. government in charge of regulating interstate communications by radio, television, wire, satellite, and cable.

First Mile Project The development, use, and engagement with broadband systems by First Nations to deliver a wide range of services to their communities.

fixed lines Also known as landlines; refers to telephone devices or systems that are operated in fixed locations.

Fordism Refers to a system welding the principles of scientific management to standardize work processes.

Fordist culture Describes the postwar mass culture of the 1950s and 1960s in which items were mass produced in a homogenized manner to appeal to the lowest common denominator.

French Revolution The social and political upheavals that took place in France in the late eighteenth century, demarking the loss of power of the monarchy and church.

friending The act of requesting someone's affiliation on a social networking site.

friendship Voluntary and informal relationships established between two or more parties who have interacted socially with one another. Whereas traditional friendships occur between friends who have shared localized experiences together, contemporary friendships may develop across a virtual sphere between individuals who interact via the Internet.

Friendster A social networking site similar to Facebook that allows members to share messages and media.

frontstage Those elements of an individual's identity that are revealed in public.

gatekeepers Individuals who bring information about a new innovation or technology into a social group.

Gemeinschaft Generally translated as "community" and refers to a cohesive social entity that is united by pre-existing social bonds.

gender resegregation A situation that occurs when women are assigned to jobs that are perceived as more feminine, while jobs performed by women are labelled as "women's work."

Gesellschaft Translated as "society" or "association" and describes the coexistence of individuals who are self-serving units and come together because of an overarching goal.

gizmo Baudrillard's term to characterize a technology that lacks a meaningful purpose within society.

global digital divide Differences in access to the Internet and other digital tools among nations and regions.

globalization The move toward the interconnectedness of human affairs—economic, cultural, social, and political—transcending national boundaries, governments, and laws.

global village A term popularized by McLuhan to describe the possibility that electronic forms of media and communication have compressed spatial distances by enabling people to remain connected to activities and individuals throughout the world.

goal A term used by Heidegger to represent the desired end-product to which an act is originally directed.

Great Man Theory A popular nineteenth-century theoretical idea popularized by Carlyle that supposes history can be largely explained and understood through the impact of notable individual leaders and heroes, who were often predominately male.

green revolution An unprecedented growth occurring in the 1960s in the production of food resulting from R&D and technology transfer, primarily affecting developed nations.

gross domestic expenditure on R&D (GERD) A measure the OECD uses that takes into consideration the total expenditure (current and capital) on R&D accrued by a nation over a one-year period, including expenses by companies, research institutes, universities, and government laboratories.

hack-a-thon An event where computer programmers and others interested in software, graphics, and interface design get together for collaboration on a software project.

hacktivist groups Networks of activists on the Internet that engage in protest, activism, and civil disobedience (sometimes criminal) through the use of computer networks, codes, and other digital means.

haves and have-nots In connection with the digital divide, the "haves" relate to those who have the ability and the skills to access information and communication technologies, while the "have-nots" relate to those who, while lacking the ability to access these technologies, may demonstrate an interest in obtaining the skills related to information literacy or technical competence.

hegemonic elite A dominant political, social, economic or cultural group that exerts power and influence over the remaining members of a society.

hierarchical observation Describes how people's behaviour can be controlled through simple observation by those in positions of power.

hierarchical organizations Entities or organizations that operate using a systematic power arrangement that positions one single individual or group at the top with the remaining members or participants in various levels of subordination.

hieroglyphs Simple writing forms where graphical figures are used to depict words or objects.

high-definition media A term McLuhan used to describe media that provide their users with well-defined and detailed data.

holistic approaches Approaches to the study of phenomena through multiple perspectives, often relying on multiple sources of data and data collection and analysis methods.

holoptism An open approach to problem solving in which all participating members have equal insight into the problem's components.

hominin material culture artifacts used by the ancestors of modern humans.

horticultural societies Societies that relied on simple tools to plant and tend crops on a small scale.

hot media A term used by McLuhan to describe forms of media that require little effort on the part of viewers to process and understand the content.

how-to knowledge An understanding of how an innovation is properly used and employed.

human agency The belief that humans have the ability to make, choose, shape, and act upon decisions that have a genuine impact on the world.

human controlled The ability of humans to control, design, and shape the actions of a technology or technological system.

hunter-gatherer societies Communities or societies in which the primary method of subsistence involves having its members obtain food by way of hunting animals or gathering edible plants without participating in the domestication of either.

hyper-post-Fordist culture The ability of people to customize and individualize their lives through consumer culture.

ideal speech situation Jürgen Habermas's term for a situation where individuals can openly express their thoughts as they are being evaluated solely on the basis of reason.

idioms of practice The social norms that evolve over time around media use.

imitation (or **cyclical fluctuations**) In Schumpeter's model of economic development, innovation does not occur evenly spread over time but, rather, in spurts or episodes.

immaterial labour A form of labour that creates products or services that are not tangible and readily observable, such as knowledge or information.

implementation stage The period in which an individual begins to use an innovation.

income quartile A statistical method used to categorize the population into groups based on average household income from poorest to richest. The division is based on the distribution of incomes, with each quartile representing 25 per cent of the overall population.

Industrial Revolution A historical period beginning in eighteenth-century Western Europe spearheaded by changes in manufacturing, transportation, and technology, which markedly affected the production and distribution of goods as well as socio-economic conditions.

inequality Differences in society in terms of access to social goods, such as the labour market, income, education, and the health-care systems, as well as means of political participation. The discrepancies exist along socially defined grouping, including gender, age, social class, and ethnicity.

information In Rogers's diffusion of innovations model, it is knowledge, fact, or advice communicated to an individual about an innovation.

information age Also known as the computer age; relates to an era in which individuals are able to access and manipulate information with a high degree of sophistication and speed through the advent of information and communication technologies, such as computers, the Internet, and cellphones.

Information Assurance (AI) mission Also known as the Information Assurance Technology Analysis Center (IATAC), it is in charge of managing a wide range of data security tasks in the U.S. Department of Defense (DOD).

informational production or **informational** A term used by Castells and Halls to describe an economy where economic development depends directly on the flow and processing of information and, ultimately, on the creation of new knowledge.

information and communication technologies for development (ICT4D) Describes the use of technologies that facilitate communication, the storage and reuse of information, and data analysis for the purpose of improving the economic and social conditions in poor countries.

information commons A system, community, or institution designed to develop, store, share, and conserve knowledge and information. Physical libraries represent a traditional model of an information commons. In contemporary use, the term can also refer to digital services and/or virtual spaces that promote and adhere to these ideals, such as Wikipedia.

information literacy The ability to successfully utilize, navigate, and operate information resources and information and communication technologies.

information overload The large amount of information that a single individual manages in a day as a result of information and communication technologies (ICTs).

information revelation The disclosure of personal information on the Internet, for instance on social network sites.

information revolution The changes that have occurred in the types of technologies needed and their related services and products as a result of the shift toward the information society.

information society A society in which the utilization, dissemination, diffusion, and development of information is an integral component in social, economic, and cultural life.

information systems development Customized software development, where software is designed to meet the needs and requirements of a particular client or user group.

information technology (IT) The development and application of computer-based technologies designed for the principal purpose of creating, exchanging, and storing electronic information.

informed consent Acquiring consent from participants prior to the initiation of a research study.

innerworldly asceticism Refers to the Puritan ethic of self-discipline and self-control and its associated behaviours, norms, and values.

innovation An idea, a practice, or an object that members of a social group perceive as being new.

innovator-entrepreneur In accordance with Schumpeter's model of economic development, the innovator-entrepreneur is the most important driver of economic growth. This is an individual who develops new ideas, practices, or objects despite the risks and uncertainties associated with these innovations.

inquiry-in-performance The use of art and specifically performance to investigate and create awareness around a critical topic, such as surveillance.

in real life (IRL) These are behaviours and activities that take place offline and are often contrasted with behaviours that occur on the Internet.

institutional privacy Protection of personal information from companies and institutions (e.g., access to personal information by Facebook and its partners).

instrumentalism A theory that analyzes technology as neutral tools or instruments whose purpose is to fulfill the specific tasks of their user.

intellectualization A term introduced by Weber to describe a shift in how decisions are made; instead of relying on superstitious or mystical beliefs, decisions are based on knowledge and rational choice.

intelligent agents Entities capable of accruing knowledge and displaying intelligence to achieve goals related to their environment.

interactivity The ability of users to provide content in response to a source or communication partner.

interconnectedness The extent to which social groups are geographically or socially connected to one another, allowing for the flow of goods and the exchange of ideas, information, knowledge, and innovations. A high degree of interconnectedness allows for the easy transfer of technologies and technological know-how.

interconnectors A role serviced by the early majority, who act as a bridge between early and late adopters and provide relevant information on new innovations to the latter.

interdependence Describes the high level of connectivity currently existent in the world, which makes events that happen in one part of the world have a short- and long-term trickle-down effect on all other parts.

International Telecommunications Union (ITU) An international agency linked to the United Nations (UN) and concerned with questions about information and communication technology.

Internet censorship Measures used by various countries to control the information that flows both into and out of a country, radically undermining citizens' ability to access and distribute information.

Internet dictator's dilemma The dilemma confronted by oppressive regimes who on the one hand want to be active participants in the information society and on the other hand are concerned about the political repercussions of the open exchange of information and communication.

Internet kill switch Refers to the act of shutting down the Internet to control access to information and communication primarily by governments.

interpretive flexibility A term that refers to how the meaning of artifacts is always created in a socio-cultural context.

invention Considered a creative process, in which a person discovers a new behaviour, way of understanding, process, or object. Contrary to *innovation*, where a completely new idea is developed, in the case of invention the process consists of combining already existing elements in unexpected ways.

inverse surveillance Practices that can be subsumed under sousveillance, but that emphasize surveillance as inquiry into social norms and expectation; involves the recording, monitoring, analyzing, and questioning of surveillance technologies and their proponents, and also the recording of how surveillance takes place by authority figures, such as police officers, guards, and border patrols.

invisible audience Audiences that are not known to the creator of content when content is posted on the Internet.

iron cage A concept introduced by Weber to describe how society through the introduction of rules of rationalization and bureaucratization has limited the ability of individuals to make their own choices and exert free will.

Kickstarter A website that facilitates the activities entailed in crowdfunding for a project.

killer app (or **application**) Describes a computer program that people consider to be essential and valuable, and results

in their purchasing the technology on which the program runs.

knowledge stage In Rogers's model of the diffusion of innovations, this is the period in which an individual learns about an innovation for the first time.

labour saving technology The use of technology to reduce the amount of time and effort a person spends on a specific task.

latent ties Latent ties consist of those social relations—including friends, acquaintances, and family—with whom we are not currently communicating or interacting but with whom we could reinitiate contact at any given point in time.

Layton's model of technology An idea of technological development in which ideas are translated into designs. In the model, technology is embodied in ideas, techniques, and design.

literate societies Societies that use writing as a means to preserve information as compared to oral societies, which rely on oral communication.

LiveJournal A popular free social media site that allows users to keep a blog.

local virtualities Geographically bounded places where individuals use computer-mediated communication to facilitate the exchange of information and the formation of social relationships.

low-definition media A term McLuhan used to describe media that provide users with less information, requiring them to fill in the blanks.

Luddites A social movement that emerged in nineteenth-century England, formed by textile artisans who protested against the increased mechanization of labour through sabotaging industrial machines and sites.

machine breaking The process of sabotaging or destroying industrial machinery in response to inferior working conditions and the threat posed by mechanization to workers' crafts or livelihood.

mainstreaming of the Web The notion that the Internet has become an integral component of society, including the development of social phenomena and relationships.

makerspace Physical spaces where those with an interest in for example technology, science, computing, and digital art come together to chat, look at artifacts, or create artifacts.

markets An economic infrastructure or system that allows and encourages the practice of selling or exchanging goods and services for payment.

Marxist tradition A critical theoretical approach to society based on the writings and ideas of Karl Marx.

mass consumption A socio-economic system that nurtures a yearning to purchase increasing amounts of mass-produced goods under the auspices of social improvement and personal gratification.

mass production The production of large quantities of standardized materials, made possible by streamlining the manufacturing process and adopting technology such as the assembly line.

material substance Viewing technology as being its physical or material properties separate from its interactions with society.

mechanical solidarity A society based on social cohesion, where

members share similar social norms and expectations, as they occupy similar social roles.

mechanism Designated by Heidegger to represent the means through which to achieve a goal.

media bias Innis's term to describe the effect of media on how societies operate. He distinguished between a space and a time bias.

media ideologies A term Gershon used to describe the beliefs users form about media and how these affect their use.

the medium is the message An aphorism coined by Marshall McLuhan that proposes that the type of medium through which an individual encounters content may affect the manner in which an individual understands this content. McLuhan underlined the need to examine the impact of media on people instead of focusing only on the influence of content.

megacities Metropolitan areas containing more than 10 million inhabitants, such as New York City.

model of regressiveness Baudrillard's term for the manner in which society, distracted by ideas of technological progress, morally degenerates due to a lack of critical discussion about social inequalities and injustices brought about by the system of production.

modern technologies Technologies that affect nature and human kind in radical ways; they have an active process and a dynamic impetus.

moral backwardness Baudrillard's term to indicate the stagnation of morality brought about by ideas of technological progress and the trappings of materialism.

moving assembly line A sequential manufacturing process that enables parts to be assembled within a specific order to create a product. This process was made famous by Henry Ford's production line, which allowed for the mass assemblage of automobiles.

mutual shaping A term used in STS to describe the close interrelation that exists between social and technological factors.

MySpace A pioneering social networking site that prior to the advent of Facebook was the most popular social networking site in the United States.

MySpace band A rock or pop band that has become famous as a result of its MySpace profile, only to lose its notoriety as it became perceived as being of low quality and catering to the masses.

National Security Agency (NSA) The U.S. agency whose mission consists of the global monitoring, collecting, decryption, and analysis of massive amounts of data for foreign intelligence and counterintelligence.

National Telecommunications and Information Administration (NTIA) An agency of the U.S. Department of Commerce whose information-based functions and policies relate to issues of telecommunications access and development.

nation-state Self-identified and sovereign entities that cover a territorial unit, integrating individuals who live in a specific geographical area and who share an identity.

Ned Ludd A weaver and mythical leader of the Luddites, who, according to folklore, destroyed his knitting frame in response to ill-treatment from his master. Ludd's name was adopted by workers who resented the imposition of technology in their places of work.

Neolithic period An era of technological development beginning around 9500 BCE characterized by the transition from hunter-gatherer societies, which encompasses the advent of farming and settlement practices and ends with the widespread employment of metal tools.

Neolithic Revolution The first agricultural revolution, which precipitated the shift from hunter-gatherer societies toward settlement and agricultural development.

Neo-Luddism Individuals or groups who either openly reject or critique the role of technology in society.

netiquette The social norms around communication and behaviour that have developed on the Internet. These norms are also linked to how language on the Net is unique, as exemplified by the use of acronyms such as LOL.

Netlytic A software developed for the collection and analysis of social media data coming from tools such as Twitter, Facebook, and YouTube.

Net neutrality The premise that all data have equal rights to flow through data networks, without any preferential treatment to data from specific carriers.

network A term used by Latour to denote relationships or interactions between people, objects, and organizations whose shared purpose transforms these connections into an extensive collection of resources and participants that enables them to function as a single unit.

network of security partners A theory that describes how various security partners, such as the police, private security, and the public, need to work together to deal with societal threats.

networked individualism Sees society as moving away from a model where people are embedded in groups toward more loosely connected social networks.

networked organization New forms of management that do not rely on a hierarchical structure of organization to achieve organizational goals; instead, employees are loosely associated.

neutrality of technology argument Technology is considered impartial because it lacks a set of moral values and direction.

neutral point of view (NPOV) A guiding principle of Wikipedia that stresses the expectation that participants will input information that is reliable and objective.

newly industrializing nations Nations whose economic, technical, and social development is outpacing developing nations, particularly through an emerging industrial sector. China and India represent newly industrializing nations.

new surveillance The application of technical means to collect and record personal data.

nomadic tribes Communities of people who prefer to roam from one area to another rather than settling in a single specific location.

nondiffusion When an innovation or technology fails to be adopted by a social group.

normalizing judgment A term Foucault used to describe how

individuals are evaluated against set societal standards to determine if they can be considered normal (or are categorized as abnormal).

observability The visibility of an innovation and its effects on members of a social group. By observing the innovation, members are more likely to discuss and gain information about it.

One Laptop per Child (OLPC) A U.S. non-profit organization whose guiding principle is to create educational opportunities for the world's poorest children through information technologies.

online communities Virtual communities whose members interact primarily online via synchronous or asynchronous forms of communication.

online persona The virtual self-projected by individuals through their online activities, such as their avatar, post history, status updates, and so forth.

opinion leaders Individuals within the early adopter category whose influence and opinions help guide the decision-making process of others in the social group.

oral societies Non-literate societies that preserve culture, knowledge, and norms via oral means.

organic solidarity A quality of modern and industrial societies that feature a specialization of social roles, division of labour, and diverse social norms.

Organisation for Economic Co-operation and Development (OECD) An international organization, consisting of 34 country members, that uses evidence-based analysis to promote policies on economic development and trade, with the aim of improving the economic and social well-being of people around the world.

organizational chart A diagram featuring an organization's structure, rankings, levels, and components.

organization of thought Secondary element determined by Havelock to be a fundamental response in the shift from an oral to literate society, which relates to how main and subordinate ideas are connected.

oversharing The sharing of intimate or personal information via social media without much consideration of social norms.

packaged software development Software that is produced in large quantities and can be obtained off the shelf.

Panopticon A building that functions as a prison, providing complete control over the inmates. It also denotes an entire social system based on techniques of control through surveillance.

para-social grieving The act of grieving for an individual with whom one has established a connection through media.

para-social interaction A form of one-sided social interaction mediated via technology in which one individual has developed a personal bond with the other. This type of relationship is evident in the bond between celebrities and fans.

party line A form of telephonic communication originating in the early twentieth century that enabled multiple users to be connected via the same circuit. Incoming calls for specific users could be differentiated through a distinctive ring assigned to each customer.

pasteurization A process developed by Louis Pasteur by which food or drink is heated in order to slow microbial growth.

pastoral era (or **pastoral societies**) A utopian characterization of pre-industrialized life, where communities were composed primarily of locally based interactions in closely bounded groups.

penetration rate The percentage of users of a technology in relation to non-adopters. It is used as a standard measure for comparing user groups when discussing the digital divide and global digital divide.

perpetual beta The release of software to users before being complete, under the understanding that the software would continue to be improved based on user feedback.

persistence Describes how data on social media and other digital tools are archived for later retrieval and use.

perspective effects The development and application of techniques designed to provide the impression of depth and symmetry.

persuasion stage A period when potential adopters actively seek out information about an innovation.

phablets A term combining the words *phone* and *tablets* to describe cellphones with all the features common to this technology, but larger in size and therefore closer to tablets in this respect.

political economic theory A field of study that has different meanings. Often, the term refers to analysis based on Marxian theory. Other times, the term refers to studies influenced by the Chicago school.

post-Fordist (or **post-industrial**) A system of production and consumption that features greater technical and individual specificity in production and labour roles.

post-typography A society that after having relied on print as a form of communication moves again toward a heavy reliance on orality.

primary orality A term coined by Havelock to describe societies that rely only on oral forms of communication to transmit knowledge, information, and culture.

principle knowledge An understanding of the mechanisms behind an innovation.

privacy The right of individuals to choose what personal information they want to disclose to which audiences.

privacy paradox How users disclose large amounts of personal information on the Internet, despite concerns about their privacy.

probes Aphorisms consisting of ideas designed to inspire critical thinking about the media.

process of circular flow A term Schumpeter uses to describe phases in the economy characterized by stability and a balance between demand and supply.

produsage A term coined by Bruns describing the movement toward user-led areas of development, content creation, and collaboration

of technologies and services, such as open-source software and interactive virtual communities.

prosumer A term introduced by Toffler in 1980 to describe the merging of producers and consumers.

prosumption Modes of production in which consumers perform a significant role in a product's design, development, and use.

public sphere Public spaces where citizens can gather to share their perspectives and voice their opinions.

punishment-as-spectacle The exertion of discipline in the Middle Ages through the use of techniques such as torture, decapitation, and burning.

qualitative methods Contrasted with quantitative methods, these methods rely on numerical analysis and answer questions of causality, while qualitative methods rely on interviews, focus groups, and other text-based sources and answer why and how questions.

rational choice A theory that models and attempts to understand social and economic behaviour.

rationalization A new mode of operation in society, where social action is aimed at increasing efficiency and supporting a capitalist system of production rather than based on grounds of morality or tradition.

reflectionism Ideas and procedures of using technology to mirror and confront surveillance.

regressive force An influence that causes an entity, such as society, to degenerate or reverse from its established course, way of life, or mode of thinking.

relative advantage The process by which the merits of an innovation are examined in relation to those of a previously existing idea, practice, or object.

relevant social group Social constructivist concept pertaining to the group who gives meaning to an artifact.

replicability Capabilities provided online to reproduce content (text, pictures, and videos) and insert it in other contexts.

research and development (R&D) Characterized by a focus on the design, development, and implementation of innovations and inventions.

retro-analysis The analysis of a situation after it has occurred; hence, it relies on memory, archives, and other documentation.

return on investment (ROI) Describes the economic gain to be made as a result of capital investment. It is usually measured as the ratio of monetary input to output.

revenge effect An unintended effect occurring directly in an area of technological intervention.

reverse salient (or **salience**) In the context of system theory, when a system grows unevenly, some components develop quickly, creating imbalances.

rhetorical closure Occurs when instead of solving a technological problem, the meaning given to the problem is simply changed.

rich get richer hypothesis That the Internet will primarily benefit those who are already connected and have large social networks instead of those who are isolated and have small social networks.

science and technology studies (STS) An interdisciplinary field concerned with the study of how scientific and technological change intersect with society.

scientific management A theory of management which attempts to use scientific methods to improve worker efficiency and productivity. Pioneered by Frederick Winslow Taylor in the late nineteenth century, it is often referred to as Taylorism.

searchability The ability to quickly locate information on people via the Web.

search history Search and toolbar logs recorded by search engines and Internet browsers.

secondary orality A term coined by Havelock to describe societies that move away from print and toward sound as a result of electronic media (including radio and television).

second order communication A term Gershon used to convey the formality and nature of a medium.

sedentary societies Small or large types of permanent settlement that are entirely immobile.

SGT STAR A chatterbot used on the U.S. Army website to provide visitors with information about army life.

side effect An action or effect that occurs in an area unrelated to the one the technology was designed to function within.

Signals Intelligence mission (SIGINT) A department of the U.S. NSA, with a mandate to gather intelligence by intercepting of signals. These signals can come from people-to-people communication or from other electronic signals. Central piece is the use of cryptanalysis to decode encrypted signals.

simulation Creating and enacting technologies that imitate the human mind or body within a computerized form.

skills divide The gap between those who have the necessary skills to utilize information and communication technology and those who do not.

social accessibility The ability to control how others can contact us either in real life or in the digital sphere.

social affordance Characterizes the relationship between the features of a system and the social characteristics of a group, facilitating or undermining particular social behaviours.

social after-effects The social results of selecting or adopting one technology over another, which influence social relations and experiences.

social capital The relationships forged through social interactions, networks, and connections, and the resources available through these relationships.

social change Major change of structured social action or social structure taking place in a society, community, or social group.

social construction of technology (**SCOT**) The belief that technology is shaped by human needs and social factors. The cultural norms and values within a social system influence the construction, diffusion, and utilization of the technological product.

social determinism The idea that social factors alone determine and shape uses of technology.

social media Web-based technologies, such as Facebook and YouTube, designed for social interaction; they often include a user profile, links between users, and virtual spaces for users to express their ideas.

social networks The social structures formed by individuals' patterns of social interaction.

social networking sites (**SNSs**) Online websites, applications, or platforms centred on developing or maintaining virtual social relationships between individuals with shared interests, experiences, or connections.

social privacy Protection of personal information from other people that we know, such as friends, co-workers, and family.

social structure The arrangement of social organizations, institutions, and relationships within a society.

socio-technical perspective The study of how social factors affect technological and scientific developments.

software cowboy Programmers and developers of software who excel in their ability to write code and design software products.

sousveillance The recording of events and activities via mobile technologies, such as cellphones, tablets, or wearable technologies.

space bias Emerges in literate societies and favours imperialism and commerce. A space bias emerges because writing allows for the easy dissemination of ideas and information over vast distances.

spiral of silence A theory proposed by Elisabeth Noelle-Neumann to describe how individuals who feel that their opinion is in the minority will not speak up because of fear of being excluded and ostracized.

S-shaped curve of adoption The form that the adoption curve takes when we plot frequency of adoption rate on the *y*-axis and time on the *x*-axis.

stabilization The point in which a relevant social group has assigned a very specific meaning and use to an artifact.

Stanford Industrial Park An industrial park, today known as Stanford Research Park, located in Palo Alto, California, on land owned by Stanford University. Its aim is to bring together basic and applied research to develop cutting-edge products in the high-tech industry.

startup companies Companies that start their operations based on a promising idea, often with limited capital and no revenue. The label *startup company* became well-known during the 1990s technology boom, when a new company surfaced every day.

Stone Age A prehistoric era typically defined by the use of stone in the construction of tools.

strategic action Planned action aimed at accomplishing specific goals with optimal results.

subculture A small cultural group within a larger culture, often defined by things that make them stand out.

substantivism A theory arguing that technology brings forth new social, political, and cultural systems, which it structures and controls.

supplement argument of the Internet Argues that the Internet does

not completely change social structure but, rather, becomes embedded in existing patterns of interaction.

supplier factory Factories are dedicated solely to the mass production of goods that are then sold to consumers by vendor companies.

surrounding awareness capabilities A knowledge and understanding of ambient conditions outside of one's physical self.

surveillance The monitoring of a person's behaviour or information, often with the use of technologies for recording and storing data.

system A configuration of components that are joined through linkages into a network.

systems theory The field that studies social and biological systems that are self-regulating through, for example, feedback mechanisms.

Taylorism A system of management developed by Taylor that aimed to make work more efficient and to increase productivity through the application of scientific standards and processes.

technical competence The knowledge and/or skills required to demonstrate an understanding of the practices and tasks necessary to effectively utilize and master information and communication technologies.

technical (or **technocratic**) **elite** A class of people who, according to social theorist Bell, emerge as the technocratic elite in a post-industrial information society because of their understanding of theoretical knowledge, technology, and information.

technique A term used by Heidegger to describe how technologies constitute an object, a goal that the object fulfills, and a mechanism through which the goal is achieved.

technocracy An organization, group, or collective comprising individuals from scientific, technological, and research-based fields, whose knowledge and technical expertise either influences or performs a defining role in making decisions regarding technical or scientific development.

technological determinism A theory proposing that technology is the driving force in developing the structure of society and culture.

technological inequality The gap between the haves and the have-nots, resulting in disadvantages for the latter.

technological regression Rare cases where a technology is adopted and then later abandoned for social, political, cultural, or religious reasons. The social group then rejects the technology and returns to previously established practices and habits.

technological society The pervasiveness and intrinsic centrality of technology in contemporary society.

technological utopianism A belief that views technology as a largely positive force with the potential to create an idealized world through improved work conditions and lifestyles.

technological waste The waste that results from obsolete, out of fashion, or broken gadgets that are no longer used.

technology transfer The flow of technological innovations from one country or region to another.

technopoles Cities built within cities in order to produce the content, devices, and applications for the information society.

technotrash Consists of the accumulated material waste resulting from either obsolete or out of fashion electronics.

thanatechnology A term Sofka uses to refer to the Internet; an instrument through which people can express emotional responses to death.

third places Places that give people the opportunity to be social. Examples include coffee houses, taverns, restaurants, bars, libraries, and other locations that people visit routinely.

3D printers Machines that allow for the printing objects in 3D format with various materials from a digital blueprint.

time bias Innis's term to describe oral societies in which there is an emphasis on community and metaphysics. In these societies, change occurs slowly because the only transfer of culture, information, and knowledge is through oral means.

time–space compression This is the sense that constraints of time and space have been lifted as a result of technologies that bridge these barriers.

time study A concept developed by Taylor involving the recording and detailing of a worker's movements to aid in the development of processes to improve efficiency.

Tor Free software that allows Internet users to surf the Web anonymously without being traced or data recorded.

Toronto School of Communication A group of scholars working at the University of Toronto from about the 1940s to the 1970s, whose scholarship focused on the impact of media—including the alphabet, writing, television, and the radio—on society.

traditional technologies
Technologies of the pre-industrialized era, which are described as stationary and passive and having little effect on the natural environment.

transformation The ability of separate entities in actor network theory (ANT) to convert into a single unit through a network.

transhumanism A belief in the convergence of technology and the human body by using biotechnological components to augment or substitute existing physical human characteristics or parts with technological replacements.

transistor A semiconductor that is used to route electronic signals.

trialability Provides potential adopters with an opportunity to reduce the uncertainty associated with new innovations by gathering evidence about its potential value and risks.

triple revolution a theory proposed by Rainie and Wellman to describe changes in society resulting from mobile technologies, social relations, and digital technologies.

Turing Test A test developed by Turing to determine a machine's ability to showcase human intelligence.

Twitter Revolution A term that describes the central role that Twitter played as an information and communication platform to organize and mobilize the citizens of a country to protest against their government.

uncertainty A state of being unclear about the outcome of a particular innovation.

unfriend describes behaviour typical to facebook usage, where a Facebook friend is deleted.

unintended effects Consequences of technological invention or application, which are often only realized and understood after the technology has been used.

United Nations Development Programme (UNDP) A global development program enacted by the United Nations to assist in solving global and national socio-economic problems related to education, poverty, and the environment.

unverifiability of power Refers to the principle that one cannot determine whether or not one is being observed.

user-generated content Content that is created, modified, and shared by end-users through Web 2.0 applications.

utopian perspective of technology The belief that technology has a positive role in society and can be harnessed to create a more perfect world. Utopians embrace technology to improve efficiency and progress.

utopian perspective of the Internet Views the Internet as leading toward positive social change, in particular by strengthening social relations and communities.

value-laden A belief that technology is actively shaping or being shaped by culture, politics, or social values.

venture capital firms Firms that specialize in investing in startup companies that have a high potential for growth.

virtual mourning The use of Web-based media to mourn, commemorate, or provide support following the death of a family member, friend, or colleague.

virtual self Contrasted with the in real life (IRL) self, describes the creation of a self through posts, pictures, etc. on the Internet, particularly social media sites.

virtual stranger loss The means through which people mourn the death of individuals who may be strangers or whom they may not have met in person.

visibility of power The principle that power is centrally displayed with the aim of intimidating.

voyeurism The act of finding pleasure in secretly observing others engaged in private behaviours, such as undressing, sexual activity, etc.

wearable computing Types of computers that are worn on the body. For instance, the WearComp is a type of wearable computer.

WearComp A wearable computing system developed by Mann.

Web 2.0 Web-based applications that encourage and make possible interaction, information-sharing, and collaboration among users and producers.

WELL Stands for Whole Earth 'Lectronic Link and is one of the first online communities to emerge on the Internet, based primarily in the San Francisco Bay Area.

Wheeler method An archaeological excavation process that involves developing trenches in a series of rectangular boxes with balks in between them. The boxes assist in improving the organization of labour

and comparing the origin of artifacts in relation to the adjacent layers of earth.

white-collar workers Professional or educated workers whose job does not involve manual or physical labour.

wider context Describes, in the context of social construction of technology (SCOT), how the value system of a social group influences the meaning given to and the use of a technology.

WikiLeaks An international, non-profit, journalistic website whose purpose is to make secret information from anonymous sources available to the media and the public at large

Wikimedia Foundation A non-profit organization founded in 2003 by Wikipedia co-founder Jimmy Wales that operates various collaborative wiki-based projects on the Internet, such as Wikipedia.

Wikipedia A popular editable and collaborative non-profit, Web-based encyclopedia administered by the Wikimedia Foundation.

write community into being Through friending—i.e., making friends on social network sites—users establish the boundaries of their virtual community.

write themselves into being The idea that through online participation a user's profile can represent and his or her virtual self.

XO laptop A sturdy and low-cost laptop that employs open-source software designed specifically for the One Laptop per Child program.

Notes

Chapter 1

1. This reference to *Star Trek* was used previously in Hogan and Quan-Hasse with reference to the rapid changes occurring in the realm of social media (2010).
2. The definition of *artifact* was taken from *The Concise Oxford Dictionary of Archaeology* and focuses primarily on the distinction between objects created by humans and objects occurring naturally. (*The Concise Oxford Dictionary of Archaeology*. Timothy Darvill, ed. Oxford University Press, 2008. Oxford Reference Online. Oxford University Press.)
3. Information on the cyborg models comes from the Wikipedia entry on Terminator (character). http://en.wikipedia.org/wiki/Terminator_(character). Retrieved 4 June 2012.
4. For a similar list describing the challenges associated with studying the effects of the Internet on society, see Quan-Hasse and Wellman (2004).

Chapter 2

1. Information from the Stone Age comes from the Southern Africa entry from the Encyclopaedia Britannica Academic Edition Online, www.britannica.com/EBchecked/topic/556618/Southern-Africa?cameFromBol=true. Retrieved 13 October 2010.
2. Further information is available on the CBC McLuhan archives. Retrieved from http://archives.cbc.ca/arts_entertainment/media/topics/342-1818/.
3. A review of Pertierra et al.'s book *Txt-ing Selves* (2003) can be found in A. Quan-Haase (2004), "Book Review of Pertierra, R., Ugarte, E.F., Pingol, A., Hernandez, J., & Dacanay, N.L. (2003). *Txt-ing selves: Cellphones and Philippine modernity*. Manila: De La Salle University Press," *Canadian Journal of Sociology*.

Chapter 5

1. The GDP measures a nation's standard of living as it is an indicator of the value of goods and services produced, usually within a one-year period, and it was first introduced by Simon Kuznets in 1934. It is usually calculated as GDP = consumption + gross investments + government spending + net exports.

Chapter 6

1. *Scholars Portal* is a database that contains a comprehensive selection of e-journals and is available to all universities in Ontario. See http://journals1.scholarsportal.info/discuss.xqy.
2. This information comes from Arvind Singhal's speech for the introduction of the award ceremonies for Professor Everett M. Rogers when he was named the 47th Annual Research Lecturer at the University of New Mexico, Ohio University, 24 April 2002. Retrieved 5 July 2010 from www.insna.org/PDF/Connections/v26/2005_1-2-2.pdf.
3. Cultures are constantly changing, and, as a result, the values and meanings given to technologies also constantly need updating.
4. This phenomenon has recently been observed with the BlackBerry, where users switched to other devices but then realized that they preferred the features offered by the BlackBerry and so switched back.

Chapter 7

1. Often, software products are updated as new features are developed and integrated into the system.

Chapter 8

1. Data come from the 1995 Household Facilities and Equipment Survey and exclude residents from Yukon and Northwest Territories, Indian reserves, and Crown land and institutions (Dickinson & Sciadas, 1996). At the time of the survey, owning a TV without cable was still fairly common.
2. Further information on E-Rate and the source of the quote can be found at www.fcc.gov/learnnet/ (retrieved 2 May, 2011).
3. These numbers are per 100 inhabitants.

Chapter 10

1. The concept of friendship is also closely linked to the distinction made by Granovetter (1973) between weak and strong ties. Strong ties are with individuals who one trusts, has frequent contact with, and who provide social support in times of need.

Chapter 11

1. In a normalized system, there is little room for a person to be different or unique. Nonetheless, fitting into the system is not always a measure of success. For instance, Bill Gates, Mark Zuckerberg, and Steve Jobs are all extremely successful entrepreneurs in the technology sector who dropped out of the school system.
2. Also see the discussion in Chapter 10 concerning the four characteristics of social network sites identified by boyd in her research on Friendster (2006).

Chapter 12

1. Many AKs in use were variants such as AK-74, AKSU (Bin Laden's little gun), AKM, as well as foreign copies with different names (Chinese Type 56, Yugoslav M90). Powers other than the USSR sold the AK-47, such as China.
2. The weapon was designed based on the impetus of the German invasion: however, by the time trials and early production were complete, the AK was several years too late to influence the war. Two primary Soviet arms developments that changed the nature of World War II were the invention of the T-34 tank (fast, well armoured, and easy to mass-produce) and the PPSH-41 submachine gun (high rate of fire, cheap, and reliable).
3. This is particularly true in poorer regions of the world, which barter materials rather than purchase goods in cash. Moses Naim points out that in 1986 an individual in Kenya would have had to trade 15 cows for an AK-47; in 2005 it would have cost the same individual only 4 cows (Naim & Myers, 2005).

References

Aboujaoude, E. (2011). *Virtually you: The dangerous powers of the e-personality*. New York: WW Norton & Company.

Abrams, J. J. (2009). *Star Trek* [motion picture]. Retrieved from www.imdb.com/title/tt0796366/quotes

Acar, G., Eubank, C., Englehardt, S., Juarez, M., Narayanan, A., & C. Diaz. In Proceedings of, N. F. (2014). The Web never forgets: Persistent tracking mechanisms in the wild 21st ACM Conference on Computer and Communications Security. Scottsdale, Arizona, November 3–7.

Adams, P. (2011). Why I left Google. What happened to my book. What I work on at Facebook [Blog post]. *Think Outside In*. Retrieved from www.thinkoutsidein.com/blog/2011/07/why-i-left-google-what-happened-to-my-book-what-i-work-on-at-facebook/

Agger, B. (2004). *Speeding up fast capitalism: Cultures, jobs, families, schools, bodies*. Boulder, CO: Paradigm Publishing.

Albanese, P. (2012). Sexuality. In L. Tepperman, A. Kalyta & P. Albanese (Eds.), *Reading sociology: Canadian perspectives* (2nd ed.). Don Mills, ON: Oxford University Press.

Anderson, C. (2012). *Makers: The new industrial revolution*. New York: Crown Business.

Andrejevic, M. (2004). *Reality TV: The work of being watched*. Lanham, MD: Rowman & Littlefield.

Anthis, K. S. (2002). On the calamity theory of growth: The relationship between stressful life events and changes in identity over time. *Identity: An International Journal of Theory and Research, 2*(3), 229–240.

Back, M. D., Stopfer, J. M., Vazire, S., Gaddis, S., Schmukle, S. C., Egloff, B., et al. (2010). Facebook profiles reflect actual personality, not self-idealization. *Psychological Science China, 21*(3), 371–374.

Bamman, D., O'Connor, B., & Smith, N.A. (2012). Censorship and deletion practices in Chinese social media. *First Monday, 17* (3–5). Retrieved from http://firstmonday.org/ojs/index.php/fm/article/view/3943/3169 doi:10.5210/fm.v17i3.3943

Bánáthy, B. H. (1997, February 28). A taste of systemics. Retrieved from www.newciv.org/ISSS_Primer/asem04bb.html

Bandura, A. (1973). *Aggression: A social learning analysis*. Englewood Cliffs, NJ: Prentice-Hall.

Barker, G. (2006). *The agricultural revolution in prehistory: Why did foragers become farmers?* Oxford: Oxford University Press.

Barnes, S. B. (2006). A privacy paradox: Social networking in the United States. *First Monday, 11*(9). Retrieved from http://firstmonday.org/htbin/cgiwrap/bin/ojs/index.php/fm/article/view/1394/1312

Barrett, M., Grant, D., & Wailes, N. (2006). ICT and organizational change. *The Journal of Applied Behavioral Science, 42*(1), 6–22.

Basalla, G. (1988). *The evolution of technology*. Cambridge: Cambridge University Press.

Batson, A. (2010). China's GDP: Still number three. *The Wall Street Journal*. Retrieved from http://blogs.wsj.com/chinarealtime/2010/07/02/chinas-gdp-still-number-three/

Bauchspies, W. K., Restivo, S. P., & Croissant, J. (2006). *Science, technology, and society: A sociological approach*. Malden, MA: Blackwell.

Baudrillard, J. (2005). *The system of objects*. London: Verso.

———, & Gane, M. (1993). *Baudrillard live: Selected interviews*. London: Routledge.

Bauwens, M. (2005, November 4). P2P and human evolution: Placing peer to peer theory in an integral framework. Retrieved from http://integralvisioning.org/article.php?story=p2ptheory1

Baym, N. K. (2010). *Personal connections in the digital age*. Cambridge, UK: Polity Press.

BBC. (2006, November 27). Star Wars kid is top viral video. BBC *News*. Retrieved from http://news.bbc.co.uk/2/hi/entertainment/6187554.stm

BBC Technology. (2014, 9 June). Computer AI passes Turing test in "world first." BBC News. Retrieved October 25,

2014, from www.bbc.com/news/
technology-27762088

BBC. (2014, January 17). Edward
Snowden: Leaks that exposed U.S.
spy programme. Retrieved October
22, 2014, from www.bbc.com/news/
world-us-canada-23123964

Beckett, A. (2010, July 12). Inside the
Bill and Melinda Gates foundation.
The Guardian. Retrieved from www.
guardian.co.uk/world/2010/jul/12/
bill-and-melinda-gates-foundation

Bell, D. (1973). *The coming of a post-industrial society: A venture in social forecasting.*
New York: Basic Books.

Berg, M. (1994). *The age of manufactures,
1700–1820: Industry, innovation and
work in Britain* (2nd ed.). New York:
Routledge.

Bertot, J. C., Jaeger, P. T., McClure, C.
R., Wright, C. B., & Jensen, E. (2009).
Public libraries and the Internet 2008–
2009: Issues, implications, and challenges. *First Monday, 14*(11). Retrieved
from www.uic.edu/htbin/cgiwrap/bin/
ojs/index.php/fm/article/view/2700/2351

Bijker, W. E. (2009). Social construc-
tion of technology. In J.-K. B. Olsen,
S. A. Pedersen & V. F. Hendricks
(Eds.), *A companion to the philosophy of
technology* (pp. 88–94). Malden, MA:
Wiley-Blackwell.

———, Hughes, T. P., & Pinch, T. (1999).
General introduction. In W. E. Bijker,
T. P. Hughes & T. Pinch (Eds.), *The
social construction of technological systems:
New directions in the sociology and history
of technology* (pp. 1–6). Cambridge, MA:
MIT Press.

Bill and Melinda Gates Foundation. (2011).
About the foundation. Retrieved from
www.gatesfoundation.org/about/Pages/
values.aspx

Bilton, N., & Rusli, E. (2012). From founders to decorators, Facebook riches.
Retrieved 15 February 2012, from www.
nytimes.com/2012/02/02/technology/for-
founders-to-decorators-facebook-riches.
html? pagewanted=all

Bimber, B. (2000). Measuring the gender
gap on the Internet. *Social Science
Quarterly, 81*(3), 868–876.

Binfield, K. (Ed.). (2004). *Writings of the
Luddites.* Baltimore, MD: Johns Hopkins
University Press.

Boero, N., & Pascoe, C. (2012). Pro-
anorexia communities and online
interaction: bringing the pro-ana body
online. *Body & Society, 18*(2), 27–57.

Boehm, C. (1993). Egalitarian behavior and
reverse dominance hierarchy. *Current
Anthropology, 34*, 227–254.

——— (1999). *Hierarchy in the forest: The evolution of egalitarian behavior.* Cambridge,
MA: Harvard University Press.

——— (2000). The origin of morality as
social control. In L. D. Katz (Ed.),
*Evolutionary origins of morality: Cross-
disciplinary perspectives.* Bowling Green,
OH: Imprint Academic.

Bogart, L. (1972). *The age of television; a
study of viewing habits and the impact of
television on American life* (3rd ed.). New
York: F. Ungar.

Bolter, J. D., & Grusin, R. (1999).
Remediation: Understanding new media.
Cambridge, MA: MIT Press.

Bonabeau, E. (2009). Decisions 2.0: The
power of collective intelligence. MIT
Sloan Management Review, 50(2), 45–52.

Boradkar, P. (2006). 10,000 songs in your
pocket: The iPod® as a transportable
environment. In R. Kronenburg &
F. Klassen (Eds.), *Transportable
environments 3* (pp. 21–30). Abingdon:
Taylor & Francis.

Boreham, P., Parker, R., Thompson, P., &
Hall, R. (2008). *New technology @ work.*
New York: Routledge.

Borgatti, S. P. (1998). A SOCNET discussion on the origins of the term social
capital. *Connections, 21*(2), 37–46.

Borgmann, A. (1984). Technology and democracy. In P. T. Durbin (Ed.), *Research
in philosophy & technology : Vol. 7* (pp.
211–228). Greenwich, CT: Jai Press.

Borsook, P. (2000). *Cyberselfish: A critical
romp through the terribly libertarian culture
of high tech.* New York: Public Affairs.

Bostrom, N. (2014). *Superintelligence: Paths,
dangers, strategies.* Oxford: Oxford
University Press.

Bourdieu, P. (1977/1998). *Outline of a theory
of practice.* New York, NY: Cambridge
University Press.

——— (1973). Cultural reproduction and
social reproduction. In R. Brown (Ed.)
*Knowledge, education and social change:
Papers in the sociology of education* (pp.
71-112). London, England: Tavistock
Publications.

boyd, d. (2006). Friends, Friendsters, and top 8: Writing community into being on social network sites. *First Monday*, *11*(12). Retrieved from http://firstmonday.org/htbin/cgiwrap/bin/ojs/index.php/fm/article/view/1418/1336

——— (2007). Why youth (heart) social network sites: The role of networked publics in teenage social life. In D. Buckingham (Ed.), *The MacArthur foundation series on digital learning—youth, identity and digital media volume* (pp. 119–142). Cambridge, MA: MIT Press.

boyd, d. (2014). *It's complicated: The social lives of networked teens*. New Haven: Yale University Press.

———, & Heer, J. (2006). *Profiles as conversation: Networked identity performance on Friendster*. Proceedings of the Hawai'i International Conference on System Sciences (HICSS-39), Persistent Conversation Track. IEEE Computer Society, Kauai, HI. Retrieved from www.danah.org/papers/HICSS2006.pdf

Bradsher, K., & Mozur, P. (2014, September 21). China clamps down on Web, pinching companies like Google. *New York Times*. Retrieved 22 September, 2014, from www.nytimes.com/2014/09/22/business/international/china-clamps-down-on-web-pinching-companies-like-google.html?_r=0

Bradner, E. (2001). Social affordances of computer-mediated communication technology: Understanding adoption. In *CHI '01 extended abstracts on human factors in computing* pp. 67–8. New York: ACM.

———, Kellogg, W. A., & Erickson, T. (1999, 12–16 September). *Social affordances of Babble: A field study of chat in the workplace*. ECSCW, 99, the Sixth European Conference on Computer Supported Cooperative Work, Copenhagen, Denmark.

Braverman, H. (1974). *Labor and monopoly capital: The degradation of work in the twentieth century*. New York: Monthly Review Press.

Brenner, J., & Smith, A. (2013). *72% of online adults are social networking site users*. Washington, DC: Pew Internet and American Life.

Briggs, A., & Burke, P. (2009). *A social history of the media: From Gutenberg to the Internet* (3rd ed.). Cambridge, England: Polity.

Broll, R. (2014). *Policing cyber bullying: How parents, educators, and law enforcement respond to digital harassment* (Doctoral dissertation, Retrieved from University of Western Ontario - Electronic Thesis and Dissertation Repository (Paper 2116). http://ir.lib.uwo.ca/etd/2116

Brosnan, M., & Lee, W. (1998). A cross-cultural comparison of gender differences in computer attitudes and anxieties: The United Kingdom and Hong Kong. *Computers in Human Behavior, 14*(4), 559–577.

Brown, B., & Quan-Haase, A. (2013). 'A Worker's inquiry 2.0': An ethnographic method for the study of produsage in social media contexts. *TripleC, 10*(3). Retrieved from www.triple-c.at/index.php/tripleC/article/view/390

Bruns, A. (2008). *Blogs, Wikipedia, Second Life, and beyond: From production to produsage*. New York: Peter Lang.

Bull, M. (2008). *Sound moves: Ipod culture and urban experience*. New York: Routledge.

Bynum, W. F., & Porter, R. (Eds.). (2006). *The Oxford dictionary of scientific quotations*. Oxford University Press.

Callon, M. (1987). Society in the making: The study of technology as a tool for sociological analysis. In W. E. Bijker, T. P. Hughes & T. Pinch (Eds.), *The social construction of technological systems: New directions in the sociology and history of technology* (pp. 83–103). Cambridge, MA: MIT Press.

———, & Law, J. (1997). After the individual in society: Lessons on collectivity from science, technology and society. *Canadian Journal of Sociology, 22*(2), 165–182.

CANARIE. (2010, August 10). About CANARIE. Retrieved from www.canarie.ca/en/about/aboutus

Caperton. (2012). Why aren't there more women at STEM conferences?: This time, it's statistical. *Feministe Blog*. Retrieved September 15, 2014.

Carmel, E. (1995). Cycle-time in packaged software firms. *Journal of Product Innovation Management, 12*(2), 110–123.

———, & Sawyer, S. (1998). Packaged software development teams: What makes them different? *Information, Technology & People, 11*(1), 7–19.

Carroll, B., & Landry, K. (2010). Logging on and letting out: Using online social networks to grieve and to mourn. *Bulletin of Science, Technology and Society, 30*(5), 377–386. Retrieved from http://bst.sagepub.com/content/30/5/341.full.pdf+html

Carter, C., Steiner, L., & McLaughlin, L. (Eds.). (2013). *The Routledge companion to media and gender*. New York: Routledge.

Carey, A. (1967). The Hawthorne studies: A radical criticism. *American Sociological Review*, 403–416.

Castells, M. (1996). *The rise of the network society*. Cambridge, MA: Blackwell Publishers.

——— (2001). *The Internet galaxy: Reflections on the Internet, business, and society*. Oxford: Oxford University Press.

———, & Hall, P. G. (1994). *Technopoles of the world: The making of twenty-first-century industrial complexes*. London: Routledge.

Ceruzzi, P. E. (2005). Moore's law and technological determinism: Reflections on the history of technology. *Technology and Culture, 46*(3), 584–593.

Chakrabortty, A. (2013). The woman who nearly died making your iPad. *The Guardian*. Retrieved April 12, 2015 from www.theguardian.com/commentisfree/2013/aug/05/woman-nearly-died-making-ipad

Chen, W., Boase, J., & Wellman, B. (2002). The global villagers: Comparing Internet users and uses around the world. In B. Wellman & C. Haythornthwaite (Eds.), *The Internet in everyday life* (pp. 74–113). Oxford: Blackwell.

Cheng, H. K., Bandyopadhyay, S., & Guo, H. (2011). The Debate on Net Neutrality: A Policy Perspective. *Information Systems Research, 22*(1), 60–82. doi:10.1287/isre.1090.0257

Chesley, N. (2014). Information and communication technology use, work intensification and employee strain and distress. *Work, Employment & Society, 28*(4), 589–610.

Chesterman, S. (2011). *One nation under surveillance: A new social contract to defend freedom without sacrificing liberty*. Oxford: Oxford University Press.

Chib, A., & Chen, V. H.-H. (2011). Midwives with mobiles: A dialectical perspective on gender arising from technology introduction in rural Indonesia. *New Media & Society, 13*(3), 486–501.

China Internet Network Information Center. (2014, July 2014). *Statistical Report on Internet Development in China*. Retrieved November 22, 2014, from http://www1.cnnic.cn/IDR/ReportDownloads/201411/P020141102574314897888.pdf

City of Toronto. (2006). Toronto's racial diversity. from www.toronto.ca/toronto_facts/diversity.htmmc

China Labour Watch. (2011). Tragedies of globalization: The truth behind electronics sweatshops. Retrieved March 4, 2015 from www.chinalaborwatch.org/report/52

Clinton, H. R. (2011, February 15). *Secretary Clinton on Internet rights and wrongs: Choices & challenges in a networked world*. [Video clip.] Retrieved from http://geneva.usmission.gov/2011/02/16/internet-rights-and-wrongs/

Clynes, M. E., & Kline, N. S. (1960). Cyborgs and space. *Austronautics* (September), 26–27 & 74–76.

Cohen, E.A. (n.d.). Strategy. In *Encyclopædia Britannica*. Retrieved from www.britannica.com/EBchecked/topic/568259/strategy

Cohen, N., Comor, E., Compton, J. R., & Watts, B. (2014). Journalistic labour and digital transformation: A survey of working conditions. Paper presented at the Canadian Association of Work and Labour Studies Conference, Brock, ON.

Coleman, J. S., Katz, E., & Menzel, H. (1966). *Medical innovation: A diffusion study*. New York: Bobbs Merrill.

Collins, J. L., & Wellman, B. (2010). Small town in the Internet society: Chapleau is no longer an island. *American Behavioral Scientist, 53*(9), 1344–1366.

Connidis, I. A., & McMullin, J. A. (2002). Sociological ambivalence and family ties: A critical perspective. *Journal of Marriage and Family, 64*(3), 558–567.

Connolly, K. (2002, July 30). "I wish I'd made a lawnmower." *The Guardian*. Retrieved from www.guardian.co.uk/world/2002/jul/30/russia.kateconnolly

Constantine, L. L. (1995). *Constantine on peopleware*. Englewood Cliffs, NJ: Prentice Hall.

Corrigall-Brown, C. (2011). *Patterns of protest: Trajectories of participation in social movements*. Stanford: Stanford University Press.

Coser, R. L. (1975). The complexity of roles as a seedbed of individual autonomy. In L. A. Coser (Ed.), *The idea of social structure: Papers in honour of Robert K. Merton* (pp. 237–262). New York, NY: Harcourt Brace Jovanovich.

Costa, D. L., & Kahn, M. E. (2001). *Understanding the decline in social capital, 1952–1998*. Retrieved from UCLA website: www.econ.ucla.edu/costa/scapital8.pdf

Couch, R. (2015). Not into 'Fifty Shades'? Grassroots campaign says donate $50 to women's shelter instead. Retrieved from www.huffingtonpost.com/2015/02/05/activists-fifty-shades_n_6621840.html

Cowan, R. S. (1983). *More work for mother: The ironies of household technology from the open hearth to the microwave* (Vol. 5131). New York: Basic Books.

Crary, J. (2013). 24/7: *Late capitalism and the ends of sleep*. London, England: Verso.

Crowley, D. J., & Heyer, P. (2011). *Communication in history: Technology, culture, society* (6th ed.). Boston: Allyn & Bacon.

Cullen, R. (2001). Addressing the digital divide. *Online Information Review, 25*(5), 311–320.

Cutcliffe, S. H., & Mitcham, C. (2001). Introduction: The visionary challenges of STS. In S. H. Cutcliffe & C. Mitcham (Eds.), *Visions of STS: Counterpoints in science, technology, and society studies* (pp. 1–7). Albany, NY: State University of New York Press.

David, P. A. (1985). Clio and the economics of QWERTY. *American Economic Review, 75*(2), 332–337.

Day, P., & Schuler, D. (2006). Community practice in the networked society: Pathways towards civic intelligence. In P. A. Purcell (Ed.), *Networked neighbourhoods: The connected community in context* (pp. 19–46). London: Springer.

Dedehayir, O. (2009). Bibliometric study of the reverse salient concept. *Journal of Industiral Engineering and Management, 2*(3), 569–591. Retrieved from http://upcommons.upc.edu/revistes/bitstream/2099/8490/1/dedehayir.pdf

———, & Mäkinen, S. J. (2008). Dynamics of reverse salience as technological performance gap: An empirical study of the personal computer technology system. *Journal of Technology Management*

& Innovation, 3(4). Retrieved from www.scielo.cl/scielo.php?pid=S0718-27242008000100006&script=sci_arttext

Dewdney, C. (1998). *Last flesh: Life in the transhuman era*. Toronto: HarperCollins.

——— (2001, December 15). First Mann into cyborgspace. *The Globe and Mail*, pp. D6–7.

Diamond, J. M. (1997). *Guns, germs, and steel: The fates of human societies*. New York: Norton.

Dias, K. (2003). The Ana Sanctuary: Women's pro-anorexia narratives in cyberspace. *Journal of International Women's Studies, 4*(2), 31–45.

Dickinson, P., & Sciadas, G. (1996). *Access to the information highway*. Services Science and Technology Division. Retrieved from www.statcan.gc.ca/pub/63f0002x/63f0002x1996009-eng.pdf

Dinwiddy, J. (1979). Luddism and politics in the northern counties. *Social History, 4*(1), 33–63.

Dubé, L. (1998). Teams in packaged software development: The software corp. experience. *Information, Technology & People, 11*(1), 36–61.

Duggan, M., & Smith, A. (2013). *Social Media Update 2013*. Washington, DC: Pew Research Center.

Duggan, M., & Smith, A. (2013). *Social media matrix*. Washington, DC: Pew Research Center.

Durkheim, E. (1893/1960). *The division of labour in society* (2nd ed.). Glencoe, IL: Free Press.

Durndell, A., Glissov, P., & Siann, G. (1995). Gender and computing: persisting differences. *Educational Research, 37*(3), 219–227.

Dyer-Witheford, N. (1999). *Cyber-Marx: Cycles and circuits of struggle in high-technology capitalism*. Urbana, IL: University of Illinois Press.

——— (2001). Empire, immaterial labor, the new combinations, and the global worker. *Rethinking Marxism, 13*(3/4), 70–80.

Edmunds, S. (1991). From Schoeffer to Vérard: Concerning the scribes who became printers. In S. Hindman (Ed.), *Printing the written word: The social history of books, circa 1450–1520* (pp. 21–40). Ithaca: Cornell University Press.

Education and Library Networks Coalition. (2007). *E-rate: 10 years of connecting kids and community*. National Coalition for Technology in Education and Training. Retrieved from www.edlinc.org/pdf/NCTETReport_212.pdf

Edwards, R. (1979). *Contested terrain: The transformation of the workplace in the twentieth century*. New York: Basic Books.

Eisen, J. (2012). Q-Bio conference in Hawaii, bring your surfboard & your Y chromosome b/c they don't take a XX [Blog post] (September 11 ed.).

Eisenstein, E. L. (1979). *The printing press as an agent of change: Communications and cultural transformations in early modern Europe*. Cambridge: Cambridge University Press.

Eldridge, L. P., & Pabilonia, S. W. (2010). Bringing work home: implications for BLS productivity measures. *Monthly Labor Review, 133*(12), 18–35.

Elliott, J. E. (2004). Introduction to the transaction edition. In J. A. Schumpeter (Ed.), *The theory of economic development: An inquiry into profits, capital, credit, interest, and the business cycle* (pp. vii–lix). Cambridge: Harvard University Press.

Ellison, N. B., Steinfield, C., & Lampe, C. (2007). The benefits of Facebook "Friends:" Social capital and college students' use of online social network sites. *Journal of Computer-Mediated Communication, 12*(4), article 1. Retrieved from http://jcmc.indiana.edu/vol12/issue4/ellison.html

Ellison, N. B., Steinfield, C., & Lampe, C. (2006, June 19–23 2006). *Spatially bounded online social networks and social capital: The role of Facebook*. Paper presented at the Proceedings of the Annual Conference of the International Communication Association (ICA), Dresden, Germany (ICA).

Ellison, N., Heino, R., & Gibbs, J. (2006). Managing impressions online: Self-presentation processes in the online dating environment. *Journal of Computer-Mediated Communication, 11*(2), 415–441.

Ellul, J. (1964). *The technological society* (1st American ed.). New York: Knopf.

——— (1989). *What I believe*. Grand Rapids, MI: W.B. Eerdmans.

———, & Vanderburg, W. H. (1981). *Perspectives on our age: Jacques Ellul speaks on his life and work*. New York: Seabury Press.

England, P. (2014). *Theme for 2015 Program of the American Sociological Association: Sexualities in the Social World*. Retrieved September 8, 2014, from www.asanet.org/am2015/Theme.cfm

Epstein, D., Nisbet, E. C., & Gillespie, T. (2011). Who's responsible for the digital divide? Public perceptions and policy implications. *The Information Society, 27*(2), 92–104.

Erickson, B. H., Albanese, P., & Drakulic, S. (2000). Gender on a jagged edge the security industry, its clients, and the reproduction and revision of gender. *Work and Occupations, 27*(3), 294–318.

Espinoza, V. (1999). Social networks among the urban poor: Inequality and integration in a Latin American city. In B. Wellman (Ed.), *Networks in the blobal village* (pp. 147–184). Boulder, CO: Westview Press.

Facebook. (2011). Facebook statistics. Retrieved from www.facebook.com/press/info.php?statistics

Facebook. (2014). Company info. Retrieved from http://newsroom.fb.com/company-info/

Fallows, D. (2005). *Search engine users*. Retrieved from Pew Internet and American Life Project website: www.pewinternet.org/Reports/2005/Search-Engine-Users.aspx

Fallows, D. (2005). How women and men use the Internet: Pew Internet & American Life Project. Retrieved from www.pewinternet.org/2005/12/28/how-women-and-men-use-the-internet/

Farley, T. (2005). Mobile telephone history. *Telektronikk, 3*(4), 22–34. Retrieved from www.privateline.com/archive/TelenorPage_022-034.pdf

Febvre, L. P. V., & Martin, H.-J. (1997). *The coming of the book: The impact of printing, 1450–1800*. London: Verso.

Federal Communications Commission (FCC). (2004, May 2). E-rate. Retrieved from www.fcc.gov/learnnet/

Feenberg, A. (1982). Technology and the idea of progress. In P. T. Durbin (Ed.), *Research in philosophy & technology* (Vol. 5, pp. 15–21). Greenwich, CT: Jai Press.

——— (1991). *Critical theory of technology*. New York: Oxford University Press.

———— (1999). *Questioning technology*. New York: Routledge.

Feist, R., Beauvais, C., & Shukla, R. (2010). Introduction. In R. Feist, C. Beauvais & R. Shukla (Eds.), *Technology and the changing face of humanity* (pp. 1–21). Ottawa: University of Ottawa Press.

Ferguson, E. S. (1992). *Engineering and the mind's eye*. Cambridge, MA: MIT Press.

Fischer, C. S. (1982). *To dwell among friends*. Berkeley, CA: University of California Press.

———— (1992). *America calling: A social history of the telephone to 1940*. Berkeley, CA: University of California Press.

Flew, T. (2008). *New media: An introduction*. Melbourne, Australia: Oxford University Press.

Florida, R. (2001, December 5). *The creative class*. Lecture presented at Rotman School of Management, University of Toronto, Toronto, ON.

Fox, S., & Rainie, L. (2014). *Part 1: How the Internet has woven itself into American life*. Washington, DC: Pew Research Internet Project. Retrieved from http:// www.pewinternet.org/2014/02/27/part-1-how-the-internet-has-woven-itself-into-american-life/

Foucault, M. (1995). *Discipline and punish: The birth of the prison* (1st American ed.). New York: Vintage Books.

Fountain, J. E. (2000). Constructing the information society: women, information technology, and design. *Technology In Society, 22*(1), 45–62. doi: http://dx.doi.org/10.1016/S0160-791X(99)00036-6

Fuller, R., Tussey, E., Curtin, M., & Green, J. (2011). *HuffPo bloggers raise status and pay concerns: Responses to the AOL-Huffington Post merger*. Carsey-Wolf Center Media Industries Project.

Fowler, W. S. (1962). *The development of scientific method*. Oxford: Pergamon Press.

Francis, R. D. (2009). *The technological imperative in Canada: An intellectual history*. Vancouver: UBC Press.

Franklin, U. M. (1992). *The real world of technology*. Concord, ON: House of Anansi Press.

Franz, C. R., Roby, D., & Koeblitz, R. R. (1986). User response to an online information system: A field experiment. *MIS Quarterly, 10*(1), 29–42.

Fuchs, C. (2008). *Internet and society: Social theory in the information age*. New York: Routledge.

———— (2010). Labor in informational capitalism and on the Internet. *The Information Society, 26*(3), 179–196.

Füssel, S. (2005). *Gutenberg and the impact of printing* (1st English ed.). Aldershot, England: Ashgate Publishing.

Gardiner, M. (in press). The multitude strikes back? Boredom in an age of semiocapitalism. *New Formations, 82*(2), 31–38. doi: 10.3898/NeWF.82.02.2014

Gasher, M., Skinner, D., & Lorimer, R. (2012). *Mass communication in Canada* (7th ed.). Don Mills, ON: Oxford University Press.

Gee, A. E. (2013, July 3). U of T Lab's 3D printer gun raises disturbing questions. *Toronto Star*. Retrieved from September 15, 2014, from www.thestar.com/news/gta/2013/07/03/u_of_t_labs_3d_printer_gun_raises_disturbing_questions.html

Gershon, I. (2010). *The breakup 2.0: Disconnecting over new media*. Ithaca, NY: Cornell University Press.

Giddens, A. (2013). *The consequences of modernity*. Oxford, England: Wiley.

Gilpin, L. (2014, May 30). How recycled plastic for 3D printing will drive sustainability and improve social consciousness. *TechRepublic*. Retrieved October 28, 2014, from www.techrepublic.com/article/how-recycled-plastic-for-3d-printing-will-drive-sustainability-and-raise-the-social-conscious-of-business/

Goffman, E. (1959). *The presentation of self in everyday life*. Garden City, NY: Doubleday.

Goffman, E. (1963). *Behaviour in public places: Notes on the social organization of gatherings*. New York: Free Press.

Goodman, D. (1989). Enlightenment Salons: The Convergence of Female and Philosophic Ambitions. *Eighteenth-Century Studies, 22*(3), 329–350. doi: 10.2307/2738891

Goosey, M. (2009). Introduction and overview. In R. E. Hester & R. M. Harrison (Eds.), *Electronic waste management: Design, analysis and application* (pp. 1–39). Cambridge, UK: RSC Publishing.

Granovetter, M. S. (1973). The strength of weak ties. *American Journal of Sociology, 78*, 1360–1380.

Grant, G. P. (2002). Philosophy in the mass age. In A. Davis (Ed.), *Collected works of George Grant: 1951–1959* (Vol. 2). Toronto: University of Toronto Press.

Grant, G. P. (1986). *Technology and justice.* Toronto: House of Anansi Press.

Green, L. (2002). *Communication, technology and society.* London: SAGE.

Greenberg, A. (2008). The privacy paradox. *Forbes.* Retrieved from www.forbes. com/2008/02/15/search-privacy-ask-tech-security-cx_ag_0215search.html

Greenberg, A. (2014). The world's first 3D-printed gun. *Forbes.* Retrieved from www.forbes.com/pictures/mhl45ediih/the-liberators-copycats/

Grimes, S. M. (2014). Configuring the child player. *Science, Technology & Human Values.* doi: 10.1177/0162243914550253

Grint, K., & Woolgar, S. (1997). *The machine at work: Technology, work and organization.* Malden, MA: Blackwell.

Gripsrud, J., Moe, H., & Splichal, S. (2010). *The digital public sphere: Challenges for media policy.* GÃteborg: Nordicom.

Gross, R., & Acquisti, A. (2005). *Information revelation and privacy in online social networks.* Proceedings of the 2005 ACM workshop on privacy in the electronic society, New York. Retrieved from www.heinz.cmu.edu/~acquisti/papers/privacy-facebook-gross-acquisti.pdf

Grossberg, L. (1996). On postmodernism and articulation: An interview with Stuart Hall. In D. Morley & K.-H. Chen (Eds.), *Stuart Hall: Critical dialogues in cultural studies* (pp. 131–150). London: Routledge.

Guest, A. M., & Wierzbicki, S. K. (1999). Social ties at the neighborhood level: Two decades of GSS evidence. *Urban Affairs Review, 35*(1), 92–111.

Gurstein, M. (2007). *What is community informatics (and why does it matter)?* Milano, Italy: Polimetrica.

Gutting, G. (2010). Michel Foucault. *Stanford Encyclopedia of Philosophy.* Retrieved from http://plato.stanford.edu/entries/foucault/

Ha, L., & James, E. L. (1998). Interactivity re-examined: A baseline analysis of early business websites. *Journal of Broadcasting & Electronic Media, 42*(4), 457–474.

Haas, C. (1996). *Writing technology: Studies on the materiality of literacy.* Mahwah, NJ: Lawrence Erlbaum Associates.

Habermas, J. (1984, 2001). *The theory of communicative action: Reason and rationalization of society.* Boston: Beacon Press.

Habermas, J. (1989, 1962). *Strukturwandel der Öffentlichkeit* (2nd ed.). Berlin, Germany: Suhrkamp.

Haigh, T. (2011). The history of information technology. *Annual Review of Information Science and Technology 45,* 431–487.

Haight, M., Quan-Haase, A., & Corbett, B. (2014). Revisiting the digital divide in Canada: The impact of demographic factors on access to the Internet, level of online activity, and social networking site usage. *Information, Communication & Society, 17*(4), 503–519.

Hake, S. (2002). *German national cinema.* New York: Routledge.

Halverson, J. (1992). Havelock on Greek orality and literacy. *Journal of the History of Ideas, 53*(1), 148–163.

Hampton, K. N., Goulet, L. S., & Albanesius, G. (2014). Change in the social life of urban public spaces: The rise of mobile phones and women, and the decline of aloneness over 30 years. *Urban Studies.* doi: 10.1177/0042098014534905

Hampton, K., Rainie, L., Lu, W., Dwyer, M., Shin, I., & Purcell, K. (2014, August 26). *Social media and the "spiral of silence."* Retrieved October 20, 2014, from www.pewinternet.org/2014/08/26/social-media-and-the-spiral-of-silence/

Hanks, C. (Ed.). (2010). *Technology and values.* Malden, MA: Wiley-Blackwell.

Hargittai, E. (2002). Second-level digital divide: Differences in people's online skills. *First Monday, 7*(4). Retrieved from http://firstmonday.org/htbin/cgiwrap/bin/ojs/index.php/fm/article/view/942/864

Hargittai, E. (2002). Second-level digital divide: Differences in people's online skills. *First Monday, 7*(4), 1–20. doi: http://dx.doi.org/10.5210%2Ffm.v7i4.942

Hargittai, E., & Hsieh, Y. P. (2012). Succinct survey measures of web-use skills. *Social Science Computer Review, 30*(1), 95–107. doi: 10.1177/0894439310397146

Hargittai, E., & Hsieh, Y. P. (2010). Predictors and consequences of differentiated social network site uses. *Information, Communication and Society, 13*(4), 515–536. doi: 10.1080/13691181003639866

Harris, J. L., & et al. (2013). *Fast food facts 2013: Measuring progress in nutrition and marketing to children and teens: Yale Rudd Center for Food Policy and Obesity* [Report]. Retrieved from www.fastfood-marketing.org/media/FastFoodFACTS_report.pdf

Hartley, M. (2009, May 12). How the iPod changed everything. *The Globe and Mail.* Retrieved from www.theglobeandmail.com/news/technology/download-decade/how-the-ipod-changed-everything/article1133329/

Harvey, D. (2000). *The condition of postmodernity: An enquiry into the origins of cultural change.* Cambridge: Blackwell.

Hauser, G. A. (1998). Vernacular dialogue and the rhetoricality of public opinion. *Communication Monographs, 65*(2), 83–107.

Havelock, E. A. (1963). *Preface to Plato.* Cambridge: Harvard University Press.

Haythornthwaite, C. (2005). Social networks and Internet connectivity effects. *Information, Communication & Society, 8*(2), 125–147.

Hearn, A. (2006). "John, a 20–year-old Boston native with a great sense of humour": On the spectacularization of the "self" and the incorporation of identity in the age of reality television. *International Journal of Media and Cultural Politics, 2*(2), 131–147. doi: 10.1386/macp.2.2.131/1.

Heidegger, M. (2010). The question concerning technology. In C. Hanks (Ed.), *Technology and values. Essential reader* (pp. 99–111). Malden, MA: Wiley-Blackwell.

Henton, D., Melville, J., Grose, T., Furrell, T., Halter, G., Harutyunyan, A., et al. (2011). *Index of Silicon Valley.* Retrieved from www.jointventure.org/images/stories/pdf/The%20Index%20of%20Silicon%20Valley%202011.pdf

Hermida, A. (2014). *Tell everyone: Why we share and why it matters.* Toronto, ON: Doubleday Canada.

Herring, S. C. (2004). Slouching toward the ordinary: Current trends in computer-mediated communication. *New Media and Society, 6*(1), 26–36.

Hershbach, D. (1995). Technology as knowledge: Implications for instruction. *Journal of Technology Education, 7*(1), 31–42.

Higgins, E. T. (1987). Self-discrepancy: A theory relating self and affect. *Psychological Review, 94*(3), 319.

Hill, C. T. (1989). Technology and international competitiveness: Metaphor for progress. In S. L. Goldman (Ed.), *Science, technology, and social progress* (pp. 33–47). Cranbury, NJ: Associated University Presses.

Hippel, E. v. (2005). *Democratizing innovation.* Cambridge, MA: MIT Press.

Hobsbawn, E. J. (1952). The machine breakers. *Past and Present, 1*(1), 57–70.

Hogan, B. (2010). The presentation of self in the age of social media: Distinguishing performances and exhibitions online. *Bulletin of Science, Technology & Society, 30*(6), 377–386. Retrieved from http://bst.sagepub.com/content/30/6/377.full.pdf+html

Hogan, B., & Quan-Haase, A. (2010). Persistence and change in social media: A framework of social practice. *Bulletin of Science, Technology and Society, 30*(5), 309–315. Retrieved from http://bst.sagepub.com/content/30/5/309.full.pdf+html

Honeysett, A. (2014, 4 August). The Facebook Experiment: What it means for you. *Forbes.* Retrieved October 25, 2014, from www.forbes.com/sites/dailymuse/2014/08/04/the-facebook-experiment-what-it-means-for-you/

Horrigan, J. B. (2008). *Home broadband adoption 2008.* Retrieved from Pew Internet and American Life Project website: www.pewinternet.org/~/media//Files/Reports/2008/PIP_Broadband_2008.pdf

Horton, D., & Wohl, R. R. (1956). Mass communication and para-social interaction: Observations on intimacy at a distance. *Psychiatry 19*, 215–229.

Hounshell, D. A. (1985). *From the American system to mass production, 1800–1932: The development of manufacturing technology in the United States.* Baltimore: Johns Hopkins University Press.

Howard, P. E. N., Rainie, L., & Jones, S. (2002). Days and nights on the Internet: The impact of a diffusing technology. In B. Wellman & C. Haythornthwaite (Eds.), *Internet and everyday life* (pp. 45–73). Oxford: Blackwell Publishers.

——— (2011). *The digital origins of dictatorship and democracy: Information technol-*

ogy and political Islam. Oxford: Oxford University Press.

Huey, L., Walby, K., & Doyle, A. (2006). Cop watching in the Downtown Eastside: Exploring the use of (counter) surveillance as a tool of resistance. In T. Monahan (Ed.), *Surveillance and security: Technological politics and power in everyday life* (pp. 149–166). New York, NY: Routledge.

Hughes, T. P. (1983). *Networks of power: Electrification in Western society, 1880–1930*. Baltimore: Johns Hopkins University Press.

Huynh, K.-P., Lim, S.-W., & Skoric, M. M. (2013). Stepping out of the magic circle: Regulation of play/life boundary in MMO-Mediated romantic relationship. *Journal of Computer-Mediated Communication, 18*, 251–264.

Huws, U. (2003). *The making of a cybertariat: Virtual work in a real world*. New York: Monthly Review Press.

Ihde, D. (2010). *Heidegger's technologies: Postphenomenological perspectives*. New York: Fordham University Press.

Innis, H. A. (1951). *The bias of communication*. Toronto: University of Toronto Press.

International Telecommunication Union. (2009). *Mobile cellular subscriptions*. ITU World Telecommunication/ ICT Indicators Database. Retrieved from www.itu.int/ITU-D/icteye/ Reporting/ShowReportFrame.aspx? ReportName=/WTI/CellularSubs cribersPublic&ReportFormat=H TML4.0&RP_intYear=2009&RP_ intLanguageID=1&RP_ bitLiveData=False

Jacobs, J. (1961). *The death and life of great American cities*. NY: Random House.

Jarvenpaa, S. L., & Ives, B. (1994). The global network organization of the future: Information management opportunities and challenges. *Journal of Management Information Systems, 10*(4), 25–57.

Jarvis, J. (2009). *What would Google do?* (1st ed.). New York, NY: Collins Business.

Jewkes, Y. (Ed.). (2003). *Dot.cons: Crime, deviance and identity on the Internet*. Portland, OR: Willan Publishing.

Jobs, S. (n.d.). To all iPhone customers. Retrieved from www.apple.com/ hotnews/openiphoneletter/

Johns, A. (1998). *The nature of the book: Print and knowledge in the making*. Chicago, IL: University of Chicago Press.

Jonas, H. (1984). *The imperative of responsibility: In search of an ethics for the technological age*. Chicago: University of Chicago Press.

——— (2003). Toward a philosophy of technology. In R. C. Scharff & V. Dusek (Eds.), *Philosophy of technology: The technological condition: An anthology* (pp. 191–204). Malden, MA: Blackwell Publishers.

Jones, S. E. (2006). *Against technology: From the Luddities to neo-Luddism*. New York: Routledge.

Kahaner, L. (2007). *AK-47: The weapon that changed the face of war*. Hoboken, NJ: John Wiley & Sons.

Kaplan, A. M., & Haenlein, M. (2010). Users of the world, unite! The challenges and opportunities of social media. *Business Horizons, 53*(1), 59–68.

Kasapoglu, C. (2015). Turkey social media ban raises censorship fears. *BBC*. Retrieved April 15, 2015 from www.bbc. com/news/world-europe-32204177

Katz, J. E., & Rice, R. E. (2002). Syntopia: Access, civic involvement, and social interaction on the net. In B. Wellman & C. Haythornthwaite (Eds.), *The Internet in everyday life*. Oxford: Blackwell Publishers.

Katz, J. E., Rice, R. E., & Aspden, P. (2001). The Internet, 1995–2000: Access, civic involvement, and social interaction. *American Behavioral Scientist, 45*(3), 405–419.

Khan, S. S., Lodhi, S. A., Akhtar, F., & Khokar, I. (2014). Challenges of waste of electric and electronic equipment (WEEE): Toward a better management in a global scenario. *Management of Environmental Quality: An International Journal, 25*(2), 166–185.

Kim, S. H. (2008, December 31). Max Weber. *Stanford Encyclopedia of Philosophy*. Retrieved from http://plato. stanford.edu/archives/fall2008/entries/ weber/

Kirby, P. (2002). *The Celtic Tiger in distress: Growth with inequality in Ireland*. New York: Palgrave.

——— (2010). *Celtic Tiger in collapse*. New York: Palgrave.

Kirkpatrick, D. (2010). *The Facebook effect: The inside story of the company that is connecting the world.* New York: Simon & Schuster.

Kirkup, G. (1995). Gender issues and learning technologies. *British Journal of Educational Technology, 26*(3), 218–219. doi: 10.1111/j.1467-8535.1995.tb00344.x

Klemens, G. (2010). *The cellphone: The history and technology of the gadget that changed the world.* Jefferson, N.C.: McFarland & Co.

Kraemer, K. L., Dedrick, J., & Sharma, P. (2009). One laptop per child: Vision versus reality. *Communications of the ACM, 52*(6), 66–73.

Kramer, A. D. I., Guillory, J. E., & Hancock, J. T. (2014). Experimental evidence of massive-scale emotional contagion through social networks. *Proceedings of the National Academy of Sciences of the United States of America, 111*(29), 10779–10779. doi: 10.1073/pnas.1412583111

Kraut, R. E., Kiesler, S., Boneva, B., Cummings, J., Helgeson, V., & Crawford, A. (2002). Internet paradox revisited. *Journal of Social Issues, 58*(1), 49–74.

Krishnan, M. S. (1998). The role of team factors in software cost and quality: An empirical analysis. *Information, Technology & People, 11*(1), 20–35.

Landivar, L. C. (2013). *Disparities in STEM employment by sex, race, and Hispanic origin.* U.S. Census Bureau.

Lampe, C., Ellison, N. B., & Steinfield, C. (2007). *A familiar face(book): Profile elements as signals in an online social network.* CHI 2007 Online Representation of Self, San Jose, CA. Retrieved from www.msu.edu/~steinfie/CHI_manuscript.pdf

Latour, B. (1987). *Science in action: How to follow scientists and engineers through society.* Milton Keynes: Open University Press.

Latour, B. (1987). *Science in action: How to follow scientists and engineers through society.* Milton Keynes: Open University Press.

——— (1988). *The pasteurization of France.* Cambridge, MA: Harvard University Press.

——— (1993). *We have never been modern.* New York: Harvester Wheatsheaf.

——— (1999). On recalling ANT. In J. Law & J. Hassard (Eds.), *Actor network theory and after* (pp. 15–25). Boston, MA: Blackwell Publishers.

Law, J. (2009). Actor network theory and material semiotics. In B. S. Turner (Ed.), *The new Blackwell companion to social theory* (pp. 140–158). Malden, MA: Wiley-Blackwell.

Layton, E. T. J. (1974). Technology as knowledge. *Technology and Culture, 15*(1), 31–41.

Lazzarato. (1996). Immaterial labour. In P. Virno & M. Hardt (Eds.), *Radical thought in Italy: A potential politics* (pp. 133–147). Minneapolis, MN: University of Minnesota Press.

Lenhart, A., & Duggan, M. (2014, February 11). *Couples, the Internet and social media.* Retrieved October 20, 2014, from www.pewinternet.org/2014/02/11/main-report-30/

Lenhart, A., Purcell, K., Smith, A., & Zickuhr, K. (2010). Social media and young adults. *The Pew Internet and American Life Project.* Retrieved from The Pew Internet and American Life Project website: www.pewinternet.org/Reports/2010/Social-Media-and-Young-Adults.aspx

Lewchuk, W. (2005). Mass production. In J. Mokyr (Ed.), *The Oxford Encyclopedia of Economic History.* Oxford: Oxford University Press.

Li, N., & Kirkup, G. (2007). Gender and cultural differences in Internet use: A study of China and the UK. *Computers & Education, 48*(2), 301–317.

Livermore, O.R. (2013). *The academic grind: A critique of creative and collaborative discourses between digital games industries and post-secondary education in Canada.* The University of Western Ontario, London, ON, Canada. Paper 1128. Retrieved from http://ir.lib.uwo.ca/etd/1128

Lorimer, R., Gasher, M., & Skinner, D. (2010). *Mass communication in Canada* (6th ed.). Don Mills, ON: Oxford University Press.

Lukacs, V., & Quan-Haase, A. (2015). Romantic breakups on Facebook: new scales for studying post-breakup behaviors, digital distress, and surveillance. *Information, Communication & Society, 18*(5), 492–508. doi: 10.1080/1369118X.2015.1008540

Lyon, D., & Zureik, E. (1996). Surveillance, privacy, and the new technology. In D. Lyon & E. Zureik (Eds.), *Computers, surveillance, and privacy* (pp. 1–18). Minneapolis, MN: University of Minnesota Press.

MacKinnon, R. (2011). Internet wasn't real hero of Egypt. *New America Foundation*. Retrieved from http://articles.cnn.com/2011-02-12/opinion/mackinnon. internet.egypt_1_heroes-printing-press-digital-technologies?_s=PM:OPINION

Madden, M., Lenhart, A., Cortesi, S., Gasser, U., Duggan, M., Smith, A., & Beaton, M. (2013). *Teens, social media, and privacy*. Retrieved November 24, 2014, from www.pewinternet.org/2013/05/21/teens-social-media-and-privacy/

Mann, S., & Niedzviecki, H. (2001). *Cyborg: Digital destiny and human possibility in the age of the wearable computer.* Toronto: Doubleday Canada.

———, Nolan, J., & Wellman, B. (2003). Surveillance: Inventing and using wearable computing devices for data collection in surveillance environments. *Surveillance & Society, 1*(3), 331–355.

Marcuse, H. (1982). Some social implications of modern technology. In A. Arato & E. Gebhardt (Eds.), *The essential Frankfurt school reader* (pp. 138–162). New York: Continuum.

Markus, L. M., & Robey, D. (1988). Information technology and organizational change: Causal structure in theory and research. *Management Science, 34*(5), 583–598.

Marvin, C. (1988). *When old technologies were new: Thinking about electric communications in the late nineteenth century.* New York: Oxford University Press.

Marx, G. T. (1996). Electric eye in the sky: Some reflections on the new surveillance and popular culture. In D. Lyon & E. Zureik (Eds.), *Computers, surveillance, and privacy* (pp. 193–233). Minneapolis: University of Minnesota Press.

——— (2007). What's new about the "new surveillance"? Classifying for change and continuity. In S. P. Hier & J. Greenberg (Eds.), *The surveillance studies reader* (pp. 83–94). Maidenhead: Open University Press.

Marcia, J. E. (1966). Development and validation of ego-identity status. *Journal of Personality and Social Psychology, 3*(5), 551.

Marx, K. (1996). *Das Kapital* (Vol. I). Washington, DC: Gateway Editions.

———, & Engels, F. (1970). *Marx/Engels selected works, volume 3.* Retrieved from www.marxists.org/archive/marx/works/1880/soc-utop/

McCarthy, J. (2007). What is artificial intelligence? *Stanford University.* Retrieved from www.formal.stanford.edu/jmc/whatisai/whatisai.html

McCrae, R., & Costa, P. (1990). *Personality in adulthood.* New York: Guilford Publications.

McGaw, J. A. (1982). Women and the history of American technology. *Signs,* 798–828.

McGinn, D. (2011, January 27). Does social media speed up romances? *The Globe and Mail.* Retrieved from www.theglobeandmail.com/life/the-hot-button/does-social-media-speed-up-romances/article1885457/

McGinn, R. E. (1978). What is technology? In P. T. Durbin (Ed.), *Research in philosophy and technology* (Vol. 1, pp. 179–197). Greenwich, CT: Jai Press.

McKinsey & Company Report. (2014, June 25). *Offline and falling behind: Barriers to Internet adoption.* Retrieved November 28, 2014, from www.mckinsey.com/~/media/McKinsey/dotcom/client_service/High%20Tech/PDFs/Offline_and_falling_behind_Barriers_to_Internet_adoption.ashx

McLuhan, M., McLuhan, E., & Zingrone, F. (1995). *Essential McLuhan.* Don Mills, ON: House of Anansi.

McLuhan, M. (1962). *The Gutenberg galaxy: The making of typographic man.* Toronto, ON: University of Toronto Press.

——— (1964). *Understanding media: The extension of man.* New York: McGraw-Hill.

——— & Powers, B. (1989). *The global village: Transformations in world life and media in the 21st century.* Oxford: Oxford University Press.

———, & Quentin, F. (2003). *The medium is the massage: An inventory of effects.* Toronto, ON: Penguin Canada.

McMahon, R., Hudson, H., & Fabian, L. (2014). The First Mile Connectivity Consortium and Digital Regulation in Canada. *The Journal of Community Informatics, 10*(2). http://ci-journal.net/index.php/ciej/article/view/1123

McMullin, J. A. (Ed.). (2011). *Age, gender, and work: Small information technology firms in the new economy.* Vancouver: UBC Press.

McPherson, M., Smith-Lovin, L., & Brashears, M. E. (2006). Social isolation in America: Changes in core discussion networks over two decades. *American Sociological Review, 71*(3), 353–375.

Mehdizadeh, S. (2010). Self-presentation 2.0: Narcissism and self esteem on Facebook. *CyberPsychology, Behavior, and Social Networking, 13*(4), 357–364.

Merton, R. K. (1964). Foreword. In J. Ellul (Ed.), *The technological society* (1st American ed., pp. v–viii). New York: Knopf.

Miller, C. C. (2011, July 19). Google looks for the next Google. *New York Times.* Retrieved from www.nytimes.com/2011/07/20/technology/google-spending-millions-to-find-the-next-google.html?pagewanted=all

Mod, G. (2010). Reading romance: The impact Facebook rituals can have on a romantic relationship. *Journal of Comparative Research in Anthropology and Sociology, 2,* 61–77.

Mok, D., Wellman, B., & Carrasco, J. A. (2010). Does distance matter in the age of the Internet? *Urban Studies, 47*(13), 2747–2783.

Monge, P. R., & Contractor, N. S. (1997). Emergence of communication networks. In F. M. Jablin & L. L. Putnam (Eds.), *Handbook of organizational communication* (2nd ed.). Thousand Oaks, CA: Sage Publications.

——— & ——— (2003). *Theories of communication networks.* Oxford: Oxford University Press.

Moretti, S. (2010, November 2). Facebook using Canada as testing ground. *London Free Press.* Retrieved from www.lfpress.com/money/2010/11/02/15923101.html

Mossberger, K., Tolbert, C. J., & Stansbury, M. (2003). *Virtual inequality: Beyond the digital divide.* Washington, DC: Georgetown University Press.

Mumford, L. (1967). *The myth of the machine: Technics and human development.* London: Secker & Warburg.

——— (1981). *The culture of cities.* Westport, CT: Greenwood Press.

Murray, W. C., & Rostis, A. (2007). "Who's running the machine?" A theoretical exploration of work stress and burnout of technologically tethered workers. *Journal of Individual Employment Rights, 12*(3), 249–263.

Naim, M., & Myers, J. J. (2005). Illicit: How smugglers, traffickers and copyrights are hijacking the global economy. *Carnegie Council.* Retrieved from www.carnegiecouncil.org/resources/transcripts/5279.html

National Center for Women & Information Technology. (2014a). *Girls in IT.* Boulder, CO: Author.

National Center for Women & Information Technology. (2014b). *NCWIT's Women in IT: By the numbers.* Boulder, CO: Author.

National Public Radio (NPR). (n.d.). *Stories about net neutrality.* Retrieved 12 April 15, 2015 from www.npr.org/tags/132227849/net-neutrality

National Security Agency (NSA) (2015). *Welcome page.* Retrieved 12 April 15, 2015 from https://www.nsa.gov/

National Telecommunications and Information Administration. (2011). Internet and computer use studies and data files. Retrieved from www.ntia.doc.gov/data/index.html

Nelson, D. (Ed.). (1992). *A mental revolution: Scientific management since Taylor.* Columbus, OH: Ohio State University Press.

Nielsen. (2009, May 20). Americans watching more TV than ever; web and mobile video up too. Retrieved from http://blog.nielsen.com/nielsenwire/online_mobile/americans-watching-more-tv-than-ever/

Nierenberg, C. (2014, August 4). With kids and video games, moderation is key. Retrieved November 11, 2014, from www.livescience.com/47171-kids-video-games-moderation-mental-health.html

Noelle-Neumann, E. (1974). The spiral of silence: A theory of public opinion. *Journal of Communication, 24,* 43–51. doi: 10.1111/j.1460-2466.1974.tb00367.x

Norman, D. A. (1988). *The psychology of everyday things.* New York: Basic Books.

Norris, M. L., Boydell, K. M., Pinhas, L., & Katzman, D. K. (2006). Ana and the Internet: A review of pro-anorexia websites. *International Journal of Eating Disorders, 39*(6), 443–447. doi:10.1002/eat.20305

Norris, P. (2001). *Digital divide: Civic engagement, information poverty, and the Internet worldwide*. New York: Cambridge University Press.

Nowotny, H. (1994). *Time: The modern and postmodern experience*. Cambridge, UK: Polity Press.

Oakley, A. (1974). *The sociology of housework*. New York: Pantheon Books.

Oberg, A., & Walgenbach, P. (2008). Hierarchical structures of communication in a network organization. *Scandinavian Journal of Management, 24,* 183–198.

OECD. (2009). *OECD factbook 2009: Economic, environmental and social statistics*. Retrieved from www.oecd-ilibrary.org/economics/oecd-factbook-2009_factbook-2009-en

Oldenburg, R. (1999). *The great good place: Cafes, coffee shops, community centers, beauty parlors, general stores, bars, hangouts, and how they get you through the day*. New York: Marlowe & Co.

Oliveira, M. (2014, February 19). 10 million Canadians use Facebook on mobile daily. *The Globe & Mail*. Retrieved October 20, 2014, from www.theglobeandmail.com/technology/10-million-canadians-use-facebook-on-mobile-daily/article16976434/

Ollman, B. (1976). *Alienation: Marx's conception of man in capitalist society* (2nd ed.). Cambridge, UK: Cambridge University Press.

One Laptop per Child. (2010a). Education. Retrieved from http://laptop.org/en/vision/education/index.shtml

——— (2010b). Vision. Retrieved from http://laptop.org/en/vision/index.shtml

Ong, W. J. (1991). *Orality and literacy: The technologizing of the word*. London: Routledge.

Ono, H., & Zavodny, M. (2003). Gender and the Internet. *Social Science Quarterly, 84*(1), 111–121. doi: 10.1111/1540-6237.t01-1-8401007

O'Reilly, T. (2005). What is Web 2.0: Design patterns and business models for the next generation of software. Retrieved from http://oreilly.com/pub/a/web2/archive/what-is-web-20.html?page=1

Pacey, A. (1983). *The culture of technology* (1st MIT Press ed.). Cambridge, MA: MIT Press.

Palfrey, J. G., & Gasser, U. (2008). *Born digital: Understanding the first generation of digital natives*. New York: Basic Books.

Pavlik, J. V., & McIntosh, S. (2011). *Converging media: A new introduction to mass communication*. New York: Oxford University Press.

Pennock, G. A. (1930). Industrial research at Hawthorne. *Personnel Journal, 8,* 296–313.

Pertierra, R., Ugarte, E. F., Pingol, A., Hernandez, J., & Dacanay, N. L. (2003). *Txt-ing selves: Cellphones and Philippine modernity*. Manila, Philippines: De La Salle University Press.

Pinch, T. (2009). The social construction of technology (SCOT): The old, the new, and the nonhuman. In P. Vannini (Ed.), *Material culture and technology in everyday life: Ethnographic approaches* (pp. 45–58). New York: Peter Lang.

———, & Bijker, W. E. (1987). The social construction of facts and artifacts: Or how the sociology of science and the sociology of technology might benefit each other. *Social Studies of Science, 14*(3), 399–441.

Plummer, T. (2004). Flaked stones and old bones: Biological and cultural evolution at the dawn of technology. *American Journal of Physical Anthropology, 125*(S39), 118–164.

Prensky, M. (2001). Digital natives, digital immigrants. *On the Horizon, 9,* 5. Retrieved from www.marcprensky.com/writing/Prensky%20-%20Digital%20Natives,%20Digital%20Immigrants%20-%20Part1.pdf

Privacy Commissioner of Canada. (2009). Facebook agrees to address privacy commissioner's concerns. Retrieved from www.priv.gc.ca/media/nr-c/2009/nr-c_090827_e.cfm

Pruijt, H.D. (1997). *Job design and technology: Taylorism vs. anti-Taylorism*. London: Routledge.

Przybylski, A. K. (2014). Electronic gaming and psychosocial adjustment. *Pediatrics, 134*(3), e716–e722.

Puma, M. E., Chaplin, D., & Pape, A. D. (2000, September 12). *E-rate and the digital divide: A preliminary analysis from the integrated studies of educational technology.* Retrieved from Urban Institute website: www.urban.org/publications/1000000.html

Putnam, R. D. (2000). *Bowling alone: The collapse and revival of American community.* New York: Simon & Schuster.

Quan-Haase, A. (2009). *Information brokering in the high-tech industry: Online social networks at work.* Berlin: F Publishing.

———, & Collins, J. L. (2008). "I'm there, but I might not want to talk to you": University students' social accessibility in instant messaging. *Information, Communication & Society, 11*(4), 526–543.

———, Cothrel, J., & Wellman, B. (2005). Instant messaging for collaboration: A case study of a high-tech firm. *Journal of Computer-Mediated Communication, 10*(4). Retrieved from http://jcmc.indiana.edu/vol10/issue4/quan-haase.html

Quan-Haase, A., Martin, K., & Schreurs, K. (2014). Not all on the same page: E-book adoption and technology exploration by seniors. *Information Research, 19*(2). Retrieved from www.informationr.net/ir/19-2/paper622.html#

Quan-Haase, A., Nevin, A., & Lukacs, V. (2014). *Romantic breakups on Facebook.* Paper presented at the American Sociological Association, San Francisco, August 16–19.

———, & Wellman, B. (2004). How does the Internet affect social capital? In M. Huysman & V. Wulf (Eds.), *Social capital and information technology* (pp. 151–176). Cambridge, MA: MIT Press.

——— & ——— (2006). Hyperconnected network: Computer-mediated community in a high-tech organization. In C. Heckscher & P. Adler (Eds.), *The firm as a collaborative community: Reconstructing trust in the knowledge economy* (pp. 281–333). London: Oxford University Press.

——— & ——— (2008). From the computerization movement to computerization: Communication networks in a high-tech organization. In K. L. Kraemer & M. S. Elliott (Eds.), *Computerization movements and technology diffusion: From mainframes to ubiquitous computing* (pp. 203–224). Medford, NJ: Information Today, Inc.

———, & Young, A. L. (2010). Uses and gratifications of social media: A comparison of Facebook and instant messaging. *Bulletin of Science, Technology and Society, 30*(5), 350–361.

Rainie, L., & Wellman, B. (2012). *Networked: The new social operating system.* Cambridge, MA: MIT Press.

Rainie, L., Kiesler, S., Kang, R., & Madden, M. (2013). *Anonymity, privacy, and security online.* Retrieved November 24, 2014, from www.pewinternet.org/2013/09/05/anonymity-privacy-and-security-online/

Randall, A. J. (1991). *Before the Luddites: Custom, community and machinery in the English woolen industry 1776–1809.* Cambridge: Cambridge University Press.

Rao, A., & Scaruffi, P. (2010). *A history of Silicon Valley: The greatest creation of wealth in the history of the planet.* Palo Alto, CA: Omniware Press.

Rasmussen Neal, D., & Hoffman, C. (2011). *Online mental health information behaviours of emerging adults: A web usability and user experience study.* 39th Annual CAIS/ACSI Conference. Retrieved from www.cais-acsi.ca/proceedings/2011/18_Neal_Hoffman.pdf

Ratnagar, S. (2001). The bronze age: Unique instance of a pre-industrial world system? *Current Anthropology, 42*(3), 351–379.

Raynes-Goldie, K. (2010). Aliases, creeping, and wall cleaning: Understanding privacy in the age of Facebook. *First Monday, 15*(1), January. Retrieved from http://firstmonday.org/htbin/cgiwrap/bin/ojs/index.php/fm/article/viewArticle/2775

Reese, L., Faist, J., & Sands, G. (2010). Measuring the creative class. *Journal of Urban Affairs, 32*(3), 345–366.

Regional Surveys of the World. (2004). *The Far East and Australia* (35 ed.). London: Europa Publications, Taylor and Francis Group.

Rentschler, E. (1996). *The ministry of illusion: Nazi cinema and its afterlife.* Cambridge, MA: Harvard University Press.

Reskin, B. F., & Roos, P. A. (2009). *Job queues, gender queues: Explaining women's inroads into male occupations.* Philadelphia: PA Temple University Press.

Restivo, S. P. (2005). *Science, technology, and society: An encyclopedia.* Oxford, England: Oxford University Press.

Rheingold, H. (2000). *The virtual community: Homesteading on the electronic frontier* (Rev. ed.). Cambridge, MA: MIT Press.

Rich, L. (2010). Shiny new things. *Ad Age Insights.* Retrieved from http://adage.com/images/bin/pdf/shiny_new_things.pdf

Roberts, J. (2007, July 6). AK-47 inventor says conscience is clear. CBS *News.* Retrieved from www.cbsnews.com/stories/2007/07/06/world/main3025193.shtml?source=RSSattr=World_3025193%29

Robinson, L. (2007). The cyberself: The self-ing project goes online, symbolic interaction in the digital age. *New Media & Society, 9*(1), 93–110.

Roebuck, J. (1982). *The making of modern English society from 1850* (2nd ed.). London: Routledge.

Roehrs, J. (1998). *A study of social organization in science in the age of computer-mediated communication.* Unpublished doctoral thesis, Nova Southeastern University.

Roethlisberger, F. J., & Dickson, W. J. (2003). *Management and the worker* (Vol. 5). Michigan: Psychology Press.

Rogers, E. M. (2003). *Diffusion of innovations* (5th ed.). New York: Free Press.

Rogers, E. M. (1983). *Diffusion of innovations* (3rd ed.). New York, NY: Free Press.

Rogers, T. W. (1994). Detournement for fun and (political) profit. *Ctheory.* Retrieved from http://ctheory.net/text_file.asp?pick=242

Rohrbeck, R., Döhler, M., & Arnold, H. M. (2009). Creating growth with externalization of R&D results-the spin-along approach. *Global Business and Organizational Excellence, 28*(4), 44–51. Retrieved from http://papers.ssrn.com/sol3/papers.cfm?abstract_id=1472133

Rubin, V. L., Chen, Y., & Thorimbert, L. M. (2010). Artificially intelligent conversational agents in libraries. *Library Hi Tech, 28*(4), 496–522.

Russell, R. (2011, July 26). An inconvenient truth about Toyota. *The Globe and Mail.* Retrieved from http://m.theglobeandmail.com/globe-drive/car-tips/safety/an-inconvenient-truth-about-toyota/article2104879/?service=mobile

Russell, S. J., & Norvig, P. (2003). *Artificial intelligence: A modern approach* (2nd ed.). Upper Saddle River, NJ: Prentice Hall.

Sacks, D. (2011, January 31). How YouTube's global platform is redefining the entertainment business. *Fast Company.* Retrieved from www.fastcompany.com/magazine/152/blown-away.html

Sale, K. (1995). *Rebels against the future: The Luddities and their war on the industrial revolution: Lessons for the computer age.* Reading, MA: Addison-Wesley.

Sanderson, J., & Cheong, P. H. (2010). Tweeting prayers and communicating grief over Michael Jackson online. *Bulletin of Science, Technology and Society, 30*(5), 328–340. Retrieved from http://bst.sagepub.com/content/30/5/328.full.pdf+html

Saslow, L. R., Muise, A., Impett, E. A., & Dubin, M. (2013). Can you see how happy we are? Facebook images and relationship satisfaction. *Social Psychological and Personality Science, 4*(4), 411–418.

Schulte, B. (2014). *Overwhelmed: Work, love and play when no one has the time.* Toronto: Harper Collins.

Schummer, J. (2006). Societal and ethical implications of nanotechnology: Meanings, interest groups and social dynamics. In J. Schummer & D. Baird (Eds.), *Nanotechnology challenges: Implications for philosophy, ethics and society* (pp. 413–449). London: World Scientific Publishing.

Schumpeter, J. A. (2004). *The theory of economic development: An inquiry into profits, capital, credit, interest, and the business cycle* (1934 ed.). New Brunswick, NJ: Transaction Publishers.

Sciadas, G. (2002). *The digital divide in Canada.* Science Innovation and Electronic Information Division. Retrieved from http://dsp-psd.pwgsc.gc.ca/Collection/Statcan/56F0009X/56F0009XIE2002001.pdf

Scola, N. (2014, July 16). U.N. human rights chief: Surveillance is now world's "dangerous habit." *Washington Post.* Retrieved November 26, 2014, from www.washingtonpost.com/blogs/the-switch/wp/2014/07/16/u-n-human-rights-chief-surveillance-is-now-worlds-dangerous-habit/

Scott, J., & Marshall, G. (2005). *Oxford dictionary of sociology*. Oxford: Oxford University Press.

Scragg, G., & Smith, J. (1998). *A study of barriers to women in undergraduate computer science*. Paper presented at the ACM SIGCSE Bulletin.

Sears, A., & Jacko, J. A. (2008). *The human-computer interaction handbook: Fundamentals, evolving technologies, and emerging applications* (2nd ed.). New York: Lawrence Erlbaum Associates.

Sedikides, C., & Spencer, S. J. (Eds.).(2011). *The self: Frontiers of social psychology*. Michigan: Psychology Press.

Segal, H. P. (1985). *Technological utopianism in American culture*. Chicago: University of Chicago Press.

Sellen, A., & Harper, R. H. R. (2002). *The myth of the paperless office*. Cambridge: MIT Press.

Servaes, J. (1999). *Communication for development: One world, multiple cultures*. Cresskill, NJ: Hampton.

Servaes, J. (2010). Social change. *Oxford Bibliographies Online*. Retrieved from www.oxfordbibliographiesonline.com/view/document/obo-9780199756841/obo 9780199756841-0063.xml;jsessionid=8D56E1250611451078B7224F60235FC6

Service, E. R. (1971). *Primitive social organization: An evolutionary perspective* (2nd ed.). New York: Random House.

Shade, L. R. (2014). Missing in action: gender in canada's digital economy agenda. *Signs, 39*(4), 887–896. doi: 10.1086/673342

Shaheed, A. (2014). *Layers of Internet censorship in Iran. UN Special Report*. Retrieved April 15, 2015 from http://shaheedoniran.org/english/blog/layers-of-internet-censorship-in-iran/

Shashaani, L. (1997). Gender differences in computer attitudes and use among college students. Journal of Educational *Computing Research, 16*(1), 37–52.

Shorter, E. (1991). *Women's bodies: A social history of women's encounter with health, ill-health, and medicine*. New Brunswick, NJ: Transaction Publishers.

Simpson, L. C. (1995). *Technology, time, and the conversations of modernity*. New York: Routledge.

Singer, P., & Friedman, A. (2014). *Cybersecurity and Cyberwar: what everyone needs to know*. New York, NY: Oxford University Press.

Smentek, K. (2010). Mind and hand (mens et manus) illustrated in Diderot's "Encyclopédie." Retrieved from http://techtv.mit.edu/videos/5141-mind-and-hand-mens-et-manus-illustrated-in-diderots-encyclopdie

Smith, B. D. (1995). *The emergence of agriculture*. New York: Scientific American Library.

Smith, A. (2014, February 3). 6 facts about Facebook. *CNN*. Retrieved October 20, 2014, from www.pewresearch.org/fact-tank/2014/02/03/6-new-facts-about-facebook/

Smith, A., & Duggan, M. (2013). *Online dating and relationships*. Washington, DC: Pew Research Center.

Smith, C. (July 22). The creepiest Internet tracking tool yet is "virtually impossible" to block. Retrieved November 24, 2014, from http://bgr.com/2014/07/22/canvas-fingerprinting-internet-tracking-tool/

Smith, S. (2005, December 1). The $100 laptop—is it a wind-up? *CNN*. Retrieved from http://edition.cnn.com/2005/WORLD/africa/12/01/laptop/

Snezhurov, Y. (2011, April 12). Museum Kalashnikov. Retrieved from www.kalashnikov-museum.udmnet.ru/kalash5e.htm

Social Bakers. (2011, March 17). Interesting digital marketing trends in the Middle East. Retrieved from www.socialbakers.com/blog/130-interesting-digital-marketing-trends-in-the-middle-east/

Sofka, C. J. (1997). Social support "Internetworks," Caskets for sale, and more: Thanatology and the information superhighway. *Death Studies, 21*(6), 553–574.

Sorensen, C. (2010, July 29). Toyota's latest repairs. *Maclean's*. Retrieved from www2.macleans.ca/2010/07/29/toyotas-latest-repairs/

Sonnenfeld, J. A. (1985). Shedding light on the Hawthorne studies. *Journal of Organizational Behavior, 6*(2), 111–130.

Sproull, L. S., & Kiesler, S. B. (1991). *Connections: New ways of working in the networked organization*. Cambridge, MA: MIT Press.

Srinivasan, R. (2011, February 15). The net worth of open networks. *The Huffington*

Post. Retrieved from www.huffington-post.com/ramesh-srinivasan/the-net-worth-of-open-net_b_823570.html

Stanworth, M. (1987). *Reproductive technologies: Gender, motherhood and medicine.* Cambridge: Polity Press.

Statistics Canada. (2013, November 26). Canadian Internet Use Survey, 2012: *The Daily.* Retrieved October 25, 2014, from www.statcan.gc.ca/daily-quotidien/131126/dq131126d-eng.htm

Statistics Canada. (2009). *Canadian Internet use survey 2009.* CANSIM. Retrieved from www.statcan.gc.ca/daily-quotidien/100510/dq100510a-eng.htm

Stedmon, A. W. (2011). The camera never lies, or does it? The dangers of taking CCTV surveillance at face-value. *Surveillance & Society, 8*(4), 1477–7487.

Steiner, G.A. (1963). *The people look at television: A study of audience attitudes.* New York: Knopf.

Stevenson, S. (2009). Digital divide: A discursive move away from the real inequities. *The Information Society, 25*(1), 1–22.

Stone, B. (2007). Microsoft buys stake in Facebook. *The New York Times, Technology.* Retrieved from www.nytimes.com/2007/10/25/technology/25facebook.html

Street, J. (1992). *Politics and technology.* New York: Guilford Press.

Suler, J. (2004). The online disinhibition effect. *CyberPsychology & Behavior, 7*(3), 321–326.

Sundén, J. (2003). *Material virtualities: Approaching online textual embodiment.* New York: Peter Lang Publishing.

Sundström, P. (1998). Interpreting the notion that technology is value-neutral? *Medicine, Health Care and Philosophy, 1,* 41–45.

Sunstein, C. R. (2001). *Republic.Com.* Princeton, NJ: Princeton University Press.

Sward, K. (1948). *The legend of Henry Ford.* New York: Rinehart.

Swartz, J. (2011, April 21). Tech jobs boom like it's 1999. *USA Today.* Retrieved from www.usatoday.com/tech/news/2011-04-20-tech-jobs-booming.htm

Tapscott, D., & Williams, A. D. (2006). *Wikinomics: How mass collaboration changes everything.* New York: Portfolio.

Taylor, F. W. (1947/2003). *Scientific management.* New York, NY: Taylor & Francis.

Tenner, E. (2003). *Our own devices: The past and future of body technology.* New York: Alfred A. Knopf.

Tenner, E. (1996). *Why things bite back: Technology and the revenge of unintended consequences.* New York: Knopf.

Terazono, A., & Yoshida, A. (2013). Current international flows of electronic waste, future tasks, and possible solutions. In K. Hieronymi, R. Kahhat, & E. Williams (Eds.), *E-waste management: From waste to resource* (pp. 137–163). London: Earthscan.

The Bureau of Investigative Journalism (n.d.). Drone warfare. Retrieved from www.thebureauinvestigates.com/category/projects/drones/drones-war-drones

The Canadian Press. (2008, December 31). Canadian Internet usage at home in 2007. *CBC.* Retrieved from www.cbc.ca/news/interactives/cp-internet-use/

The real digital divide. (2005, March 10). *The Economist.* Retrieved from www.economist.com/node/3742817?story_id=3742817

Thirsk, J. (1983). The horticultural revolution: A cautionary note on prices. *The Journal of Interdisplinary History, 14*(2), 299–302.

Thrift, N. (1996). New urban eras and old technological fears: Reconfiguring the goodwill of electronic things. *Urban Studies, 33*(8), 1463–1493. doi: Doi 10.1080/0042098966754

Toffler, A. (1970). *Future shock.* New York: Random House.

——— (1980). *The third wave.* New York: Morrow.

Tönnies, F. (2004). *Community & society (Gemeinschaft und Gesellschaft).* New Brunswick, NJ: Michigan State University Press.

Tófalvy, T. (2014). "MySpace bands" and "tagging wars": Conflicts of genre, work ethic and media platforms in an extreme music scene. *First Monday, 19*(9–1). Retrieved from: http://firstmonday.org/ojs/index.php/fm/article/view/4354/4115 doi: http://dx.doi.org/10.5210/fm.v19i9.4354

Tokunaga, R. S. (2010). Following you home from school: A critical review and synthesis of research on cyberbullying victimization. *Computers in Human Behavior, 26*(3), 277–287.

Tokunaga, R. S. (2011). Social networking site or social surveillance site?

Understanding the use of interpersonal electronic surveillance in romantic relationships. *Computers in Human Behavior, 27*(2), 705–713.

Trimborn, J. (2007). *Leni Riefenstahl: A life.* New York: Faber and Faber.

Tufekci, Z. (2007). Can you see me now? Audience and disclosure regulation in online social network sites. *Bulletin of Science, Technology & Society, 28*(1), 20–36.

Tufekci, Z. (2008). Grooming, gossip, Facebook and MySpace. *Information, Communication and Society, 11*, 544–564.

——— (2010). *Who acquires friends through social media and why? "Rich get richer" versus "seek and ye shall find."* Presented at 4th Int'l AAAI Conference on Weblogs and Social Media (ICWSM, 2010). ICWSM '09.(Washington, DC, May 23–26: AAAI Press).

Turkle, S. (1984). *The Second Self: Computers and the Human Spirit.* New York: Simon & Schuster.

Turkle, S. (1995). *Life on the Screen: Identity in the Age of the Internet.* New York, NY: Simon & Schuster.

Turing, A. M. (1950). Computing machinery and intelligence. *Mind, 59,* 433–446.

Vanek, J. (1974). Time spent in housework. *Scientific American, 231,* 116–120.

Vanhemert. (2014, January 13, 2014). Why HER will dominate UI design even more than minority report. *Wired.*

Van Dijck, J. (2007). *Mediated memories in the digital age.* Stanford, CA: Stanford University Press.

Vehovar, V., Sicherl, P., Husing, T., & Donicar, V. (2009). Methodological challenges of digital divide measurements. *The Information Society, 22,* 279–290.

Venture Outsource (n.d.). Top 10 EMS providers and ODM rankings, reviews, ratings. Retrieved April 12, 2015 from https://www.ventureoutsource.com/contract-manufacturing/top-10-cms-odm-reviews-ratings/

Verbeek, P.-P. (2005). *What things do: Philosophical reflections on technology, agency, and design.* University Park, PA: Pennsylvania State University Press.

Viseu, A. (2002). *Augmented bodies and behavior bias interfaces.* Proceedings for the Society for Social Studies of Science, Milwaukee,

Rushe, D. (2011). Facebook's value swells to $50bn after Goldman Sachs invest-ment. In *Proceedings of the Guardian Online.* Retrieved from www.guardian.co.uk/technology/2011/jan/03/facebook-value-50bn-goldman-sachs-investment

Viseu, A. (2002). *Augmented bodies and behaviour bias interfaces.* Paper presented at the 26th annual meeting of the Society for Social Studies of Science. Milwaukee, WI, November 7–10. Retrieved from www.yorku.ca/aviseu/pdf%20files/viseu_4S2002.pdf

Viseu, A. Clement, A., & Aspinall, J. (2004). Situating privacy online: Complex perceptions and everyday practices. *Information, Communication & Society, 7*(1), pp. 92–114.

Wajcman, J. (2013). *Feminism confronts technology.* Hoboken, NJ: Wiley.

Walsham, G. (1997). Actor-network theory and its research: Current status and future prospects. In J. I. DeGross, A. S. Lee & J. Liebenau (Eds.), *Information systems and qualitative research: Proceedings of the IFIP TC8 WG 8.2 international conference on information systems and qualitative research, 31st May–3rd June 1997, Philadelphia, Pennsylvania, USA* (1st ed., pp. 466–480). London: Chapman & Hall.

Wang, H., & Wellman, B. (2010). Social connectivity in America: Changes in adult friendship network size from 2002 to 2007. *American Behavioral Scientist, 53*(8), 1148–1169.

Wasserman, I., & Richmond-Abbott, M. (2005). Gender and the internet: Causes of variation in access, level, and scope of use. *Social Science Quarterly, 86*(1), 252–270. doi: 10.1111/j.0038-4941.2005.00301.x

Weber, M. (1920/2003). *The Protestant ethic and the spirit of capitalism* (Rev. 1920 ed.). Mineola, NY: Dover Publications.

Weinstein, J. (2010). *Social change* (3rd ed.). Lanham, MD: Rowman & Littlefield.

Wellman, B. (1979). The community question. *American Journal of Sociology, 84,* 1201–1231.

———, & Berkowitz, S. D. (Eds.). (1988). *Social structures: A network approach.* Cambridge: Cambridge University Press.

——— (2001). Physical place and cyber place: The rise of personalized networking. *International Journal of Urban and Regional Research, 25*(2), 227–252.

———, & Frank, K. (2001). Network capital in a multilevel world: Getting support from personal communities. In N. Lin, K. Cook & R. S. Burt (Eds.), *Social capital: Theory and research* (pp. 233–273). Hawthorne, NY: Aldine de Gruyter.

———, & Haythornthwaite, C. (2002). Introduction. In B. Wellman & C. Haythornthwaite (Eds.), *The Internet in everyday life*. Oxford: Blackwell Publishers.

———, Quan-Haase, A., Witte, J., & Hampton, K. (2001). Does the Internet increase, decrease, or supplement social capital? Social networks, participation, and community commitment. *American Behavioral Scientist, 45*(3), 437–456.

———, & Wortley, S. (1990). Different strokes from different folks: Community ties and social support. *American Journal of Sociology, 96*(3), 558–588.

Westin, A. F. (2003). Social and political dimensions of privacy. *Journal of Social Issues, 59*(2), 431–453

Wikipedia. (2011). Neutral point of view. Retrieved from http://en.wikipedia.org/wiki/Wikipedia:Neutral_point_of_view

Wilson, C. (2014, January 27). How much time have you wasted on Facebook? *Time magazine*. Retrieved October 29, 2014, from http://time.com/6107/how-much-time-have-you-wasted-on-facebook/

Winner, L. (1999). Do artifacts have politics? In D. Mackenzie & J. Wajcman (Eds.), *The social shaping of technology* (pp. 28–40). Buckingham: Open University Press.

——— (2003). Social constructivism: Opening the black box and finding it empty. In R. C. Scharff & V. Dusek (Eds.), *Philosophy of technology: The technological condition: An anthology* (pp. 233–244). Malden, MA: Blackwell Publishers.

Witte, J. C., & Mannon, S. E. (2009). *The Internet and social inequalities*. New York, NY: Routledge.

Wolak, J., Mitchell, K., & Finkelhor, D. (2007). Does online harassment constitute bullying? An exploration of online harassment by known peers and online-only contacts. *Journal of Adolescent Health, 41*, S51–S58. doi: 10.1016/j.jadohealth.2007.08.019

World Health Organization (WHO). (2014). What do we mean by "sex" and "gender"? Retrieved September 15, 2014, from www.who.int/gender/whatisgender/en/

Wysocki, R. K. (2006). *Effective software project management*. Indianapolis, IN: Wiley Publishing.

Yeshua-Katz, D., & Martins, N. (2013). Communicating stigma: The pro-ana paradox. *Health communication, 28*(5), 499–508.

Young, A. L. (2008). *Defacing the 'book: Examining information revelation, Internet privacy concerns and privacy protection in Facebook* (Unpublished master's thesis). University of Western Ontario, London, ON.

——— & Quan-Haase, A. (2009). Information revelation and Internet privacy concerns on social network sites: A case study of Facebook. In J. M. Carrol (Ed.). *Fourth International Conference on Communities and Technologies (University Park, PA, USA, June 25–27)*, pp. 265–274. Dordrecht: Springer Verlag.

Yu, X. (2008). Impacts of corporate code of conduct on labor standards: A case study of Reebok's athletic footwear supplier factory in China. *Journal of Business Ethics, 81*(3), 513–529.

Zachary, P. G. (1998). Armed truce: Software in an age of teams. *Information, Technology & People, 11*(1), 62–65.

Zackariasson, P., & Wilson, T. L. (2012). *The video game industry: Formation, present state, and future* (Vol. 24). New York, NY: Routledge.

Zimmerman, M. E. (1990). *Heidegger's confrontation with modernity: Technology, politics and art*. Bloomington, IN: Indiana University Press.

Zoeteman, B. C. J., Krikke, H. R., & Venselaar, J. (2010). Handling WEEE waste flows: On the effectiveness of producer responsibility in a globalizing world. *International Journal of Advanced Manufacturing Technology, 47*, 415–436.

Zuckerman, E. (2011, January 14). The first Twitter revolution? *Foreign Policy*. Retrieved from www.foreignpolicy.com/articles/2011/01/14/the_first_twitter_revolution?page=full

Index